WATER-COLOUR PAINTING
IN BRITAIN

I   THE EIGHTEENTH CENTURY

'View on the Galleria di Sopra, above the Lake of Albano'
Coll. Mr & Mrs Paul Mellon   14¼ x 20¾ : 362 x 527   *Water-colour*
John Robert COZENS

Water-colour Painting in Britain

1 The Eighteenth Century

Martin Hardie

Edited by Dudley Snelgrove *with*
Jonathan Mayne *and* Basil Taylor

B T BATSFORD LTD LONDON

First published 1966
Second Edition 1967

© The Estate of the late Martin Hardie 1966, 1967

Made and printed in Great Britain
by William Clowes and Sons, Limited, London and Beccles,
Collotype plates printed by L. Van Leer and Co. N.V.,
London and Amsterdam,
for the publishers B. T. BATSFORD LTD
4 Fitzhardinge Street, Portman Square, London W1

CONTENTS

THE ILLUSTRATIONS

Acknowledgment

The Publishers wish to express their gratitude to the owners of the original drawings for their permission to reproduce them as illustrations in this book and their names are given in the captions to the plates.

Figures 76, 81 and 212 are reproduced by gracious permission of Her Majesty The Queen.

Figure 203 is reproduced by permission of the Syndics of the Fitzwilliam Museum, Cambridge; figures 200, 201 and 202 are reproduced by courtesy of the Trustees of the Tate Gallery and figure 185 is reproduced by courtesy of the Victoria Art Gallery, Bath.

INTRODUCTION

Martin Hardie
C.B.E., R.E., R.S.W., Hon. R.W.S.

(1875-1952)

by

Basil Taylor

INTRODUCTION

This book, of which two further volumes will appear, was Martin Hardie's *magnum opus*. He had completed the original draft soon after the last war and continued to revise it until his death in 1952 but the circumstances of publishing in those years had made impossible the publication of such a large illustrated work which was then, as it remains, the most extensive study of the subject.

Hardie's qualifications, while by no means uncommon in his generation, would now be most rare and in some unreasonable opinions treated as a handicap. He was a museum keeper and a scholar who, like D. S. MacColl, Sir Charles Holmes and Arthur M. Hind, combined the historical study of art and expert connoisseurship with artistic practice. He studied etching with Sir Frank Short and produced a body of prints which will certainly have their place among the engraved works of the twenties and thirties and which brought recognition to more famous artists such as Muirhead Bone, D. Y. Cameron and James McBey. He was also a productive water-colourist exhibiting constantly at the R.A., the R.W.S. and the R.I. For him his study and his studio were one and the same place. He served for 37 years on the staff of the Victoria and Albert Museum, always in the combined Departments of Painting and of Engraving, Illustration and Design as it was then called, of which he became Keeper in 1921. As I remember him in the years of his retirement—he left the Museum in 1935—his desk and the table where he worked on his drawings and prints stood side by side in a room which also housed a large part of his fine collections of water-colours and prints. Many of his acquisitions had been made, as he liked to remind younger enthusiasts, by saving pennies from his lunch money in a period when spectacular acquisitions could be made at small expense. As student and collector he belonged to the generation which undertook the fundamental investigation of English drawings and included such men as C. F. Bell, Laurence Binyon, Randall Davies, A. J. Finberg, C. E. Hughes, Thomas Lowinsky, A. P. Oppé, Iolo Williams and J. Leslie Wright. Each one of them, whether as author or collector, brought to their activity an individual enthusiasm, knowledge and sensibility. Binyon, who first catalogued the British Museum collection of English drawings, also responded to them with the apprehensions of a poet. Oppé treated them with a rigorous, often relentlessly critical connoisseurship which was not then common in England. Williams had a special interest in the obscure and minor figures, so many of which found treatment in his study published in 1952.[1]

Hardie, a man of delightful modesty, regarded his rôle in this enterprise too modestly. In

[1] *Early English Watercolours*, Iolo Williams, 1952.

the draft of his own introduction to this book he expressed not only gratitude for the friendship of these colleagues, especially Oppé and Bell, but disclaimed any originality for his own research. He regarded his book as being founded upon the discoveries of others and as being essentially directed to the general reader. But we must acknowledge that his own contribution was considerable and important. Besides the experience derived from studying and enlarging a great national collection, he had an unrivalled understanding of the development of water-colour as a medium and of the diversity of methods employed by the innumerable English artists who used it. This gave him a strong sense of slight differentiations of style enabling him to characterise with unusual precision the personal methods of those treated in his studies of individual artists. It also encouraged him to include the long introductory survey on materials which cannot be found elsewhere. 'I have written,' he said, 'at length upon aspects of technique which in so many books mainly through diffidence or sheer ignorance are too often overlooked.' It must be remembered that apart from his own immediate knowledge of practice he was a nephew of the nineteenth-century painter, John Pettie, R.A., and another of his uncles, Charles Martin Hardie, R.S.A., was also an artist. Perhaps it was this connection with a Victorian artistic family which made it natural for him to give substantial space to a period which others had rejected and which at the time of his writing was notably unfashionable.

As his own water-colours and the scope of his collection suggest, it was the period between the emergence of Girtin and the death of Turner which most attracted him, a period when a strong orchestration of colour, a concern with light and weather, and a vigorous freedom of touch was, as in De Wint or Cox, the primary aim, while still being achieved with the transparent washes so skilfully employed by earlier painters. Although this book takes a liberal view of what constitutes water-colour, including as it does such figures as Barlow or Alexander Cozens who worked essentially in monochrome, one cannot fail to notice Hardie's prejudice, common in his time, against the use of body-colour, Chinese white, to give solidity to the pigment, dramatize tonality and elaborate textures. Hardie's common-sensible outlook—he was an effective administrator and a good manager of the practicalities, whether as treasurer of the Artists' General Benevolent Institution, as air-raid warden, or organizer of local activities—might conceal from some a more romantic inclination which made him so responsive to, say, J. R. Cozens or Samuel Palmer; in fact, his part in the reassessment of Palmer was a most important aspect of his professional career. And he admitted that in his book 'much more space is given to artists whose work had some personal elements of originality and distinction than to those who were imitators or merely capable craftsmen without creative faculty'.

As already indicated the book does not consist of a continuous historical narrative but is constructed from studies of individuals. This is one reason why it seldom diverges from water-colour painting into a wider territory of English pictorial art, and it has been a local English peculiarity to study water-colours in separation from oil paintings. That this is an historical phenomenon is proved by the emergence, about 1800, of exhibiting societies devoted solely to the medium, something which the nineteenth century conserved and which has persisted into our own time. The outlook has also been shown in the organisation of our national collections and in art-historical studies. Although students may nowadays be less tolerant of this habit, the editors have not tried to compensate for a practice which only a few years ago would have seemed quite natural.

Our editorial task has been threefold. Hardie wrote his book in the leisure of retirement, much of it during the war, when the occupation of writing, as he himself admitted, gave relief from the anxieties of the time. This led him into many and often elaborate, luxurious discursions and quotations which would now be unsympathetic to many readers and which tend to obscure the book's main structure. We have, it is hoped with reason and propriety, excluded much of this intrusive material.

Although there has not been very much fresh research applied to this aspect of English art since Hardie's death many references have had to be brought up to date. This work, together with a thorough verification of all factual statements, has been Mr. Snelgrove's responsibility and in all which is most significant he is the editor of this book. In the case of certain minor chapters, namely those devoted to amateur artists and to the drawing masters of the eighteenth century, radical changes were demanded by the access of knowledge and new chapters on these matters will form appendices to the third volume. In addition to the indices of artists which will be found in volumes I and II, it is intended that volume III should include a full general index to the whole work and an extensive bibliography.

Hardie had not finalised his plans for the plates and so these are the editors' choice. We have tried to supply a selection which will illustrate the subject rather than exactly refer to his text, but in drawing so much upon the British Museum and the Victoria and Albert Museum we have quite deliberately followed his intention.

Martin Hardie would himself have wished acknowledgement to be given to those who contributed so much to his own knowledge and experience. In addition to those mentioned earlier in this Introduction he would have named Thomas Girtin, M. H. Grant, Sir Henry Hake, Sir Charles Holmes, Isherwood Kay, Sidney Kitson, D. S. MacColl and W. T. Whitley.

The editors are grateful to those museums and private collectors who have allowed their works to be reproduced and many of whom have given their kind assistance.

Miss Rosamond Harley, who is preparing a study of artist's materials and has uncovered much new evidence, has made useful comments upon the relevant section of Hardie's text, but any shortcomings therein should not be accounted to her. Mr. Paul Hulton has provided valuable amendments to the passages on John White and Jacques Le Moyne based upon his recent study of these artists. Miss Margot Holloway has rendered most valuable service in checking the typescripts and reading the proofs.

The editors would also like to acknowledge the sympathetic interest shown by members of the Hardie family, especially Dr. Frank Hardie, and that of Mr. Paul Mellon who initiated the publication of this book.

Martin Hardie *A selected list of publications*

1903   *V.A.M. Catalogue of Prints in the National Art Library*
           I Modern Etchings—Foreign Schools
           II British and American Schools
1906   *English Coloured Books*
1908   *John Pettie R.A., H.R.S.A.*
1918   *Boulogne—32 drawings by Captain Martin Hardie*
1919   *V.A.M. Catalogue of Modern Wood-engravers*
1921   *The Etched Work of W. Lee-Hankey R.E.*
1922   *The British School of Etching* (Print Collectors' Club)
1925   *James McBey Etchings 1902–1924* (and supplement)
1928   *Samuel Palmer Etchings* (Print Collectors' Club)
1932   *Thomas and William Daniell* ('Walker's Quarterly', with Muriel Clayton)
1938–40   *Catalogue of the Work of Sir Frank Short* (Print Collectors' Club)
1949   *English Water-colours of the XVIII century* ('Connoisseur' booklet)

Articles in the Old Water-colour Society's Club

1927	Vol. IV	*Samuel Palmer*
1932	IX	*William Turner of Oxford*
1934	XI	*Thomas Girtin, the technical aspect of his work*
1935	XII	*Constable's water-colours*
1944	XXII	*William Callow*
1945	XXIII	*Joseph Crawhall*
1947	XXV	*David Roberts*
1947	XXV	*Robert Hills 'Extollager'*

Walpole Society

1939   Vol. XXVII   *A sketch-book of Thomas Girtin*

Abbreviations

B.M.   British Museum
Diary   Joseph Farington's Diary, ed. James Greig. 8 vols. 1922–1928
L.B.   Laurence Binyon: Catalogue of Drawings by British Artists in the British Museum
     4 vols. 1898–1907
Oppé Coll.   Collection of Mr. D. L. T. and Miss Armide Oppé
Roget   J. L. Roget: History of the 'Old Water-colour' Society. 2 vols. 1891
V.A.M.   Victoria and Albert Museum
Whitley 1700–1799 I and II   W. T. Whitley: Artists and their Friends in England
     1700–1799. 2 vols. 1928
Whitley 1800–1820   W. T. Whitley: Art in England 1800–1820. 1928
Whitley 1821–1837   W. T. Whitley: Art in England 1821–1837. 1930

PART I

The nature of water-colour

'Water-Colour', as a descriptive title, seems to imply a kind of paint made just with pigment and water, but this is an impossible working process, for if colour and water only were applied to the paper, the colour would not adhere; when dry, it could be flicked from the surface even more easily than pastel. The art which actually corresponds to water-colour as an exact definition, is the form of wall-painting called fresco in which the painting is applied to a surface of fresh plaster, the pigments being mixed with water only. But a process supervenes by which the setting lime seizes upon the particles of colour, binding them to itself with a durable adhesion. In the case of 'powder colours', used widely in schools, these are already prepared with a binding material.

For painting, then, in water-colour upon paper or silk, it is essential to have some matter of a colloid nature either dissolved in the water, in which the brush is dipped before taking up colour, or, as is more usual, employed as a binding material for the pigments, whether made up in cakes, or 'moist' in tubes. Quite a number of substances, natural and artificial, have been employed for the purpose. Amongst the most useful are several varieties of gum, but use has also been made of vegetable and animal albumens in the form of flour and rice paste, the white and yolk of eggs (tempera painting), animal size (distemper), and the casein of cheese, which was probably the vehicle employed for Persian miniatures. To use ordinary ink of any colour, black, blue, brown, red, etc., is to work with water-colour. In all writing inks there must be a little gum, besides water; otherwise the ink would not adhere to the paper. On the analogy of 'Oil-Painting', therefore, water-colour should strictly be entitled 'Gum-Painting'. But it is well entitled 'Water-colour', because a vast amount of water is used with a very little gum. If water is stinted, the work is dry, opaque and messy. The brush should always be full of water, indeed De Wint used to insist that therein lay the whole secret of good water-colour painting.

In normal practice gum arabic is employed by the artist's colourman when making the powdered pigment into cakes or mixing it for use in tubes. Gum arabic, obtained from the *Acacia*, is a vegetable gum, differing from resins in that it is soluble in water. Nothing else is essential and nothing else was used in the earliest colours of this kind, but in later times it became the custom to add a little honey while grinding the colours, in order to counteract the possible brittleness of the gum, and glycerine was mixed in so as to keep the colour moist. This is, of course, particularly essential when the colours are put up in tubes of so-called 'moist colours' instead of, as was the old use, in cake form. Professor Laurie was inclined to think that in honey and glycerine there was danger that their sugars, being slightly hygroscopic (i.e. absorbent of damp) might attract moisture, but judging by the long tradition behind it, the presence of honey does no harm.

Gum arabic dissolves remarkably well in water. As a solution it flows freely, and even in diluted washes there is enough gum to prevent the colours from drying matt. But this easy solubility is troublesome when any first tint is to be covered by a second. A second touch on a wet passage of colour, in any case, causes a revolution among the molecules of pigment, which may rush together, making the tone darker and the colour more intense in some places, particularly at the edges, and thinner and paler in other parts. Even when a second wash is put over a dry one, the water in the second wash re-dissolves to some extent the gum which held the first, and the two get mixed together. Some degradation of colour always ensues when one wash is laid over another, and in extreme cases the result is an obvious mess.

Gum arabic, though it dissolves in water, does to some extent become a thin varnish, increasing the luminosity of the colours. Where honey and glycerine are used in moist colours there is possibly more risk of the colour underneath being lifted by subsequent washes. Many artists still prefer to use colour in cakes, prepared with a minimum of honey or glycerine.

There are troubles and embarrassments from which the water-colour painter, due to his medium, suffers more than the painter in oil. It is generally admitted that water-colour wash laid to full depth and allowed to dry is of finer colour and quality than the work which is produced by repeated operations. Though, in modern days especially, it has been the almost universal practice to use only water as a vehicle, certain other liquids have at times been added in order to retard or accelerate the drying of the pigment. A painter working under a very hot baking sun will find that his colours become almost insoluble and that colour placed on the paper dries so rapidly that he cannot manipulate a wash. In this case he will add glycerine to the water; and in past days chloride of calcium, gum tragacanth and fig-tree juice have been employed for this purpose. The use of sour paste, for somewhat similar purposes, is dealt with in my chapter on Cotman. To accelerate drying, alcohol may be added to the water; in the eighteenth century it was quite usual to add a little brandy, gin, or whisky for this purpose: Paul Sandby constantly used gin.

Pigments: their earlier use

The earliest list known to me of water-colour pigments is that given by Edward Norgate. About 1630 or a little earlier he wrote a treatise, *Miniatura or the Art of Limning*,[1] for Sir Theodore Mayerne. In his own words it 'broke forth and became a wanderer', and was much copied and pirated. Twenty years later, a little before his death in 1650, he revised

---

[1] Tann. 326 (MS); transcribed and edited by Martin Hardie, 1919.

and enlarged it, and a manuscript transcript of it in its best form, by a contemporary hand, is preserved in the Bodleian Library. Norgate's list is as follows:

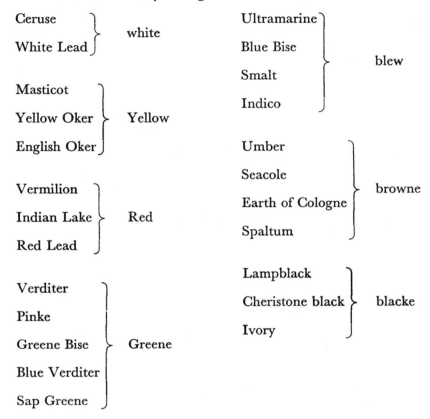

Ceruse ⎫
White Lead ⎭ white

Masticot ⎫
Yellow Oker ⎬ Yellow
English Oker ⎭

Vermilion ⎫
Indian Lake ⎬ Red
Red Lead ⎭

Verditer ⎫
Pinke ⎪
Greene Bise ⎬ Greene
Blue Verditer ⎪
Sap Greene ⎭

Ultramarine ⎫
Blue Bise ⎪
Smalt ⎬ blew
Indico ⎭

Umber ⎫
Seacole ⎪
Earth of Cologne ⎬ browne
Spaltum ⎭

Lampblack ⎫
Cheristone black ⎬ blacke
Ivory ⎭

Norgate describes the nature and use of these colours, stating which are to be prepared by grinding and which by washing in distilled water. Gum arabic is always used, and he anticipates the use of honey by employing sugar candy.

> Your colour being dry, reserve it in cleane papers & boxes for your use, and when you will fall to worke take as much as will lie in a muscle shell (which of all others are fittest for limming, or otherwise those of Mother Pearle) and with a little gum water temper it with your finger till it come to a fitting consistency or stiffnes, observing that your proporcon of Gum Arabique must bee soe as neither to make the Colour shiny which it will doe if it bee too much gumd, nor when dry in the shell it will come off with a touch of your finger, which is a signe that it is gumd too little. . . . For you must endeavor to make all your colours lie even and fast, without peeling or cracking, and this is done by adding a little white Sugar Candy in fine powder and with a few dropps of faire water temper the Colour with your finger till it bee thoroughly mixt and dissolved, and then it will be smooth and even.

In his *Graphice* of 1658 William Sanderson clearly borrows much, without acknowledgement, from Norgate or from one of the many contemporary copies of Norgate's manuscript. Speaking of 'Limning in Water-Colours', he gives 'the True Order and Names of

Colours, the means to prepare them for the Pensill and to clense them from their corrupt mixtures wherewith they are Sophisticate'. His list of colours is shorter than Norgate's, but introduces Cedar-green, Spanish-brown, and Terra Lemnia or Collins earth. He gives much the same directions for grinding them, with a mixture of gum arabic, on porphyry, marble, glass or crystal, and for putting them in a shell for use. As to actual practice his directions for 'Landskipp' are solely for painting landscape on vellum, which implies that he was dealing with a miniature method and that the art of water-colour, as practised in Holland, was not in 1658 a general English use.

W. Gore's *Art of Limning*, 1674, begins with a list of colours. Ruling out three kinds of white and six kinds of black, there are thirty-one colours mentioned: blue in six varieties, yellow in ten, green in three, red in eight, and brown in four. He adds that: 'all other colours necessary and useful in the Art of Limning, may be composed and made out of the forementioned Colours.' In *The Art of Drawing and Painting in Water-Colours*, printed in 1732, for J. Peele, London, there is an illustration of a box, to which we shall come later, capable of holding thirty-two colours. It is the greatest mistake—and one which has often been made—to suppose that the simplicity of method employed at the end of the eighteenth century was due to any lack of colours or that the restrained colour of J. R. Cozens or Girtin was enforced. Samuel Redgrave was of the opinion that about 1793 John Cozens could procure only Indian red, lake, indigo, yellow ochre, burnt umber, burnt sienna and black; but in fact Cozens probably limited his palette to those seven colours from choice. In 1746, nearly fifty years earlier, his father, Alexander Cozens, refers to thirty colours which he had in use when sketching at Rome.[1]

About 1800 Dayes wrote[2]: 'One great inconvenience the student labours under, arises from the too great quantity of colours put into his hands; an evil so encouraged by the drawing-master and colour-man, that it is not uncommon to give two or three dozen colours in a box, a thing quite unnecessary'; and Richard Wilson on being told that a new colour had been found said he was sorry for it, as there were too many already. In 1809 James Roberts evidently agreed with this verdict, and in his *Painting in Water-Colours* gives a list of 'as many colours as are ever necessary for the most vivid and elaborate painting in water-colours'. Excluding black, they are twelve in number, very much the average extent of a modern painter's palette:

Light Oker	Lake
Orange Orpiment	Prussian blue
Raw Terra di Sienna	Indigo
Gambouge	Burnt Terra di Sienna
Light Red	Vandyke Brown
Red Lead	Cologn Earth

Indian Ink.

[1] A. P. Oppé, *A Roman Sketch-book by Alexander Cozens*, Walpole Soc. XVI, 1927–1928, pp. 81–93.
[2] *The Works of the late Edward Dayes*, 1805, p. 298.

He adds the following notes:

> Lake and Indigo, or Prussian blue, make Purple.
> Light oker and Indigo, make a pale Green.
> Gamboge and Indigo, make a brilliant Green.
> Raw Terra di Sienna and Indigo, make a softer Green.
> Burnt Terra di Sienna and Indigo, make an Olive Green.
> Indian Ink, Indigo and Gamboge, make a very dark Green.
> The colour commonly called the Aerial Tint, is made with Lake, Indigo, and Raw Terra di Sienna.
> A richer tint is composed of Burnt Terra di Sienna, Indigo and Lake.
> Either of these two mixtures are very serviceable for distance.

Washes of the actual colours, and of the combinations mentioned, are given on a plate in Roberts' book, so that it is easy to see what was the artist's average palette and method of work during Girtin's lifetime. Dayes, as has been seen, had no great liking for the colour-man. He wrote as follows:

> The best way is for the student to prepare his own colors, and this may be easily done, as all that is requisite, after grinding them, if they should be wanted very fine, is to wash them: this is effected by putting the ground color into a bason of water, and letting it stand a few minutes, pouring the top gently off into a second vessel, and letting that stand double or triple the time of the former; then into a third; and so on, in proportion to the fineness of the color wanted, as each time will afford a finer sediment. This may be preserved dry in a powder, tempered with gum-water for use; or by mixing with gum, and put to dry in little card molds, may be rubbed upon a smooth stone or plate when wanted. To prevent them from cracking in the mold, some fine sugar, or white sugar-candy, should be mixed with them. Sweet-wert will answer the same purpose, and may be drawn from the malt, by boiling it in an earthen vessel till it feels sticky between the fingers. It is a mistake of those who suppose much mucilage (gum) will prevent the colors from fading; on the contrary, it is highly injurious, as when it loses its transparency, which it soon does, it deadens the colors, by preventing the transmission of the light. [1]

Worthy of mention here is T. H. A. Fielding's *Index of Colours and Mixed Tints*, published in 1830. It is interesting for its eighteen plates, each plate containing twenty-eight squares of colour actually applied by hand to illustrate different varieties of tint. The labour, care and cost involved in producing an edition of a book, each copy of which contains five hundred and four distinct colours, applied one at a time by hand, makes this an extraordinary publication.

Pure water-colour; body-colour or gouache

Colour, prepared with a colloid material, may be applied to the paper with water as the only vehicle. In this case it is usually termed 'pure' water-colour. The brilliancy of pure water-colour rises from the fact that transparent colours (and all water-colours are transparent or semi-transparent) never quite hide the white surface of the paper, and the paper remains throughout as the lighting agent. A full tint of any colour shows darker than a thin

---

[1] *The Works of the late Edward Dayes*, 1805, p. 298.

13

tint, only because less of the white ground shows through. 'Never lose your paper' is an old and sound maxim for the water-colourist. One reason for the luminous brilliance of the pure method is that the surface of most paper is granulous. Its little hollows and projections maintain an alternation of light in the latter and half light in the former. The prominences, unless loaded with colour, will always retain their reflective lustre. In pure water-colour, even dark passages, like those in De Wint's foliage, can remain luminous. Put the same wash of deep colour on a white paper and a toned paper, and the difference will be immediately apparent. All of this was understood as far back as 1735 by the writer of *Method of learning to draw in Perspective*. One of his main points is the avoidance of white paint:

> If you leave the Lights, the Whiteness of the Paper serves instead of the use of White Paint, which is an heavy colour, and would rather confound the edges of the Colours, which I have prescribed to be laid on, than do them any Service; but the Colours which I have directed, where there is no White laid on, will agreeably shine into the White of the Paper. I am more particular in this, because several, if they see a Flower of a blue Colour, will lay it all over with one Colour thick enough to hide both the Lights and the Shades, and then it remains like a Penny Picture, where there is nothing to be seen but a Jargon of Reds, Blues, and Yellows.

In water-colour, a transparent dark colour is put over a light one (a process which in oil-painting is called 'glazing', as opposed to 'scumbling', i.e. the application of opaque colour to modify or alter an effect) the paper will still act as an illuminant. Oil-painters use glazing as an occasional, or alternative, device, but it remained for water-colour painters, especially after the beginning of the nineteenth century, to develop it as an entire manner. Edward Dayes gave a good description of the purpose and value of glazing in water-colour:

> In working up a drawing, if a richness of color is wanted, it will be necessary to repeat it two or three times, or indeed as often as necessary; this will give a depth and richness, that never can be obtained by a single color. This is what the artist calls glazing, and can only be got by practice; only the most warm and transparent colors are used for the purpose. Thus a green of blue and yellow would be raw; but burnt terra de Sienna, or lake, glazed over it, will beautify it; not make it lighter, but richer. Again, if crimson drapery is wanted, it should be dead colored with vermilion, and glazed with lake: and if shadows of Indian ink are too cold, the bistre would warm and clear them.

As opposed to pure water-colour we have the use of body-colour, i.e. of pigment containing sufficient body to make it opaque. This implies that painting in body-colour is entirely a scumbling, and not a glazing, method. Some water-colours, such as cobalt, cobalt violet, terra verte, vermilion and cerulean blue, being only semi-transparent, are more opaque than others, but all colours when mixed with Chinese white, in the normal body-colour method, become semi-liquid and opaque. The oil-painter can amend a dark portion of his picture with a colour mixed with white. If a painter in pure water-colour made a surface amendment with an opaque Chinese white, it would at once look foreign to the rest of his work, where the lighting agent is under the surface of colour. Even when a drawing in black chalk on a toned paper is heightened with Chinese white, a note of falsity and dissonance is introduced. The usual practice, therefore, in body-colour painting is to mix

14

Chinese white with all the colours. All of them become opaque; the whiteness of the paper counts for nothing; body-colour can equally well be used on a brown or black paper. It becomes possible, as in an oil-painting, to reduce or obliterate a dark colour by putting a light colour over it. In pure water-colour a light colour, added over a dark, will merely darken it further, by shutting out more of the light given by the white paper. In the pure method a dark cannot be reduced or obliterated by superimposing a light colour; it must be washed down, to allow the paper to reflect more, or it must be washed completely out, to permit re-painting on the white surface. This process is dealt with later.

The term gouache (from the French *gouache* and Italian *guazzo*) is interchangeable with the term 'body-colour'. The Oxford Dictionary defines gouache as 'a method of painting with opaque colours ground in water and mixed with gum and honey so as to form a sort of paste'. The first quotation given by the Dictionary, embodying the term, dates from 1882; it was in use earlier than that.

The use of pure water-colour in transparent washes is the method in which the British School has notably excelled. Body-colour has always been to some extent subject to criticism. From the *Library of the Fine Arts*[1] comes the following paragraph:

> Mr. Ackermann of Regent-street, who has long been busied in experimental improvements in the manufacture of water-colours, has produced a permanent white of great brightness, which will be very acceptable to the professors of water-colour painting, as many of the most distinguished amongst them are at length allowed by custom to avail themselves ad libitum of its vigorous aid. Heretofore, the *cognosc* would not tolerate, upon the finest coloured drawing, a single speck of this bright pigment—no, not even to the tipping of a skimming seagull's wing. Now, the daring, dashing emulators of *oil*, splash it about at will, and most effectively. Thanks to the late Bonington for this. Why should Prejudice longer be allowed to prescribe limits to the flights of Genius?

Body-colour is scorned, or dismissed with contumely, by writers of modern manuals—such as A. W. Rich in his *Water-Colour Painting* (1918)—'body colour cannot be too severely condemned'—and Adrian Hill in *On the Mastery of Water-Colour Painting* (1939).

Body-colour was used largely in the eighteenth century, and its uses and abuses are discussed fully in a later chapter upon Paul Sandby, and elsewhere. From 1830 onwards, as the above quotation indicates, it was undergoing a revival. Turner had used it freely for drawings made upon a grey or blue paper, and frequently, when working on a white paper, he mixed some white in his water-bottle, giving the water a milky appearance and consistency. Later on, such painters as J. F. Lewis and Birket Foster, to name but two among many, consistently mixed white with their pigments. Other artists such as William Hunt, Samuel Palmer in his last period, and Arthur Melville, constantly underpainted with solid white, producing great brilliance by the use of transparent water-colours over this white surface, when quite dry. On the other hand, where De Wint used body-colour, his work is

[1] Vol. I, 1831, p. 180.

a dismal failure. Thackeray passed his opinion about body-colour with his usual outspokenness. Writing about a drawing by Fred Tayler, he said:

> We are led bitterly in this picture to deplore the use of that fatal white-lead pot that is clogging and blackening the pictures of so many of the water-colour painters nowadays. His large picture contains a great deal of this white mud, and has lost in consequence much of that liquid mellow tone for which his works are remarkable.[1]

All through the nineteenth century and in modern times body-colour, in spite of much argument, has been frequently used as will be pointed out later when the work of individual painters comes under consideration.

What has been said about gouache and body-colour applies to tempera painting, a hybrid process for the water-colourist. Some members of the Royal Academy, such as David Murray, Charles Napier Hemy and Charles Sims, were said, I think with some truth, to produce tempera paintings, exhibiting some as water-colours and others, varnished, among the oils. The subject of varnishing is dealt with in a later section.

I have frequently referred to 'Chinese White' in the sense of any white pigment used in water-colour. Actually, this title was not used till 1834, and up to that year most whites had a basis of lead and were easily blackened (by the sulphuretted hydrogen) in the smoky air of crowded cities. In 1834 Messrs. Winsor & Newton put on the market a white with the title of Chinese White. It was specially prepared for water-colour, and was based upon oxide of zinc, which is not nearly so liable as lead to change by the action of sulphuretted hydrogen and is perfectly durable. Winsor & Newton stated: 'The pigment, at present known to artists as Chinese White, is our exclusive manufacture, the name being merely a distinctive one adopted by us, as involving no description of the composition or properties of the substance to which we applied it.'[2]

The following remarks are extracted from J. D. Harding's *Principles and Practice of Art*, 1845:

> When the oxide of zinc, which is prepared by Winsor and Newton, under the name of Chinese White, was first put into my hands, some years ago, I applied to one of my friends, whose name as a chemist and philosopher is amongst the most distinguished in our country,[3] to analyse it for me, and to tell if I might rely on its durability; the reply was, that if it would in all other respects answer the purposes I required of it, I had nothing to fear on account of its durability . . . This is an invaluable pigment . . . It is hardly possible to overrate the value of opaque white in water colours when judiciously used.

[1] *Fraser's Magazine*, 1840.
[2] *Remarks on the White Pigments used by Water-Colour Painters, being a letter addressed to G. H. Bachhoffner, Esq., Lecturer in Chemistry*, published by Winsor & Newton, 1837. Bachhoffner had written, in his book on *Chemistry applied to the Fine Arts*, 1837, of whites made with zinc as 'being much inferior to the whites with a basis of lead, and but little, if any, superior to them in durability.'
[3] This was Faraday, who did not allow the publication of his name in this connection.

Colours and the artist's colourman

It is difficult to give with any certainty the date when an 'artist's colourman' began to supply his clients with paints, canvases and brushes. Northcote says that when Kneller came to this country in 1675 he brought with him a man whose sole employment was to prepare his colours and materials. 'Kneller afterwards set him up as a colourmaker for artists; and this man's success, he being the first who kept a colour shop in London, occasioned the practice of it as a trade.'[1] Sir Charles Eastlake believed that long before Kneller came to England there were persons employed here exclusively in the manufacture of painters' materials. In his *Art of Painting in Oyl*, published in 1687, John Smith speaks of artist's colourmen as if they were common in London, and says that those of his readers who do not care to be at the trouble of grinding their own colours can obtain any sort of quantity from the shops, ready ground and at reasonable prices. Another writer on painting about 1710, after mentioning the principal colours in use at the time, says[2]:

> Note that they are all to be bought ready ground at the colour shops in London, tied up in bits of bladders and of about the bigness of walnuts; and are done much finer and cleaner (and almost as cheap) than anyone can possibly do them himself. All painters generally have them thus.

W. T. Whitley could find no definite statement about the artist's colourman and his business earlier than 1749, when a writer in *The London Tradesman* mentions Robert Keating of the White Hart in Long Acre, who appears to have done a large trade:

> This gentleman deals in all the colours for the housepainter, but his chief business consists in furnishing the liberal painters with their fine colours. A painter may go into his shop and be furnished with every article he uses, such as pencils, brushes, cloths ready for drawing on, and all manner of colours ready prepared, with which he cannot be supplied either in such quality & quantity in any or all of the shops in London.

Perhaps the colourman was slower in supplying the requirements, for which there would be less demand, of the water-colour painter. Till towards the end of the eighteenth century it was quite the usual practice for the water-colour artist to prepare his own colours, grinding or washing them, and then mixing his pigments with the requisite proportion of gum arabic. In *The Art of Drawing and Painting in Water Colours*, published in 1770, minute instructions are given to the artist for the preparation of his colours from natural products— roots, minerals, animal and other compounds; and the processes of preparation, chemical and manipulative, are closely described. No mention is made at this date of the artist's colourman; the painter is referred to the druggist and the herbalist for his material. A few years later, in 1776, the well-known engraver and printseller, Matthew Darly, advertises: 'Transparent colours for staining drawings.' The colours were probably liquid, and this is possibly the beginning of the colourman's trade so far as concerns the water-colour painter.

[1] Whitley, 1700–1799, I, p. 330.
[2] Whitley, 1700–1799, I, p. 331.

Writing in 1811, two years after Sandby's death, a biographer[1] says:

> For many years after Mr. Sandby commenced landscape drawing no colours were in general use except such as were peculiarly adapted for the staining of maps and plans, and indeed it was himself who set Middleton the colour maker to prepare them in somewhat like their present state, and which are now brought to so great perfection by Reeves, Newman and others.

As was shown in the preceding section, the writer was entirely wrong about the colours available for Sandby's use, and though John Middleton of St. Martin's Lane, who supplied colours to Turner, followed out Sandby's suggestion, he had been anticipated by the founder of the firm of Reeves which is still in existence. Reeves was the first, about 1780, to make up colour in small, hard, cakes.[2] A writer in the *Repository of Arts* in 1813, says that Reeves:

> . . . about thirty years ago turned his attention to the preparation of water-colours and by his successful experiments produced the elegant invention of forming them into cakes. Until this period, every artist was obliged to prepare his own colours, which, generally for want of sufficient knowledge of their chemical properties, and leisure to grind and prepare the pigments, gave much trouble and produced but indifferent success.

The name of the firm, it should be added, was stamped on each cake. In 1781 the Society of Arts recognised the value of the Reeves' invention of soluble cakes by awarding them a premium. The firm was then composed of two partners, William and Thomas Reeves, who carried on the business at the sign of the Blue Coat Boy and King's Arms, Holborn Bridge. In 1784 they quarrelled, and for years afterwards rival announcements appeared in the newspapers in which both William and Thomas claim to have been the original inventors of the cakes; each warns artists and amateurs not to deal with the other. William's advertisements of 1784, which conclude with the assertion that 'his Colours is no copy but the original Invention', are often followed immediately in the same column by the protests of Thomas against the 'malevolent puffs' of his former partner and a definite statement that upon him alone was the bounty of the Society of Arts bestowed. Thomas Reeves retained the Holborn Bridge premises after the dissolution of partnership.

In 1801 Ackermann's *Superfine Water Colours, with Directions how to prepare and use them including Succinct Hints on Drawing and Painting* contains this note:

> To prevent mistakes in the use of colours which, when of nearly the same tint, are not easily distinguishable, I have been at the additional expence of procuring a mould for each colour, so that each cake is marked with its proper name, on one side, and my name and direction on the other, without any advance in the price.

Further entries give the price of all the cakes of colour as 1s. each, excepting Carmine Lake at 2s., Gall Stone 5s., Royal Smalt 5s., Carmine 5s., Burnt Carmine 5s.

There were other imitators of the Reeves cakes besides Ackermann at a time when

[1] 'Thomas Paul Sandby', *Monthly Magazine*, June 1, 1811, reprinted in A. P. Oppé's 'The Memoir of Paul Sandby by his son', *Burlington Magazine.*, 1946, LXXXVIII, p. 143.
[2] *Whitley*, 1700–1799, II. pp. 360–363.

water-colour painting was a fashionable pursuit. 'Other advertisers', says Whitley,[1] with regard to the decade or so after the Society of Arts' award to Reeves, 'include Middleton; George Blackman, who says that he has married the daughter of William Reeves and offers to undersell his father-in-law by twenty per cent; Kebby, who claims to have been the apprentice of Thomas Reeves; John Skidmore of Holborn; and Charles Schofield of Aldersgate Street. I have seen no advertisements of this time for Newman, who had even then a reputation for water-colours; but there are frequent and lengthy ones for the cakes of John Scott of 417 Strand, among whose customers Gainsborough was probably numbered.'

James Newman, the founder of the firm of Messrs. Newman, established himself towards the end of the eighteenth century in Gerrard Street, Soho, the street of The Turk's Head Tavern, the gathering place of contemporary painters for business and for festivals. In 1801 he removed to Soho Square, where the business is still carried on. Whitley was able to add to his prior information by quoting an advertisement in the *Morning Chronicle* April 25, 1801[2]:

> James Newman, late of Gerrard Street, artist, pencil maker and colourman, returns his most sincere thanks for the many favours he has received from the Nobility, Gentry and others; and begs to acquaint them and his friends in general that he has removed to No. 24 Soho Square, where he has fitted up extensive premises for the purpose of carrying on his business in a much more commodious manner than he has hitherto been able to do.

About 1805 a writer on art said: 'Upon the invention of Reeves others have made improvements until the preparation of water-colours has almost attained perfection' and Messrs. Roberson began to experiment with pigments ground in honey instead of being bound with gum into a hard cake.[3]

Cake colours were open to some objections, in that they dried or crumbled owing to age or to being kept in a hot climate. With more careful grinding and the addition of honey they became comparatively smooth and more durable. To remove the colour from a hard cake required a good deal of friction from a brush, and the usual practice was to dip the cake in water and rub it on a china palette or in small china saucers; the same method was used in preparing Chinese ink, which was usually made up into longish oblong sticks. These small white saucers, usually $2\frac{1}{2}$ and $3\frac{1}{2}$ inches in diameter, which have gone almost completely out of use in an artist's studio, still offer great advantages for indoor work in preparing a wash, say for a sky, whether the colour is obtained from cake, pan or tube. The troughs in a colour-box are rarely large enough or clean enough for the purpose. In the Royal Library at Windsor Castle[4] is a delightful study by Paul Sandby, made about 1770, of a young lady seated painting at an artist's table with colours set out in rows of oyster shells. The shell, used by the early miniature-painters, apparently gave place to the

[1] *Whitley*, 1700–1799, II. p. 362.
[2] *Whitley*, 1800–1820, p. 26.
[3] It should be mentioned that the firm of Rowney, established 1789, is still flourishing.
[4] No. 14377

china saucer early in the nineteenth century. A writer in the *Library of Fine Arts*, 1832, recalls amateurs 'who gave their six hours daily to the delectable daubery of mountains, mists and lakes, seated round tables spread with crockery brim full of sea-tint, sky-tint, middleground and foreground tint'. Samuel Palmer had many small china saucers which he filled to the brim with the pigments which he used the most. Ruskin somewhere scolds our water-colour draughtsmen for not keeping their saucers clean. David Cox used to impress upon his pupils the necessity of having a number of saucers to mix each separate shade in, and, much later, Violet Hunt as a child had the morning task of rubbing colours, presumably in saucers, for the day's work of her father A. W. Hunt.

The next step from the hard cakes was the making-up of colours in small white pans which, like the hard cakes, fitted into receptacles, of standard size, in a paint-box. Dayes had kept his colours in little card 'molds' possibly the origin of the china pans. The colour made up in pans was described as 'moist'; it contained more honey or glycerine. From these pans the brush charged with water lifts the colour easily with a gentle friction. For sketching from nature they superseded the hard cakes and are still in ordinary use. In his *Principles and Practice of Art*, 1845, J. D. Harding writes that: 'The Art of Painting in Water Colours has been greatly assisted by improvements in the preparation of the pigments: the greatest advantage, however, has been the introduction of moist colours, which, I believe, are a French invention, but greatly improved by Messrs. Winsor & Newton.'

Messrs. Winsor & Newton kindly lent me a small catalogue, probably the first list issued by their firm. It was in 1832 that William Winsor and H. C. Newton entered into partnership at 38 Rathbone Place, London. The catalogue contains a list of water-colours, prepared in cakes, and also *Winsor & Newton's* Newly Invented *Moist Water Colours, for sketching from Nature*:

> These colours always retain their moist state, so that the application of the smallest quantity of water brings off the colour, if required, in its full force, avoiding the delay attendant on the use of the Cake Colours. They dry on paper as firmly as any other colours, retain their full brilliancy, and keep for any length of time without forming mildew.

These colours, as Messrs. Winsor & Newton inform me, were originally not filled into pans but directly into the divisions of japanned tin sketching boxes for carrying in the pocket. China pans came into use about 1836. From a *Hand-book of Water-Colours*, issued by Winsor & Newton between 1841, when they received a Royal Warrant, and 1844, when they built their first factory in Kentish Town, comes this paragraph:

> The Moist Colour is contained in thin porcelain pans, in shape like the dry cake, but rather larger—is enclosed in foil for security and portability, and warranted to keep for any length of time without deterioration. When required for use, the foil is to be taken off the pan, which may then be fastened by a wafer, or a little gum water, into the usual japanned sketching box.

The spring method of attachment, which obviated the use of any cement, was patented soon after.

20

In 1848 the firm published a pamphlet containing testimonials in praise of their Moist Water Colours, written by Stanfield, Roberts, Etty, Constable, Harding and many other well-known painters. The following may be quoted, as showing the special properties and advantages which were found by artists of that time:

> 9 Brunswick Terrace,
> Camberwell.
> September 12, 1848.

Gentlemen,

With much pleasure I join the favourable testimony of my colleagues, on your improved Moist Water Colours. They have been in my hands ever since they were offered to artists and the public, and have had a thorough trial, which has well tested their admirable qualities. Not only are they more convenient for general use (especially in sketching), but, in my opinion, more economical than the dry cakes, as those are liable to break, and can never be entirely consumed; also considerable time is lost in rubbing, and, when a small quantity of intense colour is required, a large amount must be rubbed before the requisite depth is obtained. All these serious objections are removed in the Moist Colours, and I hope the invention may continue to receive the support it fully deserves.

> I am, &c,
> W. Collingwood Smith.

> Jan. 25, 1846

Gentlemen,

I have great pleasure in being able to add my testimony to the excellence of your Moist Water Colours, and their capability of remaining in a moist state in every climate to which I have exposed them. I have many of these colours now by me, which I have had while sketching in the Cape Verde Island, Brazil, New Zealand, and various parts of Australia, and even after having remained upwards of three years under the influence of these diversified climates, still remain in a moist and perfect state.

> I am, &c,
> George French Angus.

Another, but entirely unsolicited testimonial was given by Thackeray in *The Newcomes* published in 1853. By an allusive association of names he described the firm as Messrs. Soap and Isaac:

> Before Clive went away, he had an apparatus of easels, sketching-stools, umbrellas, and painting-boxes, the most elaborate and beautiful that Messrs. Soap and Isaac could supply. It made J. J.'s eyes glisten to see those lovely gimcracks of art—those smooth mill-boards, those slab-tinted sketching-blocks, and glistening rows of colour-tubes lying in their boxes, which seemed to cry, 'Come, squeeze me'. If painting-boxes made painters, if sketching-stools would but enable one to sketch, surely I would hasten this very instant to Messrs. Soap and Isaac! but, alas! those pretty toys no more make artists than cowls make monks.

The third step in the provision of colours for the water-colour painter came about 1847 when Messrs. Winsor & Newton, who had long years before, supplied Richard Wilson with colours, put up moist colours into metal tubes of precisely the same description as those which contain oil colours. That tubes containing oil paint had recently come into commercial use during the 1840s is shown by the fact that Messrs. Winsor & Newton in their *Hand-Book* published between 1841 and 1844 give a description of their nature and purpose:

> The oil colour is ejected from these tubes in a manner similar to that in which colour is expressed from the common bladder, by squeezing or compressing between the thumb and finger, so that the colour is always kept gathered up in a compact state; the empty part of the tube remaining closed or compressed behind it. The screw cap being replaced over the aperture, effectually excludes air, and preserves the remaining colour from injury.

Tubes for water-colour were not mentioned in Winsor & Newton's price-list for 1846, but their list published in 1849 includes 'moist water colours in patent collapsible tubes'. This fixes their introduction somewhere between 1846 and 1849.

The colour prepared for tubes must necessarily be made more moist by glycerine or honey so that moderate compression of the tube may cause it to squeeze out. Many painters to-day prefer pans, on the ground that the colour is purer and less artificially moistened.

Paint-box and palette

To the craftsman the necessary details of his work tend to become monotonous because of their regularity, and are apt to be taken as a matter of course. That was not so with Norgate who was eager, in his own words, to 'stand upon every point, and go over things at large, and to be curious in particulars'. From him we know about the palette in use during the first half of the seventeenth century:

> By this time you are ready to begin your worke, yet one thing must needs retard you a whyle, which is that in a great shell of Mother of pearle, or large peece of pure Ivory, you lay severall small heaps of Colours taken out of your shells, and dispose of them in a decent order, one by another, to serve in readiness to temper your shadowes, in imitation of the Oyle painters pallets whereon their colours are laid as these of yours must bee about the border of Circumference of your large shell.[1]

The author (presumably W. Gore) of *The Art of Limning* published in 1674, giving information 'formerly set out by the excellent Limner Mr. Gerhard of Brugge, and now much augmented and amended', seems to be unaware of the ivory palette, but suggests an improvement upon shell:

> That in the using of your colours you may keep the same clean and pure, it will not be convenient to use the same out of shells, and to take the same with your Pencil out of them, because you cannot conveniently temper your colour in them, according as your work doth require it; therefore you may for this purpose have a glass pallet, or for want of that a convenient big piece of glass of one indifferent thickness; and upon this put your several colours, and mix them, and temper them upon that Glass at your pleasure, in such manner as you shall judge them to be convenient for your use in your work; wooden pallets as Picture-drawers make use of for their oyl-colours, are not good for his use, for the wood is of a softer nature, and sucks in the water-

[1] Edward Norgate, *Miniatura* (ed. Martin Hardie), 1919, p. 22.

colour, and when you have made use of them, you cannot so conveniently cleanse your pallet again, because of its softness; but Glass is hard, and the water-colour that remaineth upon it is soon taken from it, and the Glass washt clean, as if nothing had bin upon it, and so made fit, and kept for the next occasion that you may have to make use of it again.

The first mention, so far as my knowledge goes, of a portable box and palette in combination occurs in *The Art of Drawing, and Painting in Water-Colours*, printed for J. Peele, London, 1732:

> Of a portable case for Colours; with Directions for making, Gum, Allum and other Waters. . . . Let me advise such Persons, who are curious in making Observations of the Colours of Flowers, To have always in their Pocket a small Case with Colours in it, about the Bigness of a Snuff-box, made of Ivory, about half an Inch thick, in which should be scoop'd several Concaves about half an inch Diameter each, and as deep as the Ivory would bear, without going through: These Cavities may be placed as near one another as possible, and fill'd with Colours of several Sorts; and as for the liquid Colours, they will dry, by being exposed to the Air, so that one may have them altogether in a few Days dry enough to be carried in the Pocket.

The author then prints a plan of his box, which on a scale of half an inch to each colour must be about six inches by three—a good sized snuff-box. In half of the box the cavities are five in a row; and in the other half are three rows of four. He continues:

> In the foregoing Figure one may observe the Disposition of the several Cavities for the Colours . . . and on one side a little Case for Pencils, and another for Indian-ink, Gum Arabick powder'd with white Sugar-candy, or for any thing else an Artist may have Occasion for in the painting Way.
>
> In such a Case, you may have thirty two sorts of Colour under very easy Command, besides other Necessaries: Then, as a Cover to this, let there be a piece of plain Ivory to open with an Hinge, that may serve as a Pallet, and all this will lie in a very narrow Compass; nay, even though one was to add another piece of Ivory of half an Inch thick, to open below that of the Colours, to include a small pair of Compasses, a Port-crayon, and some other such useful Materials for Drawing.

Just fourteen years later, in a sketch-book of 1746, belonging to Mr. Norwood Young, Alexander Cozens made drawings of a travelling portfolio and colour box.[1] One sketch in perspective shows a square board with a drawing on paper in the centre, and holes, presumably for colours, all round it. Below the board is a bag and attached to one side of it a sheet of pasteboard (so inscribed) equal in size to the board, and presumably intended to cover it completely and keep the sketch and colours in place. From the pasteboard hangs a larger sheet of leather (also so described) with straps attached: this would fold round the lower side of the board and the bag. In a note on a later page he speaks of 'Water Collors 30 in all in bottles in frame &c.' He notes also: 'for travelling . . . carry lamp bl: in dry balls and pouders, Gum and tin vessel of Water', and 'to paint at home have bladders of ye originall collours'.[2]

[1] A. P. Oppé, *A Roman sketch-book by Alexander Cozens*, Walpole Soc. XVI, 1927–1928.
[2] It may be assumed that the colours referred to by Cozens were pigments rather than prepared water-colours. Eds.

In 1801 colour boxes were advertised by Ackermann. 'A Neat Mahogany Box, with Six Cakes' cost 6s.; with twelve cakes, 10s. 6d.; with eighteen, 15s.; and with 24, £1 1s. Neat Mahogany Boxes, containing a marble slab, brushes, etc., and colours ranging from twelve to thirty-six, cost from £1 1s. to £2 2s. These boxes, it may be assumed, were for studio use. For his sketching expeditions, some thirty years later, Samuel Palmer carried two large but very light wooden palettes coated with white enamel and set with thick clots of colour so prepared as to be readily removed by brush or finger.

In the first catalogue issued by their firm in 1832 Messrs. Winsor & Newton advertise various kinds of mahogany boxes and also 'Japanned Tin Sketching Boxes for the Pocket, with 6, 8 or 12 Colours, Pencils, Bottle, Cups &c. complete.'

From its foundation in 1754 The Royal Society of Arts has done much for the encouragement of arts and manufactures. At its very first meeting a decision was made to provide prizes for the discovery in England of cobalt, and for the growth of madder, at a time when madder was the principal source of all red dyes and a great deal of English cloth had to be shipped to Flanders for dyeing. But one of the most popular things the Society ever did was to offer a medal for a shilling colour box. The medal was awarded to J. Rogers, of Bunhill Row, and was presented to him by the Prince Consort in 1853. The success of the colour boxes was astounding, as by 1870 no fewer than eleven millions of them had been sold.[1] Thus we arrive at the modern paint-box of japanned tin, usually opening on a hinge in the middle, and having on one half four-sided compartments to hold colours in pans, or three-sided receptacles for colours from tubes, and in the other half slight concave compartments in which colours can be mixed. The better kind has a thumb-hole, enabling the artist to use the box just as the oil-painter uses a palette. A box of this nature is sometimes made to slide into the top of a larger box containing divisions for colour in tubes. Such boxes were in use in 1849. Tin vessels for holding water are made to clip on the edge of the box: in 1746, as has been noted, Alexander Cozens prescribed 'for travelling . . . a tin vessel of water'. When the outdoor painter adds a receptacle for water, and a case containing brushes, he is fully equipped, except for his paper.

Preliminary drawing: use of ink, chalk, etc.

Most painters in water-colour have worked over a preliminary drawing made with pencil, charcoal, chalk or ink. The colour may be subservient to the drawing; it may be just a hint leaving the drawing as a statement. Or the drawing may be admitted on equal terms with the colour; ink or charcoal, for instance, cannot be entirely suppressed, whatever colour they are clothed with. The pencil basis more often completely disappears when the painter has used it for the boundaries and details of his design. When colour has been applied over

[1] G. K. Menzies; *The Story of the Royal Society of Arts*, 1935, pp. 3, 46.

pencil, the pencil marks are often obscured, and light lines in pencil can be rubbed out without any apparent removal of colour. Very rarely does the artist take a brush and start to work direct upon his paper without at least some preliminary touches in pencil, chalk or ink, to indicate the outlines of his composition.

In the eighteenth century, though Gainsborough and others worked in colour over a chalk drawing, the normal procedure was to add colour over a drawing made with pen-and-ink and a monochrome wash. Ink was formerly an integral part of the water-colour painter's equipment. In 1746, as has been seen, Alexander Cozens, when travelling in Italy, always carried lamp black and gum for making ink.

Wood soot could be used for making a black ink, and Walpole describes the seven drawings by Lady Diana Beauclerk, of which he was so proud, as being 'in sut-water'. I have made experiments with soot from the chimney of a fire-place, in which coal and wood have been burned together, and find that soot, if well washed in a little water, will dissolve leaving no grit. The result is a pleasant warm black with the quality of 'Peach Black'. There is apparently enough grease in the soot to make it cling to the paper. It has a slight tendency to smudge, but with the addition of a very small quantity of gum is as adhesive as any kind of water-colour. Gainsborough and other contemporaries of Lady Diana probably used soot-water more frequently than we think.

The finding of a good black caused other experiments. In 1797 Sandby wrote to the Rev. W. Mason about a great discovery which he had made[1]:

> A few weeks ago I had a French brick (brioche) for breakfast: the crust was much burnt in the baking, I scraped off the black, and ground it with gum-water; it produced an excellent warm black colour like mummy, and bears out with great vigour. . . . The day after this great discovery I had some split peas in the evening in a shovel over the fire, and parched them quite black. This also answers well, very dark and warm, not opaque like ivory black: you will, I know, thank me when you try it, and throw your Indian ink aside.

A browner ink can be made with bistre. Bistre is made from the soot of burning wood, resin or peat. As an ink, it is hardly distinguishable from sepia, formerly obtained from the cuttle-fish, and now used as a colour, though it once had limited use as a writing fluid. Practically all of the earlier water-colour painters used pen and ink outlines as the foundation of their 'stained', or tinted, drawings; and the use of ink either for this purpose, or as a reinforcement to finished work in colour, has continued till the present day as an occasional practice. Turner frequently added touches to his later drawings with a pen and red ink. Ink can be applied with a brush, as it was by Alexander Cozens in his 'blot' drawings, or by Gainsborough, or far back by the early Chinese and Japanese artists, not only for their drawings but for all their calligraphic writing. In earliest times, when a pen was used, it was a quill; then came the reed pen with which Rowlandson, for instance, made his drawings; and in modern times steel nibs of all kinds and widths are employed, though many artists still prefer a quill or reed pen.

[1] William Sandby, *Thomas and Paul Sandby*, 1892, p. 110.

In 1790 a writer in *The Artist's Repository*[1] states:

Drawings are tinted on the following principles:

  I. Sometimes, after being outlined with a blacklead pencil, they are stained; the sky and distances in landscape with a thin wash; the ground and front objects with body-colours; then wrought up to effect with stronger colours alone, or united with Indian ink.

 II. Sometimes they are more perfectly outlined, and washed with Indian ink; then the colours are added to finish the whole.

Drawings done in colours only, seldom look well, being usually deficient in effect and repose; for be it always remembered, glaring colours are hurtful. The best way, for slight drawings, is to procure an effect with the Indian ink, and then a brilliancy and variety with colours.

There was a revolt against the use of ink as early as 1819, when James Roberts in his *Introductory Lessons . . . for Painting in Water-Colours*, conjures the student not to use pen and ink: 'when he is proficient, he may *sketch* with those materials, but if the pen is once admitted into finished water-coloured drawings, adieu to all softness, breadth and atmosphere! The *wiry* mark of the pen, especially in distances, stares through the tender shadows and aerial tint, and gives his drawings the stiff and formal effect of bad-coloured engravings.' Roberts taught his pupils to draw in pencil outline, and then wash with Indian ink and a brush. If the drawing was to be left without colour, he thought that it should be tinted: 'There are various washes for Indian ink drawings: such as *red ink* lowered with water, and gambouge; raw Terra di Sienna; yellow oker, and tobacco steeped in water. *Porter* also is a very good general wash.'

After 1800, probably owing to the example set by Girtin and Turner, the use of Indian ink tended to decline, but its employment before that date was so constant that something should be said about its nature. Indian ink, so called perhaps because it was imported by way of India, is a misnomer for Chinese ink. It was mentioned by Pepys, who wrote in his *Diary* for November 5, 1665: 'Mr. Evelyn . . . showed me most excellent painting in little, in distemper, Indian incke, water-colours.' Indian ink has for long been the accepted term in current speech and in colourmen's catalogues, though it really is Chinese ink. Dr. Monro's interesting method of drawing with a dry stick of Indian ink on wet paper is referred to later in an account of his life and work.

Paper

Too long a dissertation would be required for dealing with the whole history of paper and paper-making. For our present purpose it is enough to say that there are two kinds of paper, hand-made and machine-made. Hand-made paper was in use from the earliest times and its manufacture was introduced into England by a German, Sir John Spielman,

[1] IV, p. 79.

in 1588. Machine-made paper (e.g. cartridge paper) was not made till the beginning of the nineteenth century when the Fourdrinier paper-making machine was first brought to this country. Though machine-made paper is adequate for newsprint and all kinds of commercial work, hand-made paper is immensely superior in quality and durability, and is still made, though to a limited extent.[1]

The materials used for hand-made paper are white linen and cotton rags, which undergo a most careful sorting to eliminate any foreign material, and are then disintegrated by repeated washing, boiling and rubbing till they become a pulp. The pulp is bleached and cleansed with pure spring water till it is free of all starch, dirt or grease. Genuine hand-made paper is manufactured by a 'vatman', who handles a 'mould', i.e. a wooden frame containing a laid wire sheet or a woven wire cloth in which the design of the watermark is embodied. Woven wire, in place of the 'laid' wires and 'chain' wires crossing each other, was introduced in 1750 by John Baskerville, the famous Birmingham printer, whose beautiful edition of Virgil in 1757 (Macaulay wrote that it 'went forth to astonish all the librarians of Europe') was chiefly printed on wove paper. Wire-wove paper has not the roughness and unevenness of 'laid' paper. Machine-made paper is never so perfectly interwoven and is much more easily torn; it often contains wood fibre as well as rag, and must always have a mechanical surface. For hand-made paper the vatman passes the mould to the 'coucher', who presses the mould on to a pile of blankets or felts, the film of paper adheres to the felt, and then he passes back the clean mould to the vatman to make another sheet. The pile of felt with sheets of paper between is then transferred to a hydraulic press, and the excess water from the sheets is pressed out. It is during the process of pressing that the familiar and characteristic grain on the surface of hand-made paper is obtained. It is really the impression, under heavy pressure, of the felting. There is no other method of making genuine hand-made paper. Firms, who make so-called 'mould-made' paper, use a cylinder machine which gives a rough edge but a mechanical surface, and a mould-made paper tears much more easily one way than the other. 'It is difficult', says Mr. Barcham Green, 'to state in words the difference between hand-made and machine-made paper. It may be compared to the difference between an original water-colour drawing and a cleverly printed reproduction. It cannot be easily explained, but the artist can tell which is which at a glance.'

In order that ink or colour may not spread when applied to the surface of the finished paper, the newly-made sheets (known as 'waterleaf'), which are as absorbent as blotting-paper, must be sized. This is done by passing them through a trough of animal or gelatine

[1] For much information with regard to hand-made paper I am indebted to Lt.-Col. C. H. Balston of Springfield Mills, Maidstone, who kindly sent me a brochure published by his firm in 1831 and articles written for trade publications. By the kindness also of Mr. J. Barcham Green of the Hayle Mill, Maidstone, I have made free use of his booklet, *Notes on the Manufacture of Hand-Made Paper*, published in 1936. It is of interest to note that the so-called 'O.W.S. paper' was made at Hayle Mill from 1895 onwards, first to the requirements of J. W. North, A.R.A., R.W.S. and later issued by the firm of F. D. Head. North went into business as chairman of the 'O.W. Paper and Arts Company' in 1895. He wanted, and obtained, a pure and sound paper made entirely of linen, and finished with purified, and sterilized size (not everybody's paper, whatever he may have thought, because it was almost too good in its hardness and resistance).

size, and the excess size is squeezed out by rollers. The drying of sized paper is difficult. The paper is hung in a cold drying-loft and dried entirely by air. First steam is turned on, and the temperature is raised slowly to about ninety degrees Fahrenheit. Should the temperature go down or the moist air not be able to escape quickly enough, the paper may become greasy or stained. Sized paper dries in about forty-eight hours, and the louver boards are then opened to allow the paper to mature, which takes about twenty-four hours. The sized paper then stands for a few days in a cool place.

From earliest times the paper to which colour was to be applied required sizing, and the painter often had to attend to this himself. Here is a quotation from Gore's *Art of Limning*:

> After what manner you ought to prepare or order your paper, whereupon you intend to Limn, that your colours may not sink thorow. Before I proceed to the use of the water-colours themselves, to teach in good order all things, it is necessary that I should say somthing concerning the preparing, or making the paper firm, that it may receive the colour without sinking, in regard it often happens (in Prints especially, which are undertaken for to colour) that the colours sink: otherwise there are also papers, which are so firm of themselves, which nevertheless may be prepared, chusing to be certain rather than uncertain of a good firm ground, that you may not make imperfect and defective work; but upon parchment it is altogether unnecessary. And the preparing is performed after this manner: Take of the best white glew, boil it in fair rain water, to the consistencie of calfs broth or gelly, warm this again, and take a clean sponge dipt in this warm size, and with the same wipe over your paper, in all places equally and alike, and put it to dry, and keep it from dirt and dust; and this manner is very commodious for such work, which you do intend not to varnish.

Every painter has had his favourite type of paper; some have liked it thick and highly sized; some have preferred to strain out a thinnish paper; some have preferred a smooth surface, and some a rough. Both hand-made and mould-made paper are made of varying thickness to suit every requirement, and are supplied with three surfaces, 'Hot-pressed', 'Not' and 'Rough'. The term 'hot-pressed' is a misnomer, because no heat is used in the process, the glossy surface being obtained by putting each sheet between smooth zinc plates under the high pressure of several tons to the square inch. The 'Not' surface, which is half way between glazed and rough, is obtained by pressing one sheet against another, and maintaining that pressure for several days. When 'Rough' surface is required, no pressure is applied, the sheets merely standing in a heap under their own weight for several weeks until they are sufficiently flat. The grain on the surface of the rough paper is simply a reproduction, as has been said, of the grain of the felting with which the paper comes into contact when it is first made. Some artists have a preference for a half-sized absorbent paper; some have done good work even on a wet 'waterleaf' or 'plate' paper, which to all intents and purposes is blotting-paper. John Varley said: 'With regard to the painter in water-colours a very great portion of his time is employed in overcoming the peculiarities and defects in paper.' All of this must be borne in mind when we come later to consider the papers used by Varley, Girtin, Cox and others in relationship to their work.

28

The papers used throughout the seventeenth and eighteenth centuries were hand-made of the description termed 'laid'. Papers of this kind had a lovely quality and tone, but were entirely unsuited in texture and solidity for the manipulative methods of washing-out, scraping, etc. which came into practice later. They were of limited size and were folded into quires, so that if a large sheet were used the mark of the fold tended to appear in the drawing. A crease is apparent in several of Girtin's drawings.

As early as 1760 the Society of Arts, as the poet Gray states in a letter to William Mason, turned its attention to the manufacture of paper, and succeeded in producing a material said to be made from silk rags[1] 'and intended for the uses of drawing', possibly with a finer surface than the ordinary wire-wove then in use. It was, moreover, made in large sheets so that the necessity of joining paper for large drawings might not be felt.

In the British Museum are two drawings made in 1780 by Hearne on paper of from 27 to 29 inches in length. When James Basire in 1774 engraved *The Field of the Cloth of Gold* on a copper plate of 47 × 27 inches, the paper for printing it, which must have been over 50 × 30 inches, had to be specially made. Cozen's *Nemi* and *Albano* subjects of 1778 to 1780, unusually large for their time, measure 15 × 20 inches, and some as much as 25 × 36 inches. Turner's eight views of Salisbury Cathedral, executed for Sir Richard Colt Hoare between 1797 and 1801 are 26 × 20 inches. Some of his Fonthill Abbey drawings and the *Falls of the Reichenbach*, 1804, measure as much as 28 × 41 inches, and in all these cases there is a margin of paper outside the actual drawing. These facts are of interest not only with regard to the size of paper but, as C. F. Bell has pointed out,[2] 'it is obvious that such huge things had far outgrown the portfolio of the old-fashioned collector. They had also, partly on account of their needing to be protected with glass, brought confusion into the relatively homogeneous aspect of the exhibition rooms at the Royal Academy, and the creation of societies prepared to treat them with the full honours of a picture-gallery became a necessity. Various passages in Farington's *Diary* refer to the jealousy with which some of the oil-painters watched the rise of the fashion of water-colour and the pressing of claims for its particular consideration by the Academy.'

In the second half of the eighteenth century the firm of Whatman came into prominence and was the first to produce a hand-made paper which would stand up to repeated washings and scrubbings. About 1800 Messrs. Creswick were making papers of various qualities and textures suited to the special needs of the water-colour painter. De Wint was specially fond of 'Creswick paper'. The name has no connection with Thomas Creswick, R.A. During the nineteenth century the chemist was also beginning to play his part not only in the extension of colour but in the furtherance of purity in paper. Ruskin, in a lecture on the *Political Economy of Art*, said:

[1] Mr. Barcham Green is very doubtful whether silk was actually used. A paper may be silky in appearance, but rags of any material must be boiled in soda before they are made into paper, and if silk is boiled in soda it goes to a slimy mess.

[2] C. F. Bell and T. Girtin, *J. R. Cozens, Drawings and Sketches*, Walpole Soc. XXIII, 1935, p. 15.

From all I can gather respecting the recklessness of modern paper manufacture, my belief is, that though you may still handle an Albert Dürer engraving, two hundred years old, fearlessly, not one half of that time will have passed over your modern water colours before most of them will be reduced to mere white or brown rags; and your descendants, twitching them contemptuously into fragments between finger and thumb, will mutter against you, half in scorn and half in anger, 'Those wretched nineteenth-century people! They kept vapouring and fuming about the world, doing what they called business and they couldn't make a sheet of paper that wasn't rotten.'

In spite of this, the drawings seem to survive, most of them, in perfect condition. Whatever they may have suffered from the action of light upon impermanent pigments, they are not crumbling away. There is, of course, a danger that in his efforts to produce a pure and startlingly white paper the maker may have relied upon chloride of lime as a bleaching agent, a dangerous ingredient unless adequate steps are taken to annul its destructive effects. That, no doubt, or machine-made paper, is what Ruskin had in mind. The makers of paper in the days of Dürer and of Rembrandt did not bother about impurities, and produced paper of attractive texture and of lovely tints of ivory or cream. Prints and drawings by both of them show that the ordinary rag-made paper of their time has lasting quality.

During the nineteenth century papers were made of various tints, suitable for use with body-colour. A painter in pure water-colour may like a cream or ivory tone, something just 'off-white', in his paper, but will never wish to get far away from a white ground for his work. In the eighteenth century substitutes for a tinted paper were 'made several ways; by staining white paper with bistre, or with water coloured by tobacco-leaves, or by boiling brewer's clay in beer, and striking it on the paper with a spunge, as even as possible.'[1] To dip the paper in a weak solution of coffee is another way to obtain a pleasantly warm tint. For the group of drawings made in 1801 and known as the 'Scottish Pencils' in the Turner Bequest, Turner worked with chalk and pencil heightened with white on a yellowish-brown paper which, as he told Farington, was stained with a mixture of Indian ink and tobacco juice.

Artists of the past, when they found that their paper was too absorbent, were accustomed to wash 'water-leaf' (i.e. unsized) paper with alum. Sandby, as will be found later, primed his paper with isinglass jelly mixed with honey. From the earliest times the artist strained out his paper to keep it from cockling when liquid colour was applied. In 1787, as we are told, 'others prefer a more substantial kind of paper, the edges of which they paste to the drawing-board, to keep it flat and prevent its shrinking'.[2]

From the Renaissance days paper was made up by the artist into Sketch-Books, which could be carried in the pocket. Leonardo da Vinci speaks of 'your little book (*tuo piccolo libretto*) which you should always carry with you'. At Karlsruhe is a sketch-book of Hans Baldung Grün, at Dresden one of Albrecht Dürer, at Berlin one of Martin van Heemskerk. All down the centuries they were freely used, and in the Victoria and Albert Museum is a

[1] *Artists Repository*, 1787, I, p. 57.
[2] N. Solly, *Life of Müller*, 1875, p. 240.

collection of sketch-books by British water-colour painters, Francis Place, Joseph Farington, Richard Wilson, Constable, De Wint and many others. They contain not only the essence of the painter's work in his swift and vivid impressions—the 'breeding subjects', of which Richard Wilson talked—but scribbled notes of itineraries and expenses, and other odds and ends. The sketch-book supplies not only a notion of an artist's technique and the places where he worked, but often some inkling of his prejudices, his interests and his virtues.

The sketch-book was composed of sheets of the artist's favourite paper, bound up with a cover of leather or canvas, usually of a size which would go in the artist's pocket. More than 350 of Turner's sketch-books were included in his bequest to the Nation. Five or six inches by eight or nine inches was a usual size for Turner, but others were roll sketch-books, four times the size of these, the covers being made of paper, which permitted the book to be rolled up. We shall find De Wint using long-shaped sketch-books, across two pages of which he could draw his panoramic subjects.

About 1830 paper was also made up into sketch blocks, as they are now called. The name was not in use in 1832 when Messrs. Winsor & Newton advertised 'Solid Sketch Books, consisting of a body of paper compressed so as to form a solid substance, each sheet of which can be easily separated from the other by inserting the point of a penknife under the leaf'. In their Hand-Book (c.1842) they are still described as 'solid sketch books', but by 1849 are described alternatively as 'solid sketch books' and 'blocks'.

Brushes

Chaucer writes: 'With subtil pensil painted was the stone'; and from the fifteenth century till about the year 1850, 'pencil' was the normal description of an artist's paint-brush. Brushes were still called pencils in Newman's 1832 list and retain this name in at least one supplier's catalogue until the present day. In 1683 Pettus states that 'Black Lead . . . of late . . . is curiously formed in cases of Deal or Cedar, and so sold as dry Pencils'; but 'pencil', as a title for a lead pencil, did not oust 'pencil' as brush, till nearly two hundred years later. Norgate describes the brushes in use before 1650:

> Your next care must bee to provide your selfe with god pencills well chosen, cleane and sharppe pointed, not dividing into two parts as many times they doe nor stufft with stragling heires, which later (latter) you may take away with a sharpe penknife or by passing the pencill through the flame of a Candell. The best are of a reasonable length, full, round and sharpe, not too longe, nor too slender, which are troublesome to worke with. You can have noe better pencills than these what are here made at London, whereof you are to choose of severall sizes. Some great to lay grounds are as usefull and necessary as those finer and smaller sorted, and I have ever found the middle size better than the least, especially for dead colouring and laying grounds; besides they hold and keepe the colour longer, and as the rest, are to be fitted into neat and handsome stocks of brasille or such like of a convenient length.

31

Modernise the phrasing, and that might be written about our wooden-handled brushes in any manual of to-day. When, however, Sanderson published his *Graphice* in 1658, he recommended 'pensills' set in a quill, full and thick near the quill, and tapering to a sharp point. In his *Art of Painting in Oyl*, published in 1687, John Smith speaks about colour shops where brushes could be obtained:

> The largest brushes will cost sixpence, the other sizes from four pence to one penny apiece. The largest sort of pencils, made with fine hair, either in tin cases or in wooden stocks, from eight to two pence apiece, and others in goose or duck's quills are sixpence a dozen, one with another, or a halfpenny apiece.

The quill handle continued in use till past the middle of the nineteenth century, but has been superseded on the whole by the wooden handle to which the brush is fixed with a cupro-nickel or aluminium ferrule. Quill brushes, however, are still supplied, and the size of the quill is recognised by the various names of the birds which at one time supplied the quills: lark, crow, duck, goose and (the largest) swan. These titles are still to be found in colourmen's catalogues.

To avoid abrading the paper and to allow colour to flow easily from the brush, the water-colour painter cannot, like the oil-painter, employ brushes made of hog's hair for ordinary use. His brushes are made of the hair of the red sable,[1] which are particularly durable and at the same time pliant and firm. Cheaper brushes are made of camel's hair. Partly perhaps on the score of expense (for a large sable brush is costly) we do not use such large brushes as our ancestors. Samuel Palmer had one brush two inches broad; and I have inherited one, made a hundred years ago, which is nearly an inch wide, retains all its pliancy, and still comes to a perfect sharp point when wet.

In 1809, James Roberts gave the following advice in his *Painting in Water-Colour*:

> With respect to camel's-hair pencils, the larger and largest sort should be procured, and chiefly used: very small camel's-hair pencils will in time give the student a *petite* manner. Very small camel's-hair pencils are only occasionally wanted; viz. for touching the rigging of vessels, or very small figures. For general washes, large flat brushes in tins, should be used: they lay on a quantity of colour, clear and quick. Though many masters approve of a drawing-board, to fix the paper in, perhaps it will, in general, be more convenient for the student to have his paper *loose*: he can then turn it. As it is absolutely necessary to wet the drawing on *the back*, especially during the time the clouds are printing; he cannot so readily accomplish that very desirable object if it is fixed in a drawing-frame. He should procure a flat drawing-board, made of deal, perfectly smooth, especially for the outlines and penciling: the resistance of the board will enable him to pencil his drawing with firmness and a due degree of spirit.

There are great advantages in having a brush which, as in the case of sable, comes readily to a point, when put into the mouth with a slight twist. In *The Art of Limning*, however, Gore when recommending ox-gall for making colour pass over a greasy paper, adds;

[1] Early Chinese painters used brushes made from the hair of deer, fox and rabbit. Very special ones were made from the feelers round a rat's nose, and hairs taken from the beak of a kingfisher. Their brushes, fitted in ivory handles, were kept in gold and jewelled boxes.

'It has only this inconvenience in it, it is somewhat noisome to them that use to put their Pencils in their mouths, and lick the same, of which they may abstain and forbear.'

Application of colour

Colour may be applied by means of brush-strokes, i.e. by separate touches, flecks or dashes made with a wet brush. Much of the work of David Cox, for instance, was done entirely with quite separate strokes of the brush, almost in the manner of the oil-painters of the Impressionist School. Colour may also be applied by means of stipple, or in a wash. Stipple consists in the juxtaposition of minute spots or flecks of colour touched on with the point of a fine brush, or in the lifting up of spot after spot of colour from a wash so as to reduce it and break it up into an infinitesimal number of dots or specks. It is true that Norgate recommended a broader method, 'after the manner of washing, or hatching, drawing your pencill along with easy, faint, or gentle stroakes, washing and wiping it, rather than with stips, points or pricks to pincke or punch it, as some affect to do.' About the middle of the nineteenth century stipple again became a favourite technique with such artists as William Hunt, Birket Foster and J. F. Lewis. In the case of the last, Ruskin refers to a sky in one of his pictures where 'the whole field is wrought gradually out with touches no larger than the filaments of a feather . . . requiring the use of a magnifying glass for analysis with ordinary eyes'.

By a 'wash' is meant an application of colour over a larger space than can be conveniently covered by the brush at one stroke. It may be a space of only two square inches or it may be a sky stretching across thirty inches of paper. A wash can have no visible joins; it must be continued and extended while the colour is still wet. The water-colour painter must be skilled in laying down, over any required portion of paper, an even flat wash or a consciously gradated wash descending from dark to light or from light to dark.[1] This can only be done if it is done swiftly, with plentiful water and a full brush. All good water-colour painters insist upon the value of the full brush. 'The pencil', wrote Cox, 'should be full of colour in order that it may float'. Skill in laying the flat or gradated wash with fluid swiftness has been one of the main elements of good water-colour work.

John Varley and his compeers were expert in the laying of a wash. We read of the whole household being hushed in those days because father was 'skying', and the following quizzical note, which appeared about 1789, conveys some idea of the serious problems which the washing in of a sky involved[2]:

What a fine, clear morning! I will do my sky. Betty! tell your mistress, if anyone calls, I can't be seen—I'm skying. Betty! Betty! bring me up a pan of water, and wash that sponge: it really is

[1] For excellent instruction in the laying of washes, see C. Muncaster, *Student's Book of Water-Colour Painting*, 1938.
[2] W. Thornbury, *Life of J. M. W. Turner*, 1877, p. 85.

33

so hot I cannot lay my colour smooth. Where's the flat brush? Oh dear! that Prussian blue is all curdled. 'Please pa, ma says, will you take any refreshment?' Get away! get away! how ever can your ma think about refreshment, when she knows I'm doing my sky? There, you've knocked down my swan's quill, and how am I to soften this colour? It will all be dry before you wash out the dirt. Give me that brush. Oh, it is full of indigo! there is the horizon spoilt! Quick! quick! some water! Oh, that's gall! And the sky is flying away! Why did your mother send you here? She might have known that I was skying.

As that quotation indicates, the laying of a perfect wash could become a bane in more ways than one. In the case of many painters, such as Copley Fielding, their fine frenzy was too often directed not to an expressive interpretation of nature but to nice conduct in the grading of an unclouded sky.

A thin undisturbed wash of colour was used by the eighteenth century topographers, simply to add a pleasing tint to their underlying drawing. Later artists began to use a second wash over the whole or part of an underlying wash after it was dry. In placing wash over wash, leaving spaces of the lower wash to show through, Cotman excelled. Girtin, and later De Wint, ran in fresh colour, to break up and give variety to their first wash, while it was still wet. Artists who prefer to begin on wet, or damp paper are working from the start without any edges such as those belonging to a brush-stroke, but with a sort of wet mosaic of running washes. The topographer in what Horace Walpole called his 'minuting', knew and could see, exactly, what result his thin flat wash of colour would produce. The painter who runs wet colour into wet colour can never quite know what has happened till his work has dried out. The entirely 'wet' method as practised, for instance, by Romilly Fedden, is a comparatively modern procedure and requires vast experience. The successful operator must have something of the combination of skill and luck, that almost sixth sense, which enables the good navigator to make his landfall and find his moorings on a day of mist and rain. De Wint was a master in the partial use of a wet method. His irregular blots were brush blots rather than washes.

Finally, there is what may be described as the broken, or dragged, wash. The brush, only slightly damped, is charged with dry or almost dry colour and dragged on its side across the paper. This action leaves particles of pure colour, particularly where they are held by all the tiny prominences on the paper. The method is specially valuable for giving crispness and sparkle to foregrounds or to suggest texture and roughness of an architectural surface. The effect is almost that obtained in black-and-white by the crumbling atoms of chalk or crayon. This dragging of colour was used by Turner, Cotman in his middle period, Bonington, Boys and other painters. An early description of 'dragging' is quoted later in connection with the work of William Payne, and the device is discussed further in the chapter relating to Bonington.

A supplementary method deserves mention: that of using the brush charged with colour, as though it were a pen, for drawing outline, or emphasising form. The manipulation of the brush for this particular purpose will be referred to later in connection with J. F. Lewis, Bonington and other painters.

34

Colour, then, can be applied by separate brush-strokes from the side or end of a brush, by stipple from the point, by clean flat washes, by wash over wash, by a 'wet' method, or by any combination of these. There remains the final possibility of gaining further effects through lifting or merging colour by sponging, blotting, scraping or erasing. Originally these were methods of correction or alteration, as will be explained in the following section, but Turner, for instance, intentionally used them all at times, and many later artists deliberately and systematically exploited them throughout their work.

Methods of alteration

In pure water-colour any light colour put over a dark will merely make it darker by decreasing transparency, and there is no means, as in oil-painting, of diminishing a dark by covering it with light paint. If the water-colourist wishes to modify or alter a dark tone, he must lift off a portion of the colour, or must remove the colour entirely so as to uncover white paper on which he can work again. This may be done by applying a brush filled with clean water and washing it gently over the form or space which he wishes to modify or remove, and then pressing on it a clean rag which will lift the colour and the superfluous moisture. A pleasant and subtle effect may be obtained by a partial removal of the colour, but if the passage is to be quite clean the damped paper can be rubbed with a rag or india rubber till it is pure white. Blotting-paper is very valuable in lifting colour evenly and flatly from a wide damped space such as a sky. India rubber or ink-eraser is also effective when used over a comparatively large dry surface to reduce colour and to give a pleasant and mottled texture. Cotman, I believe, was well aware of this.

The eventful discovery of a method of wiping-out lights in water-colour is said to have been made by Girtin as the result of an accident:

> He spilt some drops of water on a drawing, and, fearing that it would injure the part upon which it fell, took his handkerchief carefully to sop it up; when, the colour being softened by the moisture, it came away upon the handkerchief, leaving the exact shape of the spot of water white. It struck him that this plan of getting out lights might be applied in the progress of a drawing, and he used it with so much success that for several seasons his works attracted particular attention in this respect. It was supposed that, instead of being taken out after the picture was advanced, they were stopped out in the commencement; and the colourmen got up a preparation which they sold under the name of 'Girtin's Stopping-out Mixture.'[1]

Stopping-out was not Girtin's invention. Laurence Binyon[2] points out that the smoke of a fire in a drawing of *Mount Etna*, dated 1777, when Girtin was only two years old, has obviously been expressed by removal of colour from the background by rubbing it with a

[1] J. L. Roget, *History of the Old Water Colour Society*, I, p. 93. He should have stated that the title and the idea of 'Stopping-out' were obviously borrowed from the practice of stopping-out with a 'stopping-out varnish', which had long been known to etchers.
[2] *Life and Works of T. Girtin*, 1900, p. 22.

damp cloth or wet brush. According to Pyne, the process of 'taking out the lights with bread', presumably with the use of bread rubbed on the damp paper instead of a rag, was 'a discovery which originated with Turner', whose 'magnificent effects, aided by this process, were first exhibited at The Royal Academy', when 'all the painters were puzzled to find out by what art he performed this graphic magic'. As there is little evidence of lifting colour by this practice in Girtin's work, it seems more probable that Turner deserves the credit for the development, at any rate, of a process which he constantly employed. W. H. Pyne describes it very fully[1]:

> The process is simple in its means, but requires skilful management. The principal masses in every object are laid in with all the effect that local colouring can give, similar to that of oil painting; but the finishing is totally different, as the lights instead of being painted on, as in oil, are really taken out. The local effect then is thus laid in, up to the finishing with the high lights, the forms for receiving which are produced by taking clean water in a camel hair or sable pencil, and touching with the same, all the parts destined for the lights; upon which a silk handkerchief is pressed, taking care not to spread the water. The handkerchief after absorbing the water is removed, when the parts are dexterously swept over by a bit of bread, pinched to a pellet, which removes the colour, and leaves the lights clean and sharp, and in a beautiful state when dry, for receiving the glazing tints. When this process is executed with judgment, and with a masterly hand, we feel no hesitation in saying that for the touching foliage, the bark of trees, the surfaces of stone, plaster, brick, etc., and for other parts of topographical or landscape composition, nothing can exceed it either in spirit or texture.

The method was used with consummate skill by Cotman for lifting colour from leaves and sprays of foliage, branches and tree trunks, which he wished to tell out as high lights against a dark background. It became part of the every-day practice of all water-colour artists.

Though Girtin was suspected of using a 'stopping-out' mixture, it is certain that Francis Nicholson did invent, and occasionally employ, a 'Stopping-out Process', for preserving light in a drawing. His method was communicated by him to the Society for the Encouragement of Arts and was published in their Transactions, 1799. A full account, from which the following brief extracts are taken, appears in his book on *The Practice of Drawing and Painting Landscape from Nature*, 1820:

> The intention of this process is to secure the lights, both in their sharpest touches and breadths, by covering them, as soon as they have received their proper depth of local colour, with a composition which defends them from injury or alteration, in passing over them with other tints, or the colours of the shadow. The composition may then be removed, and the lights will re-appear in their different forms and gradations, as secured by it, and of the different tints put on before its application.
>
> The composition is made by dissolving a small quantity of whitened bees'-wax in oil of turpentine, to which may be added as much flake-white as will give it sufficient body to appear opaque when the touches made with it on the paper are held between the eye and the light.
>
> The quantity of wax may be found by trial, and need not be more than will fix the flake-white so as to prevent its removal by washing over it with the colours. . . .
>
> When the whole of the water colours are dry, with a hog's-hair brush and oil of turpentine

---

[1] *Somerset House Gazette*, I, 1823, pp. 193, 194.

36

wash away the composition; as it dissolves wipe off with a rag, and continue to do so with more clean turpentine and a fresh rag until no more white appears; this will not affect the colours, because those used with gum water are not soluble in oil of turpentine.

If it be desirable to remove the oil of turpentine remaining in the paper, it may be done by washing it with highly rectified spirit of wine, both on the front and back.

When the drawing is dry, as it will soon be, it may be tinted down and harmonised where that is wanted, and the shadows may be strengthened in their deepest part if depth be required.

The advantages of this method are, the light may be expressed with all the freedom and sharpness of touch possible, and of various tints according to the colours laid on before and between the different applications of the composition; they are also more brilliant, and without the chalky effect caused in removing the colours by wetting and rubbing them up, but the latter in the representation of some objects such as rocks, etc. has peculiar advantages.

Nicholson's process of stopping-out is interesting in theory, but was not of much practical service. It is doubtful whether he made great use of it himself, though it seems clearly to have been employed in his water-colour of *Scarborough*,[1] a shipwreck with a wave breaking in the centre. What is more important is that in his book he writes also 'Of the Formation of Lights, etc. by Removal of the Colour', describing all the ordinary uses of brush, sponge, blotting-paper, india rubber, bread, etc.

From a dry water-colour it is quite possible, if the paper is solid enough, to scrape down or remove colour with a pen-knife or the blade of a safety razor. The surface which has been roughened by scraping can be smoothed down and polished with the back of a finger nail or with an ivory paper knife. The old water-colour painters for this purpose used agate, or some similar stone, fined off to a round point, and set with a silver-plated ferrule in a wooden handle like that of a water-colour brush. The credit of the first discovery of scratching-out high lights belongs to George Robertson.[2] C. F. Bell points out that scratched-out lights were used freely by Robertson in his views of Tivoli and Terni, and *Journey to Emmaus*,[3] and that Robertson died years before the first adoption of the process hitherto detected elsewhere by Girtin in the *Duff House*, 1794,[4] and by Turner in *Lincoln Cathedral*, 1795.[5] Turner, Cotman, De Wint and many other painters, as we shall see, made most skilful use of the point or blade of a pen-knife. There was a drawing, last century, in *Punch* of two unkempt artists. One says to the other: 'Do you do much washing?' The reply is: 'No, but I scrape a good deal.'

There is another process, akin to scraping, to which I cannot find reference in any of the earlier books. At one moment when water-colour is half-dry or 'tacky', but only during a very short period, it is possible to lift colour with the wooden end of the brush. The method was used, for instance, by Cotman and by Holland, but it can be dated back to 1795, for Mr. Augustus Walker showed me in 1931 two drawings both dated 1795 and signed

---

[1] V.A.M. 684–1877.
[2] C. F. Bell, *British water-colour painters*, Walpole Soc. V, 1915–1917, p. 59, and C. F. Bell, *Exhibited Works of Turner*, 1901, p. 19.
[3] B.M. 1916–3–3–5.
[4] Ashmolean Museum.
[5] B.M. Turner Bequest XXI–O.

'W. Williams': possibly the William Williams of Norwich, who exhibited at The Royal Academy from 1770 to 1792. In both drawings a large amount of the work had been done by lifting lights from wet paint with the wooden end of the brush; some broad tree-trunks had been taken out in this manner. Anyone who had not used the process might imagine that those lights were taken out in the usual way with brush, water and rag. The use of the wooden brush leaves a dark creamy edge which cannot be mistaken. The wood throws up colour at the edge, whereas rag and water soften it. Speaking of Turner's practice, C. F. Bell says that 'the furthest development of the system is found in the use of a blunt point'— obviously the artist will use the tip of the wooden end of his brush—'to mould, as it were, a heavy wash of colour in its wet state', and says that the device is not to be detected in any drawings earlier than those made by Turner after his first Swiss journey in 1802. Samuel Redgrave says: about one of Turner's drawings of 1803, 'It combines lights wiped out of the local colour in the sky, and sharply and decisively in the trees in the foreground; others scraped out with a blunt instrument whilst the full lay of local colour is in a wet state, as in the moss on the wall; lights scratched out, as in one of the waterfalls; others cut sharp and clear with a knife from the white paper, as in the housings of the mules on the mountain road; together with a large amount of surface washing, to give texture and air.'[1]

Rubbing a wet passage in water-colour with a rag, or scraping a dry portion with a pen-knife, may seem drastic methods for making alterations, but there are others which, in actual usage, seem more drastic still. A drawing may be wiped over with a soft sponge or a large brush—Dayes and Nicholson knew all about this—or even held under a running tap, to remove or modify overworked parts of its colour. Light, or hard, pressure of blotting-paper on the damp surface will help in removing, or softening, what seems harsh. By such means it is possible to quieten, suppress and equalise, or to leave a foundation on which to build anew. Over the wet drawing light washes of colour can be floated, or touches of strong colour run in. Even when a drawing has been held for some time under a running tap, some stains of colour will remain. The deliberate use of such methods for the purpose of building up rather than remodelling or altering a water-colour were mentioned in the last section. It should be obvious that, with all these methods of obtaining high light, the use of body-colour is not essential.

Varnish on water-colours

In the eighteenth century water-colour drawings on exhibition frequently hung side by side with oils, and were not always framed under glass. Efforts to make them resemble or compete with their neighbours sometimes led to the use of varnish. Gainsborough, for instance, varnished many of his drawings. Here is a description of the process[2]:

[1] *Catalogue of the Water Colour Paintings in the Victoria and Albert Museum,* 1876 (the editors have failed to find this quotation).
[2] Hesketh Hubbard, *Forgotten Methods,* Old Water-Colour Society's Club, XVII, 1940.

The drawing was first sized with isinglass dissolved in warm water, which was strained through a cloth and allowed to stand till it cooled to the consistency of hartshorn jelly. For use the size was either diluted with hot water or melted over steam until it just acquired fluidity. If the water-colour pigment had been applied with any appreciable degree of impasto the more heavily impasted parts were first sized with a medium-sized soft brush, care being taken not to disturb the pigment. When this preliminary *local* sizing had dried, two or three additional *general* washes of size were floated over the whole of the drawing with a large flat varnish brush. When these washes in turn had dried hard the drawing was slightly heated (to prevent the varnish chilling and sinking into the paper) and varnished sparingly with mastic to which a little copal was added if a very highly varnished drawing were desired. A water-colour so protected could be sponged when its surface became dirty. The varnish also brought out the beauty of deep shadows.

Most water-colour painters regarded with suspicion the use of adventitious materials to enhance their work. In the minutes of the Old Water-Colour Society for June 12, 1809, the following resolution is recorded[1]:

Some difficulty having been experienced by the committee of arrangement in the Spring Gardens Exhibition, owing to the introduction of a quantity of gum in certain subjects, it was resolved that such a mode of painting was injurious to the views of the Society relative to the admission of varnished drawings: and although the works had been admitted, it was not to be taken as a precedent for the future.

Francis Nicholson[2] said that 'many pictures have been painted with water-colours, in which the depth and force are as great as oil colour can or ought to exhibit'. Obviously this end, however mistaken, could only be attained by the use of varnish. He recommends in fact, using varnish for 'water-coloured pictures, that is, such as have all the force that is necessary for colour to give; these will not appear to lose by it; on the contrary, the shadows will be increased in strength and clearness, expressing depth, obscurity and space, as great as can be attained in oil'. Nicholson's own recipe was one part of Zapon varnish to two parts of alcohol.

In or about 1824 John Varley, perhaps under the bad influence of Nicholson, defied his Society and took a fancy to varnishing his drawings, but became dissatisfied with the result. A contemporary notice[3] says:

Mr. John Varley we have lately seen busily engaged in his study, on his new process of landscape in water-colours, heightened with white and varnished with copal. How this process would succeed for larger works is yet to be proved; but on some designs in small, the style is so effective, that they approximate to the richness and depth of painting in oil.

The writer, however, goes on to condemn varnished drawings in general, as involving of necessity the use of body-colour, and so discarding the quality peculiar to water-colours. Varley constantly, in his last period, either varnished the whole drawing or applied gum arabic to some passages of dark to give them a luminous quality. This patchy use of gum as

---

[1] Roget, I, p. 445.
[2] *Practice of Drawing and Painting Landscape from Nature in Water-Colours*, 1820.
[3] *Somerset House Gazette*, September 25, 1824.

a surface varnish appears here and there in the work of many water-colour painters until 1850, or even later. Bonington and Samuel Palmer used it frequently, and gum will sometimes be seen on the shadows cast by boats in James Holland's Venetian subjects. T. J. Gulick and J. Timbs[1] remark:

> A water-colour painting may be worked with or without the glossy appearance inseparable from a varnished-painting in oil; and the employment of gum for thus deepening and adding lustre, particularly to the shadows, is frequently considered illegitimate. We have given our reasons for believing in the legitimacy of the use of varnish in oil paintings. The same principle is here involved, but only so far as the glaze of gum may be used in passages where the grain of the paper is already with good reason sacrificed—its use is not necessary elsewhere.

It is one of the greatest possible mistakes often made in the past to think that water-colours or prints can be preserved by varnishing them like an oil painting. Paper is more perishable and more easily damaged than canvas, and water-colours sink into the paper without forming a hard surface like oil paint. In many cases, varnish can be removed from water-colours or prints, but I have known instances where all the usual methods of friction or the employment of chemical solvents have entirely failed.

In my own practice I have found that an effect of varnish can be obtained, particularly in dark shadows, by burnishing with an agate polisher or with an ebony or ivory paper knife. By this means a highly polished surface, reflecting light, can be obtained, even on a roughish Whatman, Cox, or Van Gelder paper, without any deterioration of the colour. The colour surface, in fact, becomes glossy instead of matt.

Mounts, frames, etc.

A mount is necessary because it displays a drawing to advantage, covering any stray portions of irregular work or ragged edges of paper, and enhancing the value of the drawing by its margin of contrasting white or slight tint. It has an additional value in that it protects the drawing from rubbing and soiling when it is kept in portfolio or solander, and shields it from contact with the glass when the drawing is placed in a frame.

The general practice at the end of the eighteenth century was for the artist to enclose his water-colour in a white, cream or greyish mount with a tinted border round the margin of the drawing. This border of lines and delicate washes, in which tones of the drawing were deliberately repeated, served to soften the hard and abrupt edge of the cut mount, to nullify the false notion of looking through a window, and to make drawing and mount a unified flat decoration for a wall. The practice since the eighteenth century has been much the same in France, though the French have always had a special liking for blue mounts. In the Louvre even modern water-colours have been placed in blue mounts, generally with a washed band of appropriate tint round the opening. Samuel Palmer wrote to P. G. Hamerton in 1872: 'I wonder that the French, the countrymen of the world's greatest

[1] *Painting popularly explained*, 1809 (6th edn. revised).

40

landscape-painter, the countrymen of such a triumvirate as Claude, N. Poussin, Sebastian Bourdon, should rejoice, as they seem to do, in blue mounts.' I know no instance of a gold mount in France, though they passed through a period corresponding to our Victorian epoch of gold mounts, when water-colours were nearly always set close in a frame, without mounts, and the frame, usually of dark, polished wood, had a gold slip between it and the picture. The custom of sinking a water-colour in a very thick mount with a widely cut *biseau* is common in France. The French have never had our liking for a wide margin of mount. Their tendency is to have only about two inches of margin between the washed border and the frame.

To Cozens or Sandby or Girtin the thought of a gilt mount or gold frame closing in their drawing would have been impossible. But at the time of its foundation, or very soon after, the 'Old' Water-Colour Society was encouraging the use of heavy gold frames shutting in the water-colour, without any mount. An illustration by Rowlandson and Pugin of the Society's rooms in 1808, published in the *Microcosm of London*, shows close ranks of large drawings set in deep and massive gold frames. The members evidently thought that their work could vie with oil paintings in size and strength of colour, and was worthy of a heavy frame of gold. Writing about the 1823 exhibition of the 'Old' Water-Colour Society, W. H. Pyne speaks of 'water-colours, displayed in gorgeous frames, bearing out in effect against a mass of glittering gold, as powerfully as pictures in oil'. And in the following year the same writer, with reference to small landscapes by Varley, Fielding and Cox, adds:

> It is only of late that such cabinet pictures in this material could be rendered sufficiently rich and deep in tone to bear out against those broad and superb frames, which seemed alone fitted to the power of oil pictures of the same size; but experiment has proved that water-colours, by the present improved process, have an intensity of depth and splendour of effect, which almost raises them to rivalry with cabinet pictures.

The *Memoir of Thomas Uwins, R.A.* records that in 1826 Robson commissioned one hundred water-colours by leading artists of the day on behalf of a wealthy patroness Mrs. Haldimand. In 1827 twenty-seven of these drawings were included in the Water-Colour Society's exhibition upon a separate screen. They were all 'framed alike in rich frost work', which Alfred Chalon described as 'offering in profile the appearance of an immense mass of gilt gingerbread'.[1]

William Callow, who was elected an associate of the Water-Colour Society in 1838, throws an interesting sidelight upon contemporary practice:

> It was a rule of the Society at this time that the price of the drawings should not include frames, which were much more expensive than they are now, and purchasers had the option of buying the drawings framed or unframed. In the earlier days prior to my election, The Society, in order to induce members to make large and important drawings, provided frames and plate glass complete in which members might place their works. The system did not last for long, and soon after I became an Associate it was given up. A lottery was held for the remaining frames, and I was successful in gaining one of them.[2]

[1] Roget I, 464.   [2] *Autobiography*, 1908, p. 104.

A little later the close frame with heavy rococo mouldings and *coquillage* was falling into disuse; a lighter encasement was employed, and a plain gold slip was introduced between drawing and frame. This afterwards expanded into the broad gilt flat which was in vogue all through the rest of the nineteenth century. One of the reasons for George Cattermole's retirement from the 'Old' Water-Colour Society in 1852 was his objection to the Society's rule demanding gold mounts and frames: he always held that his own drawings were seen to better advantage in white mounts. In 1852 Prince Albert, when visiting the 'New' Water-Colour Society's exhibition, was advanced enough, or unconventional enough, to advocate white mounts instead of gold,[1]—another instance of the many enlightened ideas in which, as we now realise, the Prince Consort was well in advance of his time. On the other hand, in 1857, J. F. Lewis wrote: 'I shall send my picture framed because I hate and detest those horrid white mounts which in my humble opinion reduce all finished drawings to the level of sketches.'

In his *Diary*, on June 27, 1857, G. P. Boyce records: 'To P.R.B. Exhibition in Russell Place. . . . I found my little *Sunset* Sketch in North Wales mounted in a preposterously wide gilt flat, whereas I had left it in my studio mounted on white paper. A lot of the foreground is covered by the mount which completely spoils the sketch and looks ridiculously pretentious besides.'

In all this controversy the gold mount and the ornate frame were victorious, and one cannot help thinking that their victory was maintained later by the picture-dealers, who in the prosperous eighties and nineties were supplying the *nouveaux riches* of the provinces with Birket Fosters, Coxes and Copley Fieldings in gold mounts and frames calculated to make the recipient feel that he had obtained good value for his money and a suitable accompaniment to the plush and gilt furniture of his Victorian drawing-room; as indeed he had, for a member of the Royal Water-Colour Society told me that in those times he used frequently to pay ten guineas for his elaborate frame.

It was not till about 1900 that the tide turned. Just before that date the New English Art Club was encouraging a revival of the water-colour drawing (as opposed to the Victorian water-colour painting) and reinstated the simple frame and the plain mount, sometimes with wash border, instead of the gold one. At the Royal Institute of Painters in Water-Colours the first definite claim by members for the admission of white mounts was made in 1914. The revolt was led by Mr. Terrick Williams, later to become President, and so great was the opposition of the diehard conservatives that a year passed before white mounts were permitted. Even then they were put on a separate wall, but after 1916 they were gradually mixed, and as a result of optical demonstration white or cream mounts won the day.

At the Royal Society of Painters in Water-Colours it was customary to insist on gold mounts for the Spring exhibitions and to allow white mounts in the Winter exhibitions of

[1] W. Callow, *Autobiography*, 1908, p. 107.

so-called 'sketches'. One of the most distinguished members of the Society, Sir George Clausen, used to refuse to submit work at the Spring exhibition owing to his intense dislike of a gold mount. The example set by the Royal Institute, however, was followed in 1915 when a rule was passed that gold mounts should no longer be essential, and white or cream mounts appeared for the first time at the Spring show of 1916. The Society still maintains a rule that plush frames are disallowed! The Royal Academy has never had a regulation about gold mounts, though they were *de rigueur* till about 1915, when white and cream mounts gradually began to get past the Hanging Committee.

The camera obscura and camera lucida

In Farington's *Diary* and elsewhere we find references to the use by artists of a 'camera' or 'camera obscura'. When Josiah Wedgwood was planning his great cream ware service, decorated with views of English landscape, he sent draughtsmen all over the country with a camera obscura, his partner Bentley wanting 'real views of real places'. In the Royal Collection at Windsor Castle is a drawing by Thomas Sandby, inscribed 'Windsor from the Gossels drawn in a camera', and a large camera obscura was the final lot on the first day of the T. Sandby sale, July 18, 1799. When Thomas and William Daniell, uncle and nephew, were travelling in India between 1786 and 1794, to prepare their great series of aquatint views,[1] they made constant use of the camera obscura.[2] Nowadays, it is not generally understood what this instrument was, or to what extent it might be of value to an artist. The camera obscura consists of a box, with an open side over which a curtain is hung. Opening into the box at the top is a small convex lens, set in a bellows, just as in the ordinary camera, to allow of focussing. Above the lens is a small mirror which is adjustable, and set usually at an angle of 45 degrees. The landscape, or object, to be depicted is reflected in the mirror, and the image passes down through the lens and forms a picture on a sheet of white paper placed on the base of the box. The draughtsman, with his head under the curtain, can readily trace out on the paper the outlines of the subject reflected, which would allow anyone to become a draughtsman; but experiment shows that the untrained person cannot make a picture that approaches being a work of art any more than he can produce a picture by tracing out a photograph. Very much depends on the touch, the thickening or refining of a line, the little difference of accent. To find just what could be done with the camera obscura, I made experiments with an eighteenth-century camera of this nature, preserved in the Science Museum. It is recorded to have been given by Sir Joshua Reynolds to Lady Yates, and is therefore contemporary with the instruments Thomas Sandby and the Daniells used. The box is 21 inches high, 25 inches wide and 18

[1] *Oriental scenery*, 1795–1808, six vols., 144 colour plates.
[2] M. Hardie and M. Clayton, *Thomas Daniell, R.A., William Daniell, R.A., Walker's Quarterly*, Nos. 35, 36, 1932.

inches deep, and the whole apparatus shuts up into a dummy book 18 inches by 25 inches, and about 4 inches deep. It is comparatively light and easily portable, and the Daniells carried with them and constantly employed, some instrument of this kind, probably supported on a tripod. Experiment showed that the outline of the whole of the Imperial Institute buildings could be very rapidly and exactly drawn on paper about 15 inches by 12 inches, and that, say, an Indian palace, such as many depicted by the Daniells, could be drawn in a quarter of an hour with exactness of perspective and detail, which might take hours to fix correctly without the camera's aid. It must be understood, however, that the result was merely an outline, hard and mechanical, a sort of tracing, and far from being a work of art. The younger Daniell could quite well make drawings in the camera obscura, and his uncle, with all his observation and stored knowledge, could readily work over a drawing of this nature, inserting figures and incident, and putting in the shadow washes which would give it a pictorial form. William Daniell at this time, it may be supposed, was an apprentice or assistant to his uncle rather than an originator.

The camera obscura was not an eighteenth-century invention, though it came to full use at that period. Its discovery has usually been attributed to Giovanni Battista della Porta, a Neapolitan savant of the sixteenth century, but actually it has much earlier origins.[1] The camera obscura is really the parent of the photographic camera. About 1813, J. N. Niepce was making experiments for fixing the image seen in the camera obscura on a sensitized paper, and in 1826 Daguerre claimed to have perfected a process whereby the image could be fixed. Thus photography began.

The camera lucida, invented by Dr. W. Hyde Wolleston, was patented in 1807. Like the camera obscura it gave a means of reflecting rays of light from any object by means of a peculiarly-shaped prism so as to produce an image upon paper and to allow the eye to see the movements of the pencil with which the image is being traced. It was cheap, small and portable, and its field of vision was larger than that of its predecessor. Some adaptation of the camera lucida was made by Cornelius Varley under the title of 'Cornelius Varley's Graphic Telescope'. It was used by Chantrey and others for outlining the profile of a portrait. A specimen of this type of camera lucida was given to Cotman by Sir Henry Englefield, and was used by him on his Normandy Tours for making drawings of Norman buildings on sheets of paper about 12 by 9 inches. Cotman found the apparatus difficult to manage and was forced to make many notes to supplement his architectural outlines. Mrs. Dawson Turner, with whom Cotman was travelling, found that 'there is no drawing with the camera lucida with a bonnet on, and even when that is removed it is needful to hold up the hair away from the forehead'. She reports, however, in 1818 that her daughter, Elizabeth, 'who has such excellent sight and can use the camera lucida with so much ease, has been of the greatest service to Mr. Cotman. His sight is by no means equal to hers, and she has a rapidity which is fully his equal so that, on the whole she is better qualified in the

---

[1] See the *Encyclopaedia Britannica* for a full scientific account of the camera obscura and the camera lucida.

use of this instrument than he. There were no less than five large drawings completed by this means yesterday between him and her. I do not mean finished drawings, but with all the lines in the right places and memoranda on the margins of all needful to be known towards making finished drawings.'[1]

The *St. Jacques, Dieppe*[2] is almost certainly a camera drawing. It is signed and dated 1818, and the further inscription 'Sketch'd June 22/17' refers, I suggest, to the date of the camera drawing, afterwards worked over and completed.

[1] S. D. Kitson, *John Sell Cotman*, 1937, pp. 194–208.
[2] Coll. J. Leslie Wright

PART II

CHAPTER I

Origins, antecedents and the beginnings of landscape

*Jacques Le Moyne de Morgues   John White   Inigo Jones
Isaac Oliver   Peter Paul Rubens   Anthony Van Dyck*

The vigorous and prolific life of British water-colour painting towards the close of the eighteenth century gave birth later to a widely held patriotic idea that the art had its origin in this country and began with the topographical artists who worked under the leadership of Paul Sandby. Thus, the introduction to the catalogue of the 1821 exhibition of the Society of Painters in Water-Colours states: 'Painting in water-colours may justly be regarded as a new art, and in its present application the invention of British artists, considerations which ought to have some influence on its public estimation and encouragement.' In 1823 W. H. Pyne wrote[1]: 'With reference to Water Colour Painting, we have to speak of a new art, originating with the English, and perfected within the age whence it began . . . It is something to record that the invention of painting in water colours, certainly one of the most elegant and interesting studies that has emanated from human ingenuity, is of English birth, of English growth, and on our soil has arrived to maturity.'

In an official *Descriptive Catalogue of the Historical Collection of Water Colour Painting in the South Kensington Museum*,[2] Samuel Redgrave claimed our British water-colour painters as 'a purely national and original school' and stated that their method of work was 'perfectly distinct from the manner of the Dutch, the French, or the Italian school'. Even Roget[3] speaks of 'the growth in Britain of the truly national art, known as drawing or painting in water-colours'.

Water-colour certainly came to maturity in England, and its possibilities as a medium were indeed much extended by British artists, but it was not in fact an indigenous growth. Like the art of mezzotint engraving, imported from overseas but later known abroad as *la manière anglaise*, water-colour came originally from the Continent and thereafter took root and flourished on English soil. It is a mistake to suppose that it had some spontaneous, almost miraculous, birth in England at the end of the eighteenth century. The earliest artists adopted, remodelled, and vastly extended a method which had been in ordinary use throughout Holland and Germany in the sixteenth and seventeenth centuries. They were provided with a clear starting-point, but they moved forward in a direction of their

---

[1] *Somerset House Gazette*, 1824/5 pp. 46–47.   [2] 1st edn., 1877.
[3] J. L. Roget, *History of the Old Water-Colour Society*, 1891.

49

own, and their lines of development were not parallel with those of their Continental contemporaries.

The remoter ancestry of the British water-colour school may be found in the work of the monk illustrators of manuscripts, with a direct descent from the 'Book of Kells' and the 'Lindisfarne Gospels' to the schools of Winchester and St. Albans.

Up to approximately the beginning of the fourteenth century the illuminators, as in the 'Book of Kells',[1] were working in pure water-colour. The miniatures in the 'Luttrell Psalter'[2] and other medieval manuscripts such as 'Le Bible en images', belonging to the Earl of Leicester, the 'Gorleston Psalter',[3] and the 'Historia Anglorum'[4] with drawings by Matthew Paris, are painted with transparent colours. Then came the conflict, which was to be repeated six centuries later, between pure water-colour and body-colour. Body-colour won; perhaps, as A. S. Hartrick suggests,[5] because the illuminators found that painting in body-colour, being more solid and opaque, held its place in conjunction with gold, which is not found in the earliest illuminations, but was lavishly used later. In either case the colours, protected from light in bound volumes, have been perfectly preserved. With all their brilliance of tint the designs of the painter-monks are essentially linear; colour clothes the drawing, and however different their subject and their outlook, the water-colour painters of the seventeenth and eighteenth centuries depended upon a similar use of structural line clothed with colour.

The link between medieval illuminations and later work in water-colour is supplied by the painters of miniature portraits; from Holbein, Hilliard, Isaac and Peter Oliver and Samuel Cooper onwards, down to Cosway, Engleheart, Plimer and their successors. About 1620 Edward Norgate wrote about the use of water-colours for miniature portraits, and said that 'there is noe more to doe than ever to remember that in all or most of the shadowes white is ever a dayly guest, and seldome absent but in the deepest shadowes'.[6] But Holbein's *Anne of Cleves*[7] and *Mrs. Pemberton*[8] show the use of white mixed with transparent colours and the same method will be found in the work of Nicholas Hilliard and Isaac Oliver. The earlier miniatures were usually painted on vellum, laid on the back of a playing card. It was not till the time of Bernard Lens (born 1682) that ivory came into general use for this purpose. In 1735 Vertue mentions miniatures as being 'painted on Ivory, a manner much used of late years among the limners'. We speak of these portraits and of pictorial illuminations in manuscript alike as 'miniatures'. They are the same in method, and from the aspect of technique are just as much 'water-colours' as the water-colours of the eighteenth and nineteenth centuries.

In his *Miniatura* Norgate becomes rapturous about water-colour. He holds that 'Lymning Colours' (i.e. water-colours) 'are much more beautiful than those in Oyle . . . All

---

[1] Trinity College Dublin: Fascimile in B.M. [2] B.M. Add. MS. 42130.
[3] B.M. Add. MS. 49622. [4] B.M. Roy. MS. 14. c. VII.
[5] Old Water-Colour Society's Club, 1938, XVI.
[6] E. Norgate, *Miniatura or the Art of Limning*, transcribed by M. Hardie, 1919, p. 22.
[7] V.A.M. P.153–1910. [8] V.A.M. P.40–1935.

Painting in generall I looke upon but as Lace and ornament, and without which a king-dome may subsist, yet (with submission to my superiours) I conceave this our Art of Lym-ning transcends all other of this kind, as farre as a Curious Watch doth a Towne clocke. . . . In the practize whereof, besides the singular delight to the student in improvement of his skill, the applause of the Juditious, and generally the love of all, there is gotten an honest, harmles, and innocent expense of time in a sweet and contented retirement from the Tintamara and illecebra of this drunken, perishing, and ending world, which, if ever, is now *positus in maligno*'. He does not confine his treatise to the subject of miniature portraits, but deals extensively with landscape and shows the extent to which, just before and just after the year 1600, landscapes were painted in water-colour, usually with body-colour on vellum, by such artists as Francis Cleyn, Bril, Savery and others.

But before that time, long before an English school came into existence, continental artists were familiar with the water-colour medium, whether in pure colour or body-colour, and had wide knowledge of its resources. If anyone has claim to be regarded as the father of water-colour then Albrecht Dürer deserves to be considered thus rather than Paul Sandby. He was a many-sided painter in the medium, who had a preference for certain large aspects of nature, but settled down with equal pleasure to the most meticulous study of the intricate detail of a bird's wing, the fur of a hare, a flower, or a reed by the river's brim.

When he set out in 1490 across the Alps, the many things he saw 'acted as a mighty ferment', and, like Turner later, he noted, eagerly and avariciously, the aspects new to him of mountains and valleys, of towns and fortifications. At Nüremberg on his return he made many studies of architecture, of places and people, of animals and birds and flowers. His journey to the Netherlands in 1520–1521 filled his sketch-books still more. Like Turner he seemed unable to resist, whenever he had the time, putting a wash of colour over his pen drawings, and whether he used water-colour lightly or lavishly, he used it with intelligence and understanding. His colour is often laid in thin, transparent washes; sometimes it is charged with white to make it opaque. More and more, as he added slight washes of colour to his drawings, he became interested in colour for its own sake, for its richness, its shifting and shimmering values and vibrations. In one of his notes on Painting[1] comes a passage which curiously anticipates the method which Cotman made his own:

> Be careful that thou shade each colour with a similar colour. Thus I hold that a yellow, to re-tain its kind, must be shaded with a yellow, darker toned than the principal colour. If thou shade it with green or blue, it remaineth no longer in keeping but becometh thereby a shot colour, like the colour of silk stuffs woven of threads of two colours. . . . Happen what may, every colour must in shading keep to its own class.

Dürer's use of water-colour was no isolated phenomenon; and in the century after his death painters all over Europe, from the Netherlands to Switzerland and Italy, were

[1] W. M. Conway, *Literary Remains of Albrecht Dürer*, 1889, p. 173.

51

producing water-colour drawings. Perhaps earlier even than Dürer's work in this medium is a *Study of a Grey Partridge*[1] by Jacopo de Barbari (*c*.1450–*c*.1515), with delicate tints of blue, yellow and brown over a highly finished pen drawing.

All through the Low Countries water-colour thrived during the seventeenth century in the work of artists such as Avercamp, Ostade, Cuyp, Van Borssom, Van Uden, Hans Bol, Valentin Clotz, Flinck, Blomaert and others.

Looking thus at the Dutch School of the seventeenth century in general, we find that to their drawings, whether in black or grey chalk, or pen and ink or bistre, colour was commonly added. Their colours appear to have been more limited than those of their British followers a century later. With the exception of Jordaens and Van Huysum they use colour as an imitation rather than a representation of natural colour. Yellows, greens and browns enhance and give warmth to the foreground: a note of blue indicates the depth of the sky. Colour is rarely used, as in the English topographical drawings of a century later, in washes that cover large spaces. Just as the lines of a drawing are the refinement and essence of natural form, so the colour is but an essence extracted from the natural colour. Like many of the washes in Rembrandt's drawings, they seem to have been applied with a wet finger. In drawings by Cuyp, Saftleven, Avercamp, Ostade and others, the colours serve merely to detach and solidify figures and separate objects. Ostade's *Cottage with Outhouse and Agricultural Implements* in the Ashmolean Museum is a typical example. Colour is rarely superimposed in order to give depth and variety; it conveys a hint or a clue; the drawing would be complete without it. And yet what a perfect feeling of warmth and atmosphere is given by yellow and brown in drawings such as those of Van Goyen, Cuyp or Doomer. Occasionally, as in the work of Jordaens, Swaneveldt and others, the first tints are enforced by secondary local colours. The Dutch painters of the seventeenth century are wrestling with the same problems and possibilities which faced our English water-colourists in the latter half of the eighteenth century.

At the close of the sixteenth century in England water-colour was not the exclusive domain of Hilliard, Oliver and other painters of miniature portraits. It was used sporadically by diverse painters for diverse purposes.

In the Victoria and Albert Museum is a beautiful set of sixteenth-century water-colour drawings of plants by Jacques Le Moyne de Morgues (*d*. 1588).[2] They deal exclusively with flowers and fruit then common in English gardens[3]; these drawings appear to have been the artist's material on which he based the engravings in a small oblong octavo volume with the title *La Clef des Champs, pour trouver plusieurs Animaux, tant Bestes qu'Oyseaux avec plusieurs Fleurs et Fruitz*. It was imprinted *aux Blackefriars* in 1586, an exceedingly rare book, of which there are two imperfect copies in the British Museum. The book was not registered at Stationers Hall till 1587, and was dedicated to Lady Mary Sidney by the

[1] B.M. 1928. 3.10.103
[2] V.A.M. 3267a etc.–1856. The drawings probably date from the 1560's.
[3] *Gardeners' Chronicle*, Jan. 28, 1922 and *Times Literary Supplement*, Feb. 9, 1922.

artist, who signs himself 'Vostre très-affectionné'; but it was a tragic year, for in May, Sir Henry Sidney died, followed three months later by his widow, Lady Mary Sidney, and, on October 16th, by Sir Philip Sidney, their son, on the battlefield of Zutphen.[1]

Le Moyne was a French artist, born at Dieppe of a Protestant family. He was sent by Chastillon, Admiral of France, with Laudonnière's expedition in 1564 to the relief of the French colonists in Florida. He escaped to London at the time of the massacre of St. Bartholomew, was employed by Sir Walter Raleigh, and became the friend of Sir Philip Sidney and Hakluyt. In his translation of Laudonnière's *Voyage to Florida*, Hakluyt mentions 'divers things of chiefest importance at Florida drawn in colours by that skilful painter James Morgues, sometime living in Blackfryars, London'. The original drawings in colour, with the exception of one in the New York Public Library, seem to have disappeared, but are known through De Bry's engravings of them published in 1591. The drawings of flowers and fruit survive to show Le Moyne's skill both as draughtsman and colourist. Almost as fresh as though they were painted yesterday, they show the use of pure water-colour, here and there mixed with a little white to give body; and specially noteworthy is the microscopic exactness of drawing, texture and colour in the butterflies and insects which he uses to give additional life and adornment. His drawings themselves may well be classed among the *choses bonnes et honnêstres*, which in the preface of his published work he wishes his readers to seek.

At the very time when Le Moyne was making his miniature-like studies of plants and flowers, John White (*fl.*1577–1590) was using water-colour for his drawings of scenery and natives in Virginia and Florida. In the British Museum is a series of drawings[2] previously in an album, entitled in the artist's hand-writing: *The pictures of sondry things collected and counterfeited according/to the truth in the voyage made by S*. *Walter Raleigh knight,/for the discouery of La Virginea. In the 27*ᵗʰ *yeare/of the most happie reigne of our Soueraigne lady Queene/ Elizabeth. and in the yeare of o*:*/Lorde God./1585*. John White[3] was one of the adventurers who sailed in the fleet of seven ships under the command of Sir Richard Grenville, of the *Revenge*, to found the first English colony in North America. White remained for a whole year in Virginia, returning to England with Sir Francis Drake in July 1586. His drawings are of the manners and customs of the natives, and studies of plants, birds, fishes, etc. They show keen observation and a sensitive hand, but their interest is primarily for the historian, ethnologist and cartographer. In 1587 Raleigh set out with a larger expedition to leave John White as Governor of his 'Second Colonie'. The difficulties on arrival at Roanoke were so great that White was sent back to England to obtain help and instructions. He left

[1] An album in the British Museum (1962. 7.14.1) discovered in 1962, of fifty drawings in water-colours and body-colours, dated 1585, reveal a development in the artist's technique. Another small volume, that would seem to have been used as a reference or copy book and almost certainly pre-dates those in the V.A.M., is in the Harvard University Library.

[2] 1906. 5.9.1.

[3] L. Binyon, *Drawings by British Artists in The British Museum*, IV, 1907 and *The Drawings of John White*, Walpole Soc. XIII, 1924–1925.

behind with the colony his daughter, who had become the mother of the first English child born in English North America, Virginia Dare. An expedition, which sailed in 1590 under White, failed to find any trace of the colony it had come to relieve.

Through the well-known publisher, Theodor de Bry, comes a link between Le Moyne and White. De Bry came to London in 1587 to obtain from Le Moyne materials for illustrating an edition of Laudonnière's *Journal*, and on a second visit in 1588 procured Le Moyne's drawings from his widow and was introduced by Richard Hakluyt to John White. Hakluyt persuaded the publisher to work on a larger theme than the printing of the *Journal* and to make a collection of voyages, beginning with a reprint of Hariot's *Report on Virginia*. So, in 1590, the first volume of De Bry's great work, *America*, was issued at Frankfort-am-Main and was illustrated by engravings from twenty-three of the drawings by White in the British Museum.

Another of the pioneers was Inigo Jones (1573–1652) who, in addition to his work as an architect, designed scenery and costumes for a long series of masques by Ben Jonson, Heywood, Chapman, Campion, Sir W. Davenant and others, which were produced at Court. Jones did a vast amount of work as masque producer, or pageant master, from 1605 to 1640. The medieval mumming and mimic show had developed in the hands of Ben Jonson into the masque, with its unity of design, dialogue and scenic *décor*. The great architect supplied the creative touch which made it a spectacle of beauty. A large number of his drawings for costume and scenery are at Chatsworth, part of the vast and princely assemblage of Old Master drawings collected by the Dukes of Devonshire.[1] The drawings as a rule were made with pen and ink or sepia wash, and show strongly the influence of Italian art and of such artists as Guercino. Nine, however, of the costume designs were finished in colour, laid on with a full brush. There is much landscape work in the designs which Inigo Jones made for the scenery of the masques, but it is all in black and white. On the subject of Inigo Jones as a landscape painter, the writer of a memoir prefixed to the book on Stonehenge by Inigo Jones some time after his death, speaks of the difficulty of finding particulars about his early career, and adds: 'This, indeed, we know, that he was early distinguished by his inclination to drawing or designing, and was particularly taken notice of for his skill in the practice of landscape painting.' There is a similar somewhat surprising note by Vertue: 'His Fancy led him to paint Landskap. in which he might make tollerable progress, before he travelled. which as he says (before his Stoneheng) that in his younger days he had been in Italy. enabled him to make a better choice of his Studies & undoubtedly, a better progress. The innumerable fine Views. Ruins Scituations Mountains Rocks Waters abound every where with so much beautifull Variety in those Countries, that a Young painter, that will apply himself to that kind of Study. has every where fine Moddels Nature to follow, which must certainly enrich his mind as well as his pictures.'[2] These quotations raise the two interesting points, that Jones was originally a land-

---

[1] P. Simpson and C. F. Bell, *Inigo Jones's designs for masques*, Walpole Soc., XII, 1923–1924.
[2] Vertue—I, *Autobiography*, Walpole Soc., XVIII, 1929–1930, p. 148.

scape painter and that the England of his time was not thought worth the consideration of any aspiring landscape painter.

At the beginning of the seventeenth century landscape art was still alien in England or, at best, a newcomer. Water-colour, as we have seen, was generally used for miniature portraits, and there was also a vogue for figure-subjects, known as 'histories'. Isaac Oliver (1551 or 1556–1617), the miniature painter, bequeathed in his will 'his drawings . . . and Limning pictures, be they historyes, stories,' etc.; and Norgate devotes a section of his *Miniatura* to 'Histories', mentioning specially the *Entombment* by Isaac Oliver,[1] and saying that 'Histories in Lymning are strangers in England till of late years it pleased a most excellent King to comand the Copieing of some of his owne peeces, of Titian, to be translated into English Lymning, which indeed were admirably performed by his Servant, Mr. Peter Olivier'. But, about the year 1600, landscape painting was so rare that Norgate found it necessary to 'blazon its coat and derive its pedigree'. He describes it as: 'an art soe new in England, and so lately come a shore, as all the Language within our four seas cannot find it a Name, but a borrowed one, [*Landscape* is the Dutch *Landschap*] and that from a people that are noe great Lenders but upon good Securitie, the Duch. Perhaps they will name their owne Child. For to say truth the Art is theirs.'

In this connection it is of interest to consult the *New English Dictionary* for the earliest uses of the word 'landscape', apart from its appearance in Norgate's *Miniatura*. It may be noted that 'landscape', in its variant spellings, was for a long time used only in a pictorial sense as a rendering of the land in art and not as a description of the natural aspect of land itself as in Gray's 'Now fades the glimmering landscape on the sight'. First, in 1598, comes R. Haydocke:

In a table (i.e. picture) done by Caesar Sestius where he had painted landskipes.

Then, in 1603, Joshua Sylvester writes:

The cunning painter limning a landscape, various, rich, and rare.

In 1605 Ben Jonson gives stage directions for a masque such as those in which he was associated with Inigo Jones:

First for the scene was drawn a landscap consisting of small woods.

Later, in a poem by A. Gibson appended to Guillam's *Display of Heraldry*, 1660, we find:

As in a curious Lant-schape oft we see
Nature so followed as we think 'tis she.

Another spelling occurs in 1656, when George Blount defines the meaning of landscape, obviously still regarding landscape as a mere background to a portrait, figure-painting, or 'history':

---

[1] The whereabouts of the original is not known, formerly in the collection of James II, but a drawing for the composition is in the B.M. 1945. 9.24.2.

Landskip, Parergon, Paisage or By-work, which is an expressing of the land by hills, woods, castles, valleys, rivers, cities, etc., as far as may be showed in one horizon. All that which in a picture is not the body or argument thereof is landskip, parergon, or by-work.

The word, 'seascape' was bound to follow, and in 1732 Vertue speaks of Samuel Scott as a 'sea schap painter'. The earliest example of 'seascape' (in the form 'sea-skip') given by the *New English Dictionary* dates from 1799.

Norgate himself points out how landscape had been used for 'filling up the empty Corners or void places of Figures and story', and adds: 'But to reduce this part of painting to an absolute and intire Art, and to confine a man's industry for the tearme of Life to this onely, is I conceave an Invencon of these later times, and though a Noveltie, yet a good one . . . The Art is growne to that perfection that it is as much as 20 or 30 yeares practice can doe, to produce a good painter, at this one species of painting onely. Where-withall Sr. Peter Rubens of Antwerp was soe delighted in his later time, as he quitted all his other practice in Picture and Story, whereby he got a vast estate, to studie this, whereof he hath left the world the best that are to bee seene, some where off were lately at York howse, now unhappily transplanted.' With these introductory remarks, Norgate then analyses the whole method of painting landscape in water-colours: 'all your Colours on a little pallet of Ivory or some great shell of Mother pearle, of capacity enough to containe some good quantity of Colour in severall heapes, reserving a void place in the middle for water . . . Be carefull often to wash your Pencills cleane in your saucer or shell of faire water, to bee ever on your right hand, for if your Yellow Pencill should temper the blew, you will find greene enough to spoile all.'

It would not be unreasonable to say that landscape painting, 'soe new in England', was brought to London when Peter Paul Rubens came to the Court of Charles I in 1629.[1] He had been painting in water-colour twenty years before he arrived as an Ambassador in England. A *Landscape* by him in the Oppenheimer Collection[2] (304), dated 1609, showed touches of colour in the manner of his predecessor, Pieter Bruegel, a wash of blue to suggest distant trees and water, a hint of green to give sunshine on the nearer foliage; two colours only, but with the bistre washes that warm the whole landscape, they suffice. A drawing of a *Tree-Trunk and Branches*, at Chatsworth, made about ten years later, is in red chalk, brown ink and water-colour; and another drawing in the same manner, probably done at the same place and time, is in the Louvre. Other landscape drawings by Rubens are *A Moated Grange with a Bridge-house*,[3] very delicately drawn in pen and bistre, with pale washes of transparent colour, and *A Stream with overhanging Trees*[4] in body-colour. His magnificent portrait of *Sir Theodore Mayerne*[5] combines transparent and opaque colour, another example of the conflict already mentioned.

There is no evidence to show that Rubens ever used water-colour in England, but as a

---

[1] Both Charles I and the Duke of Buckingham owned landscape paintings by Rubens.
[2] Sale Christie's, July 10, 13, 14, 1931.   [3] B.M. 1895. 9.15.1041.
[4] B.M. 1859. 8.6.60.   [5] B.M. 1860. 6.16.36.

1 'Peach Blossom'

B.M. 1962.7.14.1 (6) $8\frac{1}{4} \times 5\frac{3}{4}$: 208 × 146   *Water-colour and body-colour*

Jacques Le Moyne (d. 1588)

2 'Orange'

B.M. 1962.7.14.1 (44) $8\frac{1}{2} \times 5\frac{1}{8}$: 216 × 130   *Water-colour and body-colour*

Jacques LE MOYNE (d. 1588)

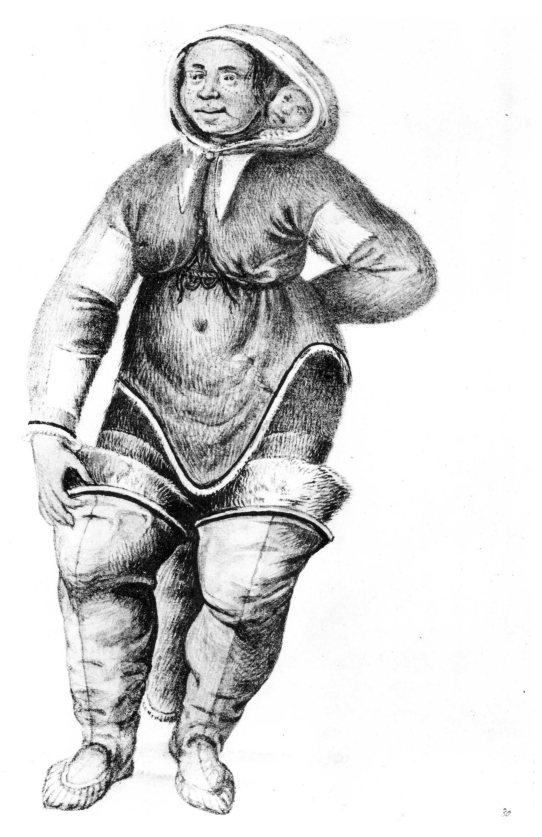

3 'An Eskimo Woman'

B.M. 1906.5.9.1 (30)   8¾ × 6½: 223 × 166   *Water-colour touched with white*
John WHITE (fl. 1577–1590)

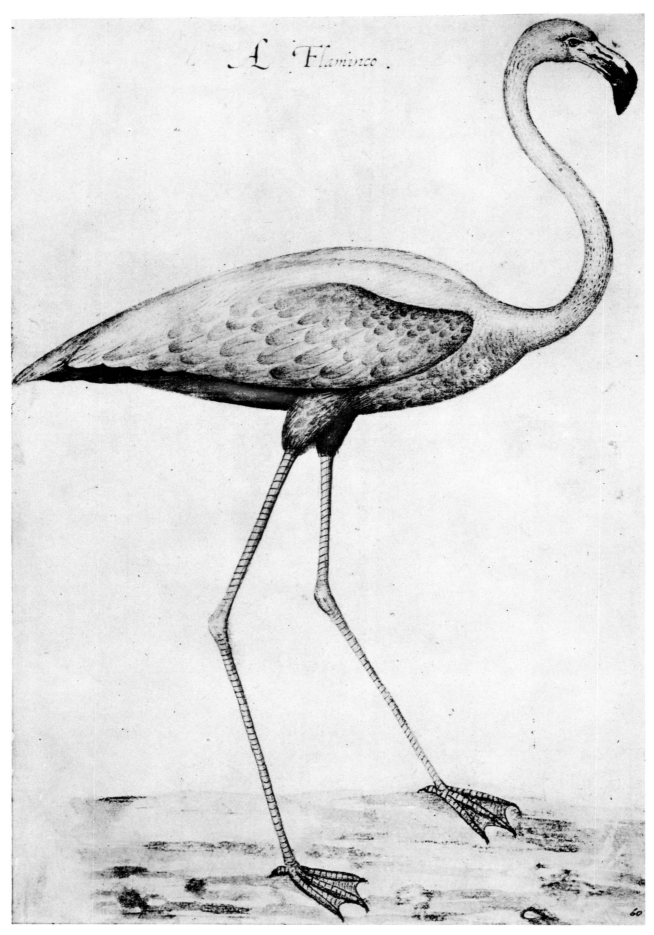

L Flaminco.

4 'A Flamingo'

B.M. 1906.5.9.1 (60) $11\frac{5}{8} \times 7\frac{3}{4}$: 296 × 197   *Water-colour touched with white*

John WHITE (fl. 1577–1590)

Pefe porco. Of this, some are 2 fote in length

5 'Queen Trigger Fish'
B.M. 1906.5.9.1 (55) $5\frac{5}{8} \times 8\frac{3}{4}$: 143 × 223
Water-colour, heightened with blue and white
John WHITE (fl. 1577–1590)

6 'A Festive Dance'

B.M. 1906.5.9.1 (10) $10\frac{3}{4} \times 14\frac{1}{8}$: 274 × 358   *Water-colour touched with white*

John WHITE (fl. 1577–1590)

7 'The Entombment'
B.M. 1945.9.24.2 $11\frac{5}{8} \times 14\frac{7}{8}$: 295 × 377
Pen and ink and wash heightened with white, signed
Isaac OLIVER (1551 or 1556–1617)

8 'Country Lane'

B.M. 1895.9.15.1067 $9\frac{5}{8} \times 15\frac{5}{8}$: 244 × 397   *Water-colour and body-colour, signed*

Anthony VAN DYCK (1599–1641)

famous landscape painter from abroad, no doubt bringing examples of his own work and works of others, both in oil and water-colour, from his own vast collections, he inspired King Charles and his court with a love of landscape art. As Norgate says, it was on the way to becoming 'a *privado* and Cabinet Companion for kings and princes'. A manuscript of the seventeenth century styled 'An Inventorie of the Personall Estate of ye late king, which was sold by Act of Parlt.' is in the Victoria and Albert Museum. It includes a landscape among the water-colours owned by Charles I, to which are appended their prices:

One piece, of Christ on the Cross Water Cullours	1. 0. 0.
A landskape with water cullours	2. 0. 0.
A picture in water cullours of the beheading of the Queen of Scotts	12. 0. 0.
Xt feeding the people watercolours	2. 0. 0.
Spanish Fleet in 88 watercolours	3. 0. 0.
Tobias in water colours by ye King's Niece	2. 6. 0.

Rubens opened the way for Sir Anthony Van Dyck (1599–1641), who followed him to London in 1632. Van Dyck struck more deeply than Rubens into English soil, and it seems probable that many of the drawings known to come from his hand were made in England. The only drawing by him, certainly made in our country, is a sketch of Rye, in the J. Pierpont Morgan Collection (Cat. pl. 178). Vertue saw it in the sale of drawings from the collection of Jonathan Richardson, sen.—'A small prospect of Rie—it is signd. A Vandyck delin. 1633 del. naturale 27 Aug.' That is in pen and ink, but some of his drawings in colour seem to be inspired by the gentle breath of our English countryside and English trees and skies. In his book on Constable,[1] Sir Charles Holmes says: 'Van Dyck's sketch in body-colour of *A Country Lane*[2] (Pl. 8), is absolutely like a drawing of the nineteenth century, rendering with the most perfect ease and accuracy the fresh, cool green of spring leafage and the faint blue mist that is the characteristic feature of our English summer sunshine'. A. P. Oppé,[3] on the other hand, thinks that some of the Van Dyck landscape drawings, mainly those at Chatsworth, may belong to his English period, but that the group in the British Museum are either of Flemish subjects or were made on visits to the Netherlands. Of the latter no monochrome is used for the underpainting of shadows. Outline is hardly used except for detail here and there. The drawings depend upon colour, and not upon line. As in the case of Girtin later, 'local colour' is painted; the tree shadows are indicated by floating a darker green or blue over a light colour. *The Unfinished Landscape*[4] is literally a sketch, left incomplete, but it is strangely modern, almost with a hint of Constable, particularly in the freshness and movement of the sky. The same qualities are

[1] *Constable*, 1903, p. 36.
[2] B.M. 1895. 9.15.1067.
[3] A. P. Oppé, 'Sir Anthony Van Dyke in England', *Burlington Magazine*, LXXIX, 1941, p. 190.
[4] Chatsworth, Duke of Devonshire's Collection.

apparent in a *Landscape*, done in body-colour, belonging to Sir W. Fitzherbert. It is not unreasonable to suppose that *A Tree Bordered Country Lane*,[1] a finely composed study of trees singly and in mass, on blue-grey paper and done in England, stands at the starting point of English landscape. It was noteworthy for the graceful feathery foliage and the *Stimmary* which Gainsborough was to make so peculiarly his own. These drawings by Van Dyck have a sparkling, thrusting quality of instinctive expression, a breadth and ease, which anticipate the landscape drawings of Gainsborough. But Van Dyck had no immediate followers; Gainsborough was the first fully to revive such a deep poetic perception. The field which Van Dyck had cultivated lay fallow, but new ground was to be opened up, and a new beginning made, by Hollar and Place. From their careful topographical work there is a continuity of tradition. There are definite links in the long chain which unites them, through Taverner, Samuel Scott, Skelton, the Sandbys, Rooker, Hearne and Dayes, with Girtin and Turner. With Hollar and Place as the fore-runners, there came into existence a national school of landscape painters, with a school of engravers to reproduce and give publicity to their work. Draughtsmen scoured the country, searching every part of the kingdom, on foot or on horseback, recording and 'minuting'—to use Walpole's expression —hill and dale, lake and river, castles, churches, country seats, ruins and antiquities.

[1] B.M. 1936. 10.10.22.

CHAPTER II

The advance guard in the seventeenth century

Wenceslaus Hollar   Francis Place   Francis Barlow   Edward Barlow

In tracing the origins of water-colour in this country, and showing its continuity, we must recognise yet another link in the seventeenth century with the schools of the Continent, to be found in the work of Wenceslaus Hollar and his follower, Francis Place.

Wenceslaus Hollar (1607–1677) born at Prague, was a pupil of Matthäus Merian, worked at Frankfort, Cologne and Antwerp, and was brought over to London in 1636 by Thomas Howard, Earl of Arundel, one of the first and greatest of English connoisseurs and patrons of art. At Chatsworth are twenty water-colour drawings by Hollar, made as a record of the Earl of Arundel's embassy to Ferdinand II in 1636. Hollar, a 'very honest, simple, well-meaning man', though 'shiftless as to the world', married an English wife and fought for the Royalist cause. Except for eight years passed in exile at Antwerp during the troubles of the Civil War, he spent the rest of his life in England. Hollar introduced to this country the method of washing pen-drawings with slight tints of colour, which had been practised by Dürer in the sixteenth century and was developed still further by the Dutch artists contemporary with Hollar in the seventeenth century. His palette is limited—blue, yellow, green, pale brown, and a rose madder for roofs; he does not seem to have used more than five colours in all. But in spite of—or because of—this limited range he produced drawings which are wholly satisfying in their colour scheme as well as in their expressive line. We may note specially *Zu Amsterdam, 1634*[1] with a sage green in the foreground, and touches of pale brown in ships and timber; or *Den Tower van London*[2] (Pl. 10); or the delicious views of *Delftshaven*[3] and *Bonn*.[4] In 1669 he was sent out by the Government to Morocco, and made many coloured drawings (some of them are in the British Museum) of the fortifications at Tangier (Pl. 12) and of British warships in its bay.[5] He must surely have come into touch with Pepys, who was very busy with a 'Committee for Tangier' from 1662 for many years, and himself went out to Tangier in 1683; but the Diary says nothing of Hollar and his drawings.

Hollar's pen-lines are often laid in the tight parallel method of the etcher or engraver, and sometimes suggest the flecks and thinning strokes of the burin. Often, however, his

[1] B.M. 1862.7.12.193.   [2] B.M. 1859.8.6.389.
[3] B.M. 1862.7.12.194.   [4] B.M. Gg. 2–245.
[5] H. Walpole, *Anecdotes of Painting in England*, 1862 edn., III, pp. 883–895, and the Vertue Manuscripts published by the Walpole Society.

line is as loose, his method almost as free, as that of Rembrandt, whose work he probably knew. As, for instance, in *By Duren* (Pl. 9).[1] It was this looser method, which Place, as we shall see, was to follow. In a drawing by Hollar such as *Richmond*,[2] with its greenish-grey wash laid faintly on the palace building and more heavily across the foreground, with its *Richmond* written tidily on the sky and *Thamesis fluvius* on the water, we have the beginnings of Francis Place. We certainly have the beginnings of the unbroken tradition of English topographical drawing, the close record of architecture and landscape, which was to be a central feature of eighteenth-century art. With his faithful and accurate representations which add so much to our historical knowledge of seventeenth-century London and its suburbs, Hollar stands at the start of this tradition. In drawings and etchings he was a recorder first and foremost, but at the same time he had an eye for the pure beauty of the English scene, as is shown by his etchings of streams and trees and rural landscape in the neighbourhood of Albury in Surrey. By his topographical art he founded a school, but the full imaginative, intimate, interpretation of landscape was to come later.[3]

Francis Place (1647–1728) was not dependent entirely on his art for a livelihood. Being provided with sufficient income by his father, Rowland Place, of Dinsdale, Durham,[4] he was destined for the law, but the outbreak of the plague cut short his studies, and he appears thenceforward to have devoted himself to drawing, etching, experiments in making porcelain and to fishing, with its often concomitant love of peaceful nature, and particularly of birds. From dates on his etchings and drawings, from mention in the letters of his friends, from the notes of George Vertue and Horace Walpole, and from a study of his work by H. M. Hake,[5] we can trace the outlines of his career. A series of drawings and a sketchbook acquired by the Victoria and Albert Museum in 1931,[6] and twenty-nine drawings owned by Mr. J. Maher[7] of Dublin, add considerably to the sparse dates given by Hake, who knew of only six dated drawings between 1694 and 1715. It can be shown that Place made an extended visit to Ireland, possibly, as Mr. Maher points out, on the invitation of the great Duke of Ormonde, though this assumption is based on the places which he visited and not on any definite information.

In 1667, at which date he was probably in touch with Hollar, Place etched two gro-

[1] B.M. 1850. 2.23.194.
[2] B.M. 1854. 5.13.7.
[3] Dr. F. G. Grossmann compiled a very informative catalogue of the Hollar material in the exhibition at Manchester City Art Gallery in 1963.
[4] Dinsdale, called Low or Nether Dinsdale, to distinguish it from Over Dinsdale on the Yorkshire side of the Tees, lies on a height overlooking the left bank of the river. The manor-house belonged to the lords of Low Dinsdale, who occasionally used the local surname, but more often called themselves Surtees (super Teisam). From this family came Robert Surtees, antiquary and author of the *History of Durham*, and R. S. Surtees of *Jorrocks* fame. In 1511 Thomas Surtees died, leaving the manor to his sister Katherine, second wife of John Place of Halnaby, Yorks. Rowland Place, a later owner, died in 1630, leaving two sons, Rowland, who succeeded to the manor, and Francis, born probably in the parish of Dinsdale, in 1647 (*The Victoria History of the Counties of England: Durham*, 1928, vol. III, pp. 217–220).
[5] *Some Contemporary Records relating to Francis Place, Engraver and Draughtsman*, Walpole Soc., X, 1921–1922, pp. 39–69.
[6] From the collection of the late Patrick Allan Fraser of Hospitalfield, Arbroath; Sotheby's June 10, 1931.
[7] Now the property of Michael J. Flynn, Esq., Dublin. Thirteen are of Dublin, six of Drogheda, five of Kilkenny and two of Waterford.

tesque heads in Hollar's manner after Leonardo da Vinci, and a tavern interior after Teniers. From 1668 to 1673 there is a blank in our knowledge of his work, but in the following years, 1674–1682, he was working in the north of England and made drawings of *Richmond Castle*[1] in 1674, *Dunstanborough Castle*[2] and *Bath bridge over the Avon*[2a] in 1678. In the same year Place went on a walking tour of 'seven thousand miles in Seaven Weekes' through South Wales with William Lodge (1649–1689), the amateur artist and engraver.[3] To 1683 belongs a set of drawings of *Peterborough House*,[4] *Lambeth and the Strand from Millbank* (Pl. 16). We find him in Ireland, making drawings at Dublin, Waterford, etc. and also at Chester and in Wales, in 1699. The sketch-book which contains these drawings, shows that he was at Middleham Castle in 1711, and was working at York and Scarborough in 1717, when he was in his sixty-ninth year. Dated drawings in the British Museum are of the *Ouse Bridge at York*[5] and *Knaresborough Castle*[6] (Pl. 13), 1703; *Knaresborough*[7] (Pl. 15) and *Middleham*[8] *Castles*, 1711; *Byland Abbey*,[9] 1713; and *Pickering Castle*,[10] 1715. Yorkshire was clearly a favourite centre owing to Place's connection with Dinsdale, just over its border, and because he took up his residence in the manor-house close to St. Mary's Abbey, York, living there for forty years. Here he was in close touch with Henry Gyles, the glass painter, and their houses were a meeting-place for the *virtuosi* of York and its neighbourhood.

In 1716 Place wrote to George Vertue a long and interesting letter containing information about Wenceslaus Hollar. Eleven years later, in 1727, Vertue visited him at York, and made this note:

> Mr. Francis Place born in Yorkshire was bred a Clerk in Grey Inn in the pipe Office. did not like the law practice. had a great inclination to drawing etching Mezotinting, painting. travelld thro many parts of England Wales. into Ireland. drew views of many places very well a great lover of fishing as was his companion Mr. Lodge & Mr. Tunstal these three travelld several months together from River to River & in Oatsplot time (1678) were taken up at Derby & put in prison for Plotters. he livd lastly near 40 years at York.

In 1728 he adds:

> 1728. This year dyd at York, Francis Place an Ingenious Gent whose works in painting drawing & engraving also Metzotint are deservedly esteemed by the Curious and lovers of Art. In the latter part of his life having means enough to live on he passed his time at ease being a sociable and pleasant companion much beloved by the gentry of those parts having in his younger days been a noted sportsman particularly for fishing but Time and a great age brought him to his Grave.

A portrait of Place by a contemporary artist, Thomas Murray (1665–1734) is in the Picture Gallery at Hospitalfield, Arbroath.

---

[1] B.M. 1850. 2.23.828. [2] B.M. 1850. 2.23.813. [2a] Whereabouts unknown.
[3] See a note in the sketchbook (V.A.M. E.1506–1931), in which Place 'drew the drafts' illustrating this tour.
[4] V.A.M. E.1507 & 8–1931. [5] B.M. 1850. 2.23.839. [6] B.M. 1850. 2.23.821.
[7] B.M. 1850. 2.23.819, 820. [8] B.M. 1850. 2.23.825. [9] B.M. 1850. 2.23.811.
[10] B.M. 1850. 2.25.826.

At an early period of his career in London, as is shown by his letter to Vertue, Place came into close touch with Wenceslaus Hollar, and was clearly indebted greatly for much of his style and choice of subjects to Hollar and to the masters of the Low Countries. In the letter to Vertue, who had asked for information about Hollar, Place says: 'He was a person I was intimately acquainted withal, but never his disciple nor anybody else's, which was my misfortune.' He was enough of a disciple, however, to absorb much of Hollar's outlook and method in his topographical views of low-lying towns fronted by river or sea, and he followed Hollar in writing the names of places on sky or water in neat and tiny script. But Hollar was 'the most indefatigable man that has been in any age as his works will testifie . . . was always indigent . . . always uneasde if not at work'. Hollar had to labour, day in and day out, to make a meagre pittance—he only got 30s. for his long plate of Greenwich—'he did all by the hour in which he was very exact for if any body came in that kep him from his business he always laid ye hour glass on one side, till they were gone . . . he always recond 12d an hour'.[1] By his own confession in a letter, Place wanted his liberty directly he had engaged to do a piece of work. This does much to explain his difference from Hollar, in spite of their similarity. Place is more free, less precise; he thinks on his paper more than Hollar, who is often slowly putting into line a formulated thought; and is more sensible to pictorial charm. In spite of the fact that he, too,—like Hollar—was an etcher and engraver, at a time when the etched or engraved line tended to be rigid and precise, his handling is looser. In his topographical views he follows Hollar both in method and in simple schemes of colour; drawing with a pen, with washes of sepia and Indian ink, and often using what are touches or notes of colour rather than any extended washes. It is worth noting that, though he uses shadow tints of ink or sepia, he does not wash colour over them in the manner of the later topographers, but leaves the shadows and adds separate touches of local colour. He comes very close to Hollar in drawings such as *View of the Coast of Lincolnshire*[2] and *One of the Block Houses at Hull*.[3] Drawings of a panoramic nature by him to be noted at the Victoria and Albert Museum are *Peterborough House, Lambeth and the Strand from Mill Bank*,[4] 1683 (Pl. 16); *The King's Victualling House from the Mast Yard at Deptford*,[5] with very slight touches of rose and brown; and, on the double page of a sketchbook, *Chester Castle*,[6] 1699. One of the most charming drawings is one of the Isle of Wight with *Insula Wigts* written on the sky, and *Oceanus Britannicus* on the water.

In another aspect of his work—a purely pictorial landscape side—seen in two drawings in monochrome of *The Dropping Well at Knaresborough*[7] (Pl. 14)—Place gets right away from Hollar, and anticipates later men, such as Alexander Cozens and John White Abbott,

---

[1] Vertue quotes an account of Hollar at work, of absorbing interest to the modern etcher, who uses acid and feather in just the same way. 'Feb. 20, 1649, I saw Mr. Hollar etching. & he laid on the water (acid) wich cost him 4s. pound. & was not half a ¼ of an hour eating. it bubled presently. he stirrd it with a feather. he lays on the wax with a clout and smooths it with a feather. he makes a Verge to keep the water wth yellow wax & Tallow melted together. & layd it on wth a pencil he always Stirrs the Aqua with a feather.' *Vertue Note Books*, I, Walpole Soc., XVIII, 1930, p. 112.
[2] B.M. 1850. 2.23.824.
[3] B.M. 1850. 2.23.815.
[4] V.A.M. E.1507 & 8–1931.
[5] V.A.M. E.1513–1931.
[6] V.A.M. E.1506–1931.
[7] B.M. 1850.2.23. 822 & 823.

in his treatment of light and shade over masses of rocks and foliage. Similarly, the bold washes of shadow and the firm design of *Scarborough Castle*[1] are more individual, leading from Rembrandt and Claude rather than from Hollar. Hake[2] has rightly pointed out that Place 'foreshadows, to a marked degree, some of the best work of the English etchers and draughtsmen of the latter half of the eighteenth century'. He etched Francis Barlow's drawings of birds and also drew them himself with great knowledge and skill as can be seen by his sheet of *Studies of Waterfowl*.[3]

Francis Barlow (*c.*1626–1704) no doubt came into touch with Place as a lover of bird life, and many of his drawings of birds were translated by Place into etchings. He came to London, and Vertue records that he was 'put prentice to one Shepherd, a Face-Painter, with whom he liv'd but few years because his Fancy did not lye that way, his Genious leading him wholly to drawing of Fowl, Fish and Beasts, wherein he arriv'd to that Perfection, that had his Colouring & Pencilling been as good as his Draught, which was most exact, he might have easily excell'd all that went before him in that kind of Painting . . . But notwithstanding all Mr. Barlows Excellency in his way, and tho' he had the good Fortune to have a considerable Sum of Money left him by a Friend, he died poor in the year 1702.'[4] Vertue is wrong as to the date, for Barlow died in 1704, and was buried in the churchyard of St. Margaret's, Westminster.[5]

A new name was added to the seventeenth-century water-colour painters in 1934, when Messrs. Bumpus exhibited the original manuscript,[6] with its illustrations in colour, of the Journal of Edward Barlow from 1659 to 1703.[7] Barlow was born at Prestwich on March 6, 1642, and began life as a farmer's boy. He was afterwards apprenticed to a 'Whitester', or bleacher, but one day put on his best clothes and ran away from home. One of the earliest drawings in this journal shows him leaving 'my ffathers house in the Whitfeld', while in the foreground his mother stands 'beckinning her hand' and calling him in vain. In London he worked for his uncle, who kept the 'Dog and Bear' at Snow Hill; but 'still my mind was to see ships and boats upon the River Thames; and sometimes I would stand where I could see the River for half an hour to see the ships and boats sail along, taking great pleasure therein'. So, very soon, this contemporary of Pepys found that chalking up scores was dull, and went to sea as a foremast hand in the *Naseby* in 1659, fought against the Barbary pirates under Lord Sandwich in 1661–1662, voyaged to Brazil in a merchantman, was pressed into the Navy again, was in the Battle of Lowestoft in 1665 (there is a large drawing of this in the journal); took part in the victory of St. James's Day; was

[1] B.M. 1850.2.23. 830.
[2] H. M. Hake, *Some Contemporary Records relating to Francis Place, Engraver and Draughtsman*, Walpole Soc., X, 1921–1922, pp. 39–69.
[3] B.M. 1857. 1.10.27.
[4] *Vertue Note Books*, II, Walpole Soc., XX, 1931–1932, pp. 135–136.
[5] *Apollo*, XIX, 1934, p. 25.
[6] National Maritime Museum.
[7] *Barlow's Journal of his life at sea in kings ships East & West Indiamen & other merchantmen from 1659 to 1703* transcribed by Basil Lubbock, with 16 colour plates and other illustrations, published by Messrs. Hurst and Blackett, 1934.

captured by the Dutch, and, while a prisoner at Batavia in 1672, began to write the story of his life up to that date. He continued as a seaman in merchant vessels, going to China on one of his voyages, and his experiences were subsequently described up to 1703, the year when our coasts were strewn with wrecks and half England was laid in ruins by a great gale. He rose gradually in his profession to quartermaster, gunner, boatswain, and, in November 1678, we find him second mate of an Indiaman at 55s. a month.

Barlow's journal is written on folio sheets in an excellent and clear hand, and considering his early life and the conditions under which he must have worked, one cannot help marvelling at this work, both in text and in drawings, of a plain seaman of the Restoration period. He was uneducated, but as apprentice to a master's mate in the *Naseby*, he did learn to write and was introduced to Waggoner's *Atlas*. In the coloured drawings, which occur all through his journal, he pictures storm-tossed galleons, or ships in harbour with their rigging and pennants drawn out with the utmost precision, or he shows ships entering port at 'Merselas' [Marseilles], 'the Iland of Sint Helena', Port Royal in Jamaica, Bangkok, Sumatra, 'Canton in Chinna', and expresses with a simple convention, rather Chinese in character, the shapes of mountains and rocks, and contours of the landscape, or cities on the banks of navigable rivers. Or he depicts birds, beasts and fishes, including the shark, 'the most Raunous fish that swimes in the sea', whales, flying-fish, a 'shovel-nose sharke-ffish', the 'Olifant' [Elephant] and a 'Risnosarse' [Rhinoceros], which animal was exhibited in London in 1684 and offered for sale for £2300.

His ability as a draughtsman increases with the progress of his journal, which becomes more and more gay and lively with his bright drawings. The subjects are drawn in with a sharp pen and a pale brownish ink. He had a love for the gay colour of flags and shows the *Royal Charles* dressed in all her bravery to receive the restored King. He puts his whole heart into a picture of the *Monk*, of which he wrote: 'A ship which deserves to be set in a ring of gold for the good services she had done . . . and she shall have my good word so long as she is a ship.' His colours were a bright viridian green, a bright lemon yellow, yellow ochre, rose madder, vermilion, brown and blue; and they show that in the seventeenth century a fairly wide range was at the artist's disposal. The colours were those used in the pictorial maps of contemporary cartographers, whose work descends in no small degree from that of the medieval illuminators of manuscripts. Barlow's bird's-eye convention, his decorative treatment of his page, his mapping of harbours and rivers, suggest that, as an apprentice, he often found excuses for looking into the chart-room and poring over maps. Pepys, who was Secretary at the time to the Navy Board, was on board the *Naseby* when she was sent to bring Charles II home.

Barlow was not of the great world like Evelyn and Pepys. His diary offers little of self-revelation or human interest, but, like the diaries of his greater contemporaries, it is a mirror of the age, none the less important because its vision includes little more than the English ships and sailors of the seventeenth century. In his work as a draughtsman he does not show the finish and refinement of Hollar and Place, especially in his studies of towns,

64

9 'Düren: The Weiler Pfort'

B.M. 1850.2.23.194 $5\frac{1}{8} \times 10$: 130 × 254   *Pen and ink and wash*

Wenceslaus HOLLAR (1607–1677)

10 'London: The Tower'

B.M. 1859.8.6.389 $4\frac{1}{2} \times 11\frac{1}{4}$: 114 × 286   *Pen and ink and water-colour*

Wenceslaus HOLLAR (1607–1677)

11 'Rheineck from the N.W.'

B.M. Gg.2–247   4⅛ × 10⅞: 106 × 276   *Pen and ink and wash*

Wenceslaus HOLLAR (1607–1677)

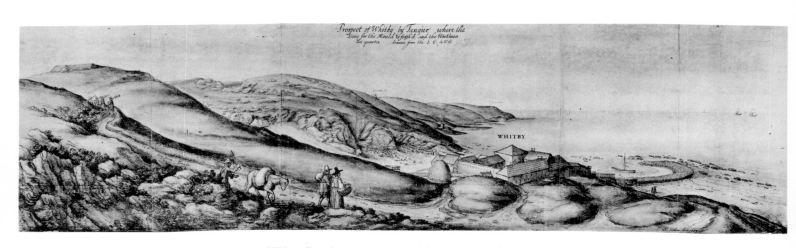

12 'The Settlement at Whitby, W. of Tangier'

B.M. 5214–21   11 × 38½: 280–979   *Pen and ink and water-colour*

Wenceslaus HOLLAR (1607–1677)

13 'Knaresborough Castle'
B.M. 1850.2.23.819   8 × 21⅛: 203 × 537   *Pen and ink and wash*
Francis PLACE (1647–1728)

14 'The Dropping Well, Knaresborough'
B.M. 1850.2.23.822   12⅞ × 16: 327 × 407
Pen and ink and grey wash, signed with initials
Francis PLACE (1647–1728)

15 'Knaresborough Castle: The Keep'
B.M. 1850.2.23.821 $12\frac{5}{8} \times 16\frac{1}{4}$: 320 × 413
Pen and brown ink and wash, signed with initials
Francis PLACE (1647–1728)

16 'Peterborough House, Lambeth'
V.A.M. E.1507, 8–1931 $6\frac{3}{4} \times 18\frac{1}{4}$: 172 × 463   *Pen and ink and wash*
Francis PLACE (1647–1728)

but he has a wide range of interesting themes, and is memorable for the variety and fancy of his art.

Some traveller must have been the author of a mysterious drawing in water-colour acquired by the Victoria and Albert Museum in 1933. It appears to date from about the end of the seventeenth century, and on the mount in an old hand is written *Scetch in Persia*. The subject is a curious, conventionalised landscape in which a blue stream, appearing low down on the right, winds its course in horizontal and zigzag stretches through a flat yellow landscape variegated with mounds like anthills, on which grow plants, shrubs and trees, and enlivened by exotic birds of various colours. Oriental influence is very apparent in this attractive drawing, which has some affinity with the decorative landscape found in Stuart embroideries. Though the whole drawing follows oriental motifs, the trees and bridge at the top seem peculiarly English, and apart from the title confirm that this most unusual drawing is by a British artist.

CHAPTER III

Early eighteenth-century painters

William Hogarth   John Talman   Charles Collins   George Edwards
James Thornhill   Peter Tillemans   William Taverner   J. Hadley
Jonathan Skelton   Francis Cotes   John Donowell

The leading artist in the first half of the eighteenth century, William Hogarth, was essentially a painter in oils, but on one occasion at least, he found use for water-colour. In a volume, *An Account of what seem'd most Remarkable in the Five Days Peregrination of the Five Following Persons vizt. Messieurs Tothall, Scott, Hogarth, Thornhill, & Forrest. Begun on Saturday May the 27th 1732 and Finish'd on the 31st of the same Month. Abi tu et fac similiter—Inscription (sic) on Dulwich College Porch,*[1] Hogarth made seven of the drawings, six of these enlivened by water-colours. The peregrination was an impromptu affair from London to the Isle of Sheppey (they visited Rochester and Queenborough) each of the travellers with a spare shirt, and the cost of the tour for the whole party being £6 6s.

If water-colour painting was still a sporadic growth in this country by the first half of the eighteenth century, discoveries in recent years have sometimes unearthed unknown talent. Attention has been drawn, for instance, to John Talman (1677–1726), the son of William Talman, architect, who flourished from 1670 to 1700. Talman spent a good deal of his life in Italy, making drawings of antiquities. Vertue speaks of him as having been in Italy with William Kent and William Locke in 1710. In Italy also he travelled with Giuseppe Grisoni, and brought Grisoni back with him to England in 1715. He became Director of the Society of Antiquaries at the first election of officers in 1717. The Royal Institute of British Architects owns an album, presented to them in 1835, containing a miscellaneous collection of architectural and topographical drawings, including a number by John Talman and by his father. In his minute work with a finely-pointed pen, and in his general method, even to the inscription of place-names in the open sky, John Talman bears a fair resemblance to Hollar. Some of the drawings from the album were exhibited at the Burlington Fine Arts Club in 1938 (cat. nos. 123–129), among them *Zalt Bommel on the Waal* (the inscriptions on it, 'ye great church', etc. are in English), which has some faint and timid touches of colour.

Francis Place's drawings of birds may be said to anticipate Charles Collins

[1] B.M. 1847. 3.20.1.

(*d.* 1744) of whom little is known except that he made drawings of flowers and birds.[1] Redgrave is most unfair to Collins,[2] partly, no doubt, because of his wish to prove that water-colour rose 'to be a purely national and original school' in Great Britain at the close of the eighteenth century. 'An early attempt', he writes, 'to colour some plates of *British Birds grouped in backgrounds*, drawn and published by Samuel (sic) Collins[3] in 1736, shows to what straits the artist must have been reduced. While the birds are fairly represented and their natural action well expressed, the tints used to colour them are mere weak stains, and the more powerful masses muddy and opaque; both have proved quite unable to resist damp and time.' Now, in speaking of 'plates', Redgrave is clearly referring to the coloured *engravings* of British birds made after Collins by H. Fletcher and J. Mynde, published in a folio volume, London, 1736; a set of twelve plates is in the British Museum Library.[4] Redgrave had probably never seen original water-colour drawings by Collins. Many of them appeared in the collection of Taylor White, F.R.S.,[5] and drawings by Collins of a *Rook*[6] (Pl. 25) and of a *Great Crested Grebe*,[7] are both signed and dated 1740. Far from the colour being muddy, it is singularly clear and strong; and far from the drawings being affected by damp or time, they are perfectly preserved and of a sparkling freshness. An illustration cannot convey the brilliant touches of red and green which fleck the blue sheen on the wings of the rook. White has certainly been mixed with the colour in the masses, but the general colour scheme is rich and luminous. There is no visible sign of pen-work—except possibly on the ground on which the bird stands, and the artist seems to have gained truth and richness by using local colour directly, without passing it over a universal shadow tint—a method which Redgrave claims as the great discovery made towards the end of the century.

A contemporary, whose life was devoted to the study of birds, and who outlived Collins by about thirty years, was George Edwards (1694–1773). He was born at Stratford, Essex, his father being of Welsh descent. Little is known of his early life, but during the years 1716–1731 he visited Holland, Norway, Belgium and France, studying works of art. In 1733, on the recommendation of Sir Hans Sloane, he was appointed librarian to the Royal College of Physicians; was awarded the gold medal of the Royal Society in 1750, later being elected a Fellow; and became a Fellow of the Society of Antiquaries in 1754. He retired in 1764 to Plaistow, where he died, and was buried in West Ham Churchyard. His chief works were *A Natural History of Uncommon Birds and Animals . . . to which is added a general idea of drawing and paintings in water colours*, published in four volumes between 1743 and 1751 (which he dedicated to God), and *Gleanings of Natural History*, published in three

[1] *Vertue Note Books*, III, Walpole Soc., XXII, 1933–1934, p. 122.
[2] Samuel Redgrave, *Catalogue of Water-Colours in the South Kensington Museum*, 1876, p. 15.
[3] Redgrave is possibly confusing Charles Collins with Samuel Collins who published in 1685 a *Systeme of Anatomy treating of the Body of Man, Beasts, Birds, etc.* with seventy-four engravings.
[4] B.M. L. 457.h.19.
[5] Sale Sotheby's June 16, 1926.
[6] V.A.M. P.137–1929.
[7] V.A.M. P.138–1929.

volumes between 1758 and 1764. These books included nearly 600 engravings of subjects never before drawn. The original drawings were purchased by the Marquis of Bute shortly before Edwards' death, and are now in the possession of the British Museum.[1] The drawings are all in gouache, in a manner probably based on French or Swiss work of the period. In their general design, most of them showing a bird completely out of scale perched on a broken tree-trunk, they have a distinct touch of the *chinoiserie* of the period. Four drawings by Edwards, of an exactly similar type, are in the Victoria and Albert Museum.[2] From the similarity of all these drawings and Edwards' handwriting where it occurs upon them, to the style and script of Plate 106 in Edwards and Darly's *New Book of Chinese Designs*, 1754, it may be assumed, with much probability, that the Edwards of 'Edwards and Darly' is George Edwards.

Sir James Thornhill (1675–1734) born of an old Dorsetshire family at Melcombe Regis, painted the interior of the domes of St. Paul's and St. Mary Abchurch, the Great Halls at Blenheim and Greenwich, and numerous walls, staircases and ceilings in country mansions with mythological, allegorical and scriptural scenes. The hundreds of Thornhill's drawings in pen and wash and colour that exist are nearly always designs for the decoration of architecture. For most people it was a surprise when the late A. E. Anderson found two Thornhill drawings of a different type and presented them to the Whitworth Institute, Manchester, in 1935. They are intimate studies of landscape, one inscribed *View from ye Toy leads at Hampton Court, July 1730, J. Th.* (Pl. 29); the other, *Clermont at a distance. A view of H. Court Ferry from my Lodging Apr. 20, 1731, J. Th.* They are thoroughly Dutch in character, the colour being used to reinforce pen work which is bolder and more in the manner of free etching than that of Hollar. They suggest that Thornhill had studied Rembrandt, and these drawings foreshadow the topographical method and spirit of Sandby more nearly than, say, the work of Hollar.

Peter Tillemans (1684–1734), the son of a diamond-cutter, was born at Antwerp. In 1708 he and his brother-in-law, Peter Casteels, were brought over to England by a dealer named Turner and employed in copying oil-paintings by Teniers and other artists. Tillemans was one of the first pupils to attend Kneller's academy when it opened in Great Queen Street in 1711, and was employed with Goupy in 1724 to paint a series of scenes for the Opera House in the Haymarket. Before this his services were retained by John Bridges to make about 500 drawings in Indian ink for his *History of Northamptonshire* (1719), for which Bridges gave him a guinea a day with board and lodging. He made many drawings of Newstead Abbey for William, 4th Lord Byron, who was his pupil. Drawings in colour by both of them are in the Oppé Collection. His *View of a Park, with Huntsmen and Deer*[3] (Pl. 32) in water-colour and gouache, is typically English in subject and sentiment, and the forerunner of many later sporting scenes. Tillemans resided for many years at Richmond,

[1] B.M. Sloane Oo–5264–6.
[2] B.M. P.67–70, 1935.
[3] V.A.M. D.557.

Surrey, in the hope of finding relief from his continual asthma. He died while executing a commission at Norton, near Bury St. Edmunds, Suffolk,[1] where he often stayed with the Chaplain to George II, Dr. Cox Macro, who was a great collector and a frequent patron of contemporary artists.

Rather more is known about William Taverner (1703–1772), who was the grandson of Jeremiah Taverner, described by Vertue as a 'face painter', and son of William Taverner, the dramatist, whom he succeeded as Procurator-General of the Arches Court of Canterbury.[2] Perhaps he should be described as an amateur, but he seems to have devoted all his spare time, and perhaps more, to art. In 1733 Vertue writes that 'the remarkable of this present young gentleman, about Aeta 30 (besides his practice in the Law) [is that he] has a wonderfull genius to drawing of Landskap in an excellent manner, adorned with figures in a stile above the common & paints in oil in a very commendable & masterly manner, a fine geneus blending the arts of his Ancestors in Painting & Poetry and his happy stile of Painting'.[3] Farington reports Sawrey Gilpin as saying that 'Taverner had much quaiking about shewing his pictures, which raised their reputation'.[4] After his death a writer in the *Gentleman's Magazine* called him 'one of the best landscape painters England ever produced', but time has toned down that view, though Taverner's work, as may be seen at the British Museum and the Victoria and Albert Museum, is pleasing and at times wholly admirable. He was prone to follow classical examples too slavishly, and is an imitator of Claude and Poussin in his interlocking forms of trees and foliage, and his breadth and massiveness of light and shadow. Following his models he was too ready to insert in his landscapes rather feebly drawn mythological or pastoral figures, as in *Aglaurus discovering Ericthonius*[5] (Pl. 37). Unfortunately, very little of his work is dated, and as he lived till 1772, it is difficult to place his drawings exactly, except by conjecture from comparison of style and paper. He worked usually with a slight tinting of sepia over pencil or chalk, followed by washes of pale colour. His touches with black ink on foreground foliage or figures were probably an accent added at the last. Of this side of his work—and he may be claimed as our first regular and systematic painter of free landscape in water-colour, *Leg of Mutton Pond at Hampstead Heath*[6] (Pl. 35) is a good example. On the back of this was found the date 1770, and Mr. L. G. Duke's *Hampstead Heath*, also a pleasant drawing in pure transparent water-colour, may be placed in the same year. A sparkling drawing, *Landscape with Ladies Bathing*,[7] in sepia and water-colour touched with gouache, is probably of a much earlier date. (These last three drawings were included in the exhibition of British Art at the Royal Academy, 1934.) In the Whitworth Art Gallery, Manchester, is another

[1] Vertue knew it as Edmundsbury. The known facts about Tillemans are supplied by him. *Vertue Note Books*, III, Walpole Soc., XXII, 1933–1934, pp. 14, 21, 73.
[2] The Court of Arches is now presided over by a Judge, and is the supreme ecclesiastical court of the Church of England.
[3] *Vertue Note Books*, III, Walpole Soc., XXII, 1933–1934, p. 68.
[4] *Diary*, I, 1923, p. 190.
[5] B.M. Gg. 3–367.
[6] V.A.M. P.8–1915.
[7] B.M. 1953. 5.9.4.

pure water-colour, an extensive and beautiful landscape, seen from Richmond Hill. This and the *Sandpits, Woolwich*[1] (Pl. 34) both belonged once to Paul Sandby, and later to Dr. Percy.[2] We shall return later to Taverner as one of the protagonists in the use of body-colour. Here let it be added that Taverner won the warm approval of Smollett. A letter from M. Bramble to Dr. Lewis, dated May 19, in *Humphrey Clinker* (1771) contains the following passage:

> I shall to-morrow set out for London. Although I am no admirer of Bath, I shall leave it with regret; because I must part with some old friends, whom, in all probability, I shall never see again. In the course of coffee-house conversation, I had often heard very extraordinary en-comiums passed on the performances of Mr. Taverner, a gentleman residing in this place, who paints landscapes for his amusement. As I have no great confidence in the taste and judgment of coffee-house connoisseurs, and never received much pleasure from this branch of the art, those general praises made no impression at all on my curiosity; but, at the request of a particu-lar friend, I went yesterday to see the pieces which had been so warmly commended. I must own I am no judge of painting, though very fond of pictures. I don't imagine that my senses would play me so false as to betray me into admiration of anything that was very bad; but true it is I have often overlooked capital beauties, in pieces of extraordinary merit. If I am not totally devoid of taste, however, this young gentleman of Bath[3] is the best landscape-painter now living; I was struck with his performances in such a manner as I had never seen by paint-ing before. His trees not only have a richness of foliage, and warmeth of colouring, which de-lights the view; but also a certain magnificence in the disposition and spirit in the expression, which I cannot describe. His management of the *chiaro oscuro*, or light and shadow, especially gleams of sunshine, is altogether wonderful, both in the contrivance and execution; and he is so happy in his perspective, and marking his distances at sea, by a progressive series of ships, vessels, capes and promontories, that I could not help thinking I had a distant view of thirty leagues upon the back-ground of the picture. If there is any taste for ingenuity left in a de-generate age, fast sinking into barbarism, this artist, I apprehend, will make a capital figure, as soon as his works are known.

With this group may be included J. Hadley, probably born in the seventeenth century. He was unknown till the Victoria and Albert Museum acquired a series of his drawings in 1932[4] (Pl. 42). Probably he was an amateur, and may have been a descendant of the family of Hadley which, up to the middle of the sixteenth century, owned the manorial rights of Withycombe, near Dunster. The drawings cover the dates 1729 to 1758, and were laid down on sheets in an album, presumably by the artist himself, as he has written a descriptive title on one of the underlying sheets. Most of the drawings were made in Hampshire and the Isle of Wight, though Wells and Glastonbury are subjects of the 1729 drawings. In 1730 he was at Watchet; in 1740 at Wilton and Shaftesbury. Among his un-dated drawings are views at Winchester, Bath, Hotwells near Bristol, and Netley Abbey. Hadley, about whom no information can at present be found, may be compared with Place,

---

[1] B.M. 1890. 5.12.140.
[2] Another drawing which seems to justify the celebrity enjoyed by Taverner in his day is the *Landscape with Horsemen* (Huntington Art Gall. California). Agnew's in February, 1948, exhibited *The Ferry*, quite an ambitious panorama of river, houses and trees, over three feet wide, on three pieces of paper joined together.
[3] Smollett, is here recording his experiences at Bath, which he left in 1752, when Taverner was forty-nine.
[4] V.A.M. E.3684–3736–1932.

in subject, manner and the writing of names in the sky. He was not a great draughtsman, but an enthusiastic topographer, and his drawings have considerable charm in their naïve simplicity.

An artist who remained in obscurity till recent years is Jonathan Skelton (*c.*1735–1759). In 1909 a series of drawings by him appeared in a sale at Messrs. Hodgson's, and some of them were acquired by the British Museum. Other drawings by Skelton were sold in 1925, and two fine examples were purchased by the Victoria and Albert Museum.[1] From these two sources alone it became clear that Skelton's work was an important landmark in the earlier stages of English water-colour and that Taverner can no longer be allowed to stand alone. About Skelton's life very little is known. From the dates on his drawings it is clear that he was working at Croydon in 1754 and London and Rochester in 1757. He is known to have been in Canterbury, and also to have worked in Surrey. He went to Italy in 1757, and died in Rome two years later.[2] Skelton's work shows that the 'stained drawing', with local colour applied over a shading of Indian ink, had reached full development before 1758, but it is important also to note that in some of his drawings, as in some by Taverner, there is variety of colour and no monochrome under-painting. His *View on the Medway*[3] (Pl. 39) has a ripeness and luminous beauty very unusual for a drawing made in 1757. His *Castel Gandolfo and the Lake of Albano* (Pl. 41) of 1758, in the Ashmolean, foreshadows J. R. Cozens, just as his view of Rome[4] bears a close resemblance to Sandby; and in 1758 Cozens was only six years old, and Sandby thirty-three. It would be of great interest to discover Skelton's date of birth, and something about his upbringing and earlier work, and thus to know whether he and Sandby ever came into relationship.

By the middle of the eighteenth century we should expect artists to be known and their powers recognised, but Skelton came as a surprise as did Francis Cotes, R.A. (1726–1770) another addition to the list of landscape painters in water-colour. His oil portraits are many and distinguished. At the British Museum are two portrait studies by him in Indian ink, slightly touched with colour, one of them a charming group of Queen Charlotte[5] with her baby sleeping in her lap, and the Duchess of Ancaster, the other of a group of children on a garden terrace.[6] But his position as a water-colour painter rests on a single example of his work, a view *Landscape, with Country Seat*[7] (Pl. 43), signed and dated 1756, which was acquired by the Victoria and Albert Museum. This complete and highly finished drawing does not suggest a sudden adventure and shows too much knowledge to be the work of a man who made one water-colour only. Perhaps other similar water-colours, done as a relaxation, have been swallowed up under the name of Paul Sandby. The subject is, in the main, pure landscape, the trees being drawn with the utmost delicacy. The figures, put in with elegance and refinement, are like those of Dayes and Sandby at their best. It is a 'blue

[1] *View of Rome* (P.11–1925). *Tivoli* (P.12–1925).
[2] S. R. Pierce, *Jonathan Skelton and his water-colours* (a check list): B. Ford, *Letters of Jonathan Skelton from Rome, 1758*, Walpole Soc., XXXVI (1956–1958), 1960.
[3] B.M. 1909. 4.6.12.   [4] V.A.M. P.11–1925.   [5] B.M. 1885. 5.9.1629.
[6] B.M. 1847. 3.6.5.   [7] V.A.M. P.35–1932.

drawing', in the orthodox tinted manner, more blue than the blue drawings of Dayes or of Turner in his earliest period; even the green meadows surrounding the country seat are blue. Anticipating much of Sandby's later work in outlook and design this remains an isolated document of 1756 in the history of British water-colour. Little is known of Cote's personal life and character, and a good deal of his work in pastel and oil is still hidden or partly absorbed under the name of Reynolds, to whom he approximated closely in style. Such facts as remain tell us that he was born three years after Reynolds and a year before Gainsborough; was apprenticed to George Knapton; stood supreme as a painter of pastel portraits; became a formidable rival to Reynolds with his portraits in oil; with Reynolds and Paul Sandby was among the founders of the Royal Academy. It is also clear that he was a friend of Paul Sandby, for he painted portraits both of him and of his wife.[1]

Another surprise is given by a water-colour painted about 1755 by John Donowell (dates unknown). He seems to have had considerable practice as an architect, and built Wycombe House, Bucks, for Lord de Spencer, exhibiting a drawing of the completed building at the Royal Academy in 1786. His architectural drawings and designs for country houses were exhibited in 1761 at the Free Society of Artists, from 1762 to 1770 at the Incorporated Society, and from 1778 to 1786 at the Royal Academy; and he published some of them as engravings. None of the architectural societies were founded much before the end of the eighteenth century, and research has failed to produce any information about his life. Of his water-colour drawings nothing was known till one was acquired by the late Leslie Wright in 1935.[2] This is a *View of Marylebone Gardens as seen from the Head of the Grand Walk with its beautiful Orchestra & a Pavilion, etc.* (Pl. 44). Donowell's original price is given on the back: 'View—£2 2s. od., figures 15s. od., £2 17s. od.' The buildings, trees, and figures are all somewhat in the manner of Sandby. The lively figures in their attractive costume, walking or conversing in natural groups, give animation to the pleasant scene, and were cheap at the price of 15s. Donowell is said to have published an engraving of the Garden Walk, Marylebone Gardens in 1761, and at the British Museum is an engraved *View of the Orchestra with the Band of Music, the Grand Walk, etc. in Marylebone Gardens*, published in 1775 by J. Tinney.

Two other artists whose work belongs to the first half of the eighteenth century are Peter Monamy (*c.*1670–1749), and Samuel Scott (*c.*1702–1772). Both were concerned mainly with seascape and shipping, and on this account a study of their work is deferred to a later chapter (see pp. 229–231).

---

[1] C. Winter, 'Francis Cotes, R.A.', *The Connoisseur*, XXXVIII, 1914, pp. 170–177.
[2] Coll. Mrs. Dorian Williamson.

17 'An Eagle Carrying off a Chicken'

B.M. 1874.8.8.2257   5 × 6⅞: 128 × 175   *Pen and brown ink and grey wash*

Francis Barlow (c. 1626–1704)

18 'Partridge Stalking'

B.M. 1859.7.9.2   7⅞ × 11⅝: 199 × 295   *Brush drawing in grey wash, signed*

Francis Barlow (c. 1626–1704)

19 'A Group of Birds in a Garden'
B.M. 1920.4.20.19 $8\frac{3}{8} \times 12\frac{3}{8}$: 212 × 313   *Pen and brown ink and grey wash*
Francis BARLOW (c. 1626–1704)

20 'A Cat and Kittens'
Witt Collection, Courtauld Institute of Art, London $5 \times 7\frac{1}{4}$: 127 × 183
Pen and bistre, grey wash, on buff paper, signed and dated 1684
Francis BARLOW (c. 1626–1704)

21 'The Queen Katharine'
National Maritime Museum, Greenwich. JOD/4   Ellipse $5\frac{3}{8} \times 5\frac{1}{8}$: 137 × 130
Water-colour and body-colour
Edward BARLOW

22 'The Ducal Crown of Venice'
B.M. 1893.4.11.10 (15)   14 × 11¼: 356 × 285
Water-colour and body-colour
John TALMAN (1677–1726)

23 'Hampton Court: "Trianon" Pavilion'
Royal Institute of British Architects (G.2/13)
13½ × 18¾: 343 × 476   *Pen and water-colour*
John TALMAN (1677–1726)

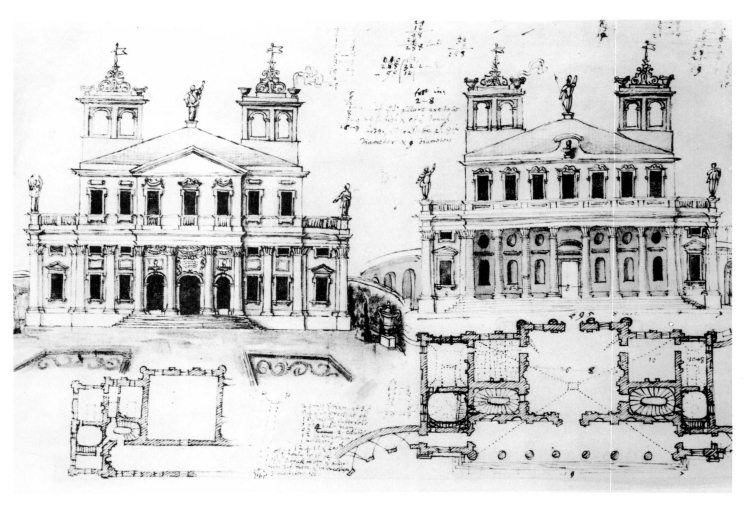

24 'A Bittern'
Coll. Mr D.L.T. and Miss Armide Oppé   21¼ × 15: 540 × 382
Body-colour, signed and dated 1735
Charles COLLINS (d. 1744)

25 'A Rook'
V.A.M. 137–1929   14¾ × 21¼: 375 × 540
Water-colour, signed and dated 1740
Charles COLLINS (d. 1744)

The Cock Sparrow

26 'The Cock Sparrow'
Coll. Mr & Mrs Paul Mellon   11⅛ × 8¾: 283 × 222   *Body-colour*
George EDWARDS (1694–1773)

27 'Bullfinches'

B.M. 1881.11.12.176 $11\frac{5}{8} \times 9\frac{1}{8}$: 295 × 232

Water-colour and body-colour on vellum

George EDWARDS (1694–1773)

28 'Scene at Windsor 1719'
Coll. Mr & Mrs Paul Mellon $4\frac{1}{8} \times 6\frac{3}{8}$: 103 × 162   *Pen and ink and brown wash*
Sir James Thornhill (1675–1734)

29 'River at Hampton Court'
Whitworth Art Gallery, University of Manchester $10\frac{7}{8} \times 18\frac{1}{2}$: 276 × 470
Pen and ink and wash, signed with initials and dated 1730
Sir James Thornhill (1675–1734)

30 'Hanbury Hall, Worcs.'

B.M. 1864.5.14.272 $11\frac{1}{4} \times 17\frac{1}{2}$: 285 × 444   *Pen and brown ink and wash*

Sir James Thornhill (1675–1734)

31 'A Feast of the Gods'

B.M. 201.b.8 fol. 107 *recto* $9\frac{1}{2} \times 8\frac{1}{4}$: 241 × 210   *Pen and ink and body-colour*

Sir James Thornhill (1675–1734)

32 'Park with Huntsmen and Deer'
V.A.M. Dyce-557   7 × 8¾: 178 × 222   *Water-colour*
Peter TILLEMANS (1684–1734)

33 'Landscape with Horsemen'
Coll. Mr & Mrs Paul Mellon   7½ × 10¾: 191 × 273   *Water-colour*
Peter TILLEMANS (1684–1734)

34 'Sandpits, Woolwich'
B.M. 1890.5.12.140 $14\frac{1}{4} \times 27\frac{5}{8}$: 362 × 803   *Body-colour*
William TAVERNER (1703–1772)

35 'Leg of Mutton Pond, Hampstead Heath'
V.A.M. P.8–1915 $12\frac{3}{4} \times 22\frac{1}{4}$: 314 × 565
Water-colour, signed and dated 1770 (at the back)
William TAVERNER (1703–1772)

36 'Classic Landscape'
V.A.M.—443 $12\frac{3}{4} \times 17\frac{7}{8}$: 324 × 454   *Water-colour*
William TAVERNER (1703–1772)

37 'Aglaurus discovering Ericthonius'
B.M. Gg. 3–367 $18\frac{7}{8} \times 14\frac{7}{8}$: 480 × 378   *Water-colour*
William TAVERNER (1703–1772)

38 'Rome: The Castle of S. Angelo and St Peter's'
V.A.M. P.11–1925   14½ × 20⅞: 369 × 530   *Water-colour, signed and dated 1758*
Jonathan SKELTON (c. 1735–1759)

39 'View on the Medway'
B.M. 1909.4.6.12   9 × 22⅝: 228 × 575   *Water-colour*
Jonathan SKELTON (c. 1735–1759)

40 'Tivoli: The Great Cascade'

V.A.M. P.12–1925   20 × 14¼ : 508 × 362   *Water-colour, signed and dated 1758*

Jonathan SKELTON (c. 1735–1759)

41 'Castel Gandolfo'

Ashmolean Museum, Oxford $14\frac{1}{2} \times 20\frac{7}{8} : 369 \times 530$ *Water-colour*

Jonathan SKELTON (c. 1735–1759)

42 'Landscape with Church and Buildings'

V.A.M. E.3716–1932 $8\frac{1}{4} \times 13 : 210 \times 330$ *Pen and ink and water-colour*

J. HADLEY (fl. 1729–1758)

43 'Landscape with a Country Seat'

V.A.M. P.35–1932 $14\frac{1}{2} \times 21\frac{1}{8}$: 368×537 *Water-colour, signed and dated 1756*

Francis COTES, R.A. (1726–1770)

44 'Marylebone Gardens'

Coll. Mrs Dorian Williamson 10×16: 253×407 *Pen and ink and water-colour, signed*

John DONOWELL (fl. 1755–1786)

CHAPTER IV

The eighteenth-century romantics

Richard Wilson   Thomas Gainsborough   William Gilpin   John Hoppner
Alexander Cozens   George Barret I   Richard Cooper II   William Pars
George Robertson   Philip James de Loutherbourg   Johann Conrad Gessner
Edward Edwards   Thomas and Benjamin Barker

Writers about water-colour have been prone to suggest that its rise and development in England should be entirely attributed to the topographers—to use an accepted but somewhat unfair term for Sandby and his followers. Roget's first chapter, for instance, is entitled 'Early Topographic Prints' and deals with eighteenth-century engravings of landscape and architecture. His second chapter, 'Sandby and the rise of Exhibitions', begins: 'Such was the condition of topography in the middle of the last century, when a draughtsman (Sandby) came into the field who had taste and originality enough to bring new influences to bear upon the work, and infuse an element of fine art into this kind of illustration'. Other writers have followed him in the easy course of tracing a continuous tradition of landscape based strictly upon topography, or what may be called the recognisable 'view', from Hollar and Place, through Sandby, Dayes, Rooker, Hearne, to a culminating point with Girtin and Turner at the end of the eighteenth century. To accept that neat and orderly progress is to ignore another tradition, of a romantic or poetic approach to nature, from Van Dyck and Taverner, through Wilson and Gainsborough, and then in varying forms through J. R. Cozens, Turner, Blake, Samuel Palmer and Constable. Because this poetic approach is more subjective and the painters more individual and personal in their outlook, there is less flow of stylistic continuity in this tradition and much greater diversity in subject and method. The topographers, as we shall see later, worked almost entirely in a uniform method, with thin washes of colour over a careful monochrome under-painting. The romantics were experimental, sometimes eccentric, in their technique, ready to seize any means of giving rapid expression to their impulsive thought.

Just as it must be accepted that the art of water-colour was not a British discovery, it must be accepted that from its beginning in this country there are two streams, separate and distinct; the one relying for its main interest on a careful and realistic recording of places and buildings; the other depending not so much on topographical interest as on the sentiments aroused by the painter's personal interpretation of some aspect of Nature seen or imagined. Ruskin made a distinction between 'simple' and 'Turnerian' topography, as being two separate branches of landscape art, the one *historical*, the other *poetical*.[1]

In order to see how these two tempers and systems exist side by side in our early water-colour art, we have but to turn from Hollar and Place to Van Dyck and Taverner, from Skelton and Sandby to Wilson and Gainsborough. Wilson and Gainsborough cannot figure largely in any history of water-colour, except for their general influence upon the trend of British art. Both of them were essentially painters in oil, but they made many studies and sketches in pencil and chalk, and both added colour to their monochrome. In spite of isolated examples of their work in colour, they were not systematic painters in water-colour, like Taverner or Sandby. But they did leave several examples of their colour work, and Finberg, when emphasising Wilson's powerful formative influence over Turner and Girtin, is wrong in saying that Wilson 'does not seem to have worked in water-colour himself'.

Richard Wilson (1714–1782) was in Italy from 1749 to 1755, and it may be supposed that a body-colour drawing, *Moonrise on a River*,[2] which came to the British Museum in the William Sandby Bequest belongs to a later period than this. It is inscribed 'Sandby from Wilson' and was catalogued originally as being after Wilson by Sandby, but Binyon rightly decided later that the inscription implied that it was Wilson's work and a gift from him to Sandby. The subject is a moonlight scene, very attractive with its tones of grey-blue and cream. The crisp touch in the drawing of the castle jutting out into the lake, is Wilson's, and the figures are less defined, less individually attractive, than Sandby would have made them. It is obviously the work of an oil-painter, the colour being applied thinly with a hog's hair brush.[3] With this drawing must be considered Wilson's *Landscape*[4] (Pl. 45) probably a study for *The Destruction of Niobe's Children* at the National Gallery. No fewer than seventy sketches and studies by Wilson were included in the sale of Sandby's collections after his death, and possibly this was No. 80, described in the catalogue: 'A drawing: the effect of a storm'. It was from this sketch that Wilson took the idea of painting his celebrated picture, the *Niobe*. It was thought once that this landscape might be described as a work in thin oil on paper, but it seems that it is probably body-colour, in Sandby's method of dry colour with size as a medium. At the Ashmolean is a large *Landscape with Pastoral Figures* in sanguine, with touches here and there of blue, yellow and green, the indicative, suggestive notes of pure colour being applied separately. In the same museum is another drawing by Wilson, a lovely sketch *View of Capo Coroglio and the Bagni di Virgilio*, almost entirely in an outline of brown ink, with slight touches of grey shadow and just a dash of vivid green at the top of the cliff and in the foreground. Mrs. Richard Ford, owner of many works by

[1] *Modern Painters*, IV, 16 (part v, Ch. II).
[2] B.M. 1904. 8.19.12.
[3] This drawing has since been re-attributed by the B.M. authorities to Paul Sandby, which is also the opinion of Mr. Brinsley Ford. The ambiguous inscription was on an old mount which no longer exists.
[4] V.A.M. P.15–1915.

Wilson, has two landscapes by him in black chalk, worked over with very dry colour, giving a pastel appearance. They have all the freedom and charm, the light touch and the poetry, which belong to Wilson's art. Of an earlier period and of a more classical type in subject, but with a breezy freshness in the treatment of the trees, is an *Italian Landscape* in the Whitworth Art Gallery, Manchester.

Thomas Gainsborough (1727–1788) is not occupied, like Wilson and the topographers, with an intellectual searching out of form or with any arbitrary simplification. He improvises as much as he studies; he imagines rather than calculates. He is not too much concerned with what the end of his brush or chalk is doing; it is almost as if he were drawing with his eye on nature more than on his paper, or as if he were working with eyes shut and painting his vision or his dream. Out of his profound sensibility springs a natural music of colour and design. He is far nearer to eighteenth-century France, to Watteau and Fragonard, than to his contemporaries in England. Something graceful, rapturous, elegant in his work is French in spirit and character. This was, we may be sure, a natural instinct, unaffected by the fact that his first master in London was Hubert Gravelot, for the connection between them did not last long and was never intimate. Perhaps he learned something from J. B. Chatelain (1710–1771), a drawing master in London, who, though not of high importance, gained considerable popularity with his spacious views of rural scenery. Occasionally Chatelain worked upon coloured paper of a greyish brown or blue-grey tint, using black chalk, and adding washes of black, warmed towards the foreground with tints of brown, and heightening the lights with white. It is also said that he piled lumps of coal on a table when drawing a rocky landscape. In the same way, Gainsborough worked on a blue or grey paper, and constantly arranged on his table stones, twigs, and pieces of moss, from which he sought ideas of form and composition. His drawings are full of memories of cottages with sparse thatch, a pathway across a field, a board-bridge with single rail across some running brook, a stump of a tree, a tangle of weeds and flowers. In his evenings at Bath he used to entertain his guests by experimenting with subjects such as these, letting his romantic imagination have full play in compositions glowing with light and air and radiant freshness. They afterwards declared that 'some of the moppings and grubbings are such emanations of genius and picturesque feeling as no other artist has conceived, and certainly such as no other has compassed'. What they called his 'magic dash' created a furore among the dilettanti. Many years afterwards W. H. Pyne[1] wrote that: 'The Gainsborough mania was long the rage, and there are some yet antique beaux and belles of haut ton who recollect their many friends who, with themselves, were stricken with the sketching frenzy, and smile at Bath and its vanities, as they talk of the days that are gone'.

Of Gainsborough's work in pure water-colour washed over a drawing in charcoal and Indian ink there could be no better example than the *A Country Lane*[2] (Pl. 47). *A Woodland Road*, lent to the Royal Academy exhibition of British Art in 1934,[3] is a typical

---

[1] *Somerset House Gazette*, 1823.   [2] B.M. 1899. 5.16.10.   [3] Plate CXLVIII in the catalogue.

drawing in chalk worked over with water-colour and pastel. The Victoria and Albert Museum has a *Landscape: Storm Effect*,[1] in chalk and water-colour, varnished, and a *Landscape, with Archway of Rock*,[2] with sparing touches of body-colour over the under-painting. A *Landscape with Pool*[3] is worked in pure water-colour, pale greys and yellows—a lovely drawing in its tender grace. One of the most enthralling Gainsborough drawings is the *Landscape with Boat* which belonged to Laurence Binyon. It is in Indian ink and sepia wash, with no colour in it, and yet full of colour. Finally, it may be said that Gainsborough was one of those painters who gave thought to his paper. He found that Anstey's well-known *New Bath Guide* was printed on a paper which he had long been in search of for making washed drawings, and he wrote to Dodsley, the publisher, who tried to procure some for him: 'I wish, Sir, that one of my landskips, such as I could make you upon that paper, would prove sufficient inducement for you to make still further enquiry'. In another letter he says: 'Upon my honour, I would give a guinea a quire for a dozen quires of it.'

After Gainsborough's death his widow and his nephew, Gainsborough Dupont, held an exhibition at Schomberg House in the spring of 1789, consisting of Gainsborough's collection of works by Old Masters, together with pictures and drawings by his own hand.[4] It is interesting that 153 drawings by Gainsborough formed the second part of the catalogue, and that twenty-six, all entered singly, were in 'Water-Colours', of which no fewer than twenty-three were varnished. Seven more were described as in 'chalk and water-colours'; three as in 'water-colours and chalk'. A separate group of six had the heading, 'Crayons and water-colours varnished', and was bought by Queen Charlotte.

Gainsborough's potent influence is seen in some of Sandby's work and in one aspect of Girtin's art. His closest follower was Dr. Monro, to whom reference is made in a later chapter. Another artist associated with Gainsborough and his period is the Rev. William Gilpin (1724–1804), who was the brother of Sawrey Gilpin and published five treatises on the picturesque, illustrated by aquatints from drawings made during his summer tours in the Highlands, North Wales and the Lakes. Many of these drawings exist and are made on paper warmly tinted with reddish yellow, but all are in monochrome. He was an advanced educationalist and head-master for many years of a school at Cheam. By the proceeds of his books and by the sale of his drawings at Christie's in 1802 for £1,560, and again in 1804,[5] he made sufficient money to build a poor-house and to erect and endow a school (which still exists) for the education of the children of gipsies and day labourers at Boldre in the New Forest, during the period when he was vicar. Gilpin exercised considerable influence upon the taste of his day by providing elegant rules for the amateur with a

[1] V.A.M. D.678.
[2] V.A.M. D.695.
[3] Coll. Mrs. Dorian Williamson.
[4] 'Gainsborough's collection of pictures', *Burlington Magazine*, LXXXIV [Editorial], 1944, p. 107.
[5] The drawings included in these sales bear a circular embossed stamp W.G. Two from the 1802 sale in my own possession (now in the collection of Mr. and Mrs. Paul Mellon) and others in the Dyce Collection, Victoria and Albert Museum, have Gilpin's autograph descriptive notes on sheets attached to the back of the drawing.

water-colour box, and a system for the aesthetic observer. But besides being romantic and visionary, and unduly verbose, he inculcated some sound sense into his readers. Even as late as 1830 David Cox quotes him when giving instructions to a pupil, who was proceeding on a sketching tour up the Rhine. He copies for her a passage from Gilpin's *Landscape Scenery*:—'In passing through a country you may not have opportunities of giving the exact portrait of any one particular scene, but this is not necessary; perhaps the most useful illustrations of local scenery are those which give the *character* of the views by a pleasing arrangement of ideas taken from the general face of the country.   A portrait characterises only a single spot, and the recollection of it becomes indistinct and confused as soon as the place is passed'. That passage surely describes the concepts of Wilson, Gainsborough and Alexander Cozens. Edmund Burke's essay on *The Sublime and Beautiful* (1756) and Sir Uvedale Price's *Essay on the Picturesque* (1796) are only two of a number of works on artistic theory including those of Gilpin which aroused a dilettante interest in scenery and landscape painting. But those who looked upon mountain scenery saw it through the eyes of Claude, Poussin and Salvator Rosa, not as a personal experience. For them the mountains were tremendous, sublime, horrific, a purely pictorial background for classical figures and classical architecture. The Lake poets (Wordsworth settled at Grasmere in 1799) were responsible for a new kind of sympathy with natural scenery. By his publications their contemporary, William Gilpin, stirred in many an increased awareness of beauties to be found among the mountains and the lakes. He supplied his readers with definite standards and with aesthetic terms for the expression of their sentiments in a sentimental age. Fanny Burney, one of Gilpin's enthusiastic admirers, found the *Observations on the Lakes of Cumberland and Westmorland* (1786) the most picturesque reading she ever met with. She forgot she was just reading and fancied that she saw Gilpin's landscapes before her coloured by the hand of nature. The seriousness with which this deliberate cult of the picturesque was pursued, and its effects upon our water-colour school are well indicated by the following quotation[1]:

> Within the last thirty years a taste for the picturesque has sprung up;—and a course of summer travelling is now looked upon to be as essential as ever a course of spring physic was in old times. While one of the flocks of fashion migrates to the sea-coast, another flies off to the mountains of Wales, to the lakes in the northern provinces, or to Scotland; some to mineralogize, some to botanize, some to take views of the country,—all to study the picturesque, a new science for which a new language has been formed, and for which the English have discovered a new sense in themselves, which assuredly was not possessed by their fathers. This is one of the customs to which it suits a stranger to conform. My business is to see the country,—and, to confess the truth, I have myself caught something of this passion for the picturesque, from conversation, from books, and still more from the beautiful landscapes in water-colours, in which English excel all other nations.

Although John Hoppner, R.A. (1758–1810) has small claim to inclusion among water-colour painters he made a large number of landscape drawings with black and white

---

[1] Robert Southey, *Letters from England*, II, letter XXX, 1807, pp. 12–13.

chalk and stump on bluish paper, thus finding relaxation like Gainsborough from his in-cessant portrait work. One of these, a *Mountainous Landscape*[1] (Pl. 57), is washed broadly with tints of a reddish brown, green and blue; and in the Victoria and Albert Museum are examples of his work where slight colour has been added. There is a similar surprise and rarity about a little seapiece in the Tate Gallery by Nathaniel Hone, the portrait-painter (1718–1784). In the subtlety of its fluent and light washes and its free notes of darker accent it anticipates Wilson Steer.

Another artist with a profoundly romantic outlook was Alexander Cozens (*c.*1717–1786). His own work in colour was slight, but his methods of monochrome were new and exciting. His 'blot' drawings and the principles which they illustrated exercised such potent in-fluence and stirred such unfair comment in his time that, even in a book dealing with water-colour, I have not hesitated to describe them fully. Above all he deserves an important place in any history of British art because of his formative influence upon many artists in the eighteenth century and particularly upon his son and pupil, John Robert Cozens, the subject of chapter VII. Popular legend for long held that Alexander Cozens was the natural son of Peter the Great by a Deptford woman, daughter of a publisher called Cozens; that he was born in Russia, and sent by the Tsar to Italy for the study of painting; and that the Tsar had, by the same mother, another son who became a general in the Russian service.[2] It was conjectured that, as Peter was working in the dockyard at Deptford in 1697, Alexander Cozens was born about 1698. The story cannot possibly stand in view of A. P. Oppé's exposition of its fallacy.[3] That Cozens was born in Russia is certainly true, and probably true that he studied in Italy. It may even have been the Tsar who paid for his education, but his own British contemporaries, to whom the Imperial patronage would have been a most attractive piece of scandal, never refer to it in any way, although they knew of his Russian birth. The facts given by Oppé were amplified in a letter written to *The Times* (March 25, 1931) by Mr. V. Poliakoff:

The father of Alexander Cozens, the Blotmaster, who is mentioned in *The Times* to-day, was Richard Cozens from Deptford. He went out to Russia in 1705 to take charge of a shipyard on the river at Voronesch, where the Tsar, Peter the Great, was building a fleet against the Turks. Richard Cozens's first ship was a frigate named the Lion, the launching of which was made the pretext for a great feast. From 1710 to 1733 Richard Cozens, whom the Tsar treated with favour, was in charge of shipbuilding at Cazan on the Volga, and superintended the dis-patch of masts and other materials for the Emperor's shipyards to the new capital, St. Peters-burg. After that he was sent to Archangel on the White Sea, to carry out a large building pro-gramme for the Russian fleet. Lord Whitworth, the famous Ambassador, in his *Account of Russia*, had much to say about Richard Cozens, and Perry, in his *Present state of Russia*, also mentions him. Russian State documents of the period speak about him very frequently as a man of conse-quence. A second son became a general in the Russian Army.

[1] B.M. 1847. 6.9.21.
[2] C. R. Leslie, *Handbook for young Painters*; 1st edn. 1855; 2nd edn. 1870; J. L. Roget, *History of the 'Old' Water-Colour Society*, I, 1891, p. 52; Burlington Fine Arts Club Exhibition, 1871, *Catalogue of Water-Colour Drawings*.
[3] A. P. Oppé, 'The parentage of Alexander Cozens', *Burlington Magazine*, XXXV, 1919, p. 40.

Nevertheless Alexander seems, as a boy, to have been closely attached to the Russian Court. C. F. Bell drew Laurence Binyon's attention to a letter written by Beckford, in the Morrison Collection[1] in which Beckford writes to Cozens recalling 'your early years, when every month was marked by some great spectacle or splendid feast, when you still retain a faint idea of the gilded halls, bright lights, and a long train of nobles led by the Empress. . . . Is the mournful sight of Peter the Great's funeral forgotten, when you kissed his pale hand?' As Peter died in 1725, and the letter points to Alexander then being a young boy, Binyon deduces that he may have been born somewhere about 1715.[2] This is a much more probable date than the surmised 1698 or 1700, for he died in 1786, and it is difficult to believe that, in those days, a man of eighty-five or thereabout could have been so active in literary and artistic pursuits as Cozens was in the last three years of his life. The earliest known date in connection with him, but giving no clue to the date of his birth, is contained in a few words written by himself on a little sketch found among the papers of William Beckford. The paper has on one side a drawing of dancers and musicians, and on the other three ibexes and a leopard, and the inscription: *Given A. Cozens by Agamine the Persian at Petersburg 1730*.[3]

The year 1746 has always been given as the date of Alexander Cozens' arrival in England after a period of study in Italy. Finberg,[4] however, discovered in the British Museum an engraving by John Pine from a drawing by Cozens of *The Royal College at Eton*, dated 1742, so that he was already in England by that date. Some time before 1746 he must have gone back to Italy, since his arrival in England from Rome in that year is definitely known. He married a daughter of John Pine, and his son, John Robert, whom Constable claimed to have been 'the greatest genius that ever touched landscape', was born in 1752. In 1751, perhaps through Pine, who was a Herald as well as an engraver, he was nominated *Rouge Croix*, but seems never to have undertaken the duties attached to the office.[5] No more is known of his early life, save for the combined discovery of W. T. Whitley and C. F. Bell that from 1749 to 1754 he held an appointment as drawing master at Christ's Hospital.[6] He was soon to be regarded as a man of considerable importance in the social world. The patronage which William Beckford of Fonthill showered upon so many artists developed in the case of Alexander Cozens into a close intimacy lasting for many years. There can be little doubt that Beckford's early instructor in drawing, whom his biographer Cyrus Redding describes as 'one of the first artists of the day', was Alexander Cozens. Beckford, at the age of nineteen, knew him well enough to make him the recipient of his most intimate and extravagant imaginings. In his letters to Cozens he pours out all his dejection

[1] Laurence Binyon, *English Water-Colours*, 1933, p. 39.
[2] Oppé refers to an addition of a date, 1717, in a family genealogical tree, as being inferential rather than established fact.
[3] Burlington Fine Arts Club Exhibition, 1922–1923, *Drawings by J. R. Cozens*, Introduction by C. F. Bell, p. 9.
[4] A. J. Finberg, *The Development of British Landscape Painting in Water-Colours, Studio* (special number), 1917–1918, p. 10.
[5] Archibald Russell, 'Alexander Cozens at the Burlington Fine Arts Club', *Burlington Magazine*, XXX, 1917, p. 66.
[6] Whitley, 1700–1799, II, p. 316; C. F. Bell and T. Girtin, *J. R. Cozens*, Walpole Soc., XXIII, 1934–1935, p. 3.

and morbid longings. Writing from Italy (January 4, 1783) he recalls with regret 'the lovely green country of England', and pictures how at Fonthill 'Cozens creeps about like a domestic Animal—'twould be no bad scheme to cut a little Cat's door for him in the great Portals of the Saloon'. Beckford and Cozens, indeed, were on such friendly terms that Cozens was included as confidant in the dangerous and romantic friendship between Beckford and the Hon. William Courtenay, later third Viscount and Earl of Devon. To Lady Hamilton, Sir William Hamilton's first wife, Beckford wrote: 'I have no friend like you to sustain my spirits and receive my ideas except Mr. Cozens. . . . Not an animal comprehends me'.[1]

From 1764 until his death Cozens lived in London, and from 1763 to 1768 was drawing-master at Eton, where among his pupils he had Sir George Beaumont and Henry Angelo. He worked also at Bath, but the tradition that he went there only after Gainsborough's departure in 1774 seems to be no more worthy of belief than the other traditions attached to Cozens. Probably he paid short visits to Bath during the season, and never remained there any length of time. In London he exhibited fairly regularly until 1781 at the Incorporated Society of Artists, of which he was a member, the Free Society of Artists, and the Royal Academy. At the Society of Artists in 1769 he exhibited two drawings of landscapes, which Walpole noted as being 'bold & very good', and in 1770 another landscape, noted as 'bold & masterly'. At the Royal Academy he exhibited eight subjects between 1772 and 1781, giving his address as Leicester Street, Leicester Fields. His subjects of 1772, 1773 and 1779 were described as 'Landscapes in Chiaro-obscuro', and it is possible, therefore, that much of his exhibited work was in monochrome. He was twice a candidate for Associateship of the Royal Academy, obtaining two votes in 1778, and three in 1779.[2] From 1781 till his death he is officially noted in royal records as Instructor in Drawing to the Young Princes. His drawings were held in esteem but his oil paintings, of which only the four small landscapes on paper in the Oppé Collection are known to exist, were not rated highly. *An Essay on Landscape Painting*, published anonymously in 1782, says of him: 'As a painter we only lament that he so seldom employs his brush upon canvas. The drawings of this artist are, for composition, keeping (i.e. tonality) and effect, superior to anything of the kind. They have a peculiar excellence in which they resemble painting, for the effect is not, as is usually the case, produced from outline filled up; but is worked into light, shade and keeping by a more artful process, the masses being determined in the first making out or designation of the parts, and afford an harmonious effect unlike the ordinary compositions of scratches and lines just connected by a flimsy washing'.

Although John Robert Cozens has always been well known and highly appreciated, Alexander was little more than a name and a legend until half a century ago. Even in 1891 Roget regarded him as the 'father of the school-masters' rather than the 'father of our water-colour school', and as 'employing his talent in fostering a kind of practical dilet-

[1] J. W. Oliver, *Life of William Beckford*, 1932, p. 59.
[2] Whitley, 1700–1799, I, p. 317.

tantism'. Public attention was really drawn for the first time to the importance of Cozens' work by the *Historical Collection of British Water-colours*, an exhibition organised by the Walpole Society at the Grafton Galleries at the end of 1911. This was followed, in 1916, by an exhibition of Herbert Horne's Collection, which included twenty-nine drawings by Cozens, at the Burlington Fine Arts Club, probably their first introduction to many people. The first really comprehensive exhibition of his art occurred at the Graves Art Gallery, Sheffield, in the autumn of 1946, showing over one hundred paintings and drawings gathered from private collections. The exhibition was brought from Sheffield to the Tate Gallery in January 1947. The British Museum contains a large number of Cozens' early drawings, apparently done between 1743 and 1746, and a note in his own handwriting says: 'Alexander Cozens, in London, author of these Drawings, lost them and many more in Germany by their dropping from his saddle when he was riding on his way from Rome to England in the year 1746. John Cozens his son being at Florence in the year 1776 purchased them. When he returned to London in the year 1779 he delivered the drawings to his father'. Another Roman sketch-book of 1746, belonging to Mr. Norwood Young, a direct descendant of the artist, has been fully described by A. P. Oppé,[1] and adds the new information that Cozens worked in Vernet's studio while in Rome. In the 1746 sketch-book, to quote Oppé, 'the written notes are all schemes or analyses of the various possible ways of sketching from nature and completing pictures from the sketches. It is to be noted that Cozens is not here concerned, as later, with the construction of ideal compositions, but is setting down the actual stages at which pencil, pen, monochrome, and colour can be used in the open, or in the studio in the production of what he would call landscape views. Where another man might have set down the stages as alternatives in their various contexts, he sets forth each process in a systematic scheme, carefully numbering each step. The result is a kaleidoscopic series of variations on the theme of outline, mass, tone and colour, difficult enough to follow but immensely interesting as showing the variety of method open to the landscape painter at this date'. Here is a typical entry, from page 6:

1. Yᵉ whole on stained paper.
2. with brush with one tint those objects next yᵉ skye.
3. at home or if convenient abroad with brush do all yᵉ rest of yᵉ whole with same tint of yᵉ outside objects.
4. Coppy yᵉ parts in large from yᵉ whole sketch on white paper.
5. yᵉ parts from life in large.
6. Correct yᵉ whole from yᵉ parts in large.
7. from life shade yᵉ whole in common and naturall circumstance.

The early drawings in the British Museum are very uneven in merit. Many are done in Indian ink, many are pen-and-ink sketches, occasionally very tight in handling, while a few are in quite bright colours with a delicate pen outline. The outline is sometimes absent in the monochrome drawings, but nearly always appears when colour is used. The most

[1] A. P. Oppé, *A Roman sketch-book of Alexander Cozens*, Walpole Soc., XVI, 1927–1928, p. 81.

highly finished of the drawings in colour are *On a Country Road*[1] and *Italian Hamlet*[2] (Pl. 52). The former is entirely in transparent colour over a faint pencil outline; the latter has a pen outline as well as colour. Cozens is not concerned, as later, with the construction of ideal compositions, but is eager to secure accuracy in representation of detail, and repro- duction, on the spot, of accidents of tone and colour. The subjects are topographical, mainly of rivers, corners of streets, buildings, and ancient tombs; and though the location is not always very apparent, the majority of them were done in Italy. Several are signed and dated 1746. One, a very formal little landscape, is dated 1743, and though there is no clue as to the place depicted, the steep mountains and high-pitched roofs of the cottages have a distinctly foreign flavour. If this sketch was done abroad, then Cozens must have left England soon after executing the drawing of Eton in 1742, of which mention has been made above. Some of the pen-and-ink sketches are very free and loose in manner, and Oppé has pointed out[3] that several are deliberately executed in the style of Italian land- scape etching, with typical thickening and thinning of line, and may have been intended for transfer to the copper plate. The most remarkable feature about this early work, in view of Cozens' later performance, is its deliberate prettiness, especially in the coloured sketches. In later years he used colour sparingly and seldom. There is one example of a *Mountainous Landscape*,[4] where the crude colours of purple and pallid green have to be for- given for the sake of the underlying drawing.

His later drawings are few in number and difficult of access. The Victoria and Albert Museum has six, one a fine drawing probably of the Tyrol about 1764. Some of these drawings (Binyon has pointed out their curious affinity to certain schools of Chinese land- scape) are of comparatively large size, and are done in bistre or Indian ink on a paper stained to a yellowish tint, with ochre, sienna, tobacco or porter[5] or perhaps oiled (as was the practice then) for tracing. Such paper has doubtless acquired a darker tone, which has given a sombre mellowness to Cozens' work. The dull golden effect is so much that of a brownish ink spread over a polished copper plate by the etcher when printing, that one is momentarily tempted to the possibly fanciful suggestion that Cozens, being himself an etcher, had this in mind. In drawings of this nature, Cozens reveals himself as a follower of Claude in the romantic-classical tradition, and his large compositions are epitomised in the words of a contemporary, writing of classical, or historical, landscapes: 'Its qualities are sought in commanding situations, and bold projections; in masses of rocks and moun- tains; or whatever nature presents as solemn and stupendous; in noble fabrics, temples, palaces; in ruins of capital buildings; and the most magnificent executions of art, the lofty turret, the ivy-mantled tower, the consecrated aisle, the melancholy tomb'.[6] And, further

[1] B.M. 1867. 10.12.34.
[2] B.M. 1867. 10.12.52.
[3] A. P. Oppé, 'Fresh light on Alexander Cozens', *Print Collector's Quarterly*, VIII, 1921, p. 86.
[4] V.A.M. P.100–1920.
[5] For methods of staining tinted drawings, see W. Roberts, *Painting in Water-Colours*, 1800.
[6] F. Fitzgerald, *The Artists' Repository*, II, 1787–1790, p. 199.

to show the trend of Cozens' own mind, it is worthy of note that he copied out[1] from *Cook's Voyages*, II, a passage where Cook is speaking of the Bay of St. Barbara or Cape Desolation:

> I have before observed that it is the most desolate coast that I ever saw. It seems composed of rocky mountains without the least appearance of vegetation. These mountains terminate in horrible precipices whose craggy summits spire up to a vast hight so that hardly anything in Nature can appear with a more barren & savage aspect than the whole of this country.

In Cozens' drawings the romantic in literature and art are linked, but a fine sense of design and a genuine feeling for the sublimity and grandeur of mountain scenery, which was poeticised and refined by his son John Robert, raises his work above the lifeless merit of the average classical composition.

Cozens devoted a good deal of his time to writing on artistic subjects, and characteristic of his mentality must be the scheme put forward in 1772, of which the prospectus ran:

A Sketch of a Great Work by Alexander Cozens.
Morality,
Illustrated by representations of Human Nature in Poetry & Painting.
In Two Parts.
Part I.

> This part may be carried out by forming or writing a poem, upon each of the human Virtues and Vices that may be thought important enough for the purpose. Each poem to be similar to the Iliad of Homer in comprehensiveness.
>
> Thus a system of Epic Poems would be produced. This part may be proper to be undertaken by a University. This part may be carried on by painting a picture of each of the Human Virtues or Vices that may be thought important enough for the purpose. Each picture to consist of the most extensive subject that can be procured. Thus a system of the first class of painting will be produced.
>
> This part would be proper to be undertaken by an Academy.

Unfortunately, or fortunately, the scheme never got any further, but it proves the truth of a draft letter written by Beckford at Fonthill (August 17, 1781) in which he says: 'Cozens is here, very happy, very solitary and almost as full of systems as the Universe'. In 1778 was published *Principles of Beauty relative to the Human Head*, with engravings by Bartolozzi. His most interesting book, however, of which the only complete copy is in the British Museum, is *A New Method of Assisting the Invention in Drawing Original Compositions of Landscape*[2] published about 1786 to expound his theory of 'blotting', on which till our own time his chief claim to fame was founded. The book consists of thirty-three pages with index and forty-three prints, some dated 1784 or 1785; a prospectus asking for subscriptions was issued in 1784. The first sixteen plates reproduce the Blot in aquatint. Then come five sheets of skies, each with four plates in mixed etching and engraving. The last seven plates are two more blots and five mezzotints by Pether, illustrating the finished drawings constructed from the preceding blots. Edwards described the method briefly:

[1] Inserted at the end of the *Roman Sketch-Book* of 1746 *op. cit.*
[2] Reprinted A. P. Oppé, *Alexander and John Robert Cozens*, 1952.

This process was, to dash out, upon several pieces of paper, a number of accidentally large blots and loose flourishes, from which he selected forms, and sometimes produced very grand ideas, but they were in general too indefinite in their execution, and unpleasing in their colour; for being wrought in dark brown or bister, they appeared sombre and heavy in the extreme, similar in their effect to the appearance of nature, when viewed through a dark-coloured lens. He published a small tract upon this method of composing landscapes, in which he has demonstrated his process.[1]

Cozens' aims and methods were distorted by the jealousy and ineptitude of unsuccessful and malicious artists, and Dayes' contemptuous description of Cozens as 'Blotmaster to the town' was widely circulated. It goes without saying that the method was hopelessly misunderstood, and Pyne even writes: 'Will it be believed hereafter that a professor of painting should undertake to splash the surface of a china plate with yellow, red, blue and black, and, taking impressions from the promiscuous mess, on prepared paper, effect to teach his disciples, and those persons of education and elegant minds, to work them into landscape compositions? This, however, he attempted, and the charlatanry succeeded, for he had a host of scholars for several seasons who rewarded him magnificently for his wonderful discovery!'[2] A more credible account is given by his pupil Angelo. 'Cozens dashed out upon several pieces of paper a series of accidental smudges and blots in black, brown and grey, which being floated on, he impressed again upon other paper, and by the exercise of his fertile imagination, and a certain degree of ingenious coaxing, converted into romantic rocks, woods, towers, steeples, cottages, rivers, fields and waterfalls. Blue and grey blots formed the mountains, clouds and skies.'[3] This is what the practice of blotting really amounted to: its theory is set forth in Cozens' book.

He begins with general remarks upon landscape painting, among which occurs what might well be taken as the standard defence of 'classical composition': 'Composing landscapes by invention is not the art of imitating individual nature; it is more, it is forming artificial representations of landscapes on the general principles of nature . . . concentrating in each individual composition the beauties, which judicious imitation would select from those which are dispersed in nature.' The weakness of many drawings may, he says, be attributed to deficiency of ideas, incapacity to distinguish and select ideas; and to want of quickness in execution, so that the idea has faded before it has been fixed on the paper. He hit on the blot method quite accidentally when, sketching on a stained piece of paper, he found himself working the form of the stain into his composition. He then tried deliberately making the stains, and then took to using a very dark ink on the blot, and tracing from it on varnished paper for the finished drawing. It is well known, of course, that Leonardo had advocated the method of stimulating imagination by observing the fantastic and suggestive shapes of stains and marks on walls, suggesting landscapes, battles, rocks, clouds, woods, humorous faces, draperies and so on. But Cozens points out that it was not

[1] E. Edwards, *Anecdotes of Painters*, 1808, pp. 119, 120.
[2] *Somerset House Gazette*, I, 1824/1825, p. 162.
[3] H. Angelo, *Reminiscences*, I, 1904, pp. 212–216.

until *after* the discovery of his method that his attention was drawn to Leonardo's state-ment. In any case, his own method, he thinks, is much superior, because it does not rely entirely on the chance discovery of a suitable stain on the wall. 'A blot is a production of chance, with a small degree of design; for in making it, the attention of the performer must be employed on the whole, or general form of the composition, and upon this only.' He insists on the fact that there must be at the outset a definite idea in the mind, and that this must be kept steadily in view. 'A blot in an assemblage of dark shapes or masses made with ink upon a piece of paper, and likewise of light ones produced by the paper being left blank. All the shapes are rude and unmeaning, as they are formed with the swiftest hand. But at the same time there appears a general disposition of these masses, producing one compre-hensive form, which may be conceived and purposely intended before the blot is begun. This general form will exhibit some kind of subject; and this is all that should be done designedly.' And again: 'It is a hint, or crude resemblance of the whole effect of a picture, except the keeping, (i.e.tonality) and colouring; that is to say, it gives an idea of the masses of light and shade, as well as of the forms, contained in a finished composition'. Finally: 'To blot, is to make varied spots or shapes with ink on paper, producing accidental forms without lines, from which ideas are presented to the mind. This is conformable to nature; for in nature forms are not distinguished by lines, but by shade and colour. To sketch is to delineate ideas; blotting suggests them'.

His actual rules for blotting, which are expounded in the middle of the treatise, are elaborated in five heads at the end. He made his ink with lamp black, gum arabic and writing ink, and his transparent paper was oiled with turpentine varnish. His method was 'with the swiftest hand to make all possible variety of strokes upon his paper, confining the disposition of the whole to the general subject in the mind'. He suggests a purely mechani-cal device of crumpling the paper before blotting in order to increase the number of acci-dental shapes. To test the whole process, I made a practical experiment in the Cozens manner. My blot drawings were made, without any formal planning of a subject and within a time limit of three minutes, for I felt that speed was essential, as indeed Cozens taught, if any conscious drawing was to be avoided; and they proved, I think, that Cozens was no quack or charlatan when he taught what was an entirely new method.[1] Moreover, I found that, from the purely practical point of view, the making of a blot on crumpled paper not only increases the accidental shapes, but also serves an active purpose in that the drawing of the brush over the creases breaks up the forms and tends to prevent the artist's natural tendency to make careful descriptive forms with his brush. I am sure that many of the blots reproduced in the 'New Method' were drawn on crumpled paper, and it is clear,

[1] I may be pardoned for some pride in the fact that two of my drawings were accepted by a well-known authority as the work of Cozens!
One of these experimental drawings was reproduced in *The Collector* (Dec. 1930) and two, handed over by me to Mr. Oppé for safe custody, were exhibited in 1946–1947 at Sheffield and in the Tate Gallery. My article on Cozens in *The Collector* was accompanied by many illustrations of his work.

from these and from actual drawings, that Cozens worked largely with a dragging stroke from the side of a biggish brush.

Although blot drawings by Cozens, and finished drawings presumably made from blots, are in existence, it was only possible until recently to compare the effect of blot and of finished drawing from the illustrations in Cozens' book. But since Oppé wrote in the *Print Collector's Quarterly*,[1] two pieces of further evidence have come to light. One came from the acquisition, by the Victoria and Albert Museum, in 1925, of a blot drawing in progress, with the oiled paper over it, squared out, and with part of the drawing traced in pencil. Later, in order to complete the story, H. M. Hake came into possession of four sheets where the blot and finished drawing are side by side; and another similar sheet belongs to Mr. Ralph Edwards. Anyone can make a tracing of the main lines of the blot, and by placing it over the finished drawing, can see exactly how Cozens manipulated the forms and seized on fortunate accidents, while preserving the main theme and composition of the blot.

Cozens was probably himself to blame for the legend about his accidental messes on china plates, and for his reputation as a charlatan. In reality, he was a drawing-master who wanted to teach his pupils to see and work in masses instead of niggling with line, and he was also trying, by a somewhat new and fantastic method, to stimulate their curiosity and interest. We must remember that he was teaching not only boys at Eton, but 'full-grown amateurs, polite idlers at Bath' in the gay times when the new Assembly Rooms were just opened, and there were 'congregated from all quarters of the globe not only the invalid to gain health from the thermal springs, but the idle, the dissipated, and also the lovers of the arts'.[2] Cozens may have claimed, or his pupils may have thought, that his blots were haphazard, accidental, automatic. In truth they owe little to accident for an artist cannot consciously rub ink on a piece of paper, without moving it about with an instinctive feeling for form and design. As Oppé puts it: 'The blots are most striking, as the concentrated essence—not accidental, but as the result of much mental selection and re-flection—of the purely pictorial elements of landscape vision. They fulfil Cozens' own definition of true genius as the power which conceives strongly, invents with originality and executes readily'.

Though Cozens eliminated all outline from the blot drawings, he could work with a pen line when he wished, sometimes with open lines, sometimes mingling powerful pen strokes with broad brushwork. There are many of his drawings in the manner which vaguely re-semble the freedom of his blot work, and yet, with their structural support of strong line, stand half way between the blot and the elaboration. Drawings of this type, like those of Claude, done with intention and without trickery, need no explanation. They embody the direct results of his theory, and they reach in one swift stage what the pupil was required to reach in two.

---

[1] See page 82, footnote.
[2] *Life of Sheridan,* prefixed to Bohn's edition of his Dramatic Works. Sheridan went to reside at Bath in 1771.

Other painters may be included in this chapter, first, because they were Gainsborough's contemporaries and, second, because their work shows a romantic sensibility not always apparent in the art of the topographers. George Barret (1732–1784) was born at Dublin; (according to some accounts this was in 1728). He was the son of a clothier, was apprenticed to a staymaker, and began his career as an artist by colouring engravings for a printseller named Silcock, in Nicholas Street, Dublin.[1] He commenced his study of landscape in the park of the Earl of Powerscourt near his native city, and came to London in 1762, carrying off the first premium of fifty guineas offered by the Society of Arts for a landscape painting in oil two years later. His success was extraordinary and his oil pictures sold for prices never before given for landscapes, at a time when Richard Wilson was bartering his work for bread and cheese. Barret was associated with Cipriani and Sawrey Gilpin in the decoration of a room at Norbury Park, the residence of William Lock.[2] After executing his commission he moved from his house in Orchard Street, Portman Square, to Westminster Green, near Paddington; and it is amusing to a Londoner of today to find this described in 1808 as 'a situation more congenial to his health then any town residence'. In 1768 he became one of the foundation members of the Royal Academy. His success was achieved as a painter in oils, but it was not long-lived, and in 1833 we find Allan Cunningham describing him as 'a worthless dauber'. That criticism, even if true, could not be applied to his more rare work in water-colour. Drawings such as his *Landscape with River and Figures*[3] and *Landscape with River and Horses Watering*[4] (Pl. 59), show a fine sense of drawing combined with fluency and quiet, graceful colour. As Professor Bodkin pointed out, they are less formal than his oil-paintings, which were a curious blend of the artificial and the well-observed.[5] His loosely rendered trees are fresh and natural, and there is a great sense of atmosphere among his pale autumnal tints. In spite of his large income he left his family destitute. His son, George Barret (1767–1842), seventeen when his father died, began his career under great difficulties, but was to become a flourishing member of the Old Water-Colour Society.

Richard Cooper (c.1740–1814), a neglected artist of rare distinction, belongs to this group. He was born at Edinburgh, the son of Richard Cooper, the engraver, who was practising there from about 1730. The son studied under his father, and in Paris under J. P. Le Bas, and then about 1770 went to Italy for some years. He resided for a time at Edinburgh and in London—Farington, in 1793, describes him as 'Mr. Cooper, the Drawing Master, of Charles-street, St. James's Square'—and became drawing master at Eton, a worthy successor to Alexander Cozens. His landscapes and views of Rome (*Interior of the Colosseum*),[6] Windsor, Richmond, etc. were exhibited at the Royal Academy from 1787 to

---

[1] E. Edwards, *Anecdotes of Painters*, 1808, pp. 97–99.
[2] *Country Life*, LXXV, 1934, p. 161, and J. Timbs, *A Picturesque Promenade round Dorking*, 1822.
[3] V.A.M. 1722–1871.
[4] V.A.M. 257–1875.
[5] Thomas Bodkin, *Four Irish Landscape Painters*, 1920.
[6] (2 views) B.M. 1882. 3.11.1135 & 1875. 8.14.950.

87

1809. Cooper is a very worthy predecessor of J. R. Cozens, with whom he shows a definite relationship in method and outlook, and would take a much higher place among the earlier water-colour painters if his work in colour were not so rare. He used his reed pen with free, rapid and flowing movement, and was often content with vivid descriptions of landscape in pen line with a wash of ink or sepia. His drawing is summary and impressionistic, full of what W. M. Craig condemns as 'shorthand kinds of representation—a twirl, a flourish or a zig-zag'.[1] There is slight colour, however, in the *Rocky Landscape*[2] (Pl. 58). It shows his characteristic way of breaking up his landscape and giving diversity by carefully placed spots of interchanging light and shade. The Cozens-like sky, with a little clear blue in it, completes the swing of a design which depends upon constructive pen-work and varying greys running from its admirable distance to the shadowed foreground with its slight but telling incident of figures and a boat to give the scale. A little ochre warms the sunny passage in a composition where all the values are just right.

William Pars (1742–1782) who stuck more closely to water-colour, and was a better and more prolific artist in this medium than Barret, was a contemporary of Francis Towne, a few years older than John 'Warwick' Smith, and ten years older than John Robert Cozens. His influence on the development of English water-colour was not perhaps very profound but, such as it was, it has been consistently underrated, owing probably to the prominence given to 'Warwick' Smith for his alleged invention of the application of local colours without under-painting and to J. R. Cozens for his discovery of Alpine scenery as subject matter for a British artist. With the realisation that Smith's so-called innovation had been anticipated by Skelton, Pars, Towne and others, and with the Alpine views of Towne and Pars in mind to detract from Cozens' originality in choice of subject, the work of Pars can be seen in its due place. He was not Towne's master, as stated by Redgrave and later writers, but his direct influence on both Towne and Cozens cannot be denied. Towne's early Roman drawings follow Pars' work very closely in their colouring (see *An Italian Villa* by Pars),[3] and Cozens' early Swiss drawings are not only reminiscent of Pars' characteristic restraint of colour, but may also have been influenced as to their subject by Pars' Alpine views which caused a stir when exhibited in 1771 at the Royal Academy.

Pars was the son of a metal-chaser, said to have been a Dutchman who settled in England,[4] and studied at Shipley's School, of which his elder brother was afterwards director, at the Duke of Richmond's Gallery, and the St. Martin's Lane School.[5] He was awarded several premiums by the Society for the Encouragement of Arts. In 1761 he exhibited a portrait and a miniature at the Incorporated Society of Artists, and in 1763 became a member of the Free Society of Artists. In 1764 he won a medal of the Society of

---

[1] *Instructions in Drawing Landscape*, 1814–1815.
[2] V.A.M. 1596–1871.
[3] V.A.M. 180–1890.
[4] Whitley, 1700–1799, II, p. 344.
[5] E. Edwards, *Anecdotes of Painters*, 1808, pp. 89–91.

Arts for an historical painting, and in the same year was commissioned by the newly-formed Dilettanti Society to accompany Dr. Chandler's expedition to Asia Minor and Greece.

The absorbing interest in classical antiquity which characterised English society in the eighteenth century particularly in its later decades was greatly encouraged by James Stuart (1738–1788), better known as 'Athenian' Stuart. He had made an expedition to Greece in 1751, accompanied by Nicholas Revett (1720–1804), the architect, and had spent four years in the study of the remains of ancient architecture. The first volume of their *Antiquities of Athens* was published in 1762. In 1764 the newly-formed Dilettanti Society decided to finance another expedition, not only to Greece, but also to those parts of Asia Minor which are rich in the remains of Ionian civilisation. They appointed as leader of the expedition Richard Chandler the antiquary, who had published *Marmorea Oxoniensa* at Oxford in 1763, and they commissioned Revett to accompany the expedition as its architect, and Pars as its artist. The party left England in June 1764, and returned in November 1766. Chandler afterwards published two journals of their wanderings: *Travels in Asia Minor*, which appeared in 1775, and *Travels in Greece*, 1776. The two books give a detailed and often vivid account of the scenery surrounding the ruins which they visited, and of the manners and customs of the local inhabitants, but it is disappointing to find that there is practically no reference to the artistic labours of the expedition. Its scope is, however, indicated: 'We were instructed by the committee of the Dilettanti Society not to interfere at Athens with the labours of Messrs. Stuart & Revett' (i.e. in 1751), 'But solely to attend to those articles, which they had either omitted or not completed.'[1]

The drawings made by Pars in Asia Minor were engraved in *Ionian Antiquities*, the two volumes of which were published in 1769 and 1797, and many of his Greek drawings appeared in the second and third volumes of Stuart and Revett's *Antiquities of Athens*. Some of the Greek drawings were also engraved by William Byrne for the Dilettanti Society. These drawings, many of which are in the British Museum, are rather immature and weak. They are carefully topographical, thin and flat, with delicate pen outline done either with a pencil or with a very fine pen. The colour is laid on directly, without any under-painting. The composition is good, and the handling of distance skilful, especially in *The Temple at Mylesa*.[2] The engraved versions are distinctly flattering to the originals, and suggest a depth and strength which they actually lack. Seven of the Greek drawings were exhibited at the Royal Academy in 1769.

Pars' second journey abroad was made in the suite of Henry Temple, Viscount Palmerston. The precise date of this expedition is unknown, but it was before 1771, the year in which Pars exhibited at the Royal Academy eight views in Switzerland and the Tyrol. The party travelled through Switzerland and the Tyrol, and down through Italy to Rome. The drawings which Pars brought back from this journey show a greatly increased power and the first indications of his characteristic style. There is a very lavish use of gouache, and

---

[1] R. Chandler, *Travels in Greece*, 1776, p. 131.
[2] B.M. Mm. 11–73 (L.B. 17 as 'Sepulchral Monument at Mylasa').

the darks are often varnished over. In many drawings the foreground is in gouache, while the mountainous background is in transparent colour. One drawing, *Mer de Glace, Chamouny*[1] which is in transparent greys and browns, has been repeated with the use of gouache throughout in another version.[2] The prevailing colours in the Swiss drawings are strong greens and yellows. Many of the Swiss drawings were engraved by Woollett and others were aquatinted by Sandby.

The drawings which anticipate the Swiss landscapes of Towne and Cozens, were perhaps, as Binyon points out, 'the earliest revelation of the high Alps to the untravelled English'. They are careful transcripts of nature. Towne and Cozens were to reveal, in a different sense, the grandeur and infinity of the Alps.

In 1770 Pars was elected Associate of the Royal Academy. He never attained the rank of full Academician, although in 1773 he reached the final ballot in competition with James Barry, and in 1779 was defeated by Copley by two votes.

In 1774 the Dilettanti Society determined to grant an income to an artist for the purpose of completing his studies in Rome, and Pars was chosen as the first recipient. He left London in the summer of 1775, the year in which Girtin and Turner were born. In 1776 he exhibited two portraits at the Royal Academy, giving an address in Rome. Many of the views of Rome drawn by him during his stay were executed for Lord Palmerson. He died in Rome in 1782, of a fever, according to Edwards; but Whitley quotes a letter from James Irvine, dated November, 1782, in which he says: 'We have all been in very great grief for the loss of William Pars, who was a very robust, hearty fellow. At Tivoli he was so imprudent as to stand in the water to make a drawing, and in returning to town was seized with a kind of aguish complaint & oppression on his heart, & in a few days he died of suffocation. . . . Poor fellow, I believe he was not very anxious about life, & enjoyed but little happiness in this world.'[3]

It is difficult to place Pars. He is not in the same category as Cozens or Girtin, but he should not be regarded just as one of the topographers of his day, and should claim a higher rank than that usually awarded to him. If one thinks of his work at its best, what comes to mind is a feeling of spaciousness, of the craft of line and wash employed, almost with mastery, to suggest receding planes in a spacious landscape. From this point of view some of his most notable drawings were done during a visit to Ireland before he left for Rome in 1775. Of the six Irish scenes in the Victoria and Albert Museum, two are splendid examples, *Killarney and Lake*[4] (Pl. 62) and *Londonderry*.[5, 6] Here he works with little more than grey, with which touches of a slightly warmer colour are intermingled. In the distance, especially, and in the small wet blots suggestive of trees and of broken ground, he recalls J. R. Cozens. There is a little pen work, drawn in jerky and nervous touches with a sharp

---

[1] B.M. 1868. 8.8.3158. [2] B.M. 1870. 5.14.1223.
[3] Whitley, 1700–1799, II, p. 344. [4] V.A.M. 179–1890. [5] V.A.M. 676.
[6] Also while in Ireland, Pars made a portrait drawing of *Miss Cronin of Killarney* (B.M. 1870. 5.14.1215) and a view of *The Seat of Owen Wynne*, Coll. Mr. Gilbert Davis.

point, but usually in the foreground only. The pen lines are rarely structural, and I am inclined to think that most of them were added to give form and accent after the drawing was complete. His figures are elegantly drawn and well placed; his animals are superior in form and articulation to those of J. R. Cozens. Another most interesting small drawing is *View of St. Peter's, Rome*,[1] inscribed as 'painted for Ozias Humphry 1777'. In its method of approach, its delicate colouring in greens, greys and rose, in its actual slightness and reticence, here, at first sight, is a drawing by J. R. Cozens. But it was made a year before Cozens visited Rome and is more mature than his work at that time, indeed it is like a Cozens of 1780, the *St. Peter's, Rome*, for instance, with its rosy light behind the buildings, which belonged to the late Morland Agnew. And it leaves us with the riddle as to how much Cozens learned from him. Towne had a tremendous admiration for Pars, and on his deathbed wished that his own drawings of Rome might repose in the British Museum along with those of his friend; and they went there by his bequest in 1816.

George Robertson (*c.*1748–1788) should also be considered in this context. He was born in London about 1748, the son of a wine merchant; won a premium at the Society of Arts in 1761, and studied art at Shipley's School. Under the patronage of William Beckford he went to Italy, working for several years at Rome and elsewhere, and returned to England with Beckford about 1770. Together they visited Jamaica. His life, on his return to London, was something of a struggle against ill-health and adverse circumstances. He made some large drawings which Boydell engraved and published, but is said to have had 'no very brilliant success with the publick'. He supported himself and his family by teaching, and was drawing-master to a girls' school in Queen's Square, Bloomsbury. He exhibited his work at the Royal Academy and till the end of his life at the Incorporated Society of Artists, of which he became Vice-President in 1780. Owing to a fall from his horse he was suffering for two years, and died on September 26, 1788. An obituary notice[2] of September 27, 1788, reads as follows:

On Friday died at Newington Butts, after a long series of pain and sickness, Mr. George Robertson, Landscape-painter. This admirable artist was about forty-one years of age, and a native of London; he had a strong natural genius for drawing, which at an early age he went to Rome to improve, from whence, after a long tour through Germany, Holland, &c. in company with the Duke of Dorset, William Beckford, Esq., of Sommerley, in Suffolk, (his patron and friend) and some other Gentlemen, he returned to England about eighteen years since. In this journey his drawings from Nature, and a few pictures in the Dresden and other collections, are in the possession of Mr. Beckford; those, and his many chalk drawings from Claude and other landscape painters, which compose a large part of Alderman Boydell's gallery, are unrivalled productions. Mr. Robertson was not much known to the world; his modesty, and a love of tranquility, kept him to himself and a few select friends, though he was well known to several of the first families; but what greatly contributed to Mr. Robertson's merits not being generally known, not a picture or drawing of his has met the public eye, since the Society of Arts have declined exhibiting, of which he had been a President.

[1] V.A.M. P.31–1932.
[2] *Press Cuttings from English Newspapers*, 1685–1835, II, p. 406, in the Victoria and Albert Museum.

It would be in vain to attempt a description of Mr. Robertson's drawings in water colours, these have an effect equal to oil, which he produced with an expedition and ease peculiar to himself; and added to the great knowledge of Nature, (trees in particular) he had by close study acquired—his figures of cattle had equal merit.

It would be difficult to say, whether he most excelled in oil, water colours or chalk—whether he was most to be admired as an artist, or a friend and Gentleman; but this may safely be said, that in the first character, his name is likely, one day or other, to rival the first of his predecessors, or contemporaries, of whatever school or country.

Robertson remained obscure and unaccepted until C. F. Bell wrote about his work with special reference to some drawings in the Ashmolean Museum from the collection of James Moore.[1] Lack of appreciation of his work has been due, as Bell points out, to his hybrid style. When most painters were successful in rendering atmosphere and space with transparent tints, Robertson combined the two methods most effectively. He follows Gainsborough in his love of pastoral subjects, with groups of trees, and winding roads, and waggons fording a stream. The drawing and grouping of his figures is admirable, and examples in the British Museum and the Victoria and Albert Museum show that he was particularly happy as a draughtsman of lively human figures, and of sleek and comfortable cattle in quiet solitudes. He used a very complete dead colouring of ink in monochrome, ranging from quite pale grey to dead black. Some of his work is in transparent watercolour, with little or no monochromatic under-painting, and he often uses body-colour— to this we shall refer in a later chapter—for putting bold, finishing touches, of Chinese white, or colour mixed with white, sometimes running a whole branch of a tree across the dark ink wash of his first lay-in. A notable feature of his work, to which Bell has drawn attention, is his technical innovation in scratching out high lights. This is apparent in the Moore series, and particularly in his most ambitious effort, the *Journey to Emmaus*[2] (Pl. 65), where the brook in the foreground owes all its movement and sparkle to skilful scraping with the point of a knife.

One of the true romantics, in person and in part of his work, was Philip James de Loutherbourg (1740–1812). He painted battle-pieces, landscapes and coast views in oil. His drawings, which are often studies for oil paintings of greater importance, are spirited in line and pleasant in colour, frequently with numerous figures well grouped. He had a vivid appreciation of wild scenery and storm effects. Born at Strasbourg,[3] the son of a painter of Polish extraction, he studied under his father and J. H. Tischbein at Strasbourg, and later under Carle Van Loo and F. G. Casanova in Paris, where he won a name for his landscapes and battle-pieces and was elected a member of the Académie Royale in 1767. In 1771 he came to London, bearing a letter to Garrick from the actor's Parisian friend, Jean Monnet.[4] The writer strongly advised Garrick 'to let him paint three small pictures for you;

[1] C. F. Bell, *British water-colour painters: James Moore Collection*, Walpole Soc., V, 1915–1917.
[2] B.M. 1916. 3.3.5.
[3] Though this is stated on his tomb at Chiswick, claims have also been made for Fulda and Basle. Farington says that he gave his birthplace as Basle.
[4] For this letter and for a full account of De Loutherbourg's *Eidophusikon*, see Whitley, 1700–1799, II, p. 352.

one a seapiece, another a landscape in the manner of Berchem, and the third a battle scene. In all three styles he is delightful'. In 1773 Garrick did purchase a landscape for sixty guineas, but he went further and engaged De Loutherbourg (at £500 a year, says Farington) to design scenery for Drury Lane. *A Christmas Tale*, for instance, was staged in 1773, with scenery, costume, and every detail, carried out from De Loutherbourg's designs. He introduced many revolutionary scenic devices and invented a number of the methods still in use for reproducing the sounds of thunder, waves, wind and rain. For William Beckford's voluptuous coming-of-age festival in 1780 De Loutherbourg displayed all his ingenuity in an elaborate arrangement of lighting at Fonthill, the whole house being filled with a delicate roseate glow.[1] After Garrick parted with his interest in Drury Lane in 1776, De Loutherbourg continued to work under the new management and in 1779 designed the scenery for Sheridan's comedy, *The Critic*. At the same time he had been exhibiting paintings which won high esteem, and became A.R.A. in 1780 and R.A. in 1781. His work as draughtsman and water-colourist is well represented at the British Museum.

In 1781 De Loutherbourg produced his *Eidophusikon*[2] in a large room in Lisle Street, saying in a prospectus that he had always believed that 'by adding progressive motion to accurate resemblance a series of incidents might be produced which should display in the most lively manner those captivating scenes which inexhaustible Nature presents to our view at different periods and in different parts of the globe'. A contemporary critic writes of his moving canvas, and says that 'the progressions are uniform and have the slowness and constancy of the operations which they imitate'. At his little theatre De Loutherbourg set up a new standard of comfort and luxury; 'the room is the most beautiful that can be conceived . . . the seats for the spectators are crimson stuff'; a musical performance supplemented the exhibition of the moving pictures. He had a full house every night, with Reynolds and Gainsborough sometimes among the audience. Here is a typical advertisement:

EXHIBITION ROOMS, over EXETER CHANGE, STRAND

This present MONDAY evening there will be a Representation of Mr. LOUTHERBOURG's EIDOPHUSIKON, Including the awful, pathetic, and most interesting scene of the STORM and SHIPWRECK, conveying a striking idea of the late dreadful catastrophe of the HALSWEL EAST-INDIAMAN; and the GRAND SCENE from MILTON'S PARADISE LOST, confessedly the Chef d'Oeuvre of that incomparable artist, with suitable accompaniments.

The pauses necessary to change the scenery will be supplied with English READINGS and RECITALS, BY MR. CRESSWICK.

First Seats 3s. Second Seats 2s.

The Doors to open at half past seven, and the performance to begin precisely at eight. Places for the first Seats may be taken from Ten till Five.

The Days of Exhibition are MONDAYS and FRIDAYS.

---

[1] J. W. Oliver, *Life of W. Beckford*, 1932, pp. 88, 89.
[2] A water-colour showing a performance in the *Eidophusikon* was made by E. F. Burney (B.M. 1963. 7.16.1).

In 1785 De Loutherbourg took the lease of a house in Hammersmith Terrace, which three years later became the scene of his work as a professed faith-healer for the cure of all sorts of diseases, including deafness, lameness and cancer.[1] He was a highly accomplished draughtsman, who anticipated Rowlandson in his treatment of lively groups of figures.

Johann Conrad Gessner (1764–1826) also claims a place in this chapter, and his fine work has been most undeservedly overlooked—perhaps on account of its rarity—by writers on water-colour. Born at Zurich, he was the eldest son of Solomon Gessner (1730–1788), author of the *Death of Abel* which in its English translation of 1761 had a great vogue and was read by Wordsworth, Coleridge and Byron. Geoffrey Grigson quotes passages from Gessner's writings in his anthology, *The Romantics* (1942), and suggests that he had as much effect upon English painters as upon the poets. Gessner's *New Idyl, With a letter to M. Fuslin on Landscape Painting* was a book which 'delighted Constable, who certainly must have enjoyed Gessner's charming and delicately honest illustrations'. Mr. Grigson's extracts may be quoted here:

> A thought conceiv'd in the first warmth, an effect with which we are struck at the first view, is never so well express'd as by the strokes that are drawn at that instant.
>
> There is no reputation for him to whom a taste for his art does not become his ruling passion, to whom the hours he employs in its cultivation are not the most delicious of his life, to whom the study of it does not constitute his real existence, and his primary happiness; to whom the society of artists is not, of all others, the most pleasing; whose watchings, or dreams in the night, are not occupy'd with the ideas of his art, who in the morning does not fly with fresh transport to his painting-room.
>
> My natural inclination led me to landscapes; I sought with ardour the means of satisfying my desire, and embarrassed in the route I should take, I said to myself, there is but one model, there is but one master; and I determined to draw after nature.

These quotations are interesting for their own sake as the expression of a painter's fervour in the eighteenth century, and they show the atmosphere in which Gessner was nurtured. He studied art in Dresden; in 1787 went to Italy; resided at Zurich from 1789 to 1796 when he came to England. Farington, as usual, is first with the news. On November 21 of that year he notes that 'a Son of Gesner, (*sic*) the Poet, is come to England from Zurich—Gesner is a Painter of Horses, Battles, &c. . . . In Paris, Gesner visited the Louvre, which is not yet finished as a gallery for pictures'. Gessner exhibited at the Royal Academy from 1799 to 1803. His *Horses at a Pool*[2] (Pl. 70) and *Landscape with Horses*,[3] both dated 1800, are spirited drawings executed with vigorous and flexible line and slight but pleasant colour.

In this company we may also consider Edward Edwards (1736–1806), in that he took a half-way place between Gainsborough and the topographers. He drew definite places, but he drew them romantically and with a boldness, almost a swagger, of pen work which

---

[1] Mary Pratt's pamphlet (B.M. Lib. 1418. k. 17) concerning his supposed cures; A. Pasquin, *Memoirs*; E. Hardcastle (W. H. Pyne), *Wine and Walnuts*, 1824; Whitley, *1700–1799*, I, pp. 354, 355.
[2] V.A.M. 493.
[3] V.A.M. P.2–1913.

resembles Canaletto rather than Rooker and Malton. Edwards was born at Castle Street, Leicester Square, the son of a chairmaker and carver who had come from Shrewsbury to London. He was educated at a French Protestant school in London and made his own way in life, drawing furniture patterns for an upholsterer, working at the St. Martin's Lane Academy, and opening a drawing school of his own in 1760. He exhibited portraits and subject paintings in oil at the Royal Academy and elsewhere, and became A.R.A. in 1773, but never rose to the higher rank. He was never very prosperous, being compelled to do a good deal of hack-work on painting and repairing ceilings, and at one time painting scenery for a theatre at Newcastle-on-Tyne. Perhaps he was too volatile and restless, for he illustrated books, was a proficient etcher, wrote verses, played the violin, and—what concerns us here—made some spirited topographical water-colours. During the last years of his life he was working, with Farington's warm encouragement, on a volume entitled *Anecdotes of Painters*, intended as a continuation of the *Anecdotes of Painting* by Horace Walpole, who frequently obtained the assistance of Edwards. On August 16, 1796, Farington records that: 'Edwards called on me this morning, and brought a manuscript volume of sketches of lives of modern artists written by himself. He read a few of them as specimens. He does not mean that they shall be published during his lifetime'. The book, which appeared in 1808, two years after his death, is sometimes not entirely reliable, but it contains valuable information about contemporary artists, and was not deserving of the malicious attack in the *Quarterly Review*, by Hoppner, who went out of his way to sneer at the poverty and the physical deformity from which the old artist had suffered since birth.

Edwards' drawing of *Durham Cathedral*[1] (Pl. 72), dated 1788 on the back, is a fine example of his vigorous and expressive handling of the pen, and his use of wash to give contrasts between carefully chosen lights and shadow masses. The final process of applying the local tints over the shading was begun in the sky and on the roofs of the houses, but at that point the artist held his hand. If the colour were removed, there would still remain a powerful drawing in pen and wash with a distinct resemblance to Canaletto, and this brings Edwards nearer to Girtin than to the topographers, such as Rooker, Malton and Dayes. Of another Durham subject, drawn in 1788, *North Dean, Castle Eden*, there are two versions, one in the Victoria and Albert,[2] the other in the British Museum.[3]

Within the precincts of the romantic-idealist group are the two brothers Barker, Thomas (1769–1847) and Benjamin (1776–1838). Thomas, known as 'Barker of Bath' was born near Pontypool, spent a few years at Bath copying old masters, and was sent about 1791 by Mr. Spackman of Bath to study in Italy, where he remained for some three years. He is known chiefly by his oil paintings, notably *The Woodman*, and many of his oils are strongly reminiscent of Gainsborough. After his return from Italy he settled at Bath and from 1791 exhibited at the Royal Academy. His brother, Benjamin, also lived at Bath. He exhibited

[1] V.A.M. P.1–1913.
[2] V.A.M. 23–1873.
[3] B.M. 1878. 7.13.1783.

landscapes in oil and water-colour from 1800 to 1838 at the Royal Academy, the Old Water-Colour Society, and elsewhere. He worked much in imitation of the old masters, and recorded gorges, precipices, cascades and ruins in the manner of Salvator Rosa. With reference to his *Rhaeadr Mawddach* in the National Museum of Wales, D. K. Baxandall points out in the official catalogue how scenes of this kind were recorded by the early topographers such as Grimm, 'but Barker, coming later in the development of water-colour, gives a greater weight and force to his drawing of the shadowed gorge. Grimm's drawing of the same fall (in the National Museum of Wales) is a record of it, almost a catalogue of its various parts; Barker attempts to give something of the mood of awe it inspired in him'.[1] My own experience has been that 'Barker of Bath' has been used as a convenient peg on which to hang many unidentified landscapes of a romantic type which hover between reminiscences of Gainsborough and of Crome.

[1] National Museum of Wales. *Handbook to the Pyke Thompson Gallery*, 1939, p. 37.

45 Landscape: probably a study for 'The Destruction of Niobe's Children'

V.A.M. P.15-1915   16¼ × 20¼ : 413 × 515   *Oil and body-colour* (?)

Richard WILSON, R.A. (1714-1782)

46 'Landscape Composition'

B.M. 1936.1.6.1 $6\frac{3}{8} \times 8\frac{1}{2}$: 162 × 216   *Pen and water-colour*

J. B. C. CHATELAIN

47 'A Country Lane'

B.M. 1899.5.16.10 $9\frac{3}{4} \times 12\frac{1}{2}$: 247 × 318   *Water-colour*

Thomas GAINSBOROUGH, R.A. (1727–1788)

48 'Lovers in a Country Lane'

Coll. Lord Eccles $13\frac{7}{8} \times 9\frac{5}{8}$: 352×244 *Pen and ink and gouache*

Thomas GAINSBOROUGH, R.A. (1727–1788)

49 'Landscape, River and Castle'
B.M. 1946.4.13.185 $7\frac{3}{8} \times 10\frac{1}{2}$: 187 × 267   *Grey and brown wash*
William GILPIN (1724–1804)

50 'Ruined Tower on a River'
B.M. 1946.4.13.184 $7\frac{3}{4} \times 10\frac{3}{4}$: 197 × 273   *Grey wash*
William GILPIN (1724–1804)

51 'Castle in a Landscape'
Coll. Mr & Mrs Paul Mellon $9\frac{5}{8} \times 13$: 244×330 *Brush and brown wash*
Alexander COZENS (c. 1717–1786)

52 'Italian Hamlet'
B.M. 1867.10.12.52 $7\frac{1}{4} \times 9\frac{3}{8}$: 184×238 *Pen and ink and wash*
Alexander COZENS (c. 1717–1786)

53 'Landscape with High Rocks'
V.A.M. P.6–1928 $17\frac{7}{8} \times 25\frac{1}{4}: 455 \times 642$ *Wash drawing*
Alexander COZENS (c. 1717–1786)

54 'The Cloud'
Coll. Mr D.L.T. and Miss Armide Oppé $8\frac{1}{2} \times 12: 215 \times 305$ *Grey and black wash*
Alexander COZENS (c. 1717–1786)

55 'Ruin on a Hill', blot drawing

B.M. 1951.7.14.73   6⅛ × 7⅝: 155 × 194   *Brush and brown wash*

Alexander COZENS (c. 1717–1786)

56 'Ruin on a Hill' (composition from above drawing)

B.M. 1951.7.14.73   6¾ × 7¾: 162 × 197   *Pen and brown ink and wash*

Alexander COZENS (c. 1717–1786)

57 'Mountainous Landscape'

B.M. 1847.6.9.21   13 × 18¼: 330 × 464   *Black chalk and water-colour*

John HOPPNER, R.A. (1758–1810)

58 'Rocky Landscape'

V.A.M. 1596–1871   13 × 19½: 330 × 495   *Pen and water-colour*

Richard COOPER (c. 1740–1814)

59 'River Landscape, Horses Watering'
V.A.M. 257–1875 $14\frac{5}{8} \times 21 : 372 \times 534$ *Water-colour*
George BARRET (I), R.A. (1732–1784)

60 'River Bank with High Rocks'
Coll. Mr & Mrs Paul Mellon $13\frac{3}{8} \times 20\frac{1}{2} : 339 \times 520$ *Water-colour*
George BARRET (I), R.A. (1732–1784)

61 'Valley of Chamouny'
B.M. 1870.5.14.1224   13¼ × 19¼: 337 × 489   *Water-colour*
William PARS, A.R.A. (1742–1782)

62 'Killarney and Lake'
V.A.M. 179–1890   12½ × 19: 318 × 483   *Water-colour*
William PARS, A.R.A. (1742–1782)

63 'The Temple of Venus'
Coll. Mr & Mrs Paul Mellon   11¾ × 16: 299 × 407   *Water-colour*
William Pars, A.R.A. (1742–1782)

64 'Italian Villa'
V.A.M. 180–1890   8⅞ × 12¾: 226 × 324   *Water-colour*
William Pars, A.R.A. (1742–1782)

65 'Journey to Emmaus'

B.M. 1916.3.3.5   16¼ × 11⅝: 413 × 295   *Water-colour and body-colour*

George ROBERTSON (c. 1748–1788)

66 'Landscape with Cattle'

V.A.M. 191–1890   11½ × 15⅞: 292 × 403   *Water-colour*

George ROBERTSON (c. 1748–1788)

67 'Lt. Gen. Sir William Congreve'
B.M. 1851.9.1.708   8 × 5 : 203 × 128   *Water-colour*
Philip de LOUTHERBOURG, R.A. (1740–1812)

68 'Mad Prisoner in Chains'
B.M. 1907.9.26.3   11¾ × 15½ : 300 × 395   *Pen and brown wash*
Philip de LOUTHERBOURG, R.A. (1740–1812)

69 'Cataract on the Llugwy, near Conway'
V.A.M. 170–1890   9⅛ × 12¼: 222 × 311   *Water-colour, signed*
Philip de LOUTHERBOURG, R.A. (1740–1812)

70 'Horses at a Pool'
V.A.M. 493   14¾ × 18¼: 375 × 464   *Water-colour, signed and dated 1800*
Johann Conrad GESSNER (1764–1826)

71 'Near North Dean, Castle Eden, Durham'
B.M. 1878.7.13.1783   8¼ × 12⅝: 209 × 321
Pen and water-colour, signed with initials and dated 1788
Edward EDWARDS, A.R.A. (1736–1806)

72 'Durham Cathedral'
V.A.M. P.1–1913   11½ × 18¾: 292 × 476   *Water-colour, signed and dated 1788*
Edward EDWARDS, A.R.A. (1736–1806)

73 'Shepherd and Sheep'
Coll. Mr & Mrs Paul Mellon   6¾ × 10: 172 × 253   *Water-colour and gouache*
Thomas BARKER (1769–1847)

74 'Stormy Landscape'
V.A.M. 132–1890   18⅛ × 25½: 464 × 648   *Water-colour, signed and dated 1813*
Benjamin BARKER (1776–1838)

CHAPTER V

The foundation of the Royal Academy: some painters in gouache

Thomas and Paul Sandby   Joseph Goupy   William Taverner   George Keate

In November 1760 William Mason, the biographer of the poet Gray and the close friend of Reynolds, wrote to Lord Nuneham as follows:

> Sandby has made such a picture! such a bard! such a headlong flood! such a Snowdon! such giant oaks! such desert caves! If it is not the best picture that has been painted this century in any country I'll give up all my taste to the Bench of Bishops (even to the Bishop who you know read one ode and not t'other) and ask not even a prebend in exchange.
>
> Put on your hat and feather, your red surtout, your Dresden cane, your ribband muff, put them on, my Lord, and take your *chaise de poste* and be pelted all the road for a French Marky, and depend on it you'll be amply rewarded by the sight of this picture. Then there's Roche Abbey too, every side and nook of the charmingest ruin in England. In a word Sandby improves as much in painting as your Lordship does in caprice, or Miss Chudleigh in fat, or Miss West in—in—charms; and in a short time will be that Claude Lorraine that Browne assured him he was at Lord Scarboro's in my hearing, and therefore desired him not to spoil a Claude by eating too many filberts.[1]

About two years later Gainsborough wrote to Lord Hardwicke describing Sandby as 'the only man of genius' who has painted 'real views from Nature in this country'.[2] Sir Richard Colt Hoare, writing in 1822 about the same early period in Sandby's art, said 'during my younger days Paul Sandby was the monarch of the plain, and esteemed the best artist in this line'.[3]

Nowadays, Mason's letter may seem somewhat fulsome, and other contemporary writers may appear to exaggerate Sandby's merit. With our fuller opportunities of knowledge and of comparative study we do not consider Sandby a genius, and we may admit that he has not even an indisputable claim to rank among the first half-dozen painters of our water-colour school. At the same time, it must be recognised that these contemporary estimates do indicate that Sandby developed in England something that, perhaps without knowing it, England had all along been seeking. They show that Sandby established and nationalised an art which, up till his time, had some foreign elements in it, and it was due largely to his influence that water-colour, hitherto regarded by artists themselves merely

[1] Whitley, 1700–1799, I, p. 169. Quoted from *The Harcourt Papers*, by William Mason.
[2] W. T. Whitley, *Thomas Gainsborough*, 1915, p. 358.   [3] Whitley, 1700–1799, II, p. 363.

as a useful method of making studies for oil-paintings or as a pleasant recreation, was raised to an independent status as being in itself an end worthy of serious consideration.

The popularity which Sandby enjoyed in his lifetime was, however, very transient. Cozens, Girtin and Turner were too close on his heels, and Farington, a barometer of contemporary attitudes to the arts, seldom mentions Sandby, and then with no great enthusiasm. Writing in 1811, à propos of the sale of Sandby's works after his death, he says: 'I could not but sensibly feel the great difference between His works and those of Artists who now practise in Water Colour.—His drawings so divided in parts, so scattered in effect,—detail prevailing over general arrangement'.[1] He notes in 1816 that a fellow artist 'spoke of the change which had taken place in the practice of Drawing; He observed that the modern manner had supersed[ed] the old practice. Paul Sandby some time before His death told Him that he had long been witht. a commission'.[2] Yet even after his death there were some who realised Sandby's contribution to the growth of the new art. In 1807 Benjamin West said 'that a style of drawing had been practised in this country such as had not been seen in any other, and that with Thomas Sandby it had originated'.[3] 'Thomas' may be a mistake for 'Paul', since Thomas Sandby's work in water-colour was a very minor incident in his activities, which were devoted mainly to architecture. All the same it is possible that West may have known the extent to which Thomas led the way and influenced his younger brother. Down through the years the two brothers have been constantly confused, and collectors have been too prone to attribute to Thomas all work of a purely architectural nature and to Paul landscapes and figures.[4]

Thomas (1723–1798) and Paul (1730–1809) Sandby were both born in Nottingham. The brothers showed an early talent for drawing, but James Gandon's note that they kept an academy in Nottingham is probably the result of a misapprehension, since they both left that town in their early teens for London, Thomas preceding Paul there by 7 years. In 1747, through the influence of Thomas already established and experienced, Paul was appointed to the Military Drawing Office of the Tower of London. Thomas had for some time been in the employ of the Duke of Cumberland and accompanied him on his campaigns in Flanders and Scotland. He was present at several of the Duke's battles, at Dettingen, and Fontenoy, and later at Culloden in 1746 (his sketch of the battle-field of Culloden is preserved at Windsor Castle) and was the first to report to the Government the news of the landing of the Young Pretender in 1745. After this beginning, which was so brisk and agitated, his life suddenly altered to a quieter tempo, for Cumberland, who in 1746 had been appointed Ranger of Windsor Great Park, immediately selected Thomas Sandby as his deputy, and for many years Thomas was occupied in the construction of the artificial lake and the grounds at Virginia Water.[5]

---

[1] *Diary*, May 2, 1811.   [2] *Ibid.*, Oct. 31, 1816.   [3] *Ibid.*, March 29, 1807.
[4] For a discussion of this point, see A. P. Oppé, *Sandby Drawings at Windsor Castle*, 1947, pp. 12, 13.
[5] In 1754, eight plates were published, with a dedication to the Duke of Cumberland, illustrating the works at Virginia Water. They were engraved, after drawings by Thomas Sandby, Paul Sandby and others, the prospectus being drawn and etched by Paul Sandby. The plates were republished by Boydell in 1772.

Paul Sandby, in the meanwhile, sought employment under the Board of Ordnance, as draughtsman to the Military Survey in Scotland, which followed on the suppression of the rebellion of 1745. His earliest known works are a *Prospect of the Entrance into the Tower*[1] and some copies of Bloemart and *East View of Edinburgh Castle*[2] which were presented to the Board as a specimen of his performance. He secured the post and was engaged in planning those roads which brought blessing also on the name of General Wade. Like Whistler at West Point, he grew weary of his allotted task of mechanical survey drawings and, beginning to indulge in picturesque sketches, saw in front of him a wider field and the freedom of an artist. How fine an artist he already was at this early period is shown by a group of his Scottish drawings at the British Museum. In *Draw Well at Broughton near Edinburgh*[3] (Pl. 75), 1751, can be seen his knowledge of Dutch art and the brilliant drawing of figures which characterises all his work. Coming south, he joined his brother, and for almost ten years they led a peaceful and retired existence in Windsor Park, Thomas being busy with architectural work and landscape gardening for the Duke, and Paul in sketching and etching. He had already begun to etch in Scotland, and several etchings of Scottish views were sold by a relation, William Sandby, bookseller, of Fleet Street, between 1747 and 1751.[4] Among his other etchings was a series of caricatures, published anonymously in 1753–1754, which drew their inspiration from Hogarth's *Analysis of Beauty*, issued in 1753. Paul had a very neat gift for caricature, which he again employed against Hogarth in 1762 in reply to two plates of a political nature published by Hogarth with the title, *The Times*. Later, on seeing Hogarth's paintings of *Marriage à la Mode*, he conceded that so great a painter should not be made the subject of ridicule and burlesque, and withdrew from sale all his satirical prints dealing with Hogarth's work.[5] He also did much reproductive etching, producing the illustrations to Ramsay's *Gentle Shepherd* from drawings by David Allan, and, in collaboration with Rooker, the plates for Tasso's *Jerusalem Delivered*; among his original work he published in 1760 twelve etchings of the *Cries of London*. He found time, however, to produce very many water-colour drawings of Windsor Castle and its surroundings, and obtained for these a munificent patron in Sir Joseph Banks, the President of the Royal Society. Banks bought about seventy of his drawings, which were carefully preserved in a folio by his descendants and were sold,[6] sixty-seven of them being purchased for the Queen's collection at Windsor by the Royal Librarian, Sir Richard Holmes. His successor made further additions deriving from the same source. With others acquired at different times in the past, notably a series of small figure subjects, the collection of Sandby's work at Windsor is the most important that exists. The drawings at Windsor, some four hundred and fifty, have been fully catalogued and described by A. P. Oppé,[7] whose introduction provides a close analysis of the artist's work.

[1] V.A.M. 1119–1931.   [2] B.M. 1880. 9.11.1229.   [3] B.M. 1904. 8.19.95.
[4] These, and other etchings by P. Sandby, were collected and published in a folio volume in 1765.
[5] *Library of the Fine Arts*, II, 1831, p. 345.
[6] Christie's, May 23, 1876.
[7] A. P. Oppé, *The Drawings of Paul and Thomas Sandby . . . at Windsor Castle*, 1947.

In 1760 both brothers came to town, Thomas taking a house in Great Marlborough Street, and Paul residing at Mr. Pow's, Dufour's Court, Broad Street, Carnaby Market, where his neighbour was James Gandon, architect of the Customs House and the Four Courts in Dublin. The Sandbys held a good position in the society of the day, largely owing, no doubt, to opportunities given by Royal patronage during their residence at Windsor, and Paul, in particular, was extremely sociable and hospitable. 'His house and his hand were ever at the call of his friends. They found a ready and a hearty welcome at his hospitable board'.[1] Gandon notes this aspect of his life: 'Sandby's vast store of knowledge in the fine arts, added to his high professional character, and the conversational powers which he possessed, being highly attractive, drew round him a circle of intellectual and attached friends, comprising the most distinguished artists and amateurs of the day.'[2] Gandon is speaking of a rather later time, when Paul Sandby had his home at 4 St. George's Row,[3] overlooking Hyde Park, where he lived from 1772 till his death; but even in his early days in London, he must have already begun to lay the foundations of his extensive acquaintanceship in high circles. On Sundays, after Divine Service, the great and the learned alike thronged the house in St. George's Row with its pleasant view looking over Hyde Park to the Surrey Hills. The house was near Tyburn turnpike, a little westward of the spot where the Marble Arch now stands, and among Sandby's drawings in the Victoria and Albert Museum will be found some depicting the main road, then a rural approach to London, and the Bayswater Tea Gardens. Other sketches of the neighbourhood are in the British Museum, and one drawing shows Sandby's studio on a terrace above a charming garden embowered among tall trees, behind which Paddington was approached by way of fields.

Considering their position, then, it was natural that both brothers should play a part in the agitations and convulsive efforts which culminated in 1768 in the foundation of the Royal Academy. When Paul came to London there were no facilities whatever for artists to exhibit their works. Artists at this period, were 'generally speaking the property of picture dealers (at that time their chief employers) and held by them in somewhat the same kind of vassalage and dependence as many authors are by booksellers'. The subscription studio in St. Martin's Lane was the only place where painters had an opportunity of meeting and exchanging views, and for many years there had been much talk of organisation with the object of founding an Academy. The Dilettanti Society supported the project, and in 1753 the first of the meetings of artists took place at the Turk's Head Tavern, Greek Street, to elect twenty-four of their number to act as a committee for the establishment of an Academy.[4] In 1755 a pamphlet was issued by the Committee, among whom were Reynolds, Hudson, Roubilliac, Robert Strange and Thomas Sandby, entitled *The Plan of*

---

[1] *Library of the Fine Arts*, II, 1787–1790, pp. 342–343.
[2] T. Mulvany, *Life of Gandon*, 1846.
[3] Afterwards it became 23 Hyde Park Place, and was demolished in 1901.
[4] The Turk's Head Tavern then stood at the corner of Greek Street and Compton Street, Soho. It was here that Johnson, Garrick, Reynolds and others joined in the meetings of the famous literary 'Club'. Later, the Turk's Head was removed to the neighbouring Gerrard Street, and in Wilson's time, as Pasquin states, was the common rendezvous 'for all the metropolitan artists who professed ability approximating to renown'.

an Academy for the Better Cultivation, Improvement and Encouragement of Painting, Sculpture, Architecture, and the Arts of Design in General: the abstract of a Royal Charter as proposed for establishing the same, and a short Introduction. In the introduction comes the statement that: 'we voluntarily yield the palm to every petty state that has produced a painter, and by the language generally used on this subject, one would think England the only country in the world incapable of producing one.' 'This country does not always err in vaunting its own productions,' Horace Walpole had already said. The Dilettanti Society, however, wanted to have a majority in the voting, and the whole project fell through.

At a meeting at the Turk's Head in 1759 it was decided to organise an exhibition every April. The hospitality of the Society of Arts was obtained, and the first show was held in April 1760 at the Society's rooms in the Strand. The enterprise was justified by its popularity, but almost immediately a hitch occurred in the friendly relations with the Society of Arts, and the exhibition of 1761 was held in an auctioneer's rooms in Spring Gardens, a shilling being charged for a catalogue with three characteristic designs by Hogarth, the purchase of which was compulsory. Among the contributors were Reynolds, Hogarth and Gainsborough, and the exhibition was described as being held by the 'Society of Artists of Great Britain'. The Society of Arts continued for a time to hold an exhibition of its own, but it was never of much importance. The split from the Society of Arts resulted in a further rift among the artists themselves, and in 1762 the Free Society of Artists was formed. It held its first exhibition in 1763, in the rooms of the Society of Arts.[1]

The Society of Artists continued to flourish, and on St. Luke's Day, 1763, at the Turk's Head, held its first dinner. Paul Sandby was among the distinguished company, which included Reynolds, Wilson, Hudson, Dance and Cotes. In 1765 the Society obtained the grant of a Charter, and was known thenceforward as 'The Incorporated Society of Artists of Great Britain'. Twenty directors were appointed, Paul Sandby among them. But in this Society, too, violent dissensions occurred and caused, in 1768, the resignation of eight of the original directors—Joseph Wilton, Edward Penny, Benjamin West, Richard Wilson, Paul Sandby, William Chambers, George Michael Moser and Francis Newton. Out of the anarchy and revolution came a permanent benefit, for the dissenting directors decided to make a further appeal for royal support for an Academy. Chambers, who had been tutor to George III, suggested the scheme to the new monarch in the autumn of 1768. The royal assent was obtained and on December 10, 1768, was founded the 'Royal Academy of Arts in London'. There was also a provision of money, of which Chambers took charge as Treasurer. Reynolds accepted the offer of the Presidency, and the first exhibition was opened in Pall Mall on April 26, 1769. The first Hanging Committee was composed of Paul Sandby, Edward Penny and George Barret, and Thomas Sandby was the Academy's first Professor of Architecture.

---

[1] Algernon Graves: *The Society of Artists of Great Britain 1760–1791; The Free Society of Artists, 1761–1783*; Whitley, *1700–1799*, I & II, *passim*; Hugh Gatty, *Notes by Horace Walpole . . . on Exhibitions*, Walpole Soc., XXVII, 1938–1939, pp. 55–88.

The Incorporated Society was bitterly annoyed by this development, which immediately reduced it to the rank of a second-rate body, but it continued to survive. The Free Society, however, fell upon chequered days. It was less attractive to artists of repute than the Incorporated Society, and it led a struggling existence, hampered in every way. Resenting the authority, none too tactfully exercised, of the Society of Arts, the Free Society held its exhibitions of 1765 and 1766 in Maiden Lane, and those of 1767 and 1768 in the 'Great New Room in Pall Mall, late Mr. Lamb's'. In 1769 the Society rented a room from Christie the auctioneer on a twenty-years' lease, but its last exhibition was held in 1783.

Let us note here that these exhibitions inaugurated a complete change in the status and prospects of water-colour art. Hitherto, the draughtsman had worked for the engraver; his commissions came from the publishers of prints; and it was through the engraving that his work was presented to the public eye. The advent of the public exhibition meant that the position was reversed. The artist, instead of working in simple tints, could enlarge his scope and give himself complete freedom of colour. He could become independent of the engraver and work for a new class of patrons and collectors. The engraving now became the accessory to the drawing, instead of being the principal end. Exhibitions also allowed the wealthy and cultured amateur to give to water-colour the patronage which had hitherto been confined to pictures in oil. The artist as exhibitor, as producer for the publisher of prints, and as teacher, had three markets for his work, and from this time forward we find the water-colour painter firmly established as a prosperous professional man.

Paul Sandby, as a member of the newly-founded Royal Academy, was at the height of his career by 1768, and in that year was appointed Chief Drawing Master at the Royal Military Academy, Woolwich, a post which he held until 1796, when he was succeeded by his son Thomas Paul, already known as a drawing-master practising with his father at St. George's Row. Benjamin West designed for him and Bartolozzi engraved a beautiful advertisement card, giving his terms as two guineas for eight lessons. Sandby was also chosen by George III as drawing-master to the young princes, 'another master of great talent, (J. A. Gresse) though inferior to Sandby, being selected as teacher to the female branches of the royal family'.[1] Apart from royalty he had an extensive circle of private pupils among the leading families of the time. One of his patrons was the Hon. Charles Greville, with whom, as well as with Sir Joseph Banks, he made many sketching-tours in England and Wales. It was Greville who passed on to Sandby the secret of the process of aquatint engraving, which he had learned from Jean Baptiste Le Prince. Sandby immediately began to experiment with the new process, and W. Sandby refers to a paper, written by his ancestor, described as *A Mode of Imitating Drawing on Copper Plates discovered by P. Sandby, R.A., in the Year 1775, to which he gave the Name of Aquatinta*.[2] The claim to the discovery of the process may seem an unfair assumption in view of the fact that Greville is said to have purchased the secret from Le Prince, but the paper, from which W. Sandby quotes at some

[1] *Magazine of the Fine Arts*, II, 1832, p. 434.
[2] W. Sandby, *Thomas and Paul Sandby*, 1892, p. 136; A. P. Oppé, 'Memoir of P. Sandby by his Son', *Burlington Magazine*, LXXXVIII, 1946.

length, shows that what Sandby did discover was the use of a spirit ground instead of the dust ground which had been previously employed.[1] Both methods are still in use to-day, each offering its own advantages and possibilities; aquatint, being a tone process, provides an ideal means of reproducing water-colour drawings, and was very extensively employed towards the close of the eighteenth century for this purpose. Extracts from two letters, written by Sandby to John Clerk of Eldin, an amateur etcher of repute,[2] show Sandby's pride and delight in his first experiments with the aquatint method.

London Sepr 8th 1775.

I perceive you have been trying at Le Prince's Secret, know my good Friend I got a key to it and am perfect master of it, you will perceive by the inclosed first trials of mine I soon made a progress in it, I have already done 24 views in Wales and 4 Large Warwicks which I will send you soon as they are published. I own no hobby horse in the world woud suit me eaqual to this, indeed I have rid so cloesly these 4 months past I have scarcely done anything else, the work is so delightful and easy to me now in the execution I do it with the same ease but with more pleasure than on paper. . . .

Your
much obliged and
most humble serv^t
P. Sandby.

(Not dated, but obviously later in 1775)

Dear Sir,
. . . If I shoud be so happy to bend my course to the North I will lay close siege to Edinb^r. unless you will save me the trouble by letting me have some of your sketches which I woud execute in Aquatinta. I dare not disclose to you any part of the method being sworn to secrecy, but I will venture to acquaint you so far, they are done on copper with aquafortis such as common brass or Bell Metal. Iron you may operate upon with a hair pencil after the outline is etch'd with great ease, thus far my Dear Friend I venture to communicate to you, tho' it is not the method I now use and dare not disclose to any body, I can assure you fine effects may be produced by these ways, you may also make the most agreable out line in the following way,[3] after the ground is lay'd on the copper and before you smoke the plate with a candle put the dabber into the Tallow, and dab the Etching ground well all over while the plate is hot, when you have lay'd it pretty eaqual and thin, smoke it as usual, when the plate is cold lay some thin post paper over it, taking care not to bruise the ground by pressing too hard. Draw your design or view with a black lead pencil, which will press thro' the ground and lay the out line bare to the copper which you may bite in with Aquafortis to what strength you please, this is a most enchanting method of making your out line for you will understand it saves all the trouble of Etching with a needle, and will produce an out line like fine Italian Chalk, if you make use of a needle upon the paper it will produce an out line bit in like a pen, I have inclosed a specimen of my own, which you have already with the Tints to it. now my worthy Friend I think you will be much pleased on trial of these hints which I beg you will not tell to any save the young Artist your son.

[1] Rimbault Dibdin, *Liverpool Art and Artists*, Walpole Soc., VI, 1917: proved that in 1773 P. P. Burdett exhibited a print giving the effect of a stained drawing attempted by printing from a plate wrought chemically, 'without the use of any instrument of sculpture'. It seems clear the P. P. Burdett, working at Liverpool with S. Chubbard anticipated Sandby in the use of aquatint, but Mr. Dibdin does not give definite proof that they discovered a liquid ground.
[2] E. S. Lumsden, 'The Etchings of John Clerk of Eldin', *Print Collectors' Quarterly*, XII, 1925, p. 15. The letters written by Sandby are in the Library of the Victoria and Albert Museum and were published in full in the *Print Collectors' Quarterly*, XX, 1933, p. 362.
[3] i.e. a description of the method of soft-ground etching.

I must now lay down my pen having several persons come to dine with me but will take it up again the first opportunity. . . .

I shall only take up a few moments more of your time to acquaint you I have done some Large Views of Warwick and Windsor which I shall send you about Christmas, I flatter my self you will be much pleased with them. . . .

I remain your Much Obliged Friend
P. Sandby.

In 1775 Sandby published *Twelve Views in Aquatinta from drawings taken on the spot in South Wales,* and followed these with further sets of Welsh views. In 1776 appeared *Four Views of Warwick Castle* and *Five Views of Windsor Castle,* mentioned in the above letter. He may be considered as the artistic discoverer of Wales as a sketching ground, and he opened a way which was later widened by Varley, Cox, Samuel Palmer and many others.

It is no small compliment to Sandby that the sets of aquatints served to some extent as a model to Turner for his *Liber Studiorum,* and it may be recalled that, though Turner changed over to mezzotint, he began his projected series in aquatint. Turner must have been impressed by the wide range and variety of Sandby's subjects; their ingathering of new material (for Sandby does not hesitate to make a dull *Iron Forge between Dolgelly and Barmouth* into an inspiring picture); their combination of superb architectural drawing with a genuine sympathy for life; and a powerful grasp of atmospheric effect. In these aquatints topographical draughtsmanship is no longer used for a cold rendering of show-places, but is instinct with warmth and emotion. The method may have induced him to employ for his drawings a broader style with greater perception of bold effects of light and shade. In dealing with skies and trees his work began to show much greater freedom and amplitude, with more truth in the reflected lights and clearness in the shadows. His son, indeed, assigns to this decade his finest tree studies. Gainsborough's painter of real views from Nature was becoming more personal and perceptive.

The remainder of Sandby's life was uneventful. He was a tireless worker, as we are told by his friend Gandon, who notes: 'Sandby was indefatigable in cultivating his powers as an artist. He commenced painting in water-colours very early in the morning; the pencil, and frequently the pen, seldom quitted his hand until evening, allowing himself only those hours dedicated to his repasts—at which merit frequently met with patronage and assistance, and his friends uniformly departed from his hospitable board delighted with his wit, conversation and manners.' Sandby himself writes in one of his letters to Gandon[1]: 'His Majesty was graciously pleased to say that I am never idle, but can turn my hand to anything: like a fox, I have many shifts, but none will make me independent, so that I must drive on until death drops me in a hole

In a house low and small
Here remains your friend Paul.'

His many portraits (there is an admirable one, by Francis Cotes, in the Tate Gallery) show

[1] W. Sandby, *op. cit.,* p. 174.

him as a man of average height and good figure, of fair complexion with slight colour, in youth thin, but in age stouter, wearing powdered hair and a peruke, with a slight double chin, somewhat puffy under his laughing brown eyes, wearing the coloured coats of his day, with ruffles, and the old three-cornered hat.

He exhibited regularly at the Society of Artists from 1760 to 1768, and at the Free Society in 1782 and 1783, in response to a cry for help from that moribund body. At the Royal Academy he exhibited almost every year from 1769 to 1809, and at the British Institution, which held its first exhibition in 1806, he exhibited in 1806 and 1808. In the latter year he was seventy-eight and still active and alert. Hazlitt noted with envy what happiness attends the old age of painters—'their minds keep alive to the last'; and that was certainly true of Paul Sandby.

Paul Sandby's work falls into two styles, concurrently used. In one he is following the Franco-Italian school of Claude and the Poussins, with a slight influence of Salvator Rosa. Here he is pandering to the traditional taste of the cultured classes who had been taught to believe that the essence of the sublime and beautiful in scenery (Burke's *Essay* was published in 1756) was distilled in the classical models. So it comes about that in one division of his work—usually in his pictures executed in body-colour—he deals with scenic landscape ornamented with stage trees and temples in the foreground, and ruins or a bridge in the middle distance against a mountainous background. Such was the formula of 'Elegant Pastoral' which Turner also revived in emulation of Claude. It is fortunate that Sandby, for the second division of his work, and particularly in his transparent water-colours, took off his classical-romantic spectacles and saw with his natural eyes, like the painters of the Dutch School. All through his work we find these two disparate aims, one looking to the Franco-Italian tradition for the ideal and imaginative, the other objective, imitative and bred of loving familiarity. As Cosmo Monkhouse pointed out,[1] Sandby probably never thought that his simpler, natural style would be considered the more deeply imaginative of the two.

These two aspects of his work are, as has been indicated, largely involved with two aspects of his technique. In one phase he was using transparent water-colour, where the whiteness of the paper remains as a ground giving brightness to transparent colour. In the other phase he employed body-colour, i.e. either distemper or gouache. Distemper—not to be confused with tempera, which implies the use of an egg medium—means the use of powdered colour mixed with some form of size or isinglass jelly and honey. The colour remains on the surface as in oil painting, and is not absorbed into the paper, as in pure water-colour painting. Gouache is the term usually applied to the use of colour ground in gum and water and mixed with Chinese white. In the employment of either method the colour has 'body'; it is opaque, and not transparent. When using body-colour the artist is working more or less as he does in oil, and can paint on a dark paper, or a paper 'dead-

[1] C. Monkhouse, *Earlier English Water-Colour Painters*, 1897, p. 16.

coloured', with any tint mixed with white. In the first method—the use of transparent water-colour—a painter is working from light to dark, every touch of colour adding a darker tone and obscuring his white paper still more, though with a certain amount of transparency. In the gouache or body-colour method he can work from dark to light, being able to add his most brilliant white in his final touch. The difference between the gouache and distemper method and that of oil-painting, is that an oil-painter can glaze a dark with a transparent colour, whereas every over-painting in body-colour implies the addition of a new opaque tint. There is always in distemper or gouache a somewhat dull, matt surface. Unfortunately, Sandby—or his patrons—thought that there was something more noble or classical about the body-colour method; at any rate, he seems to have used it by preference for his exhibited works and to have employed what we may consider the finer, transparent method for his own pleasure or when working for the engraver. A. J. Finberg, who was no admirer of the dull surface given by gouache or distemper, recommends a comparison of two drawings by Sandby in the British Museum, the transparent *Windsor*[1] (Pl. 77) and the distemper *Carrick Ferry*,[2] finding that 'the *Windsor* produces a quite remarkable illusion of light and air, while the *Carrick Ferry* seems mere dead, opaque paint . . . the poverty of the distemper medium is most conspicuous in the darker parts, the rocks, trees and castle standing dark against the sunset . . . there is no illusion of reality'. In 1832 it was still possible for a writer to say about Sandby: 'His superior style, and that on which he hoped to establish a lasting reputation, was that in which he wrought in body-colour painting.'[3] His drawings where he uses gouache, not in elaborate classical composition, but simply and lightly, with a pleasant feeling of pastel—*Windsor Castle: the North Terrace*[4] is a good example—appeal more to the modern mind.

As it is my purpose to dwell on the technical aspect, I need not hesitate to quote in full a description of Sandby's method of painting in body-colours, contained in the diary of his friend, Colonel Gravatt, R.E.[5]

> *October 25, 1802.*—Went to Mr. Sandby's by appointment, at eleven in the forenoon, to see him paint a picture in water colours—subject: A View inland of Conway Castle (18 in. × 13 in.).
> *Method.*—The pasteboard being tacked down to a board, he first washed it over with isinglass jelly, mixed with a little honey, to prevent the paper from sinking or absorbing the colours, and, when nearly dry, he painted the *whole* of the paper over with azure (composed of verditer, common powder blue, and white). I observed he painted it with a soft *hog's hair tool*, pretty thick towards the top of the picture, and diluted it more with isinglass as he approached the horizon and lighter parts of the sky; but all the picture beneath the horizontal line was painted (in azure) with a good body of colour. He did not repeat the operation to form his sky, as the colour laid perfectly even, but would have done so if there had been a necessity, and with a soft large hog's hair tool.

[1] B.M. 1878. 7.13.1280 (L. B. 109).
[2] B.M. 1890. 8.6.6.
[3] 'On the study of landscape and nature', *Magazine of the Fine Arts*, I, 1832, p. 122.
[4] V.A.M. 1832–1904.
[5] W. Sandby, *op. cit.*, pp. 116–122.

106

He next laid in the seat of the sun with yellow ochre and white, diluting it with gin, melting it gradually into the azure (previously dry) by adding more gin; he then sketched the design (omitting the foreground) with care and fidelity, using for this purpose a black-lead pencil; and having composed a neutral tint of Prussian blue, Indian ink, and white, with isinglass, he proceeded to shadow the picture exactly as is done in forming transparent drawings, making the tint thin with gin, sometimes adding a little gum water, adding also more blue (verditer) or more black in proportion as the objects in the picture receded or approached the eye. In this operation he left the broad lights (as in tinting), but entirely neglected those small sharp touches which form as it were the *glitter* of the picture, they being more advantageously expressed by white plump touches.

I particularly remarked he did not, even in the nearest lights, allow the azure (previously painted as a ground) to appear, so that the whole landscape was of a lower tone than the sky, which is what gives such admirable clearness to his skies, and which (by the way) cannot be obtained to perfection except on a *white ground*, i.e. the paper.

After he had laid on two shades to (say) the half-tint and shadow, over the whole drawing, and which he did with a *small* camel's hair pencil, and so thin that the pencilled outline could be easily discerned, he pencilled in his foreground, consisting chiefly of a large tree, which reached nearly to the top of the picture; he then shadowed it as before, adding of course more black, and making the branches, or as it were the anatomy, of the tree first. To express the foliage he diluted the tint with gin, to form a strength of tint proper for the *middle tint*, with which he covered the whole place of the foliage, without regarding lights, leaving them for the opaque colours, and the shadows for a second operation. As this tree was against the great light of the sky, he added a little yellow ochre to the tint, to express that semi-transparency which leaves so situated assume. This, of course, did not apply to the capacity of the stem and branches.

I observed in working his picture he usually *began* with the second shades, and laid in the demi-tints afterwards; but that is a matter of no moment, except that by so doing the outline was probably better preserved.

30th October; second day.—He worked his design up a good deal with transparent colours, forming a neutral tint, and then added local colours, beginning with the distance, in which his greens were formed of Naples yellow, verditer, and such-like semi-transparent colours, and in proportion, as he advanced nearer the foreground, added brown ochre, sap-green, and any strong colour that suited the purpose. The whole was laid in rather thin in the broad lights, and still more diluted in the shadows, many places being left entirely without colour, which gives great air to the picture. In some places he helped this vapourish appearance by the addition of a little verditer laid thinly over the shadows.

The green in the front tree was sap-green, used thin. The whole picture being thus dead-coloured, had that sort of appearance which an artist would gladly conceal from those who are unversed in painting.

31st October.—The bluish shadows in the distance were added of verditer, Prussian blue, lake, etc. with a mixture of white done thin; next came the plump touches in the lights of white mixed with the local colour; these which form the heightening of the dead-colouring (not laid in masses), gave astonishing life to the picture; in doing these he added isinglass. Then came the sharp touches of bistre, etc., and after them thin washes, laid over the bistre touches, plump lights, and, in short, wherever the picture wanted harmony, and again plump touches over these where the picture wanted to be heightened. Last of all came the figures: these being sketched in pencil, he shadowed with darkish colour, quite transparent (using no Indian ink tint in those quite in front), and then added thick white in the lights, and upon them the local colours, and pretty much in a body, and worked up the whole to effect by treacle-brown and other strong colours.

In a subsequent note by Colonel Gravatt, there is a further description of Paul Sandby's manner of tempera painting when in his seventy-fifth year:

Saturday, 7 December, 1805.—Spent the day with my friend, Paul Sandby, Esq., who made me a present of a painted sketch of an oak-tree, which he painted whilst I was with him in about two hours. He began by mixing liquid black, verditer, and white for a dull sky, which he covered the paper with. Sketched the subject, and having made the ramifications with the neutral tint, diluted it, and just gave the rounding of the foliage, leaving the broad lights on the leaves as in staining; laid aside the black and finished with colours, which he recommended me to do in order to get out of a black manner I was sensible I habituated myself to. The tree (an oak) was dead-coloured, this with brown ochre and a little blue (verditer), and the deeper shadows with a brownish-green, Spanish liquorice, and indigo, broken with red in some places, and then the extreme heightenings added with patent yellow and white with a little blue. Towards the top of the foliage he deadened it a little by adding gamboge—lastly, ran over and mellowed the whole with transparent browns, greens, etc.

Following on this description we may repeat that nowadays we use the term body-colour to cover both the use of distemper, i.e. dry colour with size as a medium and the so-called gouache method of using colour mixed with water and Chinese white, though in many cases size and Chinese white may both be employed. Colour mixed with Chinese white and worked wetly on the paper is absorbed more readily; and flaking in some of Sandby's work and in body-colour drawings by Keate and Laporte is clearly due to the use of distemper. Colour mixed with size will lighten and become duller than colour mixed with Chinese white, and this accounts probably for the pastel-like appearance of work by Sandby and also by Wilson and Taverner. In much of his work, we constantly find Sandby, like George Robertson, hybridising pure water-colour with the elements of body-colour technique.

In transparent water-colour his methods were those of his time. He drew his outline with the pen and, being an etcher from the start, seems to have had a preference for a fine point, working with a thin, even line like that produced by the etching needle. It must not, however, be thought that this was an invariable habit, for Sandby, both in line and colour, was widely experimental. In one of his most charming drawings, the *Woodyard, Windsor Great Park*,[1] with its perfect harmony of grey, green and yellow in low tones that are far from excluding sunshine, he used a broad reed-pen for the free sketching of his subject in line. And in many of his larger drawings of tree subjects, trunks, branches and foliage are dashed in with wide strokes of the reed-pen. On the whole, however, he drew with a fine line. The shadows were then washed in with Indian ink and the local colour applied last of all. In this class of work he was very sparing of colour, using only enough to differentiate objects and to add a certain gaiety. His drawing is so refined that with a limited palette—apparently little more than ivory, black, indigo, burnt sienna and yellow ochre—he gives complete satisfaction with his colour scheme. There were no over-bright local colours to interfere with the tonal effect. Washes were laid in an orderly way and left to dry; there was no

[1] B.M. 1904. 8.19.24.

chance of one blurred colour breaking into the next; 'broken colour' was unknown. One thing that Sandby and the early topographers secured by this method was a just and proper management of values in their true sequence from foreground to remote distance; and it was on this basis of knowledge that Girtin and Turner rose to much greater heights.

Two further points with regard to his technique may be briefly noted. One is his clear grasp of perspective (probably absorbed from his architect brother) which enabled him, like Malton, to give to his architecture a true construction and recession, and not merely a picturesque aspect. His drawing in the Windsor Library of the *Upper Ward of Windsor Castle, from the North Terrace*, in 1777, has not been carried further than a pencil outline, but its perspective is carefully studied and is drawn with all the measured accuracy of an architect. It is partly, perhaps, from his knowledge of perspective that his figure groups are always admirable in composition, individuality and scale, a point in which so many landscape painters go astray, as will be found in the case of Dayes. And let us say here that, though Malton's perspective is sound, Sandby is more alive to see distinction and individuality in the character and shapes of buildings, trees or figures. Though he is observant and accurate like Malton, he is more human and genial. Malton could never have made that charming drawing of the little daughters of Lord Waldegrave with Miss Keppell,[1] all in a row like marigolds, in the grounds of Windsor Castle.

The second point is that from constant study in Windsor Forest he had gained a thorough understanding of trees and their growth. He had difficulties, in dealing with foliage. Girtin had not yet shown the way to massive simplification, and Sandby tries various formulae. You cannot instantly identify a Sandby drawing by the handling of foliage, as is possible with, say, Payne or Glover. One group of his work—*The Round Ruined Temple*[2] is a good example—would seem to resemble Gainsborough, drawing free horizontal lines and flecks across his trees, and breaking the contours into loops and feathery edges. In another mood he might seem to owe something to Ruisdael in the use of crisp, angular edges, possibly gaining vitality at the cost of repose. Down to about 1800, this handwriting or shorthand comes into nearly all water-colours, for they depend for the most part on a precise underlying structure of line drawing in pencil or ink; the colour is restrained, and rarely obscures the drawing. From the time of Girtin onwards certain artists started to treat their subjects in a painterly rather than a linear manner. Sandby comes into both camps, for in his pure water-colours there is always the basis of line, whereas in his body-colour method he is studying masses in the manner of the painter in oil.

The value of Sandby's work in water-colour derives from its own intrinsic, and somewhat limited, merits. When he died, Girtin's brief life had already ended, and Turner was in the ascendant. Sandby is the last, as he is the greatest, of the topographers. But his work, if judged, as it must be, by what preceded it, is perhaps the finest in the strict English tradition. He was not an original artist like Turner or Cozens; he was of his age and gave

[1] V.A.M. 1855–1904.
[2] V.A.M. 561.

it what it liked and could understand. The rapid development of water-colour, which began before his death, left no longer any room for such an art as Sandby's. But we like to give one last look at him, as Henry Angelo saw him, seated at his window, in his late seventies sketching effects of light and shadow in Hyde Park, opposite to his house. And we like to think of him, in his eightieth year, painting small landscape designs in body-colours on little cards, as New Year gifts to ladies who had been favourite pupils in early days. It was but a step from the window where he sat, so happily engaged, to the burial-ground of St. George's, Hanover Square, behind the Chapel of the Ascension in the Bayswater Road. When Paul Sandby died Turner was thirty-four, Constable thirty-three, Varley thirty-one, Cotman twenty-seven, Cox and Prout twenty-six, and De Wint twenty-five. Rowlandson, always young in outlook, was a veteran of fifty-three.

Though there are many good examples of Paul Sandby's work in the Victoria and Albert Museum, the student is advised, in order to see him at his best and in his full range, to study the fine collections of his work at the British Museum and in the Library of Windsor Castle.

We have described the methods which Sandby employed and have quoted a contemporary account of his work in body-colour, but it remains difficult to say how he came to adopt a process which had not previously been employed in English landscape drawing. It was, of course, no new thing. The old painters of illuminations were familiar with it. Gaspard Poussin (1613–1675) employed it for a well-known series of his works. In Holland artists such as Jordaens, Van Huysum, P. de Koninck, and many others, worked in body-colour. Among the first who introduced to this country the art of painting in body-colour were possibly the members of the Goupy family. Joseph Goupy (1689–1763), of French extraction, and nephew of Louis Goupy who was established in England as a well-known teacher of drawing, was born in London and lived there till his death. He became a favourite of George I, and was often invited to dine at the Palace, when the King would send him dishes from his own table, and bottles of his favourite wines.[1] Among his pupils were George I's grandson, Frederick, Prince of Wales, the Princess of Wales and their eldest son. Frederick remained a staunch patron, and Goupy's continued connection with royalty made him for years the most fashionable of drawing-masters. Goupy, like many other artists of his time and later, was occupied occasionally with scene-painting, for which distemper has always been employed. His practice as a scene-painter may have led him to experiment with the size process on a small scale. His *Landscape with Figures*[2] (Pl. 87) is a good example of his work in body-colour. The blue of the sky has a powdery, pastel-like appearance, suggesting that the method was distemper and not ordinary gouache.

Another painter who, as Vertue suggests, helped to introduce the method into England was Marco Ricci (1676–1729), who was born at Belluno and came to London in 1710. In a long series of landscapes, Ricci employed gouache effectively and with considerable

[1] Whitley, 1700–1799, I, p. 75.
[2] B.M. Gg. 3–365.

distinction. He died at Venice. At Windsor or in London Sandby may have seen body-colour paintings by Goupy or Ricci in the classical manner, with ruins or temples in a carefully composed setting of landscape. Charles Clérisseau (1721–1820), Sandby's senior by three years, and Jean Pillement (*c.* 1728–1808) both worked extensively abroad for English patrons, and both came to England, the former about 1770, the latter about 1757. Walpole describes Clérisseau as a Frenchman lately arrived, famous for the beauty and neatness of his drawings from the Antique. He was master of Mr. Adam when at Rome. Francesco Zuccarelli (1702–1788), painted decorative landscapes in body-colour, with pastoral scenes of shepherds and their flocks and herds, and became very popular throughout Europe. In Venice he found a patron in Consul Smith, who recommended him to visit England. Remaining here for five years he returned to Venice, but stayed in London for the second time from about 1752 to 1773. Zuccarelli and Sandby were foundation members of the Royal Academy and, with Clérisseau, members of the Society of Artists. Three landscapes by Zuccarelli in the Victoria and Albert Museum[1] show his use of body-colour. Sandby, then, might well have seen paintings by Goupy, Ricci, Zuccarelli, or early work by Clérisseau or Pillement. Painting in gouache which could be a quick and showy method of making popular landscapes, degenerated later on the Continent into a tourist-traffic of fan-painting and of lurid views of Naples and Vesuvius.

Sandby's inventive and experimental mind enabled him to paint in body-colour examples, such as *Carrick Ferry*,[2] exhibited at the Royal Academy in 1801, that could hang side by side with oil-paintings with more effect than the delicately tinted drawings of that time.

Enough has been said to show that body-colour painting had considerable vogue in the last half of the eighteenth century and that Sandby was not alone in his use of it. That he was one of the first native born artists to employ the method is proved by the fact that there are touches of body-colour in drawings made by him in Scotland in 1751; and in 1753 he used body-colour for picturing a *Chinese junk on its way to Virginia Water*.[3]

We have already mentioned William Taverner who, to some extent, may challenge Sandby's claim to be the father of the English school both of pure water-colour and of body-colour. Unfortunately, we do not know the date of a body-colour by him at the British Museum of *Sandpits, Woolwich*[4] (Pl. 34), formerly in the possession of Sandby, and bought by the British Museum at the Percy Sale in 1890, or of his *Classic Landscape*[5] (Pl. 36), also in body-colour, at the Victoria and Albert Museum. The *Sandpits, Woolwich*, is probably an early work, being made on three pieces of paper joined together. With its grandiose style it suggests Salvator Rosa taking a stroll at Woolwich; and it has a somewhat scattered interest of hillocks, figures and Salvator trees; but it is all bound together

[1] V.A.M. D.697–699.
[2] B.M. 1890. 8.6.6.
[3] V.A.M. 113–1898.
[4] B.M. 1890. 5.12.140.
[5] V.A.M. 443.

by the heavy waggon coming round the bend of the road, with a flash of light on the white horse, the cart and driver being left dark against the sunlit background. The waggon and road are thoroughly English and a fine detail in a noble drawing.

George Keate (1729–1797), intended originally for the Bar, was an amateur like Taverner, and a writer. With Sandby and Zuccarelli he was a member of the Incorporated Society of Artists, and is linked with Sandby at an early stage in the use of body-colour, e.g. his *Bridge over the Rhone at Avignon*[1] (Pl. 89) is dated 1754. His *Distant View of Southampton taken from Pear Tree Green,*[2] painted in 1767 and exhibited at the Royal Academy in 1780, shows that he was equally at home with pure water-colour. Other artists working in body-colour contemporary with Sandby, who should be mentioned are John Laporte (1761–1839) *View at Shalfleet, Isle of Wight*[3] (Pl. 90); Thomas Walmsley (1763–1805) *Bowness and part of the lake of Windermere*[4]; W. Fearnside (Exhibited R.A. 1791–1801) *Landscape and watermill*[5] (Pl. 88); Richard Reinagle R.A. (1775–1862) *View in the Island of Capri*[6] 1799 (Pl. 93); George Cuitt (1743–1818) *Aysgarth Bridge, Yorkshire*[7] (Pl. 92).

[1] V.A.M. 685–1877.
[2] V.A.M. P.30–1933.
[3] V.A.M. 816–1877.
[4] V.A.M. P.21–1925.
[5] V.A.M. 1811–1900.
[6] V.A.M. 188–1890.
[7] B.M. 1881. 11.12.175.

ADDENDUM

Since the production of this volume started the Editors have had the opportunity to consult the doctoral thesis on the Sandbys by Dr. Johnson Ball, deposited in the Library of the University of Nottingham. This study has usefully corrected certain traditional biographical information on these artists and has especially served to establish their dates of birth. It has been possible to adjust the dates in the foregoing chapter in accord with Dr. Johnson Ball's findings and make certain other amendments, but students of the subject are recommended to consult his thesis.

75 'Draw Well at Broughton near Edinburgh'
B.M. 1904.8.19.95   6¼ × 8⅞: 159 × 225   *Water-colour, signed and dated 1751*
Paul SANDBY, R.A. (1730–1809)

76 'A Country Girl'

H.M. The Queen (14438) $7\frac{5}{8} \times 5\frac{3}{8}$: 195 × 135   *Water-colour*

Paul SANDBY, R.A. (1730–1809)

77 'Windsor'

B.M. 1878.7.13.1280 $10\frac{7}{8} \times 22\frac{1}{8}$: 276 × 562   *Water-colour*

Paul SANDBY, R.A. (1730–1809)

78 'The Magic Lantern'

B.M. 1862.10.11.1890 $14\frac{3}{4} \times 21\frac{1}{4}$: 375 × 540   *Water-colour and body-colour*

Paul SANDBY, R.A. (1730–1809)

79 'The Gate at Reading'

Coll. Mrs Cecil Keith   8¾ × 13¾: 222 × 349   *Water-colour*

Paul SANDBY, R.A. (1730–1809)

80 'An Ancient Beech Tree'

V.A.M. 383   27⅝ × 41⅝: 702 × 1058   *Gouache, signed and dated 1794*

Paul SANDBY, R.A. (1730–1809)

81 'View through Queen Elizabeth's Gate, Windsor'
H.M. The Queen (14546)   12½ × 18⅜: 318 × 467   *Water-colour*
Paul SANDBY, R.A. (1730–1809)

82 'A Woman Attacked by a Bear'
B.M. 1904.8.19.10 (L.B.121)   12¼ × 19¾: 312 × 502   *Pen and water-colour*
Paul SANDBY, R.A. (1730–1809)

83 'The Meteor of Aug. 18, 1783, seen from the Terrace at Windsor Castle'
B.M. (album) 1904.8.19.34   11¼ × 18: 285 × 459   *Water-colour*
Thomas SANDBY, R.A. (1723–1798)

84 'Figures for the same Design'
B.M. (album) 1904.8.19.35   12⅝ × 20: 320 × 510   *Water-colour*
Thomas SANDBY, R.A. (1723–1798)

85 'Design for Triumphal Bridge across the Thames at Somerset House'
B.M. (album) 1904.8.19.418 $9\frac{7}{8} \times 18\frac{3}{4}$: 252 × 475   *Water-colour, signed*
Thomas SANDBY, R.A. (1723–1798)

86 'Landscape, with a Country Festival'
B.M. 1910.2.12.41 $10\frac{3}{4} \times 16\frac{3}{8}$: 273 × 416   *Body-colour*
Francesco ZUCCARELLI, R.A. (1702–1788)

87 'Landscape with Figures'

B.M. Gg.3–365   7¼ × 8¾: 184 × 222   *Body-colour*

Joseph GOUPY (1689–1763)

88 'Landscape, with Water Mill and Figures'

V.A.M. 1811–1900 $16\frac{1}{2} \times 22\frac{3}{8}$: 420 × 594

Water-colour and body-colour, signed and dated 1791

W. FEARNSIDE (Exhibited 1791–1801)

89 'The Bridge at Avignon'

V.A.M. 685–1877   10¾ × 14½: 260 × 369   *Body-colour, signed and dated 1754*

George KEATE, F.R.S. (1729–1797)

90 'View at Shalfleet, Isle of Wight'

V.A.M. 816–1877   16¾ × 25: 426 × 635   *Body-colour, signed and dated 1790*

John LAPORTE (1791–1839)

91 'West End of Netley Abbey'
V.A.M. 480–1875   10⅜ × 16: 264 × 407   *Body-colour*
Thomas WALMSLEY (1763–1805 or 1806)

92 'Aysgarth Bridge, Yorkshire'
B.M. 1881.11.12.175   14 × 19¾: 355 × 502   *Indian ink and water-colour*
George CUITT (1743–1818)

93 'View in the Island of Capri'

V.A.M. 188–1890 $21\frac{3}{4} \times 16\frac{1}{2}$: 553 × 420   *Body-colour, signed and dated 1799*

Ramsay Richard REINAGLE, R.A. (1775–1862)

CHAPTER VI

Francis Towne and his followers

John 'Warwick' Smith   Francis Towne   John White Abbott
John Baverstock Knight

This chapter, whose main subject is Towne, may well begin with John 'Warwick' Smith; he forms a link between Pars and Towne, and was Towne's friend and rival. John Smith (1749–1831) became known as 'Warwick' Smith either because he had the Earl of Warwick as his patron—this is the explanation given by Roget and others—or, as is more likely, because he resided at Warwick from about 1781, was married there in 1783, and became known as 'Warwick' Smith, as Joseph Wright was known as Wright of Derby. The details of Smith's life are given by Farington.[1] He was born at Irthington (Farington calls it Hetherington) in Cumberland, and was son of the gardener to Mrs. Appleby, sister of Captain John Bernard Gilpin, an amateur artist and father of William Gilpin and Sawrey Gilpin, R.A. Smith had some lessons from Captain Gilpin, who then sent him to study under Sawrey Gilpin. While staying with the latter at Sir Harry Harper's seat in Derbyshire, Smith made the acquaintance of Lord Warwick, the second Earl (Harper's brother-in-law), then about twenty-nine years of age, and himself a keen draughtsman. Pyne describes Lord Warwick as having 'acquired a rapid and masterly style of sketching landscape. His fancy in designing rocks and waterfalls, and that species of romantic scenery which abounds in the mountainous parts of Switzerland and Italy, was so prolific that many subjects could have been selected from his numerous portfolios which might, in the hands of an able artist, have been wrought into magnificent pictures'.[2]

Lord Warwick was so pleased with some sketches made by Smith at Matlock that he offered to send him to study in Italy, and supported him there for five years. A collection of water-colours made in Switzerland by 'Warwick' Smith was acquired by his patron and was preserved in albums at Warwick Castle, little known and little seen until 1936. The existence of similar albums elsewhere suggests that Smith himself may have assembled them. His drawings which have been protected in this way and saved from the destructive effects of sunlight are in perfect and unfaded condition. In 1936 the Swiss Drawings from the Warwick collection, which had never changed hands since the artist parted with

---

[1] *Diary*, February 14, 1797: See also *Roget*; W. Jackson, ed. *William Gilpin's Memoirs*, 1879; B. S. Long, *John Warwick Smith* (with list of his exhibited works), Walker's Quarterly, 24, 1928; Iolo Williams, 'John Warwick Smith', *Old Water Colour Society*, XXIV, 1946.
[2] *Somerset House Gazette*, 1824–1825, I, p. 30.

113

them, were sold.[1] One album, containing twenty-one views in Rome, and twenty-two drawings in the neighbourhood of Tenby (the Welsh drawings mostly dated 1787), was acquired by the British Museum. In many of these drawings the formal design and flat patterning, echoes the grey-blues and grey-greens of Cozens. It may be assumed that the Swiss drawings were made in the autumn of 1781, when Smith was travelling homewards through Switzerland in the company of Towne, or perhaps on a later visit to Italy,[2] with his patron. In these Swiss drawings his colour, however clean and translucent in its washes, seems timid and his drawing somewhat lacking in force. He was among the pioneers, but the praise lavished upon Smith as a colourist at the beginning of the last century was not quite merited.

Till these drawings came to light, little had been known of Smith's activities in Italy during this period, 1776 to 1781, but a drawing of *The Crater of Vesuvius*[3] is dated 1778. At Rome he was probably in close contact with Pars, who was living there from 1775 till his death in 1782, and also with Towne, who travelled back in his company through Switzerland in the autumn of 1781. Pars had long been an intimate friend of Towne, and the three of them probably went sketching together, each unconsciously absorbing something from the other and fusing it into his own method. All three have obvious phases of affinity. I believe that Smith, nine years younger than Towne, already the possessor of an individual and original style, was very strongly influenced by the method and outlook of his older companion.

On his return to England Smith made Warwick his headquarters, and contributed six drawings for illustrations, which were engraved in 1784 and 1785, to Middiman's *Select Views in Great Britain*. Smith was at work in Wales in 1784 and 1785.[4] Basil Long describes all of his Welsh tours, and the only new information to be added is that Mrs. Chance owns a collection of drawings by Smith of scenery in the Lakes, with dates ranging from 1789 to 1792. These drawings have been preserved in a large album and retain all the original freshness of their brilliant colour. The *Entrance to Borrowdale*, lent by Mrs. Chance to the 200th exhibition of the Royal Water-Colour Society in March 1933, was a fine and typical example.

[1] Sotheby's, June 17, 29, 30, 1936.
[2] Redgrave, Roget, Long, the B.M. and the D.N.B. all suggest different dates for a visit to Italy in the company of the Earl of Warwick. Iolo Williams suggests that Smith's only visit to Italy was for the years 1776 to 1781. If so, the Chamonix drawings (B.M. and V.A.M.) dated 1786, must have been made (as is quite possible) from earlier sketches. Williams can find no evidence that Warwick ever visited Italy, but it is difficult to believe that a cultured aristocrat of Warwick's type and period never made the grand tour. Possibly he was in Italy, as Smith's patron, at some time between 1776 and 1781.
[3] B.M. 1871. 11.11.1.
[4] During the next twenty years or more Smith made frequent tours in Wales. Long (*op. cit.*) gives details, based upon dated drawings of his itineraries in different years. Seven hundred or more drawings were bought from the artist by Lord Warwick, but have since been dispersed among his heirs and their descendants, while many have been sold. Long's information was based on those drawings, 360 of which belonged in 1928 to L. Kashnor. Several drawings from the Warwick Collection were exhibited at the Fine Art Society in 1941. The largest of them (it had been folded in one of the three portfolios from which they came), *The Piedmont descending the Val d'Aosta*, with windswept trees below and tall cliffs on the right, had something of the Cozens spirit in its grandeur and austerity.

114

In 1792 began the publication of Smith's *Select Views in Italy*, illustrated by engravings bearing dates up to 1799. In 1794 appeared W. Sotheby's *Tour through Parts of Wales*, with admirable aquatints by S. Alken from Smith's drawings taken on the spot. In December 1805, Smith was elected an associate of the Old Water-Colour Society, formed in the previous year. He had been very hesitant about joining in its formation owing to his unwillingness to incur any financial liability. Farington wrote that: 'He [Sawrey Gilpin] told me that the Artists who are members of the Brook Street Society for exhibiting drawings, have taken more money this year than the last, abt. £200 more. They divide the whole of what is left after paying the Expences. Their rule is to divide in proportion to the amount of the price of the whole of what each member exhibits . . . Warwick Smith now means to belong to them.' Smith was elected a full member of the Society in December 1806, but maintained his cautious attitude till 1807, when he sent nineteen drawings, one of which, a view of the Colosseum, was considered by Sir George Beaumont to be the best in the room.[1] In the following years most of his exhibits were drawings of Italian and Swiss scenes, worked up from his earlier material. In 1812 a split occurred in the Society, partly with regard to the admission of oils. It was dissolved on December 3, but reconstituted soon after, Smith being appointed Secretary. He was President in 1814, 1817 and 1818. In 1823 he exhibited for the last time. From 1807 or earlier he was living at 7, St. George's Row, Oxford Street: Sandby was still at No. 4, and Girtin had lived at No. 2 or 9. In 1814 or 1815 he removed from St. George's Row to 25, Bryanston Street, and left there at some unknown date, for his death occurred at Middlesex Place, Marylebone Road. He was buried in the vault under St. George's Chapel, Uxbridge Road, 'by the little row of houses', says Roget, 'which contained his old studio and those of Paul Sandby and Tom Girtin, between whose schools of painting, he had in a former age fashioned a connecting link'.

About Smith's method of work and his influence there is a good deal of contemporary evidence. Sir Richard Colt Hoare, in his *Tour through the Island of Elba*, 1814, pays a tribute to Smith as a teacher, and a passage already quoted in full from his *Modern History of South Wiltshire*, 1822, says that, after Sandby, 'The next marked improvement in colouring was recognised in the drawings of Mr. John Smith.' In 1808 Farington felt that Smith amended nature considerably in his topographical drawings and that, in one case, 'His view was in every respect incorrect'.[2] 'In tinted drawings,' wrote Julius Caesar Ibbetson, 'no one, I believe, ever came so near the tint of nature as Mr. John Smith; they will always retain their value when the dashing, doubtful style has been long exploded, in which everything appears like a confused dream of nature.'[3] It has been said that[4]:

[1] *Diary*, May 8, 1807.
[2] On Sunday, November 16, 1799, Farington recorded that: 'Turner called—He reprobated the mechanically systematic process of drawing practised by Smith and from him so generally diffused. He thinks it can produce nothing but manner and sameness . . . Turner has no settled process but drives his colours about till he has expressed the idea in his mind.'
[3] *An Accidence or Gamut, of Painting in Oil*, 1828, p. 11.
[4] Ackermann, *Repository of Art*, VIII, 1812, p. 260.

Smith was the first artist who attempted to unite depth and richness of colour, with the clearness and aerial effect of Cozens. He studied the paintings of Claude de Lorraine, Poussin, and other eminent Italian artists, with great attention, and thereby rendered himself master of the principles of his art. Thus prepared, Smith made excursions amidst the beautiful, the wild, and the grand scenery of Italy, and explored these classic regions that had been trodden by the painters whose works he had recently contemplated: here he made studies in colour of the effects of nature, and acquired that power which raised him much above his competitors. Splendour of colour and richness of effect had not yet been exhibited by any professor of his department; the richness of Smith's hues surprised and delighted every lover of the art. Indeed, it may with truth be said, that with this artist the first epoch of painting in water colours originated.

W. H. Pyne says of Smith[1]:

Next on the list is John Smith, cognomened 'Warwick Smith' . . . It is due to this ingenious draughtsman of the old school, to assign to him the credit of being the first who successfully aimed at producing that force in water colours, which assumed the appearance of a picture, properly so designated, some of his Italian scenery, although the *chiaroscuro* was prepared with grey, being tinted almost up to the force of oil painting. To use the phrase of Gainsborough, Smith was the first professor of water colour art, who had 'carried his intention through'. His most successful works, though not many in number, certainly surpassed in the union of light, shadow, and colour, all that had been produced before.

These laudatory notices appear to require qualification when we come to examine his actual work. He seems usually to have sketched in his landscape with pencil before applying his colour. In many cases he was adding colour over a preliminary drawing in ink, as was Towne's practice, but Smith frequently uses no obvious outline at all, as in his *Bridge of Augustus, Rimini,* 1795,[2] and *Glacier des Bossons, Chamouni,* 1786.[3] The drawings, which were made in the Lake district from 1789 to 1792, are carefully drawn in with pencil, and if ink is used, it is only for dark touches in the foreground. There is no first wash of monochrome; the local colour is painted direct, and the shadows added at the last. His colouring in these and other drawings is bright but lacking in richness and subtlety. However great the impression which he made in his life-time, as shown by the quoted accounts of his work, he was not quite so much of an innovator as they suggest. He was following tradition in his use of monochrome under-painting, and even when he made use of a direct application of local colour, obtaining depth not by underlying grey, but by superimposing wash on wash of pure colour, he was not actually doing more than Taverner and Skelton, Pars and Towne, had already done. In his *Cumae* of 1793 and his *Tivoli* of 1795, he was passing beyond mere tinting and seeking a fuller use of pigment, but in his *Val d'Aosta,* dated 1803, he returns to the more cautious tinted manner. The earlier water-colour painters, even Girtin, hovered between the traditional and the advanced method.

---

[1] Arnold's *Library of the Fine Arts,* I, 1833, p. 311.
[2] B.M. 1871. 11.11.9.
[3] B.M. 1871. 11.11.3.

Smith's earlier Alpine and Italian drawings are marked by a grey-blue colour scheme, with touches of dark green, russet and red. One feels that he was influenced first by Cozens, and then much more strongly by Towne, whose Roman drawings far surpassed in colouring anything that Smith achieved. It must be concluded that Towne, almost unknown as an exhibitor and completely unassuming so far as his water-colours were concerned, altogether escaped the discerning eye of Sir Richard Colt Hoare, and was not discovered by contemporary critics. The emergence of his drawings in bulk caused a new assessment of his art, and proves beyond doubt that Smith was in Towne's debt for anything new and remarkable in his colouring. Farington seems to give the opposite impression by quoting Patch, an Exeter clergyman, to the effect that Towne 'went to Italy with W. Smith of St. George's Row, Oxford Turnpike, and afterwards imitated his manner of drawing',[1] but it is now quite clear that Towne's style had crystallised, though not reaching its fullest expression, by the time of his Welsh drawings in 1777, while Smith's Roman drawings, made much later, show very strong traces of Towne's manner. In Towne's very individual work there are no obvious traces of the influence of Smith, but several drawings by the latter are definitely in the style of Towne. *Terracina*[2] is almost a deliberate imitation of Towne, showing his strength of line and flat planes of colour, but tailing off into the more trite and pretentious manner characteristic of Smith. It seems that 'Warwick' Smith, or 'Italian' Smith, as he was sometimes described, on account of his large output of Italian subjects, had a somewhat undeserved vogue, but in his own way he helped to introduce direct colour and reflects the process of departure from classic formalism which was finally completed by Girtin.

Until the 1920's the three artists—Francis Towne, White Abbott and Baverstock Knight—remaining to be dealt with in this chapter, were, like Alexander Cozens, practically unknown. Their contemporaries did not rate them very highly, and an even more profound obscurity shrouded them after their death, for until 1920 they are barely mentioned in any of the publications dealing with the history of water-colour. With each of them the reason is the same: their clientèle was largely local; they were primarily, and not very successfully, painters in oils; and their water-colours, which they made either as a basis for an oil painting or an engraving, or else simply for their own pleasure in handling the medium, embodied qualities which were less appreciated in their time than in ours. In the case of each of them, the chief quality of their drawings lies in their search for structure and their simplification of method. The water-colours of Towne, of his followers, White Abbott and Baverstock Knight, depend upon refinement of pattern and design. Their work, with its delicate precision of outline, its flat washes of subdued colour, and its skilful handling of receding planes, awakened an immediate response in the minds of those in the early twentieth century to whom Japanese art had been an inspiring revelation. But anyone whose ideal was embodied in the full-blooded landscapes of Poussin and

[1] *Diary*, November 11, 1810.
[2] V.A.M. 581.

117

Claude must have thought their work thin, weak and insipid. Not that their own age was given much opportunity to judge, for none of them ever attempted to exhibit his water-colour drawings. Consequently, their influence on the contemporary development of water-colour was negligible, and they form a small isolated group, immensely interesting for their approach to methods of design which were never completely understood till more than half a century after the last of them was dead. Their resurrection and sudden leap to fame are due mainly to A. P. Oppé, who published a long critical article on Towne[1] and followed it up with a similar article on Abbott[2]; while J. B. Knight owes his revival to an article by D. S. MacColl,[3] and to the acquisition in that year of several of his drawings by the Victoria and Albert Museum.

Francis Towne (1739 or 1740–1816) was the earliest and the most important of the three. Very little is known about hs early life, but he began to paint in oils at the age of fourteen, according to his own statement in a letter to Ozias Humphry in 1803. When he made this first essay in oils, he appears to have been a pupil at W. Shipley's School[4] in the Strand, as were Joseph Nollekens, William Pars and Richard Cosway. Redgrave states that Towne was a pupil of William Pars, but this is probably due to a confusion. William Pars was Towne's life-long friend, and at least two years his junior, and it was probably *Henry* Pars under whom Towne studied at Shipley's.[5] White Abbott informed Farington that Towne 'was a pupil to Shackleton (Kent's successor as principal painter to George II) and joined with Cosway in taking a house in Somerset-street, Portman Square, when they embarked in the world of artists'.[6] In 1759 he gained the first premium at the Society of Arts, of which Shipley was Secretary, for 'an original design for Cabinet makers, Coachmakers, manufacturers in Metals, Chinas and Earthenware', and from 1762 to 1773 he constantly exhibited landscapes in oil at the Society of Artists, of which he became a member in 1772. He was elected to the Free Society of Artists in 1762, and exhibited his first two pictures at the Royal Academy in 1775. They were of sufficient interest to be singled out by the *General Advertiser*, which said that 'Mr. *Town* has *countryfied* these views with judgment and taste'. He seems to have worked mainly at Exeter until 1780, and the pictures which he exhibited in London were sent from the address of William Pars until 1775, the year in which Pars settled in Rome. Towne always retained a very close connection with Devonshire, whose lovely country had nurtured also his friends Downman, Cosway and Ozias Humphry.

Though Towne had worked in oil and had made many studies in pen and wash, it is

---

[1] A. P. Oppé, *Francis Towne*, Walpole Soc., VIII, 1919/1920.
[2] A. P. Oppé, *John White Abbott*, Walpole Soc., XIII, 1924/1925.
[3] D. S. MacColl, 'John Baverstock Knight', *Burlington Magazine*, XXXIV, 1919, pp. 171, 172.
[4] For W. Shipley and his School, see E. Edwards, *Anecdotes of Painters*, 1808, pp. xv and 91. Shipley's drawing classes, the best of their kind in England, were carried on after his retirement by his former pupil, Henry Pars, brother of William Pars. The room where the classes were held, afterwards became the show-room of Ackermann. Whitley, 1800–1820, pp. 154, 155.
[5] A. P. Oppé, *op. cit.* p. 96.
[6] *Diary*, July 14, 1797.

in 1777 that his water-colours proper begin. In that year he made a tour in Wales with his Exeter friend and pupil, James White, and brought back a whole series of numbered and dated drawings, in various stages of finish, very frequently done on a double sheet of a sketch-book with a fold in the middle, or on two or more sheets pieced together. On the back of some of the drawings are noted the orders for copies in water-colour or for pictures in oil. His method of working was to make a pencil outline on the spot, and afterwards to go over the outline in ink, and to wash in the colour while the natural aspect was still fresh in his memory. The shadows were generally indicated with Indian ink, and some of the drawings have not been carried beyond this stage. On their Welsh tour Towne, for the first time, came into contact with that mountain scenery which he handled later so magnificently in his drawings of the Alps, but these early drawings, naturally enough, do not show the qualities of his mature style, and are rather timid in handling. At the same time, it is to Towne's credit that he was one of the first artists in England to recognise that the character and contours of English mountain scenery could give material for a picture that need not be a *pastiche* of the Poussins or Salvator Rosa. Wilson, too, used to say that everything the landscape painter could want, was to be found in North Wales. Of the Welsh drawings, *The Salmon Leap*, 1777,[1] is a lovely composition, serene in colour, and with the essential contours of the towering cliff-face definitely marked in outline and Indian ink wash. The beginnings of his austerity of design, his love of form and structure, are in this drawing. A drawing of 1778, *In Peamore Park*, is interesting as being the earliest example of a phase of his activity on which his pupil, John White Abbott, chiefly concentrated. In the foreground is a large fallen tree; its foliage and twisting boughs carefully drawn with a fine pen outline, fill the composition, except for a glimpse of landscape in the background. The colouring is undistinguished, and the general effect attractive but weak. Towne was later to attempt this type of subject with much greater skill.

In the next few years he reached the apex of his achievement. Like many other water-colour painters, he found in the scenery of Italy a stimulation which Britain had not been able to provide, and his reputation rests very largely on the drawings he made in his single tour abroad in 1780–1781. In 1780 he went to Rome, where his friend Pars was already settled, and this Italian visit resulted in four sets of drawings of a similar description to those he had brought back from Wales. Most of the Italian drawings—seventy-four of them, to be exact—are in three volumes now in the British Museum, to which they were given in 1816, after his death, by his friends James White, his Executor, and J. H. Merivale, his residuary legatee, as is recorded on a label on the fly-leaf of volume I, 'in compliance with the desire of the Artist, that his "Roman Drawings" should be deposited with those of his friend Pars in the British Museum'. Apart from the Rome drawings, there are other sets of Naples, Italy and Albano, and all are numbered and dated. It is possible that some were coloured much later, but the normal proceeding for an artist

---

[1] Coll. Mr. D. L. T. and Miss Armide Oppé.

119

would be to colour his sketch very soon after he had made his outline and while the natural colours were still fresh in his mind's eye. There are no notes as to colouring inscribed on the drawings, a fact which lends weight to the assumption that this was his practice, and we may, therefore, take it that a definite development of his style is illustrated in this series. On the other hand, like Constable, he frequently adds the hour of the sketch, a guide in adding the colour later.

The earlier drawings of the series show very strongly the influence of Pars in their clear, light, yellow-grey colouring. Pars' method of treating old stonework is almost exactly followed in *Part of the Ancient Roman Wall between Porta Salaria and Porta Pinciana, 1780.*[1] Two of the most attractive water-colours of this year, *On the Banks of the Tiber, near Ponte Molle*[2] and *Temple of Bacchus, two miles from Rome,*[3] illustrate, in their restrained and transparent colour and delicacy of handling, the culminating point of his previous manner, untouched by the influence of Italy and (what is strange for a painter of his generation) owing nothing to Claude. In 1781 a considerable change came over his style. It is tempting to attribute this partly to the influence of J. R. Cozens. Cozens had left Rome in 1779, a year before Towne's arrival, but Towne may quite possibly have seen his work either in Rome, or in London before he set out. At all events, his attempts at depicting the wide panoramas of the Roman plains show relationship to Cozens' handling of similar themes, though they lack the pure poetry and subtlety of Cozens; and *Rome, looking towards the Sabine mountains*[4a] combines an attempt at a wide view, such as Cozens loved, with the colouring of his friend Pars. By 1781 he was adopting a scheme of colour which was much brighter in key and richer in range. Occasionally, there is a preponderance of rather harsh violet or purple tones, and an attempt to handle foliage, not with the flat patterning in which he was so successful, but with more unity in the masses, and in a naturalistic manner, in which he certainly seems to have been influenced by Cozens. Two drawings of *Monte Cavo*[4b] are strikingly akin to the style of Cozens, both in the treatment of distance and in the soft heavy foliage of the trees. Among the best drawings of the early part of 1781 are two of *The Baths of Caracalla*[5] (Pl. 101) which unite his characteristic delicate free outline with rich masses of subdued glowing colour. In both of these one notes— what is strongly characteristic of much of Towne's work—that the greater part of the drawing is in low and subdued tones, or in shadowed masses with a few isolated specks and passages of golden evening light giving brilliance to the whole picture. In March he spent some time in Naples, but none of the drawings which he made there show him at his best, with the possible exception of the *Grotto of Posilippo*[6] (Pl. 102), which gains great dignity by its massive simplification of cliff forms. In the following month he was at Tivoli, and in some of the drawings here he wavers between the flat decorative treatment, the structural definition, which was natural to him, and a more realistic manner of hand-

[1] B.M. L.B.I.3(b).
[3] B.M. L.B.I.4(b).
[5] B.M. L.B.II.6 and 7.
[2] B.M. L.B.I.2(a).
[4] a&b Exhibited at the Burlington Fine Arts Club, 1930.
[6] B.M. L.B.III.12.

ling foliage. In *Tivoli from below the Falls*[1] and *A Distant View of Tivoli*[2] this treatment is combined with unpleasant violet tones in an unhappy effect, and perhaps the worst of his attempts in this manner is *Rocca del Papa*,[3] where the hot colour is allied to a much coarser and more indefinite pen outline. One of the best of the Tivoli drawings is *Tree Trunks at Tivoli*,[4] very subdued in colour, and satisfying in the strong design of the twisted roots.

In the early summer of 1781 he returned to Rome, and devoted himself to making further studies of the magnificent ruins there. *The Arch of Septimus Severus*[5] and *The Roman Forum*,[6] both large drawings, are not perhaps entirely satisfactory from the point of view of design, but render excellently the delicate golden charm of stone that for centuries has mellowed beneath a Roman sun. *S. Maria Nuova, with the Temple of the Sun and Moon, from the Colosseum*[7] and *The Temple of Vesta*[8] are among the best of all the Roman drawings, subdued but clear and light in colour, and showing great delicacy of fine penwork. *St. Peter's at Sunset, from above the Arco Oscuro*[9] is one of the finest of a series of drawings where landscape is enveloped in glowing and mellow light; and *L'Arricia*[10] shows a very finely designed pattern of dark trees, with the sunlight striking through beneath them. In a drawing like *The Baths of Titus*,[11] No. 37 of his Rome series, in 1781, where he uses careful descriptive outline and flat washes, the whole subject—the sky, the massive architecture with its broad shadows, and the actual handling of foliage—is a strange anticipation of Cotman.

At the end of the summer of 1781 Towne left Rome in company with 'Warwick' Smith, returning to England by way of Switzerland. The rediscovery of Towne has shown, as has been stated, that a great deal of the credit hitherto given to Smith for pioneer work in water-colour has been wrongly ascribed. Smith is supposed to have been the first to have introduced bright colouring, and as early as 1793 claimed a secret process, but Towne, his contemporary, employed in his Italian drawings even stronger colour, together with a much greater power of design which makes it more probable that Smith learned from him, rather than he from Smith. Mr. Patch, when telling Farington that Towne was an imitator of Smith, added that: 'Towne is conceited of his ability in the Art. I have a drawing by him which I wished him to change, & told him it had been remarked by others that it wd. be for his credit to do so.' Towne replied, 'I am the best judge of that', and refused to make any alteration.[12]

Towne's Swiss drawings are undoubtedly his finest work. Among the solitudes of the frozen Alps a new spirit seized him. His power of realising structure and simplifying mass found ideal scope in the superb mountain scenery, in the grandeur of vast rocky piles and slowly moving glaciers. His talents had by this time come to their full development. By 1781 he has learned that vivid colour, the full effects of *plein air* painting, may make the

[1] B.M. L.B.III.6. [2] B.M. L.B.I.9(b). [3] B.M. L.B.III.13.
[4] Coll. Mr. D. L. T. and Miss Armide Oppé. [5] B.M. L.B.III.10. [6] B.M. L.B.III.15.
[7] B.M. L.B.II.14. [8] B.M. L.B.II.17. [9] B.M. L.B.II.13.
[10] B.M. L.B.III.14. [11] B.M. L.B.II.10. [12] *Diary*, VI, p. 178.

imagination halt instead of leaving it active and free. Among the Alps his vision is large and calm; his interpretation depends on his sense of appropriate and austere design; his colour is wisely subservient to form. In drawing he has the art of extracting symmetry and order from wild profusion. From endless shapes and contours of sky-line, ridge and scree, or rock and glacier, from infinite varieties of rich and changing colour, he chooses the immanent and eternal simplicities. He disregards the picturesque; he is less scenic even than Cozens. With unerring line he preserves the essential sublimity of mountain form, and with his brush adds quiet colour of enamelled clarity. In drawings such as *The Source of the Arveiron*[1] (Pl. 99) he seems awed before the terrors of the wild mountains. He had not the placid vision of Pars and Cozens. As Oppé puts it, 'contrary to all the accepted canons of the eighteenth century Towne did nothing to soften, but everything to accentuate the crushing grandeur of the mountains'.

Altogether, 1781 was a vintage year, of which the *premier cru* can be found in the Oppé collection. Only a few of the Swiss drawings are in public collections, but an exhibition of Towne's work, held at the Burlington Fine Arts Club in 1930, revealed, for the first time, the full extent of his powers. He is at his surest when dealing with the solemn procession of mountain peaks, with stupendous heights retreating into the vast distance, as in *The Source of the Arveiron*[2] and *The Top of the Splügen Pass*,[2] and another view of *The Source of the Arveiron*.[3] These drawings of the Arveiron are astounding in their force and originality. No artist before Towne had ever built up a deliberate design of swinging curves, intersecting and contrasting, like figures cut by a skater's change of edge upon the ice.

Colour is limited in all the Swiss drawings, and tones of blue and violet are modulated with great skill. Towne's colour here is not just accepted by him from nature, but imposed upon nature as an arbitrary, functional part of the design. In many of his drawings the colour is as abstract as the form. A command of design was always Towne's strongest gift, and this power is strikingly shown in *Bridge in the Apennines*,[4] where the composition would fall to pieces if it were not for the shapes of the clouds, lightly indicated above the end of the bridge, which repeat the form of the tree on the extreme left. This drawing, inscribed on the back, 'A Bridge 15 miles on the Road between Florence and Bologna', was made on Towne's journey back from Rome to Switzerland. In the Swiss drawings he seems always to cling to the pen outline, as though discouraged by the result of his infrequent earlier attempts to dispense with it. Without the discipline of line his design tends to flatten out and to become uninteresting, as in *Naples and the Isle of Capri*[5] and *The Palatine Hill looking towards the Baths of Caracalla*,[6] Jan. 1781.

Towne never went abroad again, and the drawings produced after his return show a progressive decline. Evidently he found beneath foreign skies an inspiration which England could not provide. The peak of his achievement seems to have been reached and

[1] Coll. Mr. D. L. T. and Miss Armide Oppé.
[3] V.A.M. P.20–1921.
[5] Coll. Mr. D. L. T. and Miss Armide Oppé.

[2] Coll. Mr. D. L. T. and Miss Armide Oppé.
[4] Coll. Mr. L. G. Duke.
[6] B.M. L.B.I.22.

122

passed in 1781, and the only set of drawings that he made after that date are comparable more to the early Welsh series than to the Roman drawings. In 1813 he made a series of dainty, but not particularly striking, drawings of Oxford, some of which are now in the Ashmolean Museum, but after his return from Switzerland he was occupied largely with working on commission copies of his earlier sketches, most of which have completely lost all the qualities which go to form the charm of the sketches. Usually, the outline is missing, and this invariably tends, in Towne's case, to feebleness, both of design and of decorative effect. He seems to have regarded these drawings on commission more as *pictures* than as *drawings*, and therefore to have felt that his normal stylistic treatment was unsuitable and that a greater realism and elaboration should be sought.

In 1786 he made a tour in the Lake District with his Exeter friends, James White and John Merivale. The sketch-book that he used is in the possession of the Merivale family, and the drawings in it are numbered to forty. Other drawings done at this time are in various private hands. Two executed on this tour were, *Rydal Water, Taken at the going off of a Storm*[1] and *Part of Ambleside at the Head of the Lake of Windermere: Morning Effect.*[2] *Rydal Water* is an attempt to render an atmospheric effect and the flat decorative treatment produces a striking and unusual result. There is a good *Cascade at Ambleside*[3] (Pl. 98), dated 1786—all grey except for the white of the rushing water and a flash of sunshine here and there dappling the foliage into yellow. But on the whole, the level of the Lakes drawings is not very high, compared with the magnificent achievement of the Swiss subjects. The colours have lost the brightness they acquired in Italy, and are rather anaemic and weak, and though delicate pen-outline in every sketch is handled as skilfully as ever, the realisation of mountain structure, which added such distinction to the Swiss sketches, has degenerated into mere decoration. *The Cascade at Windermere*,[4] a drawing of a waterfall among tree trunks, belonging to Miss Merivale, is of interest as illustrating a later development of that type of drawing of which *In Peamore Park* was the earliest, and *Tree Trunks at Tivoli*, the finest examples.

After his return from Italy he seems to have divided his time between London and Exeter, and he married in London in 1807 a French dancer, Jeannette Hillisberg. White Abbott told Farington in 1797 that Towne 'makes £500 a year at Exeter by teaching drawing, etc.' Downman spoke of 'the great frugality of Francis Towne, who by saving had made a fortune', and Mr. Patch told Farington that Towne 'saved at Exeter £10,000, but His economy was extreme', adding 'He lived for a shilling a day'.[5] In a letter, from which Oppé quotes, Towne repudiates bitterly the stigma of being called a 'provincial drawing master', but none the less, his honour was in his own country, and his patrons throughout were Devonshire people. His prices were twenty-five guineas for an oil picture

[1] V.A.M. P.19–1921.
[2] V.A.M. P.24–1924.
[3] Ashmolean Museum.
[4] Reproduced in Walpole Soc., VIII, 1919–1920.
[5] *Diary*, I, p. 211.

and eight or ten for a water-colour. Eight was the price which, as Towne notes, Pars asked for a drawing of Rome. In 1776, 1797 and 1798 he was a candidate for the Associateship of the Royal Academy, but received no votes, although the field was far from strong. Some of the demerits of his oil paintings may perhaps be guessed at from a remark of Anthony Pasquin[1]: 'This gentleman [Towne] is similar in his pencilling to Mr. Abbott, and, like him, is too tender in his tones, especially for a multifarious exhibition. . . . We think if Mr. Towne used *a camera* occasionally, he would correct his present manner of colouring.' In 1803 Towne again tried for Associateship, but on this occasion was supported only by his friend Humphry. He never joined the 'Old' Water-Colour Society, and, indeed, boasted in 1803 that 'I never in my life exhibited a *Drawing*'. But in the spring of 1805 he held an exhibition[2] at the gallery in Lower Brook Street afterwards used by the Water-colour Society. His work was described in the catalogue as 'A Series of original Drawings of the most picturesque scenes in The neighbourhood of Rome, Naples, and other parts of Italy, Switzerland, etc. Together with a select number of views of the Lakes, Cumberland, Westmoreland and North Wales. The whole drawn on the spot by Francis Towne, Landscape Painter.' The collection of 191 drawings also included two studies made in London, *From Millbank*, and *Hyde Park, study of a tree on the ground*.[3] There is very little to say about Towne's water-colours of the later part of his life. They exhibit a great deal of variety in handling, but the most successful are those which reflect the manner of the Roman and Swiss drawings. Sometimes he works directly without underpainting, often he abandons the outline, but, on the whole, he tends to feebleness both of design and colour. His reputation must rest almost entirely on the drawings of 1780–1781. Had he been capable of development from that point, and had his work not remained in isolation, he might have been recognised in his time as one of the great figures in the development of early British water-colour.

In 1807 he moved from Exeter with his family to take up his residence permanently in London, at 39 Queen Anne Street West. Almost immediately, however, his wife died, in the spring of 1808. After her death Towne seems to have worked harder, exhibiting oils fairly regularly at the Academy and the British Institution, and going on sketching tours in the summer. Of his private life we know little, though Farington tells us that 'he does not drink tea in the *afternoon*, as it prevents his sleeping'.[4] He died in July 1816, and was buried beside his wife in Heavitree Churchyard. After the lack of recognition from which he suffered all his life, he would have found gratifying the obituary notice in the *Gentleman's Magazine*, which described him as 'an artist of great eminence as a landscape painter'. It took more than a hundred years for posterity to endorse that view.

In his bold simplification of form and emphasis upon structure, Towne seems almost to

---

[1] Anthony Pasquin, *A Critical Guide to the Exhibition of the Royal Academy*, 1796.
[2] Not known to A. P. Oppé, *op. cit.* when he wrote in 1919, but see Whitley, 1800–1820, 1928, p. 93.
[3] Coll. Mr. Gilbert Davis.
[4] *Diary*, June 15, 1803.

anticipate Cézanne. His technique is well summarised by Oppé: 'He was not a strong draughtsman, nor could he develop the contrasts of tone and the skilful shaping of the coloured blot which in Cotman's early work adds liveliness of incident to decoration. Towne's special skill lies in the management of even pen line and in subtle modulation of colour upon a flat surface. The one gives variation and tone to his large imaginative patterning, the other a charm and delicacy which vary but do not weaken it.'

Regarding the technical aspect, it should be noted that all the drawings by Towne— and by White Abbott and Baverstock Knight—were certainly tinted indoors. The drawing, or a study for it, was made in the open, but the colour scheme, more often conventional than realistic, was added in the studio. The artist never sat on a camp-stool with a low and wobbling easel before him, or held a board or sketching-frame tilted on his knees. He never mixed up his colours, as he went along, in the small space afforded by the inverted lid of a shallow japanned water-colour box. Those of us who follow the latter method know the difficulty of never being able to mix enough of any neutral tint, and know how disastrous it is to be stirring hastily a mixture of, say, yellow ochre, french blue and rose madder in the proportions required for adding to a grey wash that is speedily drying in patches on our paper. The earlier artist worked indoors with a row of china saucers (they can still be found with the older artists' colourmen) in which the requisite amount of each tone was all prepared in fluid quantity. Amateurs, we are told, 'gave their six hours daily to the delectable daubery of mountains, mists and lakes, seated around tables spread with crockery brim full of sea-tint, sky-tint, rock-tint, middle-ground and foreground-tint'. Amateur and professional of the period, alike working in this manner, could lay an even wash with unperturbed equanimity, and this accounts for the flat delicacy of the tints by Towne and others. Even as late as 1845 Samuel Palmer recommends an advanced pupil to take out of doors whole saucers full of colour.

Though Francis Towne gained his income mainly by teaching, and, as we find in Farington's diary, amassed a fortune of £10,000, we know of few pupils whose work has survived.[1] One of these is W. Mackinnon, who is represented in the British Museum by two drawings, and in the Victoria and Albert Museum by one; but these are poor imitations of Towne's work. His best known pupil, John White Abbott, is of much greater interest and importance.

The rediscovery of Abbott's work is quite recent, dating only from the publication in the *Morning Post* of the Farington *Diary* in 1922. A reference in the *Diary* to Abbott induced a descendant of his family to get into touch with James Greig, who was editing the *Diary* for the *Morning Post*, and through him, with the Victoria and Albert Museum. Owing to this introduction the Museum was able to acquire, by gift or purchase, a number of drawings by Abbott, and an opportunity presented itself, for the first time, for a critical

---

[1] A. Bury, *Francis Towne*, 1962, p. 112, mentions the following pupils: Susanna Buller, Annabella Yeoman (not Rowe as printed), Mrs. Flowerdew and Captain John Dale.

study of his work. No one was better qualified to undertake this than A. P. Oppé, who had already made a complete study of Towne.[1]

John White Abbott (1763–1851), born at Exeter, was connected with Francis Towne, for his mother was the sister of James White, of Exeter, well-known for his association with John Downman, Ozias Humphry and Towne. Abbott was trained for the profession of an apothecary, and practised as such for many years, but devoted his spare time to painting, under Towne's tuition. Downman said to Farington that Abbott 'practises as a surgeon, and only paints by snatches, though by choice he would always be so engaged'.[2] Farington mentions also a report that Abbott had expectations of being 'heir to a very good fortune at the death of a gentleman his near relation'.[3] This relation was, in all probability, his uncle James White, a Bencher of Lincoln's Inn. Family tradition says that his uncle took him in his youth to London, where he met Sir Joshua Reynolds, Sir George Beaumont, Benjamin West, and other artists, but the visit must have been of brief duration and was not repeated, for Towne said to Farington that his pupil Abbott had 'much preparation for painting Landscape—by having studied nature, but that he was not much acquainted with fine works of art'.[4] Abbott spent all his life in Devonshire, and with the exception of a sketching tour in 1791 in Scotland, the Lakes, and Lancashire, seems never to have travelled far from home. In 1795 he married Elizabeth Bowling of Pembroke, and had three sons and two daughters. When, as seems fairly certain, he came into his uncle's money in 1825, he abandoned the profession of apothecary, and lived a country life at Fordland, his estate near Exeter. In 1831 he was made Deputy-Lieutenant for Devonshire.

Like most artists of his day, Abbott was ambitious of building up a reputation by his oil paintings rather than his drawings. He appears in the catalogues of the Royal Academy regularly from 1793 to 1805, and again in 1810 and 1822, always as an honorary exhibitor. His exhibited pictures were all landscapes, and his known work in oil—as Oppé has indicated—is conventional and shows strongly the influence of Gainsborough in his early period. At one time his reputation much overshadowed that of Towne, and in 1794 he received almost lyrical praise from Anthony Pasquin: 'This landscape taken in all its component parts I do not hesitate to pronounce *the very best in the Exhibition*. The repose and harmony is beautifully conducted: the cattle are nearly as good as Cuyp.' It was probably about this same picture that Ozias Humphry, R.A., wrote to James White in 1794: 'I cannot forbear to acquaint you with the pleasure I felt on Saturday last at the sight of a very beautiful little picture Mr. Abbott has sent us this year for exhibition. It is a picture which not only gave me pleasure but every member of the R.A., and certainly places him in the first class of dilettante painters at least.' In 1796 Pasquin again praises Abbott but after that year overlooks him altogether. We may perhaps conclude that Abbott's early

---

[1] *John White Abbott*, Walpole Soc. XIII, 1924, 1925.
[2] *Diary*, June 25, 1804.
[3] *Ibid.* November 2, 1810.
[4] *Diary*, June 15, 1803.

promise was not fulfilled. Possibly a fairer estimate of his ability as a painter in oils than is given by the above quotations may be formed from a draft of a letter to Abbott from Ozias Humphry, in which he criticises severely the faint colouring and mildewed and foggy appearance of Abbott's pictures.[1]

Abbott's reputation now rests entirely upon his drawings, probably none of which were exhibited in his life-time. Almost all of them are of scenes in Devonshire, with the exception of the series he brought back from his northern tour. His drawings are numbered in the manner of Towne, and one in the Victoria and Albert Museum bears the number *73*. He probably did not himself consider his water-colour work as of much account, and Downman showed an appreciation surprising for his time when he said to Farington that he preferred Abbott's drawings to his paintings 'as they are done with more spirit'.[2] The drawings show Abbott to have been a very faithful disciple of Towne in the weaker manner of his Welsh sketches, for he never attempted to imitate Towne's superb handling of mountain scenery. Towne's flat decorative treatment, the delicate frilly pen outline, the thin washes of flat colour, are all accurately reproduced, but the sense of structure which gives force to Towne's most decorative subjects is missing in Abbott's work. Consequently, Abbott is at his best when he is dealing with detailed studies of trees and forest under-growth, which allow full scope for his patient drawing, and, though he took from Towne the manner of such studies, he is in them at least as good as his master. Towne's *Hyde Park*,[3] inscribed on the back, *taken in Hyde Park, June the 19th, 1797 on the spot by Francis Towne*, is done with the formula of thin crinkled line which was closely followed by his pupil. *Canonteign, Devon*[4] (Pl. 104) and *Fordland*[5] show Abbott as a close adherent to Towne's methods, but display an elaboration and a patience of structure in dealing with intricate tracery of tree-trunks and foliage, which pass beyond the more limited confines of Towne's practice. The latter drawing, it is true, is based upon an earlier drawing by Towne of a fallen tree-trunk, but in spite of the complications caused by the joining of pieces of paper it retains a real nobility of design and is worked with an extraordinary skill of schematic colour that remains quiet and modulated. Many of his larger drawings are done, like the *Fordland*, on several sheets of paper pieced together, which shows that the actual drawing must have been executed out-of-doors, the piecing being due to the difficulty of manipu-lating large sheets of paper in a breeze. It must not be supposed that Abbott applied his colour out-of-doors. His *Finished on the Spot*, inscribed on several of the drawings, can apply to the pen outlines only. An artist can work with pen or pencil on several pieces of paper, which he joins afterwards, but no one could carry even washes of colour over separate portions of paper. In some cases colour has been carried over on to the card on which a drawing is mounted, and this also implies that the colouring was studio work. There are

[1] *Diary*, June 25, 1804.
[2] Letter in the possession of the Royal Academy, quoted by A. P. Oppé, Walpole Soc., XIII, p. 74.
[3] Coll. Mr. Gilbert Davis.
[4] V.A.M. P.60–1923.
[5] V.A.M. P.58–1924.

many drawings by him in pen and monochrome, and a large series of copies, probably made after Towne's death in 1816, from Towne's Swiss and Italian drawings.

In June–July 1938, fifty-nine drawings by Abbott, the first large exhibition of his work, were shown at Walker's Gallery, forty-four of them having been from the collection of Sir Mark Grant-Sturgis, K.C.B. Almost all of these drawings had the initials *J.W.A.* on the back of the mount, together with the name of the place depicted, and the date of execution. All but four of the drawings were dated to the exact day, and covered a period from 1792 to 1838, the artist's seventy-fifth year. Thirty-four of the drawings were of his native county of Devon, while the others told of visits to Somerset, Wiltshire, Dorset, Gloucestershire and Monmouthshire. Among the Devon drawings was a view, dated 1826, of a wood at Fordland, his residence near Exeter. Three of the Devon drawings were made on one day, July 20, 1792, and three on September 1. Those made on July 20 were of Widdicombe House (not to be confused with Widdicombe-in-the-Moor), one three miles south of Lannacombe Mills near the Start, and another of the coast near Start Point. On September 1 his first two drawings were made at Greenway beside the River Dart, and a third at the Priory of Cornworthy, three miles away.

It is not possible, on the whole, to trace any real development in Abbott's drawings. Sketches dated twenty years apart might have been executed on the same day, to judge from the exact similarity of the handling. Possibly this was due to the limitations of his artistic power, which attained at an early stage under Towne's tuition a point beyond which it was unable to advance. Or perhaps there is truth in the malicious observation of Patch, the parson, when he said to Farington that 'Mr. Abbott would have been a fine artist had he been situated differently, but at Exeter he had been so admired & extolled that he was content with copying himself'. Patch further remarked that Abbott 'does not attend to aerial perspective, but finishes his middle distances equally with his foregrounds', a fault which is apparent in *Kerswell, Devon*[1] (Pl. 105). Occasionally, Abbott dispenses altogether with the pen outline, as in *The Churchyard with the west end of the Cathedral, Exeter*, 1796 (in the family possession), and is then rather more free in his handling. His colour, though anaemic at times, has usually a pleasant clarity and freshness. When he became more ambitious and aimed at a stronger effect, his greens and yellows were liable to become crude, as was the case with Towne.

If, in the drawings of his tree-trunks, he was more graceful and flexible than Towne, he is more tepid and cloistral in his work as a whole. Both Towne and he were eminently cautious and reticent. Except in the case of Towne among the solitudes of the Alps, neither had any quick flashes of imagination, or any far-reaching and unsatisfied desire. Neither had the full-blooded vigour that was to mark Müller and De Wint, and was to become so energetic in Constable and in Cox. Their skill lay in reducing their material to an orderly abstract of calligraphic outline; and in their flat method, in their patterning of design, in their conventions of contour, they have their analogists today.

[1] V.A.M. P.59–1923.

94 'Castle Point'

Coll. Mr & Mrs Paul Mellon   5¾ × 8½: 146 × 215   *Water-colour*

John 'Warwick' SMITH (1749–1831)

95 'View of Snowdon over Anglesey'

National Museum of Wales, Cardiff   5¾ × 8⅞: 146 × 225   *Water-colour*

John 'Warwick' SMITH (1749–1831)

96 'The Church of La Trinita del Monte'
B.M. 1936.7.4.22   13¼ × 21¼: 337 × 514   *Water-colour*
John 'Warwick' SMITH (1749–1831)

97 'The Temples of Concord and Jupiter'
B.M. 1936.7.4.22   18 × 28: 457 × 711   *Water-colour*
John 'Warwick' SMITH (1749–1831)

98 'Cascade at Ambleside'

Ashmolean Museum, Oxford $14\frac{7}{8} \times 10\frac{1}{2}$: 377 × 265

Pen and ink and water-colour, signed and dated 1786

Francis TOWNE (1739 or 1740–1816)

99 'The Source of the Arveiron'
Coll. Mr D.L.T. and Miss Armide Oppé $12\frac{1}{4} \times 8\frac{3}{4}$: 312×222
Pen and ink and water-colour, signed and dated 1781
Francis TOWNE (1739 or 1740–1816)

100 'Near Ambleside'
Coll. Mr & Mrs Paul Mellon 8×13: 203×330
Pen and ink and water-colour, signed and dated 1786
Francis TOWNE (1739 or 1740–1816)

101 'The Baths of Caracalla'
B.M. L.B.II.6   12¾ × 18¾: 324 × 476
Pen and ink and water-colour, signed and dated 1781
Francis Towne (1739 or 1740–1816)

102 'Grotto of Posilippo, Naples'
B.M. L.B.III.12   12¾ × 18½: 324 × 470   *Pen and ink and water-colour, signed and dated 1781*
Francis Towne (1739 or 1740–1816)

103 'The Source of The Arveiron, 1781'
V.A.M. P.20–1921   16¾ × 12¼: 426 × 312
Pen and ink and water-colour, signed and dated 1781
Francis TOWNE (1739 or 1740–1816)

104 'Canonteign, Devon'
V.A.M. P.60–1923   14¾ × 13½: 375 × 343
Water-colour, signed and dated 1803
John White ABBOTT (1763–1851)

105 'Kerswell, Devon'
.A.M. P.59–1923   17¼ × 14¾: 438 × 375
Water-colour, signed and dated 1813
John White ABBOTT (1763–1851)

106 'Lodore, Derwentwater'

V.A.M. E.3431–1922   10¾ × 18¼: 273 × 464   *Pencil and water-colour, signed*

John Baverstock KNIGHT (1785–1859)

107 'Lake Scene'

V.A.M. P.99–1922   10½ × 17¾: 267 × 452   *Water-colour, signed and dated 1809*

John Baverstock KNIGHT (1785–1859)

At first glance it would seem inevitable to assume that John Baverstock Knight was a pupil of Francis Towne, or at least of John White Abbott, but there is, in fact, nothing but a certain similarity of style to connect his work with theirs. Like Abbott, Knight, in the next county, led the life of a country gentleman, treating his art as a serious hobby which, nevertheless, was not allowed to interfere with the social duties of his position. For him, as for H. B. Brabazon in later days, his drawings, almost surreptitiously done, were an escape from life. But it is very probable that he saw drawings by Towne and Abbott in the country houses which he visited, and the fundamental similarity of style is so striking that his work can only be discussed in relation to theirs.

John Baverstock Knight (1785–1859)[1] was the son of Captain James Forster Knight, of the 3rd Dorset Militia. Captain Knight was a well-to-do man, having inherited the lands of his great-uncle, James Forster, High Sheriff of Dorset, and he was also a connoisseur of some repute, so that from the outset he viewed with sympathy his son's leanings towards art. The boy was educated first at home, and then at a 'commercial school', after which he joined his father as assistant in his business of land-surveyor and land-agent. After the death of his father he carried on this profession, and was agent and surveyor to the Duke of Bedford, and Eton and Winchester Colleges, as well as to many owners of large estates. He settled at West Lodge, Piddlehinton, Dorset, and was a typical country squire of his time, six feet six in height, handsome, well-dressed, mistaken for the duke when he rode in a duke's company, keen on shooting, fishing, riding to hounds, knowledgeable about agriculture and stock-raising, with a wife and a family of eight children.

His artistic work, including oil paintings, water-colours, miniatures and etchings, was as versatile and prolific as his life. The etchings were mainly topographical, and some of them appeared in the *Gentleman's Magazine* from 1816 onwards, while others were published in the second edition of Hutchin's *History of Dorset*. Of his miniatures we know nothing, and little more of his oil paintings. They seem to have varied from portraits to copies of Old Masters. He says, for example, in a letter to his brother, Edward Butt Knight, dated 1821: 'I have been painting away at a great rate. Two whole lengths of Mr. and Mrs. Farquharson, 7 ft. 10 ins. × 4 ft. 10 ins., and a half length of the dowager Mrs. Farquharson were fixed in Langton dining-room in superb frames on the 18th December last, & I Have in hand a picture 9 ft. 4 ins. × 7 ft. 10 ins. of the three young Farquharsons, also two more half lengths of the elder Mrs. Farquharson, a small copy of the great picture for Mr. Grove, a cabinet portrait of Sir William Fraser's sister, a Hunting picture for Ferne House 6 ft. × 4 ft. 6 ins. . . . Among all this I stick, as usual, to the old trade, and catch all the fish I can . . . I have nearly finished a perfect copy of the celebrated Wardour Murillo. I am sent for to Bath to paint your friend Meyrick, and to Cornwall to copy Lord Grenville's Ancestors at Bosconnoe, & I have commissions at Uxbridge. . . . shot with John Wickers at Wooton the other day.' A letter that gives a good

[1] Rev. Francis Knight, *Biography of J. B. Knight*, 1908.

picture of the man, when we add that he was a churchwarden notable for his charities (once a week there was a feast for the poor at his house), and possessed a pretty turn for scribbling letters in verse. As to his copies, they were said to have been good enough to be taken for the originals even by experts. He exhibited at the Royal Academy as an Honorary Exhibitor in 1818 and 1819, the first year sending one landscape, the second year, three. Benjamin West and Fuseli praised his work, but the obscurity in which his pictures are now enfolded makes any assessment of their worth impossible.

It is by his drawings that Knight lives for us. They are comparable to the drawings of Towne rather than to those of Abbott in the frequent choice of mountain scenery, the skilful handling of receding planes and the strong feeling for composition. Knight, at his best, as in some of his smaller sketches, is almost as good as Towne, but too often he is inclined to overload with detail, more in the manner of Abbott, although there is always an underlying dignity of structure which Abbott rarely attained. He frequently works altogether without outline, and occasionally mixes the two methods, putting in the foreground with outline, and the background without. But although his style is based on that of Towne and Abbott, there are striking differences. Knight, born ten years later than Girtin and Turner, seven after Varley, and two after Cox and Prout, had a longer career than Towne and Abbott, with greater facilities for travel owing to his wealth, and with the *entrée* to many houses containing fine collections. Hence, he was able to obtain a far wider knowledge of contemporary art, and consequently to experiment and extend his style. That he fell under the influence of John Robert Cozens is clearly seen in many sketches where he has used only one or two washes of clear blue-green, with or without outline, and such drawings as *Derwentwater*[1] and *Lake Scene*[2] (Pl. 107) show definite traces of Cotman. There are the same superimposed flat washes, and the same reserved spaces of white for trunks and foliage. In *Lodore, Derwentwater*[3] (Pl. 106) the treatment of the trees on the right is almost identical with the handling of the foliage in Cotman's *Study of Trees*. Nearly all Knight's drawings are either in monochrome, or in an almost uniform blue-grey tone, but occasionally he uses a light colour. *Axbridge Vale*, in the Tate Gallery, has washes of blue and green. Occasionally, he does small sketches, obviously out-of-doors, without outline and with quite bright colour, but in these he is invariably at his worst. But that he could handle colour with precision and restraint is shown by a superb little *Landscape*.[4] If many of the other drawings have some affinity with Cotman, here it is the influence of Girtin that is apparent in the simplification of the colour, the alternation of light and shadow, and the feeling for panorama. The Museum at Dorchester, the capital of his native county, has over forty examples of his work, which is also represented at the British Museum, the Tate Gallery, and, still more fully, at the Victoria and Albert Museum.

[1] V.A.M. E.3432–1922.
[2] V.A.M. P.99–1922.
[3] V.A.M. E.3431–1922.
[4] V.A.M. P.135–1920.

130

CHAPTER VII

John Robert Cozens

In the development of English water-colour John Robert Cozens seems to hold a unique place when we regard the relationship in which he stands to both his predecessors and his successors. Until his time, water-colours in England, if we omit Gainsborough's limited contribution, may be described as mainly topographical. In the large majority of water-colours the first aim was to depict adequately a scene of pictorial or historical interest, and the use of colour served merely to heighten the effect arrived at by the artist in his drawing. In the case of John Robert Cozens the actual scene was of secondary interest, the topographical content slight. His drawings were not made for the engraver or as studies for oil paintings, but were the natural expression of his poetic genius. He was one of the first water-colour painters in our country to use the medium consistently for its own sake as a purely expressional means. In spite of the short span of his life and his small output, he ranks among the masters, beside Turner and Girtin; sometimes, even, for sheer poetry he appeals more than either. Ruskin said of him: 'There were two men associated with Turner in early study, who showed high promise in the same field, Cozens and Girtin (especially the former) and there is no saying what these men might have done had they lived; there might, perhaps, have been a struggle between one or other of them and Turner, as between Giorgione and Titian.'[1]

Cozens exercised immense influence on both Turner and Girtin, who copied many of his drawings when, as young students, they spent the evening with Dr. Monro. Turner's copies of Cozens—usually interpretations rather than copies—show to what extent he had absorbed the essence of Cozens' work, the capture of mood and poetry in his rendering of landscape. Edward Edwards said, in 1808, of Cozens' style that it 'has served as a foundation to the manner since adopted by Mr. Turner and the late Mr. Girtin'.[2] And so fine a judge as Constable was eager and enthusiastic about Cozens' work. He bought a Cozens drawing for Archdeacon Fisher in 1819[3]; and he himself owned *View in the Tyrol near Brixen.*[4] *A View on the Galleria di Sopra above the Lake of Albano*[5] was presented to Constable by Sir George Beaumont. In a letter to William Carpenter in 1835, Constable wrote:

[1] *Modern Painters,* III, 346.
[2] E. Edwards, *Anecdotes of Painters,* 1808, p. 120.
[3] C. R. Leslie, *Life and Letters of John Constable,* 1951 (Phaidon Press), p. 74.
[4] (205) Coll. Mr. Thomas Girtin. The numbers in brackets before the drawings mentioned in this chapter are those of the catalogue compiled by C. F. Bell and T. Girtin, Walpole Soc., XXIII, 1934–1935.
[5] (154) Birkenhead Art Gallery.

'I want to know when the younger Cozens was born; his name was John, and he was the greatest genius that ever touched landscape.'[1] In another letter, to Fisher in 1820, he speaks of drawings by Cozens keeping him cheerful; and, again, he says: 'In the room where I am writing there are hanging up two beautiful small drawings by Cozens, one a wood, close and very solemn, the other a view from Vesuvius looking over Portici, very lovely. I borrowed them from my neighbour, Mr. Woodburn. Cozens was all poetry, and your drawing is a lovely specimen.'[2] It is not easy to analyse precisely the qualities in Cozens' work which roused, and still rouse, such enthusiasm. They are of the spirit, and seldom has any artist succeeded with such subtlety and delicacy in evoking the spirit and sentiment of a scene. Blake said that all beautiful things have 'lain burningly on the Divine hand', and it is the task of the artist to reveal what he has perceived of that divine beauty to those who lack his seeing eye. In this respect Cozens was unique—unique, even when set beside Blake—for while Blake strove to give form and substance to his vision of the intangible world, Cozens appeared to reveal it gently, with muted eloquence, through the outward beauty of the visible world.

John Robert Cozens (1752–1797) was the son of Alexander Cozens.[3] We may presume that he profited greatly by his father's teaching, and the British Museum possesses a little book of compositions by Alexander Cozens, which, an old note records, was made for the instruction of his son. Little is known about his early life, but he seems to have developed a precocious talent, for he exhibited at the Incorporated Society of Artists in 1767 at the age of fifteen. It is said that he published in 1773 a series of tinted etchings of local views near Bath,[4] presumably done when visiting there with his father, but nothing is known of them. In 1776 he was a candidate for Associateship of the Royal Academy, although he had exhibited only one picture. He received no votes, and never tried again for election, nor did he ever again exhibit at the Academy. The solitary exhibit of 1776 was *A Landscape, with Hannibal, in his March over the Alps, showing his Army the fertile plains of Italy*,[5] and is always said to have been executed in oils. Turner, at any rate, said—but at an unknown date—that he learned more from it than from any other picture he had then seen; and Turner's own oil painting, exhibited in 1812 at the Royal Academy, of *Hannibal and his Army crossing the Alps*,[6] may have been due to his recollection of Cozens' painting.

In 1776 Cozens made his first journey abroad, in the company of Richard Payne Knight, the archaeologist and art collector, famous for his splendid bequest to the British Museum. Knight was then a young dilettante of twenty-six, and most of the sketches

---

[1] Leslie, *op. cit.* p. 241.
[2] Leslie, *op. cit.* p. 100.
[3] C. R. Leslie, *Handbook for young Painters*, 1855, p. 264, states that he had seen a drawing inscribed *done by J. R. Cozens 1761 when he was nine years old*.
[4] Burlington Fine Arts Club (Exhibition), *Catalogue of a Collection of Drawings by J. R. Cozens*, 1922–1923 (Introduction by C. F. Bell).
[5] It may be noted that John Cozens inherited the subject from his father. In the Victoria and Albert Museum is a blot drawing, by Alexander Cozens, of *Hannibal crossing the Alps*.
[6] National Gallery.

which Cozens brought back from this trip in his company were done in Switzerland, with very few North Italian scenes. Cozens must have been in Florence in 1776, for the manuscript note attached to a collection of Alexander Cozens' drawings in the British Museum says that they were purchased in Florence by his son in that year. The volume in which Cozens' Swiss sketches are originally contained is said to have been first in the Townley Collection, and then in that of the Hon. Rowland Allanson-Winn.[1] When he obtained the book, it bore an inscription: *Views in Swisserland, a present from Mr. R. P. Knight, & taken by the late Mr. Cozens under his inspection during a tour in Swisserland in 1776.* The catalogue of the Percy Collection,[2] however, states that the volume was bought by a dealer called Molteno at the Payne Knight sale, who sold it to Allanson-Winn in 1870. The volume may have been returned to Payne Knight, but a further problem is raised by the fact that two drawings of this series, dated 1776, are in the Dyce Collection at the Victoria and Albert Museum, and the Dyce Collection was bequeathed in 1869, the year before Allanson-Winn bought the book.[3] However that may be, the drawings are now widely scattered. The British Museum contains twenty-four of them, from which it is possible to trace the development of Cozens' talent. The journey on which they were made was apparently one of over a year, for he was at Terracina in 1777 and at Rome in 1778, as shown by two dated drawings inscribed *Rome*; and Northcote in February 1778, writing from Rome, says that 'Mr. Cousins, a young landscape painter', had called on him.[4] J. R. Cozens left Rome in 1779, as is shown by the memorandum attached to the drawings by Alexander Cozens in the British Museum.

Nearly all the early drawings are mainly in monochrome, and it is not hard to see in them the influence of Alexander Cozens. The prevailing colour, however, is not the grey-blue with which we associate J. R. Cozens, on the strength of his later work, but a rather yellowish, dark grey,[5] occasionally muddy in tone, but often achieving a bright clarity of effect resembling the work of Pars at his best. Cozens had not yet discovered his talent for interpreting the wide levels of the valleys and the towering peaks of the mountains, and many of these drawings, such as several of the Reichenbach River, are close-up studies of water falling through little gorges. A hint of his later triumphs appears in *Between Sallanches and Servon, Mont Blanc in the Distance*[6] (Pl. 108), which is an early and not unsuccessful attempt to render the mist-wreathed mountain top and the pine-clad slopes falling to the river. Two drawings of the *Valley of Ober-Hasli*,[7] although a little weak in handling, foreshadow the achievement of the later *Valley with Winding Streams*[8]—one of Cozens' most perfect and

[1] Burlington Fine Arts Club, *op. cit.* Note by A. P. Oppé. p. 37.
[2] B.M.: Burlington Fine Arts Club, Exhibition, 1871. Dr. John Percy's annotated catalogue, containing notes on his own collection of drawings.
[3] Burlington Fine Arts Club, *op. cit.*
[4] Whitley, 1700–1799, II, p. 309.
[5] Twelve such drawings were bequeathed to the Leeds Art Gallery by Miss Agnes and Mr. Norman Lupton in 1953.
[6] (5) B.M. 1900. 4.11.13.
[7] (28, 31) B.M. 1900. 4.11.20 and 29.
[8] (27) V.A.M. 27.

atmospheric drawings—which was worked up from an earlier sketch. It was clearly a favourite subject, for Cozens made three or four versions, differing slightly in detail. C. F. Bell describes the drawing correctly as *Bern, Lower part of the Valley of Ober-Hasli from the South East*. Nearly all of the earlier drawings are done in outline, executed with a broad reed pen, and with a very loose and free handling in which the influence of Alexander Cozens is clearly apparent. The variation in merit is considerable, and occasionally the colour is harsh and crude, and the foliage treated in a worried method of short diagonal flecks. Sometimes, too, there are faults in drawing; for example, in *Mare Morto, near Naples*,[1] the lake suddenly drops downhill, and in *The Mouth of the Garigliano*,[2] the river similarly is on different levels. Both these are done without outline, in vivid tones of blue, green and brown, and are altogether unlike Cozens' usual style, although the sky in the second is peculiarly his own.

There appears to be no record that Cozens ever went to Sicily, and therefore several drawings of Mount Etna must be copies, or compositions after sketches by Charles Gore.[3] Two versions of *Mount Etna*[4] are of great interest. One, from the Payne Knight Bequest, is clearly the first drawing and is very weak. The mountain and the slopes of land across the strait are done in spots and blobs of anaemic colour, and the rocks in the foreground look like heaps of wool. In the later drawing, the prevailing colour is the grey-blue of his later work, and the composition has been pulled together by darkening the mountain and the cloud of smoke and by inserting a fishing-boat at the right side. *Segesta, Sicily*[5] is another copy after Gore, very pleasant in its clear bright yellow-green tones, but uncertain as to the planes where the hill dips to a valley.

Cozens' second journey abroad[6] was made in 1782 in the company of William Beckford of Fonthill, who was on terms of intimate friendship with Alexander Cozens. Beckford had written to Alexander from Naples in 1780, saying: 'Does your son go on with my drawings? I hope he does—he cannot make too many. Having seen Italy I value them more than ever if that be possible.' In 1782 Beckford had just composed his famous oriental romance *Vathek*, and had come of age in the previous autumn. The journey which started in May 1782 was made in luxury, with several carriages and led horses and grooms. The party entered Germany via Cologne on May 28, and travelled rapidly to Nassereit in the Tyrol, where they arrived on June 4. Seven days after leaving Cologne they reached Innsbruck, and then went to Padua by way of Verona, with an excursion to Venice, 'in order that Cozens may sketch some of my favourite Isles with their morisco towers and waving cypresses'. From there they travelled to Count Algarotti's villa at Mirabella in the

[1] (330) B.M. 1878. 12.28.5.
[2] (343) B.M. 1878. 12.28.7.
[3] For an original sketch of (107) *Mount Etna* by Gore, side by side with Cozens' copy, see Walpole Soc., XXIII, Pl. VIII.
[4] (106) B.M. Oo.4.9.; Ag. 3–394.
[5] (105) B.M. Oo.4.8.
[6] *Memoirs of Beckford*, 2 vols., 1859; Roget, I, pp. 62, 63.

Euganean Hills, near Ferrara, and on to Rome, which they reached on June 25. On July 6 they went to Naples, where both Beckford and Cozens suffered from malarial fever. Beckford then stayed with Sir William and Lady Hamilton at Portici, sailing for Leghorn *en route* for Paris and England in September. Cozens remained for a time in Italy. In a letter to Beckford, Sir William Hamilton writes: 'Cozens passed a day with me here. The vermin plays a good stick upon the violoncello, which was a fine discovery. We played 4 hours. He has made some charming sketches, but I see by his book that he is indolent as usual.'

The sketch-books which he filled during this stay provide evidence for his movements. Between September 18 and October 1 he visited Salerno, Vietri, Raito and La Cava, and then spent some time in Naples. On October 29 he was at Capua Vecchi, and on November 7 at Paestum. On November 10 he went to Gli Astroni. The rest of November was spent in the vicinity of Naples, and on December 8 he travelled back to Rome. In the following September (1783), he set out on his homeward journey, reaching Florence on the twentieth. On the twenty-fourth he was at Bologna, and on October 10, at Lago Maggiore. On the nineteenth Miss Mary Berry, being at Lanslebourg on her way to Italy, saluted him as he was getting out of his *chaise à porteurs* in which he had just made the passage of Mont Cenis.[1] On the twenty-fourth he visited the Grande Chartreuse and made seven drawings.

Though Cozens was probably working at Rome from December 1782 to September 1783, no dated drawings have emerged as witnesses of his activities. Considerable light, however, is thrown on this Italian tour by an examination of the catalogue of a sale at Christie's on April 10, 1805, of 'A Capital and Truly Valuable Collection / of / Original high-Finished / Drawings /, the whole executed by that eminent Artist, / the Younger Cozens, / During a Tour through the Tyrol and Italy, / in company with / An Amateur of Distinguished Taste, / From whose Cabinet they are now first brought forward to / Public Inspection'. The Amateur, of course, is Beckford, as was noted by Edward Edwards in 1808.[2] The ninety-four drawings realised £509 10s. 6d. ; six of them fetched £10 or over; and the highest price was £21 for *Rome from the Villa Madama*,[3] described in the catalogue as 'undoubtedly the most elegant production of the pencil of this admired Artist'. The only other drawing entered in capital letters in the catalogue is *Sepulchral Remains in the Campagna, near Rome*,[4] and this, described as a *chef d'œuvre*, was sold to Edridge for £6 15s. od. The ninety-four drawings, following the course of the tour, can be summarised as follows: Tyrol (6), Verona (1), Padua (5), Arqua (1), Venice (1), Between Rome and Naples (1), Naples (9), Salerno (6), Vietri (4), Between Vietra and Salerno (4), Between Salerno and Evoli (1), Paestum (4), Capua (2), Cumae (1), Terracina (4), Gaeta (1),

[1] *Extracts from the Journal and Correspondence of Miss Berry*, I, 1865, 36.
[2] *Anecdotes of Painters*, 1808, pp. 120, 121.
[3] (363) Whitworth Art Gallery.
[4] (369) Coll. Mrs. A. D. Cowan. A photograph is in C. F. Bell's own extra-illustrated copy of his *Additions and notes to the 23rd volume of the Walpole Society* in the Dept. of Prints and Drawings, V.A.M.

Rome (24),[1] Frascati (4), Tivoli (3), Albano (2), Lake of Vico (1), Lago Maggiore (5), Grande Chartreuse (4).

We have few records of his life after he returned to England, but he probably supported himself by teaching, as well as by the sale of Swiss and Italian drawings, and is presumably the 'Mr. Cozens', who, in 1787–1788, was on the Royal Staff as drawing-master to the Princes Ernest and Augustus.[2] On January 26, 1794, Farington notes that 'Cozens is paralytic to a degree that has incapacitated him'. A few weeks later, an entry in the Diary runs: 'Cousins' (sic) is now confined under the care of Dr. Monro, who has no expectation of his recovery, as it is a total deprivation of the nervous faculty.'[3] Cozens had married at some unknown date, and had two children who at this time were about five or six years old. An appeal was made to the Royal Academy in 1794 for a contribution towards the expenses of the family, and Cosway, Northcote, Farington and others, signed the address. A grant of ten guineas was made by the Council, and further sums were given in 1795, 1796, and to his wife, in 1797. In 1797 Farington again mentions the plight of Cozens, referring in detail to the complicated financial affairs of Cozens' sister-in-law, from which it appears that he was then subsisting on the charity of his brother artists, and adds: 'The expense of attending Cozens is at present from £70 to £80 a year.' Sir George Beaumont, on the authority of Edward Dayes,[4] has generally been credited with the charitable act of associating himself with Dr. Monro in maintaining Cozens from 1794 until his death in 1797; but, in fact, Beaumont and Payne Knight were the principal joint agents in raising an annual subscription, to which the Royal Academy made a yearly contribution. Beckford's name does not appear. On June 17, 1797, Farington met Wyatt and 'spoke to him about Beckford and Cozens'. Wyatt said that he had heard Beckford 'commend old Cozens, but call young Cozens an ungrateful scoundrel', and added that 'Beckford is whimsical, but with so much money may be so'. Farington, always active and energetic, acted as administrator of the fund to which there were at least fifteen subscribers.[5] Cozens' death was announced to Farington on December 14, 1797, by Cozens' brother-in-law, Mr. Roberts. It may be presumed that it occurred on that or the preceding day.

The seven oblong quarto sketch-books, in red sheepskin bindings, containing the products of the tour with Beckford in 1782 and 1783 were found among Beckford's papers, and are now in the possession of the Duke of Hamilton and Brandon.[6] Very many of the

---

[1] Rome, and other place-names, include 'and neighbourhood'. Under the heading of 'Rome', come three drawings entitled 'Capo di Bové'. I took this as a geographical Cape until Mr. L. Collison-Morley pointed out that 'Capo di Bové' was the old name for the Tomb of Cecilia Metella—Caput Bovis in the medieval chronicles and Capo di Bove in the seventeenth century.
[2] Whitley, 1700–1799, II, p. 325.
[3] Diary, I, p. 37.
[4] The Works of the late Edward Dayes, 1805, pp. 324–325.
[5] For full details see Bell, Walpole Soc. XXIII, 1934–1935, p. 19.
[6] Burlington Fine Arts Club Exhibition Catalogue, 1922–1923, p. 35. Complete sets of photographs of the sketches are in the Dept. of Prints and Drawings at the British Museum, the Library of the Victoria and Albert Museum, the Whitworth Art Gallery, Manchester, and the Ashmolean Museum, Oxford.

drawings which Cozens made after his return to England in 1783 were worked up from these sketches, which are on sheets $7\frac{1}{2} \times 10$ inches, and often serve to identify the subjects of his drawings. Several of the sketches, all of which are in pencil or Indian ink, are ticked, indicating perhaps that drawings had been made from them, while others are marked with a cross, perhaps to show that drawings were still to be made from them. Many were used as a foundation for several drawings, each differing slightly from the others in matters of detail; this accounts for the frequency with which a well-known drawing is suddenly encountered in some unexpected place. *The Lake of Nemi*[1] is one of the perpetually recurring drawings (cf. *Mount Etna*, seven versions). Presumably Cozens used to submit his sketches to prospective customers, and execute their chosen subject with sufficient differences to satisfy his artistic conscience and to keep him from growing bored with the repetition. Cozens, in these drawings, and Turner, in his adaptations of Cozens, both show that the true artist can never quite recapitulate. There must always be a new horizon before his eyes. Cozens rarely painted an English landscape; the *Waterfall of Lodore*[2] and *London from Greenwich Hill*[3] are among the few known. Nearly all his drawings are of Italy and Switzerland, with one or two of Corinth which were probably worked up from sketches by James 'Athenian' Stuart. The best of Cozens is in the Swiss work, with its new vision of immense and overpowering forces.

Wordsworth, who was twenty-seven when Cozens died, wrote:

> *Two voices are there: one is of the sea,*
> *One of the mountains; each a mighty voice.*

Both voices speak through English art, but Cozens is the first interpreter of the organ voice of the mountains. Before his time—in the work of Titian, the Poussins, Claude, Salvator Rosa and the rest—mountainous landscape had qualities that were emotional and dramatic; rocks were 'horrid'; rugged grandeur induced feelings of awe, or was used as a theatrical back-cloth to the sentiment of the figures. Even in the case of Towne, it was the grandiose scene and its design which dictated his response. With Cozens comes a new element, the personal subjective emotion that was to find a like expression in the poetry of Wordsworth and his contemporaries. Cozens possessed amazing skill in coping with the technical difficulties of mountain subjects, and the convention which he adopted can perhaps be fully appreciated only by those who have painted from nature in Alpine or sub-Alpine country. Cozens looked for largeness and dignity; he found a way to symbolise and epitomise; he absorbed the infinity of obtruding detail in an impression of poetic grandeur and majesty.

Without effort Cozens deals with the enormous difficulty of scale and proportion in vast altitudes. There are few mountain pictures so dignified as the *View in the Island of*

[1] (140) V.A.M. D.706.
[2] (442) Coll. Charles E. Russell.
[3] (441) Coll. Mrs. Arthur Clifton.

Elba[1] (Pl. 112), and this in spite of its limited range of tint; and, as one of the most noble and impressive of his drawings, we may single out *Alpine Scenery: Packhorses coming up a Pass*[2] (Pl. 114). It is indeed surprising that, in the clear and bright atmosphere of Switzerland and in the sunny plains of Italy, Cozens should have remained so consistently faithful to tones of blue and grey—of grey, warm and cold, mingled with brown or yellow, running from grey-green to pure blue, with all those tints overlapping and variegated with the utmost subtlety. In his later work after his second visit to Rome—and in all his later work he uses no substructure or enforcement of ink—he was not following the older method of adding fuller colour over a monochrome ground; he was floating his colour, low in tone, but pure and full of life, over white paper. To put it quite simply, he was not putting a thin wash of pale colour, yellow or green or blue, over a monochrome dead-colouring of sepia or pale Indian ink, as so many before him had done. He was putting dark over light, a dark blue over a pale one, a brown over a grey-green, but always with colour very simple and restrained, though occasionally he used an admixture of opaque white.

A valuable example of Cozens' later technique is supplied by *View on the Galleria di Sopra, above the Lake of Albano*.[3] It is an incomplete study for a drawing of which there are two finished versions. A broken but flattish wash of pale brownish and greyish green is carried right across the tree, which occupies the main portion of the paper; and a large part of this remains just as it was first laid. Elsewhere over the wash are darker touches indicating depths in the foliage. The tree trunks have been left light in almost complete anticipation of Cotman's later system of 'left spaces'. Such was Cozens' method. His drawings, like the eyes of Swinburne's Félise, are 'the greenest of things blue, the bluest of things gray'.

This is perhaps the place for drawing attention to C. F. Bell's theories about the influence of Swiss painters, and particularly of Ducros, on the work of Cozens and Turner. Bell hinted at this source of inspiration in an article on some water-colour painters of the old British School.[4] His ideas were more fully expounded in his article on Cozens,[5] when his brilliant prescience was supported by W. T. Whitley's discovery of a passage which might be taken as confirming Bell's earlier speculations.[6] It occurs in a singularly unlikely place, Sir Richard Colt Hoare's *History of Modern Wiltshire*, 1822, and deserves quoting:

> I shall now advert to a class of art, which though from convenience of size and pleasurable effect, is favourably received by the public, yet cannot be considered as worthy of being included in the *higher* class of painting. I allude to designs in water-colours, which have made,

---

[1] (433) V.A.M. 3042–1876.
[2] (8) V.A.M. 158–1881.
[3] (154) Coll. Mr. D. L. T. and Miss Armide Oppé.
[4] C. F. Bell, *British water-colour painters: James Moore collection*, Walpole Soc., V, 1915–1917, pp. 56–57.
[5] C. F. Bell and T. Girtin, *J. R. Cozens, drawings and sketches*, Walpole Soc., XXIII, 1934–1935.
[6] Whitley, II, p. 363.

108 'Between Sallanches and Servoz, Mont Blanc in the Distance'
B.M. 1900.4.11.13   9½ × 13⅞: 242 × 353   *Water-colour, dated August 27, 1776*
John Robert COZENS (1752–1797)

109 'In the Tyrol near Brixen'
Coll. Sir Edmund Bacon Bt.   14½ × 21: 368 × 533   *Water-colour, signed and dated 1790*
John Robert COZENS (1752–1797)

110 'Naples from Sir William Hamilton's Villa at Portici'
V.A.M. 121–1894   9⅛ × 14⅜: 232 × 366   *Water-colour*
John Robert COZENS (1752–1797)

111 'Padua in a Storm'
Coll. Herbert Powell, N.A.C.F.   10¼ × 14¾: 260 × 374   *Water-colour*
John Robert COZENS (1752–1797)

112 'View in the Isle of Elba'

V.A.M. 3042–1876 $14\frac{1}{2} \times 21\frac{1}{8}$: 368×537 *Water-colour, signed and dated 1780 (?)*

John Robert COZENS (1752–1797)

113 'Valley with Winding Streams'

V.A.M. D.708 $14\frac{5}{8} \times 20\frac{7}{8}$: 372×530 *Water-colour, signed and dated 1788*

John Robert COZENS (1752–1797)

114 'Alpine Scenery: Pack Horses Coming up a Pass'
V.A.M. 158–1881   17½ × 23¼: 445 × 591   *Water-colour*
John Robert Cozens (1752–1797)

115 'View of the Campagna'
V.A.M. Dyce 705   20 × 28: 508 × 712   *Water-colour*
John Robert Cozens (1752–1797)

within these few years past, a most astonishing progress and in many instances may be said to have attained the acme of perfection; for I question if the series of architectural drawings of Salisbury, in this apartment, executed by Mr. Turner, a Royal Academician, will ever be surpassed. This rapid improvement in water-colour drawing has taken place within my own memory; for during my younger days, Paul Sandby was the monarch of the plain, and esteemed the best artist in this line. The next marked improvement in colouring was recognised in the drawings of Mr. John Smith, now living, and to whom, as an instructor, I owe the little I do know of drawing: but the advancement from *drawing* to *painting* in water-colours did not take place till after the introduction into England of the drawings of Louis du Cros, a Swiss artist, who settled at Rome; his works proved the force, as well as the consequence, that could be given to the unsubstantial body of water-colours, and to him I attribute the first knowledge and power of water-colours. Hence have sprung a numerous succession of Artists in this line; a Turner, a Glover, a Nicholson, Reinagle, De Wint, Nash, *cum multis aliis*. During a long Residence in Italy I had frequently occasion to observe the system, and mark the progress of this ingenious Artist; and with regret I found that his superior merit began to create him enemies, who endeavoured to lessen the merit of his works, by questioning their durability.

That passage may perhaps be interpreted as being written by a collector, proud of his possessions and possibly a little narrow in his views, to justify his own judgment. He may be exaggerating the importance of Ducros, just as Bell's views as to the potent inspiration of Ducros during the closing years of the eighteenth century, and particularly in connection with Cozens and Turner, may be overstrained. Colt Hoare as a contemporary advocate of the theory, seems to stand alone. Other contemporaries of Cozens, Sandby, Turner and Girtin give no hint in their writings of any possibility of Swiss influence. Nowhere, to my knowledge, does W. H. Pyne, a 'gifted proficient' and the earliest historian of the movement, refer to the influence of Ducros, though he has much to say about the water-colour drawing developing into the water-colour painting and becoming as powerful as a picture in oil. In view of my insufficient knowledge of Ducros, Bell's hypothesis must await further examination.[1]

Seldom, and perhaps never in his finest drawings, does Cozens introduce a touch of pure green, and when he experiments with warm reddish and purple notes, the result is a failure. It seems as if he had no eye except for the subtle *nuances* of his delicate greys and blues. But he handles these with such skill that not only have these drawings far greater force than many a drawing more ambitious and more grandiose in colour but they have also splendidly distributed passages of sunlight and shadow. It is, of course, absurd to suggest, as has so often been done, that Cozens' limited range of colours was due to the fact that no others were procurable at that time. Redgrave states that 'John Cozens about 1783 could only procure for his tinted works Indian red, lake, indigo, yellow ochre, burnt umber and burnt sienna with black'.[2] That list undoubtedly suggests the deliberately chosen range of Cozens' palette, but it is a mistake to suppose that he could not have

[1] A. P. Oppé, *Alexander and John Robert Cozens*, 1952, p. 139 and n., appears to discount the specific influence of Ducros on Cozens. The most important collection of Ducros' work is at the Musée Cantonal des Beaux-Arts, Lausanne, but there are also other drawings in the B.M.
[2] S. Redgrave, *Descriptive Catalogue of Water-Colour Paintings in South Kensington Museum*, 1876, p. 17.

obtained others. Francis Towne, an exact contemporary, employs at times a wide range of many bright tints. Dayes wrote, 'One great inconvenience the student labours under arises from the too great quantity of colours put into his hands; an evil so encouraged by the drawing-master and colour-man, that it is not uncommon to give two or three dozen colours in a box, a thing quite unnecessary'.[1] Alexander Cozens, in his Roman sketch-book of 1746, notes that he has 'Water Collors 30 in all in bottles',[2] and even if some of these were mixed tints or in duplicate, his note suggests no lack of colour; and for his son there were still more available. He probably had another blue, possibly Prussian blue mixed with a little black, in addition to the indigo which Redgrave gives as his only blue. If indigo was the only blue which he used, it is difficult to understand how Cozens' blues have held so firmly while the indigo of so many contemporaries has faded. It is a possible explanation that Cozens' drawings, till recent years, were considered as being for the portfolio and cabinet rather than the wall and so have escaped deterioration, but Constable, at any rate, saw them hanging on a wall, and Sir George Beaumont had one in his breakfast-room, hanging beside four Claudes.[3]

Some of Cozens' contemporaries and successors no doubt regarded his work as rather thin. W. H. Pyne,[4] in speaking of the work of Girtin and Turner, refers to them as 'two superior artists, to whose works Cozens', as regards the term paintings, bear no comparison,—his being at most little more than merely tinted chiaro-scuro, similar to mezzotinto prints thinly washed with colour'. The same writer says[5]: 'His drawings, for the want of that knowledge of the power of the pigments used with gum-water, which all were then deficient in, were comparatively weak,' and again uses the phrase that they were 'little more than tinted chiar-oscuro'. He also gives a useful description of Cozens' methods:

> Cozens compounded his cloud tints, and those for his distant mountains, of Indian red, a small portion of lake, indigo, and yellow ochre; in the middle distance he blended a tint of black; and his fore-grounds were principally of black and burnt umber. His distant trees were tinted with the warm washes used for the sky; and those for the nearer than middle distance with yellow ochre and indigo, enriched with burnt sienna; the immediate fore-ground trees and shrubs with the same, rendered one or two degrees stronger. Girtin retained more of his manner and touch than either Turner or Varley; but in the early works of each, much of the style of John Cozens is observable.

Having shown that the range of colours available was not nearly so narrow as was thought, it may be emphasized again that there was no enforced economy in Cozens' colour. He showed his own choice, in his limited palette. His general view of *Naples from*

---

[1] *The Works of the late Edward Dayes*, 1805, p. 298.
[2] In the Walpole Soc., XXIII, p. 2, C. F. Bell suggests that these 'would have been body colours for use with a gouache medium'. Why not for use with gum water, and possibly already mixed with gum and water in the bottles? Alexander Cozens worked in water-colour, but never in gouache.
[3] C. R. Leslie, *Life of Constable*, p. 109.
[4] *Somerset House Gazette*, 1824, I, p. 65.
[5] *Library of the Fine Arts*, 1832, III, pp. 11–13.

Sir William Hamilton's Villa at Portici[1] (Pl. 110), is a monochrome in blue, but with its vaporous sky is as intimate and subtle as dawn itself. He may have borrowed some of his silvery colour scheme, as well as his sense of composition, from Claude. In the Ashmolean Museum is an oil-painting by Claude of *Early Morning with the Story of Ascanius*, carried out in that scheme of greys, blue-greens and blues, which Cozens adopted. Cozens deliberately limited his colours. He chose for his theme the more spacious aspects of landscape—far-reaching horizons, deep, over-arching skies, mountains. He differed from his contemporaries in that he cared nothing for the modest contour, the pastoral fold (his animals are often shockingly drawn), or the intimacy of fragments of architecture. He followed Claude and Wilson, he forestalled Crome, in his love of air and space; but he was unlike Claude and Wilson in that he was content to let air and space make his picture without the association of castle-crowned hill, or ruined temple, or dancing nymphs and fauns. When he drew a ruin, he drew it because it was there, part of his landscape, not introduced by artifice, and he rendered not only the precise facts, but their combination with the trembling and palpitating light and atmosphere in which they were veiled. To realise his consummate power we have but to look at the work of later men such as T. M. Richardson or W. L. Leitch. They painted the same country, or country of a similar sort, but their facts are accented and theatrical, accumulated and piled up rather than organised and integrated. Painters of this type lacked Cozens' selective sense and scale of values.

Lest it should be thought that Cozens' work is uniformly placid and serene in subject, attention may be drawn to the unexpected dramatic quality in such works as his *Part of Padua from the Walls*.[2] Depicting a vivid storm scene, it has brilliant atmospheric feeling of an unusual kind. Forked lightning gleams through a stormy sky, and shows the buildings in white and radiant light against the encircling gloom of sky and trees. The original study for it is in the Beckford Sketch Books, June 1782. We may link Cozens with Girtin as being the first artist of the British school to make such a careful study of skies, now peaceful and luminous, now charged with the fury or menace of stormy clouds. And always, as Laurence Binyon has pointed out, he makes his skies 'whether peaceful or tormented, an integral part of the design pervading the whole'.[3]

In Cozens' incorporeal work the actual paint and execution count for little in comparison with Turner. Even when Turner was trusting to inspiration, he was drawing from deep wells of knowledge and experience, and he was always the incomparable master of technique, alert to every artifice. Turner may have used a method, almost equally abstract, when dealing with Swiss scenes, but he imported into them an atmosphere and a rainbow beauty of opalescent colour that perhaps just now and then—but not often, and not everywhere—the landscape may have shown. In the case of Cozens, his washes of

[1] (240) V.A.M. 121–1894.
[2] (214) Coll. Herbert Powell, N.A.C.F.
[3] *English Water-Colours*, 1933, p. 54.

colour are full of meaning, but unaided by technical device. 'Their haunting beauty and incomparable power,' as A. J. Finberg has said, 'are spiritual, not material'; and, as he wisely adds, that was what Constable perhaps meant when he called Cozens 'the greatest genius that ever touched landscape'; he did not say that he was the greatest artist.[1]

[1] A. J. Finberg, *Development of British Landscape Painting in Water-Colour, Studio* special number, 1917–1918.

CHAPTER VIII

Eighteenth-century figure subjects : portraits : book-illustrations

*John Collet   John Sanders   John Downman   George Dance
Giovanni Cipriani   Angelica Kauffmann   Elias Martin   Samuel Shelley
Adam Buck   William Hamilton   Richard Westall   Stephen F. Rigaud
Lady Diana Beauclerk   Thomas Stothard   John H. Mortimer
The Corboulds   Edward F. Burney   Francis Wheatley
Julius C. Ibbetson   Thomas Uwins*

John Collet (*c.*1725–1780), born in London, was first and foremost a figure painter and, with his taste for the humorous aspects of life, stands between Hogarth and Rowlandson. Proof of his popularity is that between 1768 and 1774 at least thirty of his pictures were reproduced as mezzotint engravings, and others in 1782, two years after his death. He began as a pupil of George Lambert, the landscape painter, and studied at the St. Martin's Lane school. He exhibited at the Free Society from 1761 to 1783, showing forty-seven works, mainly humorous pieces of considerable merit, though he also painted in water-colour a number of small landscapes and scenes of rural life such as *At the Inn Door*[1] and *On the River Bank*.[2] He was a resident of Cheyne Row, Chelsea, where he died in 1780; had an independent fortune inherited from a relative; and was said to be of shy and retiring habits, much respected, and of grave manners and conversation—little though this might be expected of the man who painted the delightful skittle-alley picture of lively *Miss Tipapin going for all Nine* while her companion blows the froth from a mug of ale, or the *Bachelor's Fare of Bread and Cheese and Kisses*.

Collet was to some extent a successor to Hogarth, and Redgrave says that he 'plagiarised Hogarth, but missed his deep moral'.[3] He was indeed less satirical than Hogarth, more anxious to convey a quiet comic sense, and more interested in the narration aspect of social matters. The wide flounced skirts and enormous piled-up bonnets of the period lend charm to his attractive descriptions of women-folk whether in town or country garb. Good examples of his work are the *Night Musicians*[4] and *An Asylum for the Deaf*[5] (Pl. 117).

[1] B.M. 1890. 5.12.27.   [2] B.M. 1890. 5.12.24.   [3] *Dictionary of Artists*, 1878.
[4] V.A.M. 508–1892.   [5] V.A.M. 1694–1871.

143

In the latter two deaf patients at a window try to hear a band, the sound of which, with other raucous noises of the street, cannot reach them. Collet's drawings (typical 'stained' drawings) are usually heavily shaded with Indian ink, his colour being very slight, as though from the first he was intentionally working for reproduction by the mezzotint engraver.

John Sanders (1750–c.1825), a portrait painter, also worked at times in the Hogarthian vein, if we may judge by what is apparently the single known example of his work in water-colour. His *Bagnigge Wells*[1] (Pl. 121), c. 1772, shows an animated company of ladies and their gallants promenading the room or seated at tables drinking tea. John Raphael Smith paid it the compliment of engraving it in mezzotint, and perhaps had it in mind when, three years later, he transcended it with a similar subject of his own, *A Promenade at Carlisle House, Soho Square*,[2] a lovely drawing in coloured crayon.

Before coming to a somewhat different group of figure-painters in the second half of the eighteenth century, we may stop to consider two portrait-draughtsmen. By the close of the nineteenth century John Downman had been forgotten, and not until recent years did anyone know that Downman deserved some attention as a landscape draughtsman. Certain reasons for a revival of interest in him can be exactly defined. In 1884 the British Museum bought a series of his drawings from the collection of Sir R. Cunliffe, and these, when exhibited about 1891 to 1894, excited great attention. In 1893 the Amateur Art Society obtained a number of his drawings from private owners and made them the centre of their exhibition at 18 Carlton House Terrace.[3] In 1905, Mrs. Julia Frankau wrote an enthusiastic article,[4] and in 1907 Dr. G. C. Williamson published his book.[5] In the same year Messrs. Graves exhibited in their Pall Mall Galleries one hundred and twenty representative examples of Downman's art.

John Downman (1750–1824) was born in Devonshire, the fifth son of a Quaker attorney from St. Neots, and went to school at Ruabon. He came at an early age to London, where he studied under Benjamin West—'my most beloved teacher', he always called him—and from 1769 at the Royal Academy. He exhibited at the Free Society of Artists in 1768 and at the Royal Academy from 1770 to 1819. In 1777 he was practising at Cambridge, and in 1778 was winning enough recognition to enable him to settle in London. He was elected A.R.A. in 1795, visited Plymouth in 1806, practised at Exeter in 1807, and after again working in London, settled at Chester about 1818 and died at Wrexham, Denbighshire. It was always a grievance with Downman that the Royal Academy did not promote him to full membership. He was for many years on bad terms with that institution because they treated his portraits as drawings and hung them in the poor light of the lower room at Somerset House.[6] In 1784 he removed all his portraits after receiving a communication

---

[1] Whitworth Art Gallery, Manchester.
[2] V.A.M. 512–1892.
[3] Catalogue B.M. N.1.9 (4).
[4] Julia Frankau, 'A note on five portraits by John Downman, A.R.A.', *Burlington Magazine*, 1903, I, p. 122.
[5] *John Downman, A.R.A.*
[6] The facts as to Downman's relationship with the Royal Academy are given by Whitley, 1700–1799, II, pp. 66, 67.

from the Secretary: 'The Council have determined your performances to be drawings, and as to the other conditions specified in your letter I am ordered to acquaint you that the Council never receive directions.' In 1786 his portraits, described at this time as 'universally admired and sought after by the first people of rank and fashion' were exhibited at Saville House, Leicester Square, to which the artist had recently removed from St. James's Street.

In 1804 he went to tea with Farington and complained that his drawings were not placed in the Council Room, which he considered the post of honour.[1] In 1807 Farington notes that Downman called to 'request my interest to be elected an Academician and hinted that if not chosen He shld. resign His Diploma of Associate. I gave him only general answers, and said His residence not being in London might be an objection.'[2]

Downman had a long career as a provider of fashionable portraits of small size, with reference to which W. T. Whitley quotes two contemporary criticisms of great interest.[3] One writer, reviewing the Academy of 1789, says:

> Downman's small heads have their usual delicacy and their usual sameness. He has but two passable faces, one face for ladies and another for gentlemen, and one or other of these prototypes all his likenesses are brought to resemble.

In 1797 a reviewer in the *Morning Post* refers to a subject picture at the Academy of *Edward the Fourth on a visit to the Duchess of Bedford*, one of Downman's attempts to break away from pure portraiture:

> This is another attempt at historical painting which moves our pity. The artist has long been known to society by his portraits of persons of fashion which were very neatly manufactured, and the ladies were mightily pleased because he tinted every cheek with a rosy effusion and washed every bosom with a semblance of Olympian dew. In the prosecution of such little likenesses he was all perhaps that his employers desired, but attempts at sublimity are above his powers.

Downman's little likenesses remain pleasing to-day for their rosily tinted cheeks and white bosoms (though his sitters were by no means all female), and by the variety of graceful costume which he depicts. Very dainty are the simple white gowns and fichus, the sashes of delicate pink and blue, the mob caps, and the great hats of straw. And very interesting, too, is Downman's record of the powdered 'sesquipedalian coiffure', which was in vogue from about 1770 to 1780. The pyramid of hair, piled up in rolls at the back, stuffed with tow, and fixed with wax, often had to last a revoltingly long time. Says a hairdresser's advertisement of 1782: 'A new method of stuccowing the hair is in the most fashionable taste, to last with very little repair during the whole session of Parliament. Price only five guineas. N.B.—He takes but one hour to build the head, and two for baking it'. And it was in 1781 that Wilson, the barber, who lived opposite Goldsmith across the market-

[1] *Diary*, June 25, 1804.
[2] *Diary*, June 5, 1807.
[3] Whitley, 1700–1799, II, pp. 212, 213.

place at Olney, joined the Baptists and refused to dress Lady Hunter's hair on a Sunday. Consequently she was obliged to call him in on Saturday evenings, and more than once sat up all night to prevent the disarrangement of her 'head'. Like his contemporary, George Dance, Downman preferred his sitters in profile. About three-quarters of his drawings show the side face and so do full justice to hair and head-dress.

Downman drew on very thin paper in black chalk with a fine point, working over the shadows with a stump, thus obtaining some of the soft half-tones of a mezzotint. Slight colouring was added to lips, cheeks and hair, in water-colour; these were days when this kind of work was described as a stained drawing. In some cases red chalk, and occasionally a wash of sepia, was used. Frequently the colour is laid on the back of the thin paper, and shows like a transparency. Williamson relates how Downman obtained the hint from a piece of mischief on the part of one of his children. A pencil drawing of Mrs. Downman lay on the table, face down, and the child picked up his father's brush and dabbed some pink on the back. Downman thought the drawing would be spoiled, but finding that a pleasing effect was given by the colour showing through the thin paper, adopted this method as his common practice.[1]

The Oppé Collection reveals that Downman, quite unexpectedly and obscurely, was a charming draughtsman of landscape, to be linked with Towne as an innovator with an entirely fresh eye for form and design. The series of studies in this collection was made when Downman was in Rome with Joseph Wright, A.R.A., in 1773 to 1774. In dealing with trees, as in *Wood near Albano*[2] and *Tree Trunk near Albano*[3] (Pl. 118), Downman selects and emphasises such patches and portions of trunk or foliage as interest him, eliminating or suppressing the rest. His tinting is very slight, almost monochrome, and used for hints of sunlight and atmosphere rather than for any effect of local colour. His *Looking across the Campagna from Marino* is a landscape painted as though he had primroses and laburnum in his mind, with little more colour than to suggest a sunny glow. He seems often to have washed a pallid yellow right across the paper on which he made his admirable drawings in pen and Indian ink. His *Gaga Park* is a powerful, but almost monochrome, study of rocks and beech trunks. A volume entitled 'A Series of sketches on the spot made by J. Downman when he took a Tour to the Lakes in Westmoreland and Cummerland (*sic*) 1812',[4] contains thirty-three sketches executed in pen and wash on tinted paper. This book was originally given by the artist to his friend, John Parry of Wrexham, and passed by successive stages to his great-niece, Miss Edgeworth, from whom it was bought by F. Wellesley.[5] So far as is known, the drawings in this book and the Roman subjects in the Oppé Collection make up the whole of Downman's landscape *œuvre*, and the sketches of 1812 show an interesting return to his ideas of 1773-1774, the years during which he was in Italy.

[1] Williamson, *op. cit.* pp. xiii, xiv.
[3] R.A. Exhibition cat. no. 65.
[5] Sotheby's, June 29, 1920, lot 239.

[2] R.A. Exhibition cat. nos. 68, 69.
[4] V.A.M. E.836–68–1928.

146

George Dance's portrait drawings have much in common with those of Downman, but though he was possibly better at accomplishing a likeness, Dance had not quite Downman's charm. Nearly all of his sitters were male. Dance (1741–1825) was the younger son of George Dance, architect and surveyor to the Corporation of London, for whom he designed the Mansion House in 1739. George Dance the Younger studied architecture in Italy and after his return succeeded to the surveyorship. He rebuilt Newgate in 1770 and designed the front of the Guildhall. He was one of the foundation members of the Royal Academy, and was its professor of Architecture from 1798 to 1805. From about 1793 he devoted himself constantly to portraits, practically all of them in profile, drawn with pencil and often slightly touched with colour on lips, ears and face, and sometimes on the costume, in the Downman manner. Seventy-six of these portraits, admirably engraved in the crayon manner by William Daniell, were published between 1808 and 1814; they include interesting records of contemporary artists, Benjamin West, John Flaxman, Richard Cosway, Thomas Banks and others. The British Museum has a series of excellent examples of his work in portraiture, many of them tinted; others are owned by the Royal Academy, notably a portrait, in a pink coat, of its first secretary, *F. M. Newton, R.A.*, one of *Paul Sandby, R.A.* in grey coat and pink waistcoat, and another of *J. M. W. Turner, R.A.* The Turner portrait was exhibited at the Academy in the year of its making, 1800.

The Farington Diary is full of references to Dance. Its opening words on July 13, 1793, are: 'Went early in company with Mr. George Dance and Mr. Samuel Lysons, of the Temple, to Lord Orford's at Strawberry Hill, where we breakfasted with his Lordship. In the forenoon Mr. George Dance made a drawing of his Lordship's profile, an excellent resemblance.'[1] From Farington and from Whitley[2] it may be gathered that Dance was a friend of Garrick, played well on the violin, the violoncello and the flute, and was something of a composer. His marching chorus for the British army, called *One and All* was performed before the King at Covent Garden in October 1798. The Prince of Wales, who was also present, said that 'it was the most appropriate music He ever heard & that He wished to have a copy of it to send to the band of his regiment'. Dance was an intimate friend of Sir George Beaumont and designed his house at Coleorton.

Though Downman and Dance used water-colour as an adventitious aid to their portrait drawings, it was not quite so fortuitously employed by other artists who worked at *genre* painting and designs of a decorative character. A whole group of eighteenth-century artists devoted themselves to figure subjects. Some of the earliest gave a quasi-classical rendering of cupids and nymphs, gods and goddesses, fauns and satyrs, or allegories of Virtue, Honour, Love and Justice, or poetic pastorals of Daphnis and Chloe, Strephon and Urania. Shakespeare, the Bible, and the English lyric and idyllic poets, provided rich material and suitable sentiment. The chief inspiration of the school was Giovanni Battista

---

[1] Dance's portrait of Horace Walpole, Earl of Orford, is reproduced in the *Diary*, facing p. 2.
[2] Whitley, 1700–1799, II, p. 255.

Cipriani (1727–1785), an Italian, born at Florence, who came to England in 1755 under the inducement of Sir William Chambers and Joseph Wilton, the sculptor. In 1768 he was one of the foundation members of the Royal Academy and was an exhibitor there till 1779. A fertile designer of figure subjects he produced a vast number of drawings showing some invention and an accomplished sense of design.

Closely associated with Cipriani was Angelica Kauffmann (1741–1807), born at Coire, Switzerland. She went to Italy with her father in 1752 and worked at portrait painting, which Dr. Johnson thought 'an improper employment for a woman'. 'Public practice of any art,' he observed, 'And staring in men's faces, is very indelicate in a female.' In 1766 she came to England in the company of the wife of our ambassador at Venice. In the following year she was deceived into marriage with a valet, who passed himself off as his master, the Count de Horn, but the impostor was persuaded to make tracks for Germany. Angelica had several admirers, and in 1808 George Dance summed up for Farington some of the gossip in connection with his brother Nathaniel, afterwards Sir Nathaniel Dance Holland:

> At Rome He (Nathaniel) became acquainted with Angelica Kauffman, and became so enamoured of Her, she encouraging His passion, that when he came to England whither she also came, it was settled between them that they shld. marry.—But in England she became acquainted with Sir Joshua Reynolds, who showed Her much attention, & it is supposed that she looked to Him, expecting that He wd. offer Himself to Her. Her reception of Dance having now become more cold, & Her intercourse with Sir Joshua being noticed by Him, He remonstrated with Her in such a manner that she complained of His temper & assigned that as a reason for now refusing to marry Him—His passion for Her was extreme & He engaged *His Father* to write to Her, but all wd. not do, Her resolution remained unaltered.—(George) Dance sd. she never was beautiful, but there was something amiable & feminine in Her appearance that engaged people to Her.[1]

She was twice painted by Sir Joshua, who sometimes entered her as 'Miss Angel' in his note-books, and with Cipriani was one of the foundation members of the Royal Academy. After the death of her first husband she married Zucchi, a Venetian painter, and was with him at Rome from 1781 till her death. Cipriani and Angelica Kauffmann, in their many water-colour drawings, produced light decorative trifles, while Bartolozzi, Schiavonetti, and other engravers, used line and stipple with an appropriate delicacy for reproducing the spirit and fancy of the original drawings. These painters and engravers formed a self-sufficient foreign group, a kind of Soho quarter in English art.

Another foreign artist of the period who worked in London was Elias Martin (1739–1818) born at Stockholm, studied in Paris from 1766 and came to London in 1768. He was elected A.R.A. in 1770, and besides working in oil, painted *genre* subjects and landscapes in water-colour. Walpole writes of him in 1772: 'A Swede, excellent for character and caricature in washed drawings. He teaches to draw, but does not draw well.' In 1780 he left London to become painter to the King of Sweden, but from 1788 to 1791 was living

[1] For Angelica's attachments see also Whitley, 1700–1799, I, pp. 371–373.

148

at Bath, and in 1808 Farington refers to him as 'being nobody knows where abroad', but he is known to have died at Stockholm. His fellow countryman, a Swedish sculptor, J. T. Sergel, made a brilliant caricature inscribed *Elias Martin, London, 1799,* showing an amusing interior of Martin's studio, where he is demonstrating to the dumbfounded Sergel a new and ingenious contrivance for displaying drawings one after the other.[1]

Samuel Shelley (1750–1808) rose from a small beginning to a place in the front rank of miniature-painters of his day. While he constantly exhibited miniatures at the Royal Academy, he was also practising what Dayes describes as 'history in small', adding that this places him 'above the character of a mere miniature painter'. He was one of the founders, and treasurer, of the newly-formed Old Water Colour Society, which was originated in 1804. While he exhibited imaginative pictures, of the nature of *Love Disappointed,* he also sent numerous portraits to the Society's gallery and resigned his treasurership in 1806, when it was decided that his portraits did not promote the Society's objects and that they did not entitle him to a share in its profits. *Memory gathering Flowers mowed down by Time*[2] (Pl. 129) is perhaps the best-known of his allegorical subjects. In the Victoria and Albert Museum are seven of his sketch-books, 1786 to 1788, filled with notes not only for portraits but for fanciful subjects from Tasso, Shakespeare and other poets. At the British Museum are three small water-colour ovals of *St. Cecilia, Hassan* and *Sicander.*[3]

Another miniature painter, who embarked on 'history in small' was Adam Buck (1759–1833), native of Cork, who passed the greater part of his career in London. He illustrated *The Sentimental Journey* (Pl. 131), and produced for the engraver a number of *genre* pieces delicately drawn in water-colour and pencil. There is much charm in his frankly sentimental and emotional treatment of *Mother and Child*[4] engraved in 1808 with the legend:

> *Mamma, don't make me beg in vain;*
> *Pray read that Pretty Book again.*

His small full-length portraits of women and girls in water-colour were immensely popular in the early years of the nineteenth century, but when he died (at the age of seventy-five) he had outlived his vogue, so that his widow and three children had to obtain assistance from the charitable fund of the Royal Academy.

Another artist who was in great demand by the engravers was William Hamilton (1751–1801). He was born at Chelsea of Scottish parents in 1751, and with the assistance of Robert Adam visited Italy, where he studied under Zucchi. On his return in 1769 he entered the Royal Academy schools. He exhibited at the Academy from 1774, being elected A.R.A. in 1784 and R.A. in 1789. His portraits and subject pictures were popular in his day, and it is proof of his success that he received six hundred guineas for painting

---

[1] Reproduced in G. Gothe, *J. T. Sergel,* 1899.
[2] V.A.M. 1754–1871.
[3] B.M. 1861. 8.10.92–94.
[4] V.A.M. P.69–1930.

the panels of the Lord Chancellor of Ireland's state carriage, now at the Science and Art Museum, Dublin. In water-colours his work was light and decorative, elegant and vapid, and is sufficiently exemplified by his *Gleaners*,[1] 1796, and *Nymphs adorning the Sleeping Bacchus with Wreaths*.[2] He made a large number of fanciful and sentimental drawings of children, clearly with an eye to their value for the purpose of stipple engraving.

Richard Westall (1765–1836) belongs to the same group, and he too painted child subjects such as his *Children dividing Fruit*, 1791, which was engraved in colour by W. Nutter. He was admitted to the Royal Academy schools in 1785, and became known by his prolific output for engraved illustrations to Milton, Gray, Crabbe, Shakespeare, etc., his original drawings being dainty in design and delicate in colour. Some larger water-colours of historical subjects are highly finished, and in the direct rendering of local colour show a departure from the mannerism of the tinted drawing. Westall followed Hamilton closely both in manner and subject. At Agnew's Gallery in 1945 *Strephon and Phyllis*, *The Bird's Nest* and *The Reaper's Child Asleep* by Westall hung beside *The Gleaners* and *Cutting Faggots* by Hamilton, and displayed similar outlook and mannerisms. Both artists were highly accomplished, but their pretentious work was forced in colour and sticky in sentiment. Westall was elected A.R.A. in 1792 and R.A. in 1794. It is of interest that he gave lessons to Queen Victoria in her young days before her accession. Smirke gave a good summing-up of this artist when he told Farington that Westall's poems 'had very much the character of His works as a Painter—not much originality or strength of conception—but express an amiable feeling and will not lessen His general character in respect of talent'. On the other hand, W. H. Pyne put on record that 'Mr. Northcote, who was a great admirer of water colour art, always maintained, and his judgment upon this subject has never been disputed, that "Westall is as much intitled to share in the honour of being one of the founders of the school of painting in water-colours, as his highly-gifted contemporaries Girtin and Turner . . . many of the finest drawings by Mr. Westall were for several consecutive years distinguished amongst the most generally attractive works of the Somerset-house exhibition"'.

Stephen Francis Rigaud (1777–1861) belongs to the same circle as Shelley, and with him was one of the original sixteen members of the Old Water-Colour Society in 1804. He studied in the Royal Academy schools, and contributed to the Academy exhibitions from 1797 to 1815, and again in 1848. His pictures were mainly imaginative or allegorical, the subjects being frequently taken from Milton, Spenser, Ossian and other poets. His connection with the Water-Colour Society, of which he had been treasurer, ended in 1815, although he made a half-hearted move towards rejoining in 1849. His *Telemachus discovering the Priest of Apollo*[3] (Pl. 137) is typical of his subject matter and his manner.

As the demand for illustrated books increased, more artists turned to this type of work.

[1] V.A.M. 1673–1871.
[2] V.A.M. 505–1892.
[3] V.A.M. 76–1873.

150

One of the first to do so apart from the foreign group, was Lady Diana Beauclerk (1734–1808), an English amateur of birth and distinction.[1] She was the eldest daughter of Charles Spencer, third Duke of Marlborough, was married in 1757 to Frederick St. John, second Viscount Bolingbroke, was divorced in 1768, and two days later married Topham Beauclerk. Her second marriage was apparently no more happy than the first. In July 1794, Farington made a note of his visit to Strawberry Hill:

> Lord Orford mentioned many particulars relative to the late Mr. Topham Beauclerc. He said He was the worst tempered man He ever knew.—Lady Di passed a most miserable life with him. Lord O, out of regard to her invited them occasionally to pass a few days at Strawberry Hill.— They slept in separate beds,—Beauclerc was remarkably filthy in his person which generated vermin.—He took Laudanum regularly in vast quantities.—He seldom rose before one or two o'clock.—His principal delight was in disputing on subjects that occurred, this He did accutely.— Before He died he asked pardon of Lady Di, for his ill usage of her.—He had one son and two daughters by Lady Di.

With all his faults, however, Topham Beauclerk was immensely popular, as will be found in the pages of Boswell's *Life of Johnson*. His eloquence and wit delighted such men as Johnson, Burke, Gibbon and Garrick. 'Everything comes from Beauclerk so easily,' said Dr. Johnson, 'that it appears to me I labour if I say a good thing.'

After her husband's death in 1780, Lady Diana seems to have taken growing pleasure in her art. Her most important work was the illustration of Burger's *Leonora* (1796) and Dryden's *Fables* (1797). Many of her studies of children and *amorini* were engraved by Bartolozzi. Her large *Gipsies and Female Rustics*[2] (Pl. 136), a companion to a similar subject painted for Horace Walpole in 1781, shows that contemporary estimation was not entirely exaggerated. Reynolds is reported to have said that 'many of her Ladyship's drawings might be studied as models'. Walpole speaks of her work with unbounded enthusiasm. Her first attempt at illustration consisted of seven designs 'in sut-water' for Walpole's tragedy, *The Mysterious Mother* (1768). These were kept at Strawberry Hill in a small chamber, christened 'The Beauclerk Closet', where they hung on Indian blue damask. He described them as 'incomparable' and 'sublime' saying that 'Salvator Rosa and Guido could not surpass their expression and beauty'. In a letter dated July 18, 1780, he says: 'I expect [Paul] Sandby every day. He is to attempt Lady Di's drawings for my play in his new aquatinta. It is a thousand pities they should exist only in one septinity, and that the world should have no idea of the powers of her genius if the originals should perish.' They did not perish, though Sandby never made his prints, and Lady Di's 'seven drawings in ebony and gold frames', when sold at Strawberry Hill in 1842, realised only thirteen guineas. Her facile and expressive draughtsmanship, obviously based on Italian models and encouraged by her friendship with Reynolds, brought force and charm into her drawings of Pan, Cupid, or little chubby children frisking in a woodland Arcady. Her pictures rely on drawing and decorative design—and she rarely fails as a designer—rather

---

[1] Mrs. Steuart Erskine, *Lady Diana Beauclerk*, 1903.
[2] V.A.M. 9-1883.

than upon colour. Her tints were often little more than a touch of rose or a wash of pale blue.

It is impossible here to record all the illustrators, many of them excelling in design and invention, who used water-colour to shade and tint their drawings made for the engraver. Outstanding, however, among them is Thomas Stothard (1755–1834) who won deserved popularity by the charm and refinement of his work. Perhaps the most prolific book-illustrator in history, he was born at the Black Horse Inn in Long Acre, and after some elementary education under the care of an uncle at Acomb, near York and Tadcaster, he returned to London. After a little more schooling at Ilford, where the father of Grimaldi the clown taught him dancing, he was apprenticed to a pattern designer for Spitalfields silk. His master encouraged him to illustrate Homer and Spenser, and in 1777 he entered the Royal Academy Schools. He exhibited at the Academy in 1778, became A.R.A. in 1791, and R.A. in 1794. Sir Thomas Lawrence was elected a full member at the same time, but took second place to Stothard. Incidentally, he was in the habit of having himself shaved at 26 Maiden Lane, and was of use in encouraging the barber to let his son become an artist. The boy was Turner. Though Stothard painted much in oil, and made many designs for goldsmiths' work, including the Wellington Shield, his greatest reputation was achieved as a book illustrator. Thousands of readers were indebted to Stothard as well as the author for their conception of favourite characters in such books as *Joseph Andrews*, *Tristram Shandy*, *Clarissa Harlowe*, *Sandford and Merton*, and *The Pilgrim's Progress*. Samuel Rogers, the poet-banker, author of *The Pleasures of Memory*, owed much to Stothard and to Turner for their illustrations to his works. The British Museum owns a large collection of Stothard's drawings, showing every phase of his work.

Among the illustrators, notably of Chaucer and Bell's Poets, 1777,[1] is John Hamilton Mortimer (1741–1779), born at Eastbourne, where his father was collector of customs. He studied under Reynolds and Cipriani. He became Vice-President of the Incorporated Society of Artists in 1773; and was elected A.R.A. in 1778 and, by special royal grant, R.A. soon after. He died of fever in Norfolk Street, Strand, not having lived to receive his diploma. There are numerous drawings by him at the British Museum, among them several of *banditti*, a favourite subject with him whether for his many etchings or for work in pen and colour.

Richard Corbould (1757–1831), born in London, exhibited landscapes, portraits and historical subjects in oil and water-colour, but was best known as a book-illustrator of great fertility and talent. *Pamela* and *Tom Jones* were illustrated by him, and some of his water-colour landscapes (three are in the British Museum) were engraved for Walker's *Copper Plate Magazine*, in 1792 and 1794. Henry Corbould (1787–1844), Richard's third son, was also known for his numerous book-illustrations. A better artist than either was Edward Francis Burney (1760–1848), born at Worcester. He studied at the Royal

[1] J. Bell (pub.), *Poets of Great Britain* 1776–1783.

152

Academy schools, worked at portrait-painting till about 1803, and afterwards devoted himself to book-illustration. He published a *Collection of Theatrical Portraits* engraved from his drawings. He was a relation of Fanny Burney, and a friend of Reynolds. Few, who knew of Burney as a book-illustrator, were aware that he produced complicated figure subjects such as *An Elegant Establishment for Young ladies*[1] and *The Waltz*[2] (Pl. 144). They show that Burney could skilfully manage an elaborate composition, for in both drawings there are upwards of forty figures. The treatment is naturalistic, but verging upon caricature. Contemporary education and dancing, at a time when the newly-introduced waltz was still suspect, are the subject of humorous satire. In the *Elegant Establishment*, the head-mistress sits at her bureau, in a small office, writing down the measurements of a new pupil. In the crowded main room instruction is being given in deportment, dancing, histrionics, shoemaking, music, painting, etc., while various physical exercises are being performed. In the background, one of the young ladies is being helped into a chaise by a gallant with whom she is eloping to Gretna Green. The drawing is full of humorous touches, such as the monkey caricature pinned on the dancing-master's back and the kitten peeping, beside the kit violin, out of his coat-tail pocket. Perhaps Fanny Burney suggested some of the material and incident in these two delightful drawings.

Charles Lamb relates how Burney delighted a maiden, unknown to him save by sight, with a Valentine 'with borders—full not of common hearts and heartless allegory, but all the prettiest stories of love from Ovid and older poets than Ovid (for E. B. is a scholar)'. He describes Burney as 'an artist of no common powers; in the fancy parts of designing, perhaps inferior to none; his name is known at the bottom of many a well executed vignette in the way of his profession, but no further; for E. B. is modest, and the world meets nobody half-way'.[3]

Michael Angelo Rooker (1743–1801) executed a charming series of water-colours, which were engraved as illustrations to the *Dramatick Works of Beaumont and Fletcher* (Pl. 178), ten vols., 1778. The British Museum owns almost the complete set of the original drawings,[4] and in the Victoria and Albert Museum are six still smaller water-colours, made in 1780 to illustrate the works of Henry Fielding.[5] Rooker, however, is reserved for consideration, later, as a topographical draughtsman. Blake, too, as figure-painter and illustrator, the greatest star in the constellation, must have a chapter to himself. Later, too, must come an account of Rowlandson, though he was the contemporary of most of the artists mentioned in this chapter, as a great illustrator, caricaturist and landscape painter. It may be noted that Downman, Shelley, Stothard, Buck, Corbould, Burney, Blake and Rowlandson were all born between 1750 and 1760.

The aspiration to achieve a national school of history painting nourished by various artists, Reynolds, Barry, Haydon for instance, as well as by some connoisseurs and critics, was no more successful in the sphere of water-colour than elsewhere and the figure painters

[1] V.A.M. P.50–1930.   [2] V.A.M. P.129–1931.   [3] *Essays of Elia*, Valentine's Day.
[4] B.M. 1859. 7.9.71–98.   [5] V.A.M. 1717–1722–1900.

in the medium, such as Wheatley, found a more ready response when they treated local contemporary and particularly rustic subjects.

Wheatley, it is true, never quite shook off the trammels of classical tradition. His obituary in *The Gentleman's Magazine*, 1801, refers to his work as 'a pleasing display of rusticks in the variety of simplicity of rural avocation', but complains that they are too often clad in 'French fripperies'. Edward Edwards[1] wrote that: 'Wheatley's chief excellence was in rural subjects with figures, which when they represented females, generally bore a meretricious and theatrical air, as is very distinguishable in a set of prints representing the Cries of London, in which the women are dressed with great smartness, but little propriety, better suited to the fantastic taste of an Italian opera stage than to the streets of London.'[2] But though he could seldom get away from stage shepherds, milkmaids and rustic lovers, what Frederick Wedmore called the 'Ophelias and Mirandas of a beatified peasantry', at times—as in his *Donnybrook Fair*[3]—he is a realist.

Francis Wheatley (1747–1801), the son of a master tailor, was born in Wild Court, Covent Garden. He studied at Shipley's School and in 1769 at the Royal Academy, and won several premiums from the Society of Arts. He was closely associated with J. H. Mortimer, whose fluent draughtsmanship was greatly admired by younger students. Subsequently he ran off to Dublin in company with Mrs. Gresse, the wife of J. A. Gresse, and, as Edwards tells us, was prosecuted and cast in the Court of King's Bench. In Dublin he caused great scandal by passing off his mistress as his wife and was obliged to return to London. He was a fellow of the Incorporated Society of Artists, with whom he exhibited from 1765 to 1783, and was elected an associate of the Royal Academy in 1790 and R.A. in the following year. Edwards speaks of his irregularity and intemperance, and proof of this is that he was bankrupt in 1793, and in 1798 he had to appeal to the Academy for financial assistance. When he died his widow, who was a miniature painter, was helped by the Academy until her marriage in 1807 to Alexander Pope, actor and miniature painter himself. Farington makes many references to Mrs. Wheatley, who in 1802 had ten pupils at 7s. 6d. an hour—'The Princess Sophia of Gloucester takes lessons twice a week, but talks half the time.'

Wheatley, more than twenty years younger than Sandby, worked very much in his manner. The whole subject is drawn in with a pen line almost as fine and firm as that made with an etching needle. The big masses of tone and shadow are carefully conceived and worked with greys which become more blue as they recede. He is content with modest lack-lustre colouring. At the Victoria and Albert Museum he is well represented. The *Donnybrook Fair*, with its many raggletaggle gipsies, is dated 1783. A similar but smaller drawing with several variations, probably made in Ireland and used as a study for the

[1] *Anecdotes of Painting*, 1808.
[2] The *Cries of London*, from Wheatley's originals in oil were engraved in stipple under the direction of Schiavonetti, and were published from 1793 to 1797.
[3] V.A.M. 45–1923.

154

larger work, was sold at Sotheby's in 1924. Two *Fair Scene* (Pl. 149) subjects, dated 1782 and 1784, are in the Leslie Wright collection. Wheatley's *Volunteers of the City and County of Dublin*,[1] as they met on College Green in November 1779, contains several careful portraits. The *Interior of the Shakespeare Gallery, 1790*[2] includes portraits of the Dukes of York and Clarence, the Duchess of Devonshire, Sir Joshua Reynolds, Sheridan, Alderman Boydell and others.

Many drawings of the finest quality by Wheatley appeared in the A. N. Gilbey Sale.[3] He painted several lake scenes for the engravings in Middiman's *Select Views in Great Britain*, 1783–1787[4] (Pl. 148).   (Two of these subjects rank among the largest of existing water-colours.) Of Wheatley's landscapes, which are sometimes spectacular with a suggestion of a theatre back-cloth, there is a good example, *Landscape and River Scene*, in the Laing Art Gallery, Newcastle.

Julius Caesar Ibbetson[5] (1759–1817) made his reputation by his able painting of animals, especially of cattle and pigs. He was a little apt to trade upon this, as in his *Llangollen and Dinas Bran*,[6] 1796, where he overloads his studio-painted picture by piling up his detail and inserting too many of his studies of cattle, skilful in themselves, but distracting from unity of design. (Wheatley had the same fault of inserting groups of cattle which had obviously been seen and studied quite separately from his main landscape theme.) The sketch for Ibbetson's larger work[7] is also in the National Museum of Wales and, as D. K. Baxandall writes in the excellent catalogue, 'has a freshness of vision and a unity of impression that are lacking in the more elaborate version'. In the kind of subject which deals with landscape and farm scenes enlivened by rustic figures, horses and cattle, Ibbetson belongs to the group containing his friends, George Morland and James Ward. At the British Museum and the Victoria and Albert Museum are good examples of this aspect of his work. In other subjects, where animated groups of figures provide the main interest, he is akin to Dayes, and shows greater robustness and less artificiality than Wheatley.

Ibbetson, the son of a clothier, was born at Farnley Moore, near Leeds. He was apprenticed to a ship painter in Hull, and came to London in 1777. He worked for a time under a picture dealer named Clarke in Leicester Fields, and obtained a thorough knowledge of the Dutch artists whose influence is apparent in his work. The story of this early part of his life is related by Farington,[8] who says:

[1] V.A.M. 834–1873.
[2] V.A.M. 1719–1871.
[3] Sale Christie's, April 25–29, 1940.
[4] One of these, a large *View of Lake Windermere* is in the V.A.M. (P. 1–1948).
[5] Roget says that the heroic praenomen was due to the fact that Ibbetson was brought into the world by the Caesarian operation. See Rotha M. Clay, *Julius Caesar Ibbetson*, 1948.
[6] National Museum of Wales, Cardiff.
[7] National Museum of Wales, Cardiff.
[8] *Diary*, January 24, 1805.

155

West shewed us a letter recd. by Him from Julius Ibbetson in 1782, in which He gives a short history of His progress in the art. He was born a few miles from Leeds in Yorkshire,—had a strong inclination to painting excited in Him he scarcely knew how,—and His Father encouraged the feeling.—Seeing an advertisement for an apprentice to a Painter, He went with His Father to Hull, 70 miles distant, to the person who advertised, and there saw all the implements of the art but nothing more. Confiding that the advertiser was an artist, Ibbetson was bound apprentice to him, but immediately found that His occupation was only to be to get His master money by painting from daylight to night the inside and outside of Ships in the Port.

. . . He could only practise drawing & other painting, at stolen Hours. He did, notwithstanding so far advance in the art as to paint several *Signs* which were much admired. At the end of 5 years . . . Ibbetson ran away from *Hull* and came to London, where He got employ from a person who had previously been under His Hull master.

While in this situation He obtained admission into Mr. West's House in Newman St. where He painted a chest for one of the Servants, & where for the first time He saw pictures which excited in Him a feeling 'which affected His *very toes*'. . . . In 1782 He wrote the whimsical letter stating all the above particulars.—He added that He had been for 4 years in the hands of those Harpies the *Picture dealers*, and described their frauds with humour and acrimony.

One point probably unknown to Farington is that in his early days at Hull, while he was only seventeen, Ibbetson was engaged to paint scenery for the Hull and York Theatres, the manager of which was prepared to accept him as an actor as well. This is a curious anticipation of the early part of David Robert's career.

In 1788, when he had been exhibiting for three years at the Royal Academy, Ibbetson was appointed draughtsman to Cathcart's Embassy to China, but returned from Java on Cathcart's death. Sir Arthur Russell, Bt., owns a series of paintings of fish, dated 1788, made during this voyage. The *Flying Fish*,[1] lent by him to the Royal Academy's exhibition of British Art in 1934, was an unusual and brilliant piece of work. Ibbetson married in 1780, but lost his wife in 1794. After much domestic and pecuniary trouble he retired in 1798 to the village of Troutbeck near Ambleside, and later to Masham, Yorkshire, where he died. He paid a visit to Scotland in 1800. In November 1801, Farington notes:

Ibbetson resides at Clappersgate, abt. ½ a mile from Ambleside & was lately married to a young woman daughter to a weaver . . . She is not 20 years of age. He is instructing her in drawing.

Roget amplifies the account by describing the contact between the Ibbetsons and the Fielding family, who were living at Ambleside in 1803, and says of Mrs. Ibbetson that 'she is described as young and handsome, and we seem to be familiar with her dark hair and bright complexion among the telling rustic groups that adorned her husband's later landscapes'. It was probably in his home near Ambleside that Ibbetson wrote *An Accidence or Gamut of Painters in Oil and Water-Colour*, published in 1803.[2]

An important drawing by Ibbetson, *Hyde Park: Winter*,[3] exhibited at the Royal Academy in 1796, is a view of the frozen Serpentine looking towards Knightsbridge, with numerous

[1] No. 113 in catalogue. Illustrated.
[2] A second edition, published in 1828, contains a memoir of the artist.
[3] Coll. Mr. Alan D. Pilkington.

116 'Scene at Cavalry Barracks'
B.M. 1875.8.14.961 $7\frac{1}{2} \times 14\frac{1}{2}$: 190 × 368   *Water-colour*
John COLLET (c. 1725–1780)

117 'An Asylum for the Deaf'
V.A.M. 1694–1871 $13\frac{3}{4} \times 21\frac{1}{8}$: 349 × 537   *Water-colour*
John COLLET (c. 1725–1780)

118 'A Tree Trunk near Albano'

Coll. Mr D.L.T. and Miss Armide Oppé   21¼ × 15¼: 540 × 387   *Pen and water-colour*

John DOWNMAN, A.R.A. (1750–1824)

119 'Mrs Siddons'
National Portrait Gallery, London   8 × 6¾: 203 × 171
Black chalk and water-colour, signed and dated 1787
John Downman, A.R.A. (1750–1824)

120 'A Singing Party'
Coll. Mrs T. G. Winter   6 × 9¼ : 152 × 235   *Pen and water-colour*
Nathaniel DANCE, R.A. (1734–1811)

121 'Bagnigge Wells, 1772 (?)'
Whitworth Art Gallery, University of Manchester   13 × 19¾: 330 × 502
Pencil and water-colour
John SANDERS (1750–c. 1825)

Aug.ᵈ 3.º 1793

Geo Dance

122 'Portrait of the Artist's Son, George'
Coll. Mr & Mrs Paul Mellon   9½ × 7½: 241 × 190
Pencil and water-colour, signed and dated 1793
George DANCE, R.A. (1741–1825)

123 'Illustration to Play or Poem'
B.M. Gg.3–385   8½ × 13: 216 × 330   *Pencil and water-colour*
Giovanni Battista CIPRIANI, R.A. (1727–1785)

124 'Mythological Scene'
B.M. 1941.11.8.11   9⅞ × 16: 251 × 405   *Pen and water-colour*
Giovanni Battista CIPRIANI, R.A. (1727–1785)

125 'The Three Graces'

B.M. 1914.2.16.150　　　Circle diam: 7⅛: 182　　*Pen and wash*

Angelica KAUFFMANN, R.A. (1741–1807)

126 'Angelica and Medoro (Orlando Furioso XIX. 36)'
V.A.M. D–740   5¾ × 7¼: 146 × 184   *Water-colour*
Angelica KAUFFMANN, R.A. (1741–1807)

127 'Interior, with Family Group'

V.A.M. 174–1890   10½ × 11¾ : 267 × 299   *Water-colour, signed and dated 1771*
Elias MARTIN (1739–1818)

128 'State Barges approaching Westminster Bridge'

V.A.M. 317–1876   13¼ × 20½ : 337 × 521   *Water-colour, signed and dated 1771*
Elias MARTIN (1739–1818)

129 'Memory Gathering Flowers Mown Down by Time'
V.A.M. 1754–1871 $22\frac{3}{8} \times 15\frac{3}{8}$: 568 × 391   *Water-colour, signed*
Samuel SHELLEY (1750–1808)

130 'Study for a Portrait Group'

B.M. 1887.3.1.19 $6\frac{3}{8} \times 5$: 162 × 127   *Pen and water-colour*

Samuel SHELLEY (1750–1808)

131 Illustration to Sterne's 'Sentimental Journey'

B.M. 1869.2.13.20   6¼ × 4½: 159 × 114   *Indian ink and water-colour, signed and dated 1801*

Adam BUCK (1759–1833)

132 Illustration to 'As You Like It'

B.M. 1944.10.14.104   8⅜ × 9⅞: 213 × 251   *Water-colour, signed and dated 1796*

William HAMILTON, R.A. (1751–1801)

133 'Roman Ruins and Figures'

Coll. Mr & Mrs Paul Mellon   13⅜ × 18⅛: 340 × 460   *Water-colour touched with white*

William HAMILTON, R.A. (1751–1801)

134 'A Shepherd in a Storm'
B.M. Oo.5–32   13 × 10½: 330 × 267   *Water-colour*
Richard WESTALL, R.A. (1765–1836)

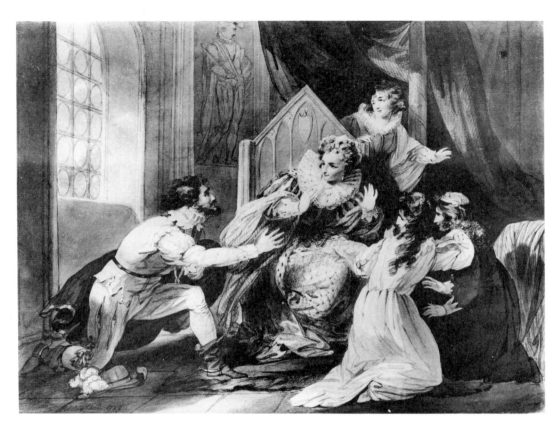

135 'Earl of Essex's return from Ireland'
Laing Art Gallery, Newcastle upon Tyne   12½ × 16½: 318 × 420   *Water-colour*
Richard WESTALL, R.A. (1765–1836)

136 'Gypsies and Female Rustics'
V.A.M. 9–1883   27½ × 35½: 699 × 902   *Water-colour*
Lady Diana BEAUCLERK (1734–1808)

137 'Telemachus Discovering the Priest of Apollo'

V.A.M. 76–1873 $20\frac{5}{8} \times 16\frac{3}{4}$: 524 × 426   *Water-colour, signed and dated 1809*

Stephen Francis RIGAUD (1777–1861)

138 'Mr Charles Ruspini'

B.M. 1961.2.11.5   3¾ × 4: 96 × 102   *Pencil and water-colour*

Thomas STOTHARD, R.A. (1755–1834)

139 'The Avon at Clifton'

B.M. 1884.2.9.25   8 × 10¾: 203 × 273   *Water-colour dated 1813*

Thomas STOTHARD, R.A. (1755–1834)

140 'The Eighth Day of the Decameron'
B.M. 1886.6.7.3 $10\frac{3}{4} \times 7\frac{7}{8}$: 273 × 200   *Water-colour*
Thomas STOTHARD, R.A. (1755–1834)

141 'Satan' (Paradise Lost, Bk. IV)

B.M. 1900.8.24.461 $11\frac{1}{4} \times 7\frac{7}{8}$: 286 × 200   *Pen and black wash*

Thomas STOTHARD, R.A. (1755–1834)

142 'Skeleton of a Sailor and Vultures on a Shore'
B.M. 198.c.10 No. 37   10¾ × 16¾ : 273 × 426   *Water-colour*
John Hamilton MORTIMER, A.R.A. (1741–1779)

143 'Bulstrode Park, Bucks.'
B.M. 1890.5.12.30   4 × 6⅛ : 102 × 156   *Body-colour*
Richard CORBOULD (1753–1831)

144 'The Waltz'
V.A.M. P.129–1931   18¾ × 27: 477 × 686   *Water-colour*
Edward Francis BURNEY (1760–1848)

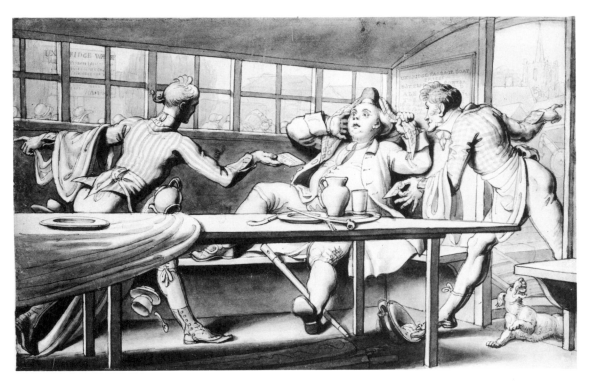

145 'John Gilpin in the Uxbridge Passage Boat'
Coll. Mr & Mrs Paul Mellon   9⅜ × 14⅝: 238 × 372   *Pen with blue and brown wash*
Edward Francis BURNEY (1760–1848)

146 'May Day'

B.M. 1960.7.16.29 $11\frac{5}{8} \times 10\frac{7}{8}$: 295 × 276   *Water-colour, varnished*

Edward Francis BURNEY (1760–1848)

147 'The Dismissal'

V.A.M. 1720–1871   13¾ × 11¼: 340 × 285   *Water-colour, signed and dated 1786*

Francis WHEATLEY, R.A. (1747–1801)

148 'Lake Windermere'
V.A.M. P.1–1948   24 × 37 : 610 × 1042   *Water-colour, signed and dated 1784*
Francis WHEATLEY, R.A. (1747–1801)

149 'Scene at a Fair'
Coll. Mrs Dorian Williamson   14½ × 21⅛ : 368 × 536   *Water-colour*
Francis WHEATLEY, R.A. (1747–1801)

150 'River Scene with Boat and Figures'
Laing Art Gallery, Newcastle upon Tyne   9 × 13⅛: 228 × 333   *Water-colour*
Francis WHEATLEY, R.A. (1747–1801)

151 'Pary's Copper Mines, Anglesey'
National Museum of Wales, Cardiff   8½ × 11¼: 216 × 285   *Water-colour, signed*
Julius Caesar IBBETSON (1759–1817)

152 'A Farmyard Scene'
Coll. Mr & Mrs Paul Mellon $10\frac{5}{8} \times 15\frac{7}{8}$: 270 × 403   *Water-colour, signed and dated 1792*
Julius Caesar IBBETSON (1759–1817)

153 'The Market'
Laing Art Gallery, Newcastle upon Tyne $8\frac{1}{2} \times 11\frac{1}{2}$: 216 × 292   *Water-colour*
Julius Caesar IBBETSON (1759–1817)

154 'Skating in Hyde Park'
Coll. Mr & Mrs Paul Mellon   10 × 14: 253 × 355   *Water-colour*
Julius Caesar IBBETSON (1759–1817)

155 'Cottage Garden and Well'
B.M. 1858.6.26.9   9½ × 14: 241 × 355   *Water-colour*
Thomas UWINS, R.A. (1782–1857)

156 'Nobleman and two Fellow Commoners'
B.M. 1858.6.26.48 $7\frac{1}{2} \times 10\frac{1}{8}$: 191 × 257   *Water-colour*
Thomas Uwins, R.A. (1782–1857)

skaters on the ice. There is a real feeling of wintry atmosphere, and the figures are in well-balanced motion. The group of the old lady and her two daughters walking on the ice, and the seated man on the bank strapping on his skates, are perfect in composition and drawing. The other, *St. James's Park, Summer*, is dated 1796, and is probably the drawing exhibited at the Academy in that year, under the title *Hyde Park: Summer*.[1] It is a view of the Park at the east end of the Mall; to the left are two soldiers on horseback, while others recline on the ground. To the right, surrounded by nursemaids and children, are the cows which supplied milk for sale at the entrance to the Park. It is a superb example of Ibbetson, but has it at some time been a little restored, and the upper part of the trees on the right refreshed with brighter greens and blues than the artist himself employed? His admirable grouping of figures and the good use he made of the attractive costume of the period are often evident.

The old tradition in figure subjects, portraits and book-illustrations was continued by Thomas Uwins (1782–1857), who followed the leadership of Stothard. Born at Penton-ville, London, he was the son of a clerk in the Bank of England. Showing an aptitude for drawing, he was apprenticed in 1797 to an engraver, Benjamin Smith, and became a student at the Academy schools in 1798. When he joined the Water-Colour Society in 1809 he was a man of twenty-seven, with some reputation as an illustrator. Not that this work put much money in his purse, for in 1809 and later he was drawing delightful fashion-plates for Ackermann's *Repository*, and the publisher paid only half a crown apiece for what in his German English, he called Uwins' 'britty vaces'.[2] Uwins seems to have been frequently employed by Ackermann, particularly for figure and costume drawings. There are, for instance, thirty-two costume plates by him in two famous publications of 1813–1814, the *History of the University of Oxford* and the companion volume on Cambridge. Uwins seems to have been inspired by the belief that all University dons are divinely tall and slender, with the exception of doctors of divinity, who alone in both volumes exhibit a comfortable portliness. During his membership of the Water-Colour Society from 1809 to 1818 Uwins exhibited scenes from Shakespeare, Fielding and Sterne, as well as small portraits and picturesque figure subjects and groups from the rural industries of his time, hop and fruit pickers, plaiters, gleaners and the like. In 1818 he began to exhibit the results of foreign travel and showed his first love for the scenery and the activities of French vineyards. After the 1818 exhibition he resigned, and following on his first visit to Italy in 1824 became a painter in oil of Italian life, character and sunshine. His work of this nature won his election as A.R.A. in 1833 and as R.A. in 1838.

[1] Ex. Coll. A. Gilbey. Present owner not known.
[2] Roget I, p. 245.

CHAPTER IX

Early topographers

John Inigo Richards   Anthony Devis   John Alexander Gresse
Samuel Hieronymous Grimm   Moses Griffith   Willey Reveley

We now return to the line of the topographers who belong to the same tradition as Hollar and Place, Scott and Sandby in the rendering of architecture and landscape. Their drawings are entered in the catalogues of the Royal Academy, commencing in 1769, as 'stained' or 'tinted'. 'Topographers' is the accepted term, and it has a pedestrian sound ; but to use this conveniently descriptive title is not to depreciate a group of original and individual artists who flourished at the close of the eighteenth century and lifted topographical art to a very high level. Farington, Rooker, Dayes, Hearne, Malton, were all artists of distinction. They were the forerunners of Girtin and Turner who, in their early work at any rate, were essentially topographers.

The taste for the topographical water-colour was enhanced by an increasing love for travel, a growing appreciation of scenery and architecture, and by a greatly expanding production of engravings. Throughout the century the English aristocracy were accustomed to tour the Continent, and became the art patrons of the world, but before the close of the century travel was not confined to the aristocracy and gentry alone. In September 1785, Gibbon was told that 40,000 English, counting masters and servants, were touring or resident on the Continent. And it was not confined to the Continent. In 1788, according to Wilberforce, 'the banks of the Thames are scarcely more public than those of Windermere'. The lure of the newly discovered or newly developed seaside resort is discussed in a later chapter dealing with Marine Painters, and it is shown elsewhere how a new wave of continental travel from about 1815 onwards produced a whole school of later topographers such as Prout and Stanfield.

It was not just snobbery which led the middle classes to follow the privileged example of the aristocracy, to travel at home and abroad, and to exercise their own taste in the acquisition of water-colours. The aristocracy and gentry associated with and gave their patronage to the living painter, as they had done to the living man of letters. Men like Gainsborough and the Cozens, Sandby and Farington, Girtin and Turner, were on close terms not only with friendly patrons of the middle class but with many of the nobility. It was an encouragement, too, for the water-colour painter that the Englishman, whether he travelled on the Continent or not, was taking a new interest in the prospect and meaning of natural scenery.

The poet Thomas Gray who had visited the Lakes in 1769 wrote that he loved 'scenes, situations, antiquities', and those three words summarise the whole endeavour of the topographical school. The enthusiasm for natural scenery had been steadily developing for at least thirty years before that and long before a poet such as Wordsworth was to give his profound interpretation of the union between landscape and the spirit and imagination of man. Burke's *Philosophical Enquiry into the Origin of our Ideas of the Sublime and Beautiful* (1756) had been but one, if the most influential, of a number of sophisticated essays which bore upon the appreciation of landscape and the forms of nature, but it was more simple and accessible works such as the various *Picturesque Tours* of the Reverend William Gilpin which were to have a wider influence upon taste and manners. They and many other topographical publications excited a remarkable interest in the visual delights of scenery and encouraged Englishmen to seek out and appreciate what was 'picturesque' in both the spectacular and the modest regions of their own country.

It is impossible to accept Roget's statement that the fashion for topographical drawings in the last quarter of the eighteenth century rose from the remarkable cream-ware table service, decorated with English landscapes, which was completed by Messrs. Wedgwood and Bentley in 1774 for the Empress Catherine of Russia. But the facts are interesting as an indication of the topographical enthusiasm. Josiah Wedgwood and his partner despatched draughtsmen over the country with a *camera obscura* (Bentley wanted '*real* views and *real* buildings'), ransacked print-shops, and sought 'the most embelished views, the most beautiful Landsckips, with Gothique ruins, Grecian Temples, and the most Elegant Buildings'. Views of country mansions were the staple part of the decorations, and Wedgwood found that he could pay some acceptable compliments in that way, though he was afraid of making enemies who might think themselves neglected by the omission of their country seat, when their neighbour's was taken, or by putting it upon a small piece, or not flattering it sufficiently. Perhaps this sort of rivalry, more than the china service, did help the artists. Sixty years before, in 1714, when *Britannia Illustrata* was published, containing *Views of several of the Queen's Palaces, as also of the Principal Seats of Nobility and Gentry of Great Britain*, the second volume contains the delightful note: 'There is a Third Volume in hand, any Gentleman paying Five Guineas towards the Graving may have their Seat inserted, it being very forward, which is only half what the former paid.' Wedgwood's magnificent table service, on which 1,282 views, no two alike, were executed 'in enamel of a delicate black, which permits a shading and finish', no doubt caused considerable stir and gratified the vanity of those whose residences were represented, but cannot have given to the art of the topographers such immense stimulus as Roget suggests.

The forms of encouragement for the water-colour painter were widespread, and opportunities of exhibiting his work were becoming more frequent. Exhibitions were a help, but the main cause for the boom was a prolific output of engraved reproductions. It was realised that engraving, by bringing art into every home at a moderate cost, was the only means by which a painter could reach more than a select few. A picture was a single example of his work, to be buried in some patron's house. A thousand prints from an engraving would multiply his name and fame. Turner realised this when, already famous, he agreed to make drawings for the *Southern Coast* series of engravings at £7 10s. each. The price, it is true, was raised later to £10 10s.; but the engraver for his part was paid £25, and later £50, for each plate. Sandby and others realised that topographical drawings made for the engraver might not bring them much money, but could satisfy their ambition. Publishers and engravers were only too ready to continue the education of the British public who were beginning to understand the spirit of place. The publishers despatched artists into every part of the kingdom to make drawings of castles, cathedrals, country estates and mountains, rivers and lakes. Nowadays the modern painter has no trouble about means of locomotion. For most painters of the time the post-chaise or a horse were beyond their means; journeys must be made on foot; a comfortable night's shelter was very uncertain; the paraphernalia of their craft must be limited in bulk. It was from personal experience that Rowlandson recorded the vicissitudes of Dr. Syntax on his tour in search of the picturesque. Artists like Sandby, Rowlandson, and Turner tramped hundreds of miles on foot and faced most difficult conditions. In Sandby's sketches you see him sometimes with a horse, sometimes with a tent, sometimes with a post-chaise waiting near by, while rustics and children are grouped round him watching him work. Samuel Palmer very much later was cumbered, as we shall see, like an Alpine climber when he set out on a sketching tour.

The itinerant artists from about 1780 onwards made thousands of drawings each year, most of them for publication in book form as aquatint plates, plain or coloured,[1] though many were issued as separate prints. Farington made seventy-six drawings for his *History of the River Thames*, published in 1794. There are twenty-five plates from drawings by Malton in his *Picturesque and Descriptive Views of the City of Dublin*, published in parts from 1792 to 1797. For his *Voyage round Great Britain*, issued in eight volumes from 1814 to 1825, William Daniell made, and himself engraved, no less than three hundred and eight drawings. Those figures—and they represent only a small fraction of the general output—show the extent to which well-known artists were working for aquatint reproduction. As an instance of colour aquatints published separately, we may take the magnificent set of six views of London, drawn and engraved by William Daniell, and published in 1804–1805; and his series, even finer, of twelve views of Eton and Windsor issued many years later, about 1830. These were printed without any date or publication line, but two sets, in the Royal Library at Windsor and in the Victoria and Albert Museum, show the prints laid down on a back of thinnish card, with a narrow grey-black line framing them after

[1] For the enormous output between 1780 and 1830, of volumes containing aquatints of topographical subjects, see *English Coloured Books*, by Martin Hardie, 1906, and the Catalogues of the J. R. Abbey Collection (now in the Mr. & Mrs. Paul Mellon Collection).

the fashion of water-colours, and the titles and artist's name written underneath in pencil. They were certainly worthy of receiving the same treatment and honour as original drawings. The plates were re-issued by William Tegg in 1862.

As its name shows, Aquatint (a new engraving, or rather etching, process introduced in England by Paul Sandby in 1775) is a method of printing a tint from a copper plate by means of biting with acid. Like mezzotint, it is a *tone* process, the plate being partially protected by specks of resin or asphaltum between which the acid bites thereby enabling the plate to hold ink. The outline of the subject is usually etched, but the finished aquatint is produced by successive bitings and stoppings-out, always in spaces of tone. The final result resembles a wash drawing, and the effect of an aquatint is extremely liquid and translucent, making it the ideal method for the reproduction of a sepia or water-colour drawing worked in simple washes. A publisher like Ackermann had a whole staff of engravers—among whom were Bluck, Stadler and Havell—each of whom could readily finish an aquatint plate in a day. The plate was printed with two or three colours, usually a blue for the sky and a brown or neutral tint for the foreground. A soft paper was employed, as a rule the best Whatman, which was then sized to prevent colour blotting. The print was finished by hand-colouring, and Ackermann had a trained body of women colourists who, with years of practice, had attained superlative skill in laying tints in even washes. Both Turner and Girtin passed a boyhood apprenticeship in tinting prints for Dayes, Malton and John Raphael Smith. Aquatints coloured by hand can be deceptively like original drawings, and have not infrequently been exhibited as water-colours. In 1813 Samuel Prout wrote that: 'It is not unlikely that the day may arrive when the connoisseur of a future age shall turn over the pages of a book, and pause upon an aquatinta print, with the same solemn delight as those of our day are wont to do upon a woodcut of Albert Dürer, an etching of Hollar, or a production of any ancient engraver.'[1]

Aquatint was an ideal medium for the topographers who inherited their method of painting in neutral washes with thin covering colour from the Dutch painters of the seventeenth century, through Hollar and Place. Their method had been used for two centuries for the tinting of maps and engravings 'with gummed colours, but tempered very thinne and bodilesse'. For their 'stained' or 'tinted' drawings the topographers drew their subject with outlines in pencil or pen-and-ink, and then added the shadows in a monochrome wash of sepia, or Indian ink, or the soot-water which Lady Diana Beauclerk used. Over this monochrome ground, which was like the monochrome under-painting of the oil-painter, the artist washed his colour, just as most of us in our young days put flat washes of thin colour over a black-and-white illustration. (In 1833 Constable spent a happy afternoon in colouring some of the pictures in Dr. Watts' *Songs Divine and Moral* (1832) 'for dear Emily, to be sent to her on her birthday'.) If the topographer was painting a red brick bridge and a tree, he drew his subject in outline; indicated the shadows on the tree and

[1] *Rudiments of Landscape*, 1813, p. 18.

under the arch of the bridge in a grey wash; finally painting a pale green all over the tree, including the shadows and a red over the entire bridge, including the shadow under the arch. He was not considering to any great extent 'local colour'. Later on, artists painted their shadows with colour, not with a neutral tint. They saw and suggested varying greens on the tree, and noted that the bridge was yellow and red and brown in parts, while the shadow under it was warm with reflected colours. In painting local colour, the later men put a dark green over a light one, a deeper red over a pale red, or laid a wash of warm yellow over tree and bridge, running darker colours into it while it was still wet. The topographers worked in the reverse way, always putting a light tint over dark.

The Bridge, Llangollen[1] (Pl. 162) by J. A. Gresse, left unfinished, is obviously a careful study from nature, and a perfect illustration of how the 'tinted' drawing was produced.[2] Outlines of form were first drawn with a pencil, as can be seen on the right, and then gone over carefully with pen and ink. Different touches and handling are used for varieties of near or distant foliage; and then the shadow tones are given by washes of diluted Indian ink. Parts of the drawing have been completed by local colour washed transparently over the monochrome ground, and parts of the middle distance on the right, and the foreground, have been left wholly untouched, thus enabling the entire process to be seen with perfect clarity. A similar drawing by Gresse of a *Waterwheel*[3] (Pl. 163) is valuable because it too is unfinished, with just one bright note provided by the vivid red brickwork, and green grass, in the centre. George Robertson's *Landscape with Cattle*[4] (Pl. 66) is also half finished, showing portions of a tree shaded with a neutral tint, partly plain and partly coloured. The method of washing colour over a monochrome under-painting was shared in common by most of the topographers up to about 1800, though each painter showed individual characteristics of style. Being dependent for its shadow effect on black and white rather than colour, it was an ideal kind of drawing for the engraver to reproduce. The engraver in aquatint, working as it were in washes of tone, and not having to break up and interpret shadow by means of lines, like the line-engraver and the wood-engraver, found it easy to make an almost exact facsimile.

On the other hand, when Turner wished to multiply, by means of engraving, his water-colour landscapes, which were painted in direct colour with little accent upon form, and which suggested in broken varied tints fleeting effects of atmosphere, he found aquatint unsuited to his purpose. He trained a school of line-engravers to reproduce delicate tones in which a multiplicity of fine lines are softly merged. Strictly, they were not line-engravers, as three-quarters or more of their work was in etched lines, faintly bitten on steel and the graver was only used for finishing accents and sharpness of detail. Their success was due to the unremitting care with which Turner supervised every stage of their work, annotating

[1] V.A.M. 1731–1871.
[2] Lucid accounts of this method are contained in William Orme's *Process of Tinting* (n.d.) and James Roberts' *Introductory Lessons. . . . Painting in Water Colours*, 1800.
[3] B.M. 1890. 5.12.92.
[4] V.A.M. 191–1890.

162

and correcting proof after proof from the plate till, however maddened the engraver might be with constant burnishing, scraping and re-biting, Turner's purpose was achieved. The period when his genius and that of his engravers was at its highest may be said to lie between the *Views of Sussex*, 1819, and the publication of *Rivers of France*, 1837, and *Picturesque Views in England and Wales*, 1838. Aquatint was defeated, and it was the Turner school of so-called line-engraving which held the field in the various popular annuals, such as the *Landscape Annual*, which employed J. D. Harding from 1832–1834, David Roberts from 1835–1838, and James Holland in 1839. *Heath's Picturesque Annual*, from 1832 onwards, contained engravings from drawings by Clarkson Stanfield, A. G. Vickers, G. Cattermole, W. Callow and other water-colour painters. It was Lady Blessington who said about some of these annuals that 'they would have been dished, if it hadn't been for the plates'. Pope put the same idea in more polished phrase:

> *Or where the pictures for the page atone,*
> *And Quarles is sav'd by beauties not his own.*

In dealing with methods of reproduction and their effect upon the uses and popularity of water-colour we have travelled a long way from the early topographers. One of the first was John Inigo Richards (1720–1810). He helped his father as a scene-painter and, after being assistant to Nicholas Thomas Dall at Covent Garden, succeeded him as head scene-painter in 1777. A scene by Richards for *The Maid of the Mill* was engraved in 1768 by William Woollett and won great popular favour. This success caused the election of Richards as one of the foundation members of the Royal Academy. He became its secretary in 1788, and died at his residence there. In his water-colours, the crumbling of old masonry, the stems and foliage of trees, the groups of picturesque rustics, are indicated in cold and vigorous line with a reed pen. He seems to have been ahead of his time, certainly ahead of Sandby, not only in this warmth of tone but in diversifying the colour in his washes and in softening their edges. Admirable examples of his work are *Orpington*, 1768[1] and *Downe Church, Kent*,[2] 1775.

After Sandby came Anthony Devis (1729–1817), born at Preston, belonging to a family of artists. His brother, Arthur Devis (1708–1787), twenty-one years older than himself, was a portrait-painter of repute in his day; and his nephew, Arthur William (1763–1822), was draughtsman in the employ of the East India Company, travelled in one of their ships which was wrecked on the Pellew Islands, returned home by way of China and Bengal, and painted the *Death of Nelson* and other historical works besides many portraits. Anthony became a teacher of drawing in London, exhibited at the Free Society of Artists in 1761 and 1763, and at the Royal Academy in 1772 and 1781. His infrequent exhibits suggest that he was little known in his own day. He retired from London in 1780 to Albury, where he died. Devis, a very charming draughtsman in his limited way, followed Dutch

---

1 Lady Lever Art Gallery, Port Sunlight, Cheshire.
2 Illus. *Nettlefold Coll. Catalogue*, 1933–1938.

models closely. In the larger works, which he probably considered more important, such as the *Landscape with Church and Cattle*[1] and *Woods at Vernon House, Glamorgan*[2] (Pl. 160), he made his drawing in black crayon, with very slight tints overlaid. These drawings are well composed in the classical tradition, with careful study of trees and foreground detail; the skies are clear and luminous; and scattered spots of light are well disposed throughout the design. His small landscape studies, particularly well represented in the Victoria and Albert Museum, are nearly all drawn in outline with a reed pen and a grey, much watered, ink; the cloud forms, if indicated, are suggested with loose pencil work. Some of the drawings are washed with thin tints of greyish ink and have slight notes of colour, often only in grey and yellow, giving a pleasant atmospheric effect in the manner of Hearne. Devis' drawing, however, was much looser than that of Hearne, and more akin, with its loops and curls, to that of Farington. Like Farington, he wanted his sketches to be 'all Van Goyenish—silver warmth—simple colour'.

Gresse, who has been mentioned, and Grimm, both helped to foster the tradition of the 'stained drawing' in England. John Alexander Gresse (1741–1794), whose father had come to London from Rolle, on the Lake of Geneva, was born in London. His name still survives in that of a back street, where his father owned property, between Rathbone Place and Tottenham Court Road. He had some instruction in etching under the engravers L. G. Scotin and T. Major (hence perhaps the etching-like lines in his *Llangollen Bridge*[3]) (Pl. 162) and also worked under Zuccarelli and Cipriani. He attended the St. Martin's Lane Academy, and from 1755 received premiums from the Society of Arts. A fat and jovial foreigner, he was known by his contemporaries as 'Jack Grease'. Having inherited a respectable income from his father, he added to it by his professional practice as a drawing-master, and from 1777 had the royal Princesses as his pupils. Perhaps the unfinished drawings referred to above, were made as demonstrations of method. His best known pupil was Robert Hills, who was to become a foundation member of the Water-Colour Society. Gresse at his death left a collection which was dispersed in a six days' sale,[4] and bequeathed his fortune to various friends. Among them was Edward Edwards, who paid a kindly tribute to his memory in his *Anecdotes of Painters*, 1808.

Samuel Hieronymous Grimm (1733–1794), though not quite so well equipped as Paul Sandby, ranks high among the minor artists of his period. Grimm[5] was the son of a Swiss notary at Burgdorf, about fifteen miles from Berne. At Berne, his uncle, Johann, a painter of miniatures and water-colours, had a drawing-school. Johann died in 1747, when his nephew was quite young, but his school was taken over by Johann L. Aberli, well-known for his colour prints of Swiss scenery, and to him young Hieronymous went as a pupil. From 1758 onwards young Grimm was writing poetry and making drawings of Swiss

[1] V.A.M. 1734–1871.
[2] B.M. 1861. 2.9.159.
[3] V.A.M. 1731–1831.
[4] Sale, Christie's, April 7–12, 1794.
[5] R. M. Clay, *Samuel Hieronymous Grimm*, 1941.

views, accurate in topography, but lacking in the imagination and power of design shown later in similar subjects by J. R. Cozens and Towne. In 1765 he went to Paris for a stay of three years, making more than one visit to Normandy, a fruitful source of his earlier drawings. In 1768 began the third stage of Grimm's roving life. The well-known French line-engraver, J. G. Wille, records in his diary: '*le 25 fév. 1768. M. Grimm, peintre et poète suisse, après avoir passé plusieurs années à Paris, a pris congé de nous et partit le lendemain pour l'Angleterre. C'étoit un bien honnête garçon que nous estimions beaucoup.*' For twenty-six years Grimm went to and fro in the land of his adoption, ceaselessly making drawings.

In England Grimm began by showing four works at the first exhibition of the Royal Academy in 1769, exhibiting there till 1784, and at the Free Society of Artists till 1793. Most of his works are topographical views in pen, pencil and water-colour, of which he produced a vast number for such private patrons as Sir William Burrell, Sir Richard Kaye,[1] H. P. Wyndham, and Gilbert White of Selborne. Of special interest is Grimm's association with White, who personally selected him to illustrate his works (the vignette on the title-page of the first edition *The Natural History of Selborne* is by Grimm). White wrote about his forthcoming visit: 'So he will have a good stroke of work. His price is two guineas and a half per week. His buildings, human figures, quadrupeds, waters, perspective among trees, are good; but his trees are not so pleasing: he has also a vein of humour, but that I shall not allow him to call forth, as all my plates must be serious.'[2]

The artist's own humour, which Gilbert White deprecated, appears in his caricatures of Georgian men and manners and in political satires. He found other topics, where his interest in figures and costume had full play—a city fire, a country fair, ceremonies attended by royalty, the Montem pageant at Eton, military reviews, camps in the park, or an election celebration. His figures, singly or in crowds, are well placed, well drawn, and intensely active and alive. A typical subject is *The Great Fair, Antwerp*,[3] a crowded market-place, in the Breughel manner, with players in a booth in the background. The figures again, under the famous Fairlop Oak (blown down in 1820), with groups and incidents as varied as those of Frith's *Derby Day*, add interest to the *Fairlop Oak and Fair*[4] (Pl. 164), exhibited at the Royal Academy in 1775. But perhaps his most attractive work is in his simple rural subjects, with slight figure incident, delicately drawn and daintily stained with colour. Some of the finest are depicted on the Thames between Putney and Richmond. There are few better examples than his delightful drawing of *The Terrace at Richmond*, 1772. Other small landscapes of this group, done with pure joy and for love of nature, are *The Thames at Brentford*[5] (Pl. 166), *Opposite Hammersmith*,[6] *Footpads attacking a Traveller*,[7] *Between Chiswick and Brentford*,[8] and *Boys Bathing at Barnes*.[9] In all of them the drawing of the trees belies White's comment. The same precision and charm are shown in

---

[1] The collections of Sir W. Burrell and Sir Richard Kaye are in the Department of MSS., British Museum.
[2] Rashleigh Holt-White, *Life and Letters of Gilbert White of Selborne*, I, 1901, p. 320.
[3] Whitworth Art Gallery, Manchester.
[4] V.A.M. P.65–1921.   [5] B.M. 1919. 7.12.25.   [6] V.A.M. 99–1894.
[7] V.A.M. P.96–1920.   [8] Coll. Mr. L. G. Duke.   [9] Coll. Mr. L. G. Duke.

a more architectural subject, *Rotherham*[1] and a *Landscape with Castle and Town*.[2] He died at his residence in Tavistock Street, and was buried in St. Paul's Church, Covent Garden.

Grimm occasionally followed the Swiss tradition of working entirely in gouache, and sometimes introduces a certain amount of body-colour into his water-colour, but most of his work is in washes of pure and transparent colour. From the pen of Gilbert White comes an interesting detailed description of his guest's technique. It might be applied to the work of the whole group of topographers at the end of the eighteenth century:

> Mr. Grimm was with me just 28 days; 24 of which he worked very hard, and showed good specimens of his genius, assiduity, and modest behaviour, much to my satisfaction. He finished for me 12 views. He first of all sketches his scapes with a lead pencil; then he pens them all over, as he calls it, with indian ink, rubbing out the superfluous pencil strokes; then he gives a charming shading with a brush dipped in indian ink; and last he throws a light tinge of water-colours over the whole. The scapes, many of them at least, looked so lovely in their indian-ink shading that it was with difficulty the artist could prevail on me to permit him to tinge them; as I feared the colours might puzzle the engravers: but he assured me to the contrary.[3]

A certain amount of Grimm's work has undoubtedly been attributed to Sandby. In his clean outline, effects of light and shade, and his use of figures, Grimm comes very near to Sandby. To see the close resemblance, we may compare his *North Foreland Lighthouse*[4] (Pl. 167) with Sandby's *Eagle Tower, Carnarvon Castle*.[5] It is sometimes also impossible to decide whether an unsigned drawing is the work of Grimm or Brandoin, another Swiss artist, who was born and died at Vevey. Michel Vincent Brandoin (1733–1790) was of French refugee parentage, and travelled in Holland, France, Italy and England. His English associations caused him to be known as 'l'Anglais', when he settled down at Vevey. In the autumn of 1786 Brandoin accompanied William Beckford on a journey through various parts of Switzerland, including Neuchâtel and Zurich, and with him climbed the great Salève.[6] Like Grimm, he had a taste for caricature as well as landscape. Grimm, on the whole, is more definite and precise, while Brandoin seems to work with a rather more full, wet brush, conducive to softer spots and edges, but they share many mannerisms and their figures have a strong similarity. Brandoin nowadays is the lesser known artist and it is possible that Grimm has been credited with some of his unsigned work. Fortunately the Victoria and Albert Museum is rich in signed and dated works by Grimm and, for comparison with them, possesses two undoubted examples of Brandoin, *The Castle of Chillon*[7] and *A Swiss Farmhouse*.[8]

The re-emergence of Moses Griffith from almost total obscurity, like that of Skelton, Towne and White Abbott, belongs to comparatively recent years. Nearly two thousand of his drawings, made for the illustration of works by Thomas Pennant and his son, David

---

[1] Coll. J. Leslie Wright.
[2] Laing Art Gallery, Newcastle.
[3] Rashleigh Holt-White, *op. cit.*, I, p. 326.
[4] V.A.M. 1730–1871.
[5] B.M. 1904. 8.19.47.
[6] J. W. Oliver, *Life of William Beckford*, 1932, p. 198.
[7] V.A.M. P.77–1927.
[8] V.A.M. P.78–1927.

Pennant, appeared at Christie's in 1938. Iolo Williams[1] gave new facts and dates, and filled up the gaps in the incomplete and inexact accounts of Griffith given in the *Dictionary of National Biography* and elsewhere.[2]

Moses Griffith (1747—after 1809), as we now know, was born at Trygainhouse in Lein or Lleyn, a peninsula on the coast of Carnarvonshire. He was descended from very poor parents and without any other instruction than that of reading and writing. Accounts of his studying in London are mistaken. Pennant made a note in 1778 that: 'the drawings marked Moses Griffith are the performances of a worthy servant whom I keep for that purpose. The candid will excuse any little imperfections they may find in them; as they are the works of an untaught genius, drawn from the most remote and obscure parts of North Wales.' Later in his *Literary Life*, Pennant adds that it was in the Spring of 1769 that he 'acquired that treasure', who 'early took to the use of the pencil, and, during his long service with me, has distinguished himself as a good and faithful servant, and able artist; he can engrave, and is tolerably skilled in music. He accompanied me in all my journies, excepting that of the present year (1791). The public may thank him for numberless scenes and antiquities, which would otherwise have remained probably for ever concealed.' Pennant has summed up nearly all that need be said, except that his journeys, with Griffiths in his company, took him to Scotland in 1769, Harrogate in 1773, the Isle of Man in 1774, the Midlands including Worcester, Kenilworth, Southwell, Lincoln, etc. in 1776, and on various journeys in Wales. Looking at Griffith's work, we see it advancing from a primitive naiveté in 1773, when he drew *Harrogate Wells*, to a definite accomplishment in *Knaresborough Castle*, 1777, and *Ludlow Castle*, 1783. His lack of training and of knowledge of the masters shows itself in frequent weakness of composition and bad figure-drawing. He is at his best in *Cowthorp Oak, Yorkshire*, 1777, which is closely akin to Grimm. His method, indeed, of drawing and colour was precisely that of Grimm, but—interesting though he may be as a discovery, and for his own sake—he is by no means of the same calibre, the same intensity as Grimm or those more brilliant topographers with whom our next chapter is concerned.

Among those who are little more than the shadow of a name in the history of British water-colour comes Willey Reveley (d. 1799). He was a topographer, a good and sound architectural draughtsman, not a great painter, but he cannot be ignored. The date of his birth is unknown; but before his death he had shown that artists were not condemned to a restricted range of colour, as most contemporary work suggests; like Pars and Towne, he certainly anticipated Girtin in his free use of local colour without any preliminary wash of tone. Even his shadows are painted in pure, warm colour, without any underlying tint

---

[1] Iolo Williams: 'Thomas Pennant and Moses Griffith, a Welsh Naturalist and his Welsh Artist in the Eighteenth Century,' *Country Life*, July 1938.
[2] Following on Iolo Williams' article and embodying his information, two fully-illustrated numbers of *Walker's Monthly* August–September 1938 (Augustus Walker had bought a large number of the Griffith drawings) gave a copious review of the artist and his work.

of sepia. A pupil of Sir William Chambers, he worked as architect and draughtsman with Sir Richard Worsley in Italy, Sicily, Greece and Egypt, from 1784 to 1788, and exhibited at the Royal Academy from 1781 to 1793. His *Reggio, Calabria*[1] (Pl. 171) and his drawings of the *Paestum, Temple of Neptune*[2] (Pl. 170) show his precise drawing of architectural elevations and are mentioned here specially as illustrating his direct treatment of local colour. One of the Paestum drawings shows a tree which bears a close similarity to the summarised handling of Towne.

[1] B.M. 1878. 7.13.1277.
[2] V.A.M. D.140–1887/1888.

157 'The Terrace, York Buildings, 1796'
Coll. Mr & Mrs Paul Mellon   14 × 20⅛: 355 × 511   *Water-colour*
John Inigo RICHARDS, R.A. (1720–1810)

158 'Bridgewater Bridge, Somerset'
B.M. 1880.2.14.316   8⅛ × 13½: 207 × 343   *Water-colour, signed*
John Inigo RICHARDS, R.A. (1720–1810)

159 'Rocky Landscape with Cascade'

B.M. 1939.2.20.6   12¾×9: 323×228   *Pen and ink and water-colour*

Anthony DEVIS (1729–1817)

160 'The Woods at Vernon House, Glamorgan'
B.M. 1861.2.9.159 $12\frac{1}{8} \times 17\frac{1}{4}$: 307×438   *Pen and ink and water-colour*
Anthony DEVIS (1729–1817)

161 'Castle of Grignon from the North'
B.M. 1920.7.13.8 $10\frac{1}{2} \times 16\frac{3}{4}$: 267×425   *Pen and ink and water-colour*
Michel Vincent BRANDOIN (1733–1790)

162 'Llangollen Bridge'
V.A.M. 1731–1871 $14\frac{7}{8} \times 21$: 378×533 *Water-colour*
John Alexander GRESSE (1741–1797)

163 'Water Wheel and Pumping Works'
B.M. 1890.5.12.92 $7\frac{5}{8} \times 11\frac{1}{8}$: 194×282 *Pen and ink and water-colour*
John Alexander GRESSE (1741–1797)

164 'Fairlop Oak and Fair'

V.A.M. P.65–1921 $15\frac{7}{8} \times 21\frac{1}{8}$: 403 × 537   *Water-colour, signed and dated 1774*

Samuel Hieronymous GRIMM (1733–1794)

165 'The Enchantresses' Cave'

B.M. 1820.5.12.95 $9\frac{3}{4} \times 15\frac{1}{4}$: 247 × 387   *Pen and ink and sepia wash*

Samuel Hieronymous GRIMM (1733–1794)

166 'The Thames at Brentford'
B.M. 1919.7.12.25 $9\frac{1}{4} \times 11\frac{1}{2}$: 235 × 292   *Pen and wash*
Samuel Hieronymous GRIMM (1733–1794)

167 'North Foreland Lighthouse'
V.A.M. 1730–1871 $9\frac{5}{8} \times 14\frac{3}{8}$: 244 × 365   *Water-colour*
Samuel Hieronymous GRIMM (1733–1794)

168 'Landscape, with Ruins and Figures on a Hill'
B.M. 1939.3.11.19 $9\frac{7}{8} \times 11\frac{1}{2}$: 251 × 292   *Water-colour*
Moses GRIFFITH (1747–after 1809)

169 'Distant View of Llandrillo'
Coll. Mr & Mrs Paul Mellon $10\frac{1}{2} \times 16\frac{1}{2}$: 267 × 420   *Water-colour*
Moses GRIFFITH (1747–after 1809)

170 'Paestum, Temple of Neptune'
V.A.M. D.140–1887/8 $20\frac{1}{4} \times 28\frac{3}{4}$: 514×731 *Water-colour*
Willey REVELEY (d. 1799)

171 'View of Reggio, Calabria'
B.M. 1878.7.13.1277 $12\frac{1}{8} \times 21\frac{1}{2}$: 308×546 *Pen and ink and water-colour*
Willey REVELEY (d. 1799)

CHAPTER X

Later eighteenth century

Theodosius Forrest   William Marlow   Michael Rooker   Thomas Hearne
John Carter   Thomas Malton II   James Malton   Thomas R. Underwood
Benjamin T. Pouncy   Joseph Powell   Edward Dayes   James Miller
Joseph Farington

While much has been written about Paul Sandby as a topographical artist, very little has appeared about his interesting contemporary, Thomas Theodosius Forrest (1728–1784), who was only three years younger. Son of Ebenezer Forrest, the friend of Hogarth, Theodosius inherited a position in a gay and cultured society, and made the most of his advantages. He was more talented than his father, but his abilities were suited rather for the entertainment of drawing-rooms than for the struggle which the arts demand, and Ebenezer probably acted wisely in making his son serve as a clerk in his own attorney's business. 'But though he was obliged to consider the Law as his wife, the Arts were the mistresses of his affection', as Thomas Tyers, one of the Proprietors of the Vauxhall Gardens, and a friend of Dr. Johnson, wrote in the appreciation of Forrest which appeared as his obituary notice.[1] Painting and music seem to have shared his heart equally, though in neither did he gain more than the status of a gifted amateur. In 1775 he wrote a 'musical afterpiece', called *The Weathercock*, which was performed at Covent Garden but withdrawn ignominiously after a run of a few nights. Following this disappointment Forrest confined himself to the composition of songs, which he himself sang very pleasingly. Like his father, he was a regular member of the Beef Steak Club. He was popular in society, his kind-heartedness and amiability gaining him many friends, while his legal experience, his sympathy and his readiness to help others, frequently involved him in the tiresome and thankless offices of trustee and executor. Again following his father, he was immensely interested in theatrical affairs and personages, and his position as solicitor to Covent Garden Theatre brought him a contract with its managers, of whom Garrick, Colman and Harris became his personal friends. He was a friend of Paul Sandby, who once addressed to him a long rhyming letter of 160 lines.[2]

---

[1] *Gentleman's Magazine*, 1784, pp. 54, 877 (as Theodore).
[2] Part of this is quoted by W. Sandby, *Thomas and Paul Sandby*, 1892.

Forrest was considered an excellent judge in matters of art, and had a fine collection of drawings. He was, moreover, a practising artist, and seems to have been rather more successful on this side of his career than in his musical ventures, for he exhibited at the Society of Artists until 1768, and afterwards at the Royal Academy. He contributed to the Academy always as an Honorary Exhibitor, but after 1774 there is a gap until his final appearance there in 1781. His exhibits were all landscapes, with one exception, a subject picture entitled *The Daughter of Damocles, King of Arcadia*. Whether there was some hidden tragedy in this life that superficially seems so carefree and successful is not hinted at by his biographer, Tyers, but nevertheless the end of his days was clouded with melancholy, induced partly by illness, and he committed suicide at his residence in York Buildings, George Street.

Almost nothing was known of Forrest's artistic work until a drawing, *St. Botolph's Priory, Colchester*, with his signature on the back, was given to the British Museum in 1930.[1] It had been exhibited at the Royal Academy in 1772. On this evidence the author identified a drawing in the Victoria and Albert Museum[2] as the work of Forrest. This proved to be a study for a water-colour once in the possession of Malcolm Laing (present whereabouts unknown) of *A View from the Terrace of York Buildings* exhibited at the Royal Academy in 1770.[3]

From these three drawings we can form an estimate of Forrest's style and method of working. The Victoria and Albert Museum drawing is a quick first sketch, and measurement shows that Mr. Laing's drawing was almost certainly traced from it. The chief interest of the sketch is that it was probably drawn out-of-doors—made, in fact, almost on Forrest's own doorstep at York Buildings—and in consequence it is much more loosely handled than is usual in work of the period. The distances, especially the broken roofs and towers beyond the river, are silhouetted in a delicate and vaporous tone of grey, and have a quality which is lacking in the careful finish of the Royal Academy drawing belonging to Mr. Laing. In his technique, notably in the preliminary dead-colouring, and in his treatment of figures, Forrest is very near to Paul Sandby, but quite individual and characteristic is the curious striation of his trees, the foliage being covered all over with parallel pencil lines. This is very noticeable in the study, and in the more finished drawing it is carried still further by being done with the point of a brush. It cannot be claimed that he approached artistic eminence, and his output was far from large, but his work has a gentle tranquillity which is most attractive, and can take its place beside the work of men who have acquired a much higher reputation.

Of the other topographers to be considered in this chapter we may begin with the oldest rather than the most eminent. William Marlow (1740–1813) was born at Southwark, the same year as Francis Towne and two years before William Pars. He told Farington that

---

[1] B.M. 1930. 12.13.1.
[2] V.A.M. P.11–1931.
[3] Both the study and the finished water-colour are reproduced in *Art Work*, VII, 1931, p. 242.

he went as a pupil to Samuel Scott about the year 1756 and was with him for five years. He studied also at St. Martin's Lane Academy, and became a member of the Incorporated Society of Artists, of which he was elected Vice-President in 1778. From 1765 to 1768 he worked in France and Italy, finding subjects for many of his later oil-paintings and water-colours, and on his return settled in London at Mr. Viall's, The Golden Head, Newport Street, Leicester Fields. He exhibited at the Royal Academy from 1788 to 1807, six years before his death. He made a vast number of sketches and studies in pencil, pen and Indian ink, many examples of which are in our museums. Like his mentor he found many of his subjects on the lower Thames, and later at Richmond and Twickenham. English castles and country-seats and views in London were among his regular themes for water-colour and his drawings of Ludlow Castle are particularly numerous. He followed Sandby in the suggestion of luminosity and clarity, which conveys the cool sunshine and limpid atmosphere of English scenery in spring or summer weather. None of the topographers would ever, like Constable, have made Fuseli call for his umbrella.

About 1788 Marlow went to live at Twickenham, in a house opposite the church and close to Strawberry Hill, with a man named Curtis, whose wife Marlow had met at Vauxhall. In 1808 Farington, who does not 'taboo a touch of scandal, If Gray or Walpole hold the candle', says there were now in the Twickenham establishment '6 or 7 children, some of them very like Marlow'. In 1813 Farington adds:

> Northcote told me that W. Marlow died possessed of property which brought Him in £100 pr. annum. He had lived at Twickenham with the family with whom He was at the time of His death, near 30 years.—He allowed them two guineas for His Board & lodging, and latterly paid for the Bread that was consumed in the family. To His Sister (an unmarried person) He allowed something,—and He was charitable, so as to expend the whole of His income.—He had long given up painting for an amusement more agreeable to Him, the making of Telescopes & other articles.

Farington describes Curtis as originally a butcher, and Whitley states that Marlow had 'only one pupil, John Curtis of Twickenham, who exhibited at the Academy till 1822'.[1]

Marlow's work follows the same method as that of Gresse and Grimm, a drawing in pencil or pen, shaded with Indian ink, and then washed over in colour, with a fairly full range. More than the other topographers he has a liking for the free use of pencil in his work. His drawing of *Avignon*[2] shows how closely at times his work approximates to that of Pars; and I recall seeing a *Conway Castle* by him singularly like a Girtin in its warm tones of gentle brown.

With Michael 'Angelo' Rooker (1743–1801) we come to a painter who was essentially more English in outlook and subject than the topographers who preceded him. Rooker drew buildings as if he loved every brick and stone, and was aware of the life behind every window; but, however old the building, he linked it with some aspect of human

[1] Whitley, 1700–1799, II, p. 206.
[2] Coll. Mr. D. L. T. and Miss Armide Oppé.

behaviour. Rooker, usually stated to have been born in 1743[1] (Marlow, Hearne, Rooker, Thomas Malton the younger, Towne and Pars were all born between 1740 and 1750), was the son of Edward Rooker, who worked as an engraver, but varied this slow and unremunerative job—he was paid three shillings a day for some of his most important work—by becoming in the evenings Ned Rooker of Drury Lane Theatre, the best harlequin of his time. His son, who had been christened Michael, was placed by his father under his friend Paul Sandby for instruction in drawing and painting landscape. 'Angelo', which was Sandby's playful nickname for his young pupil, stuck to him throughout his life, and in his will he signed himself 'Michael Rooker, commonly called Michael Angelo Rooker'.[2] He exhibited at the Incorporated Society of Artists in 1767, became a student in the Royal Academy Schools in 1769, and was elected A.R.A. in the following year along with Cosway, Pars and seven others. His training under his father and Sandby had made him a proficient engraver, and for many years he was employed as such, notably to make engravings from his own drawings of colleges, halls and ancient buildings, as head-pieces to the Oxford Almanacks. But his dislike of engraving—he is said to have found it too great a strain on his eyes—must have been innate, and hereditary instinct led him in the direction of the theatre. During a great part of his life he was employed as principal scene-painter at George Colman's theatre in the Haymarket, and the bills of some burlesque pieces announced his name to the public with an Italianised termination as 'Signor Rookerini'.

About 1788 Rooker began a series of summer walking-tours, specially in Norfolk, Suffolk, Warwickshire and Somersetshire. The studies of pure landscape which he made on these excursions are always delicately drawn, pleasant in colour, and well composed. His *Pontypridd Bridge*[3] of 1795 has a certain amount of architectural interest, but the span of the bridge, lost to-day in a welter of buildings, rises from unspoilt river banks among trees and hills. The best of Rooker is in subjects where buildings form the main theme. The large collection of drawings made during his summer tours remained in his hands, and with his pictures and painting utensils was sold by auction at Squibb's Room, Saville Row, in a four days' sale after his death in 1801, realising a total of £1240. Two notes, published within a few years of his death, may be quoted:

> Poor Michael! dejected and broken in spirit, for want of due encouragement, he drooped into eternity the last day of February, 1801 [actually, March 3], aged about fifty-seven. The ingratitude of a friend to whom he had lent a sum of money, and the neglect of an undiscerning public, broke the heart of this highly deserving and meritorious artist. The hand of folly is profuse in the purchase of old pictures; but the performances of living artists, however deserving, are too frequently treated with contempt.[4]

[1] According to his own statement, preserved in the records of the Royal Academy, Rooker was born on March 25, 1746. Whitley, 1800–1820, p. 27.
[2] E. Edwards, *Anecdotes of Painters*, 1808, pp. 264–266.
[3] National Museum of Wales, Cardiff.
[4] *The Works of the late Edward Dayes*, 1805, pp. 347–348.

A few years before his death he lost his situation as scene-painter at Colman's Theatre, which was occasioned by his refusing to join in the liquidation of the manager's debts. This circumstance affected his health, and, after lingering for some months, but without symptoms of great danger, he died suddenly in his chair at his lodgings in Dean-street, Soho, March 3d. 1801, about fifty-eight years of age, and was buried at St. Giles's in the Fields.[1]

While Rooker followed the accepted method of the stained drawing, his grey underpainting is not just in a single tint, but pleasantly varied. In his studies of architecture his drawing was lively, but scrupulously faithful, and there can be no doubt that Girtin and Turner in their early days learned much from his example. Rooker went further than his predecessors in the treatment of the local colour of separate objects, bricks, stones, tiles, timber, with all their irregularities. His work is much more a mosaic of tints, and his colour, thus broken and varied, shows great refinement of tone. As a writer in the *Magazine of the Fine Arts*[2] put it:

Rooker found that roads and paths were not necessarily to be tinted red gravel colour, nor posts and rails washed with a weak tint of orange; neither were tiles and chimneys to be coloured with the fiery red of chimney pots, nor trees with an unbroken mixture of Prussian-blue and gamboge. . . . It was by his artist-like mode of studying nature that others were taught to discover that light and shadow derived its pictorial effect from a due observance of reflection, a feature in painting now universally practised and as generally understood, but one that until then had entirely escaped the perception of all who pretended to be painters.

Rooker should certainly be credited with extending the bounds of the topographer's art. Like Towne and 'Warwick' Smith in some aspects of their work, he grasped the value of filtered light, of the play of sunshine and shadow on gold coloured walls. There is always a beautiful quality in his greys and soft greens and in the hints of yellow and dull red on brick, tile and plaster. With an eye even more penetrating than Sandby's he rendered the mellow patina imposed by the weather.

Rooker's success is also due to his observant rendering of figures, entirely in keeping with their surroundings. Like those of Dayes, they always have life and variety, and in their grouping fall happily into his design. The combination of architectural interest and warm human life, in which Rooker excels, is evident in his *Bury St. Edmunds*[3] (Pl. 179), showing the square Norman tower of St. James's Church and the frontage of the Six Bells Inn, with a timber waggon moving slowly along the dusty road, and people promenading or marketing in the open square, while sunlight plays over the whole scene, bringing dwellings and figures into a warm concerted life. And there are no more typical examples of his work than *A Game of Bowls*[4] (Pl. 176) and the *Farmyard, Thetford*[5] (Pl. 177), with the flutter of doves on the tiled roof, the girl on a balcony talking to a man with a wheelbarrow below, some goats, a dog and horses in the stable yard. In drawings like these, Rooker brought a new blend of colour, light and activity into British water-colour

[1] E. Edwards, *Anecdotes of Painters*, 1808, p. 266.
[2] 1832, I, p. 124.
[4] Coll. Mr. & Mrs. Paul Mellon.
[3] V.A.M. 51–1881.
[5] B.M. 1857. 2.28.210.

painting. He deserves a much higher place in its history than he has normally been given, and it is pleasant to think that Turner admired Rooker's work and bought more than a dozen of his sketches at the sale held after his death in 1801.

Rooker and Thomas Hearne are closely linked in their lives and in their technical practice as engravers and painters. While both were reputed men of great integrity, Rooker's manners are said to have been 'somewhat rough',[1] and Hearne's 'Agreeable, gentlemanly and modest'.[2] While Rooker's work belies his reputation by being all that is gracious and endearing, without doubt Hearne is the finer artist. Thomas Hearne (1744–1817), the topographer, was born a year later than Rooker, and coming to London from his native village of Brinkworth, near Malmesbury in Wiltshire, gained a premium at the Society of Arts in 1763, and from 1765 served a six years' apprenticeship to William Woollett, the engraver. After the term of his indentures had expired he travelled in 1771[3] to the Leeward Islands as draughtsman to the new Governor, Sir Ralph Payne, afterwards Lord Lavington. He had embarked on a five year task. Three and a half were spent in the West Indies making drawings of harbours, ports and characteristic scenery, and the remaining time after his return, in preparing his work for engraving. He was now over thirty and preferring the more original branch of his work determined to devote himself to the drawing of British topography, employing others for the task of engraving. In 1777 he combined forces with William Byrne for the production of a work, which appeared much later in two volumes, with the title *Antiquities of Great Britain. Illustrated in Views of Monasteries, Castles and Churches, now existing. Engraved by W. Byrne, F.S.A. from Drawings made by Thomas Hearne, F.S.A. with descriptions in English and French, London, Printed for T. Cadell and W. Davies, Strand, 1807.* The dates of publication on the plates, which were engraved by Byrne, S. Middiman and others, range from 1778 to 1806, and the fifty-two subjects drawn by Hearne show how widely he travelled over England and Scotland in search of surviving relics of medieval antiquities. In the Victoria and Albert Museum are the original drawings for *Wetheral Priory, Cumberland*[4]; *N.E. View of Llanthony Priory*[5]; *The Bar Gate, Southampton*[6]; *Ludlow Castle*[7]; *Priory Church, Haddington*[8]; and *Abbey Gate, Bury St. Edmunds*[9]. Further facts about this publication are supplied by Farington:

Byrne called to-day.—He pays Hearne 10 guineas each for the drawings of the 'Antiquities of Great Britain', and He becomes the sole proprietor of the 2nd volume. He sells the drawings for 8 guineas.

John Byrne called & told me that He & Hearne, joint proprietors of the first volume of Antiquities of Great Britain had sold the work to Cadell & Davis, and that He had also sold the eight numbers finished of a second volume of Antiquities, in which Hearne had no share. Cadell & Davis gave £1600 for the whole work, meaning to make one volume of it. He did not say how much of the £1600 was allowed for the *first volume.*[10]

---

[1] E. Edwards, *Anecdotes of Painters,* 1808, p. 264.   [2] Pilkington's *Dictionary.*
[3] A large water-colour by Hearne representing the Court House and the Guard House, St. John's, Antigua, is in the V.A.M. P.2–1932.
[4] V.A.M. 52–1887.   [5] V.A.M. D.771.   [6] V.A.M. 95–1892.   [7] V.A.M. D.772.
[8] V.A.M. D.773.   [9] V.A.M. D.414–1899.   [10] *Diary,* March 29, 1808.

Farington gives us a glimpse of Hearne and his home life when Hearne was sixty-four:

Hearne sd. that He usually rises at half past 10 oClock,—puts His tea in the Pot, & while it is drawing washes His face & hands, then drinks a cup of tea & eats a piece of toast, after which feeling Himself refreshed by it, He sits down & draws a while, then takes another cup of tea & some toast, which completes His breakfast.—He is not able upon an average to work more than from two hours & a half to three Hours a day.—He dines at 5,—drinks from half a pint to a pint of Port at & after dinner,—has tea, and between 9 & 10 goes to Mills's Coffee House where he remains till ½ past 12 oClock & from thence returns home to bed immediately. He complained of slow circulation & cold feet which Lamb's wool stockings worn in the night & Cloaths heaped upon him will not warm.

When Hearne was seventy-three, Farington called upon him and recorded[1]:—

I found him having the appearance of an old and nearly worn out man. He was at his Drawing table with a Black lead pencil drawing before Him. . . . He was told He looked better, but he sd. 'I best know how I am: my appetite nearly gone, only taking soup and such things. I have lost my relish for Port Wine, but wine is necessary for my support, and I mix Raisin Wine with Port Wine to make it more relishing to my taste. My debility is great, and I have giddiness in my head, which I never before felt.' I sat with Him a considerable time, and he talked without pausing, but coughed much. His spirits did not in this respect seem to be affected.—He spoke on several subjects with all the interest that he formerly felt.

Dr. Monro was present at Hearne's bedside when he died, a few weeks later.

Hearne's power as an artist, coupled with his genial nature, brought him the life-long friendship of Sir George Beaumont. This is shown in a copy of a letter in the Victoria and Albert Museum, written by Beaumont to Dr. Monro on December 20, 1816, when Hearne was ill. Beaumont refers to his forty years' friendship and its beginning:

I first became acquainted with him in the spring of 1771. I came with my tutor, Mr. Davy, to London, and as my fondness for art made me desirous of seeing the most celebrated professors in every line, he carried me to his friend Mr. Woollett. We mounted up to his garret and there sat Hearne, most assiduously employed in etching from a picture by Swanevelt, now in my possession. We passed about six weeks in London and there were few days in which we did not spend some hours in the company of Woollett and Hearne. We talked incessantly of pictures and plates, and my love for painting was completely confirmed. Mr. Woollett was prevailed upon to promise a visit to Mr. Davy in the course of the summer and bring Hearne with him; accordingly in August they arrived at his house at Henstead in Suffolk.

There we passed six weeks together, I may almost say, as far as I was concerned, in perfect happiness. We sketched all day and in the evening we were delighted with the original pleasantry and inimitable humour of Mr. Davy. I am sure you must have heard Hearne speak of him. We visited Houghton and saw that collection with delight.

The remembrance of this happy year never fails, when I think of it, to cross my mind like a gleam of bright sunshine. I was young and ardent, and admiration—the most pleasing of sensations—I enjoyed in the highest degree. I thought Woollett and Hearne the greatest artists that ever existed, and if anyone had presumed to say that Claude or Gaspar knew half so much of the matter, I should have considered it as ignorance or prejudice. Woollett I knew, and regarded to the day of his death, he was an excellent man—it is unnecessary to praise him in his line. Since that time Hearne has risen daily in my esteem, a man of purer integrity does not exist.

[1] *Diary*, February 1, 1817.

175

References in Farington's *Diary* show that Hearne made a tour of the Wye with Beaumont in 1794, was frequently in his company, and stayed with him at Coleorton in 1808.

In his technique Hearne was less inclined than Rooker to concentrate upon detail. Though he used the pen he employed it less obtrusively than his contemporary, depending often upon a soft pencil more than ink for his outline, and searching for broad effect rather than close definition. In his trees, particularly, he shows—thanks to his frequent use of pencil—more feeling of the natural growth and variety of foliage. Like Rooker, he used grey tints instead of the conventional Indian ink for his under-painting and washed pale notes of slight colour over this in a pleasant harmony. His lively skies, so much in keeping with his spirited drawing and quiet colour, are a new feature in topographic art. They are serene, with touches of blue appearing through rifts of thin and ragged white cloud, but in *St. Mary's Abbey, York,*[1] he essays a storm effect, which was quite unusual at that time among the practitioners of water-colour. He was much nearer to J. R. Cozens than to Rooker in his restrained colour, which often goes little beyond the gentlest tones of ashen green and grey. It is a mistake to suppose that Hearne's work, as is sometimes thought, has suffered from fading, or that his restraint is due to any lack of available colours. C. F. Bell emphasises this in his note on Hearne in relation to James Moore, F.S.A., and points out that drawings of *Wells* and *Glastonbury*, dated 1795, then in the Spencer Churchill collection at Northwick Park, have always been carefully guarded from light, 'But in spite of admirable draughtsmanship and a very fine sense of pictorial effect, [these] are marred by the combination of the cork coloured landscape with brightly tinted figures in the foreground'.[2] His limitation in chromatic treatment is due partly to a desire to keep his colour in harmony with pencil or a pale ink, but still more to the sympathetic desire of a man who had been an engraver himself to make the engraver's task as simple as possible. Where Rooker gives the impression of painting for his own pleasure, Hearne must always have been conscious that his drawing was going direct to Byrne or some other engraver in London, who would bless him for simplifying an irksome task.

At times Hearne gives an attractive glimpse, as in his *Carisbrooke Castle,*[3] of a stretch of distant country—here a view of the Solent and the Hampshire coast—sparkling in sunlight as it recedes to a far horizon. It was clearly his pencil work and drawings like this which exercised so profound an influence upon the young Turner when they were placed before him by Dr. Monro, who had spent what in those days was the large sum of £800 upon his collection of Hearne's work.[4] The doctor told Farington, on December 14, 1795, that he considered 'Hearne as superior to everybody in drawing'. Some of those best drawings, showing Hearne at the height of his power, are in the British Museum, among them *Elvet Bridge, Durham*[5] (Pl. 180), *Hitchin Priory,*[6] *Near Monmouth*[7] and *Near Witham,*

[1] Whereabouts unknown.
[2] C. F. Bell, . . . *Some water-colour artists of the British School*, Walpole Soc. V, 1915–1917, p. 81.
[3] B.M. 1859. 5.28.204.   [4] Farington, *Diary*, March 5, 1810.
[5] B.M. 1859. 5.28. 207.   [6] B.M. 1859. 5.28.210.   [7] B.M. 1859. 5.28.212.

Essex.[1] *The Witham, Essex,* in design no less than locality, with its cottage under trees, its running water, and carefully drawn waggon and horses, is strangely like a Constable in little, *The Hay Wain* in reverse. His two silvery views of water and shipping[2] have an atmospheric quality which few other artists of his period can match. In his noble *Durham Cathedral*[3] drawing and atmosphere are combined in a work which achieves great dignity of composition. The shortening of the shadows of the towers to make them come inside the lower margin of his drawing is untrue but forgivable; and it may be noted how perfectly the spacious sky links the tall trees on the left with the magnificent group of buildings on the right (a favourite subject with so many artists in England). In the Victoria and Albert Museum the *Durham Cathedral* by Edward Edwards, already mentioned, and painted from almost the same spot, offers an interesting comparison.

Belonging to the topographic group were draughtsmen concerned mainly with architecture, among them John Carter (1748–1817) and Thomas Malton II (1748–1804). Carter was draughtsman to the Society of Antiquaries and an enthusiastic writer on Gothic architecture. He made numerous records, dull but faithful, of ancient edifices and archaeological remains. Malton, whose task it was to portray the buildings of his own period, was a more memorable artist than Carter. His father, Thomas Malton (1726–1801), worked for a time as a cabinet maker and upholsterer in the Strand (it is quite conceivable that Edward Edwards worked under him). He drew architectural subjects, invented a 'Perspective Machine', and published a *Complete Treatise on Perspective*, 1775. About 1785 he left London and settled in Dublin. Two of his sons were trained by him and followed in his footsteps. Thomas Malton II, won a premium from the Society of Arts in 1774 and a gold medal in the Royal Academy Schools in 1782. He exhibited architectural views at the Academy between 1773 and 1803, and painted scenery for Covent Garden Theatre. Like his father, he became a teacher of perspective, and in the Victoria and Albert Museum is his charming professional card, worked in aquatint, with the inscription: 'Drawing Taught by T. Malton, No. 103 Long Acre. An Evening School.' Malton did not move to Long Acre till 1796, and Thornbury's highly-coloured account of Turner's boyish experiences there must be discounted, along with much else that he wrote. Turner studied as a boy under Malton, and his early work, where buildings are set out in careful perspective, shows the thoroughness of the tuition he received. When Turner was lecturing at the Royal Academy in 1811 as Professor of Perspective, he paid a tribute to the knowledge and skill of his former teacher.

Malton made about a hundred drawings which he engraved in aquatint for his *Picturesque Tour through London and Westminster*, 1792. The original drawing for *The Strand with Somerset House and St. Mary's Church*[4] (Pl. 186) is in the Victoria and Albert Museum. At the British Museum is the original of the *Interior of St. Paul's Cathedral*[5] and an etched proof,

---

[1] B.M. 1859. 5.28.202.   [2] V.A.M. 1699/1700–1871.   [3] V.A.M. 4–1891.
[4] V.A.M. 1725–1871.   [5] B.M. 1868. 3.28.301.

177

worked over by the artist in ink and water-colour, for his aquatint of *King's Mews, Charing Cross*.[1] (Tinted etchings of this type have frequently been sold as original water-colours.) The two drawings of The Strand and St. Paul's are typical of Malton at his best, an accomplished draughtsman, using hard, precise outlines with rigid restraint and mathematical accuracy. The under-painting in a neutral tint gives well-observed indications of light and shade, knitting the different passages together, but the colour is slight and merely gives diversity without suggestion of atmosphere or depth. He does not possess Girtin's power of realising a building, but he does give a faithful portrait of it, without any of that artificial picturesqueness which for example is at times found in Samuel Prout's drawings.

James Malton (? 1766–1803), a younger son of Thomas Malton I, was in Dublin with his father, and employed for nearly three years by James Gandon, the architect, but dismissed for irregular conduct. His *Picturesque and Descriptive View of the City of Dublin*, published in parts from 1792 to 1797, containing twenty-five plates, is one of the earliest and best of the books with coloured aquatints. Like his brother Thomas, he was an authority on perspective, and his work has a distinction of its own in addition to its value as an architectural record. He exhibited from 1791 at the Incorporated Society of Artists, the Free Society and the Royal Academy. He committed suicide in 1803, a year before the death of his brother Thomas.[2]

The Maltons were 'street-artists', to use the term in contrast to landscape-painter or sea-painter. Both brothers had eye not merely for the buildings but for the life of the street, the slow-moving horse-drawn traffic, the waggons, the brewers' drays, the hand-carts and barrows, the bustle of the pavements. Their attachments, like those of Charles Lamb, were purely local; they had no longing for groves and valleys and the countryside. The small drawing of *Queen Eleanor's Cross, Waltham Cross*[3] (Pl. 195), for a long time was ascribed to Thomas Malton. Cosmo Monkhouse draws particular attention to it. 'Nowhere,' he says, 'will you find brick-work much more beautifully painted, in shade or out of shade. It is the quality of the colour, its preservation of broad general tone, with infinite variety and play of colour within it that is perhaps the most remarkable thing in the drawing, but it is throughout not only good but choice in colour, and altogether a masterly little picture worthy to rank with the best of Van der Heyden's Dutch streets. It is to be wished—it is often to be wished—with regard to these early water-colours that it were dated. Did Turner learn this quality of colour from Malton, or did Malton learn it from him, or is this drawing by some other artist?'[4] The old inscription on the mount to Thomas Malton had been doubted by various authorities. When the drawing was re-mounted, 'T. R. Underwood, Jany. 1793/14' was found to be inscribed on the back; the date exhibited at the Royal Academy. The composition may have been based on a similar

---

[1] B.M. 1871. 12.9.996.
[2] Whitley, 1800–1820, pp. 72–75.
[3] V.A.M. 407–1885.
[4] *Earlier English Water-Colour Painters*, 1897, pp. 59, 60.

178

one Thomas Richard Underwood (1772–1835) did for J. C. Barrow's *Picturesque Views of Churches*, engraved in 1790. Little is known save that he was born in London, studied at Dr. Monro's, was a founder-member of Girtin's sketching society, and exhibited at the Royal Academy from 1789 to 1801. Charles Cundall[1] records that mention is made of Underwood in *Archives de l'Art Français, recueil de documents, inédits relatifs à l'histoire des Arts en France, publié sous la direction de M. Anatole de Montaiglon*, 1862, under the heading, '*Deux Paysagistes Anglais, prisonniers de Guerre (1803–13). Lettres communiqués par M. le Baron de Girardot.*' It appears that on returning from Italy in 1803, Underwood was taken prisoner in France. He painted for two summers at Ussé, near Tours, and in 1813 a passport was granted to him, with permission to paint landscapes at Roucy. A foot-note states, '*C'est un vrai nom de paysagiste de s'appeler M. Sous-Bois*'. The other artist to whom reference is made was M. Schmith, presumably Smith, who is said to have anticipated the Barbizon School in discovering the beauties of Fontainebleau. Underwood died at Chamaraude, near Paris.

Benjamin Thomas Pouncy (d. 1799) comes very near to Rooker and Hearne, so near that it might be difficult to distinguish some of his work unless it were signed. Pouncy was brother-in-law of Woollett, the engraver. Studying under him he produced some excellent plates, and also painted landscapes in water-colour. He contributed some Kentish views to Royal Academy exhibitions and among these may have been his neat and precise, *On the coast at Broadstairs*[2] (Pl. 189). Another good example of his work is *St. George's or Newin Gate, Canterbury*, 1795[3] (Pl. 190). His drawings are so rare that one suspects that many have been assigned to other painters. The date of Pouncy's birth is unknown, but he exhibited from 1772 to 1789. From 1780 or earlier he resided at Lambeth, where he was Deputy Librarian at the Palace. Joseph Powell (*c.* 1780–1834?) was a pupil of his, and sent in his earlier Royal Academy exhibits from Pouncy's address. Powell was much employed in teaching, but made sketching tours in most parts of England and Wales. His *West View of Worcester Cathedral*,[4] 1798, and his *Lanercost Priory*[5] show that he followed Pouncy in close observation and uninspired tidiness.

The outstanding member of the group of topographers at the close of the eighteenth century is Edward Dayes (1763–1804). Apart from his own work he usually comes into notice as the teacher of Girtin. The popular tale about the refractory apprentice and the aspersions which Dayes made upon the character of his pupil, will be dealt with in connection with Girtin. Here it may be said that Dayes was a sound and capable draughtsman, a graceful colourist in the established manner, and probably an admirable teacher. Certainly, Girtin's early work was closely founded upon the teaching and example of Dayes, and A. J. Finberg recognises the extraordinary influence which Dayes exercised

[1] *History of British Water Colour Painting*, 1928, p. 30.
[2] V.A.M. 108–1879.
[3] V.A.M. P.75–1920.
[4] V.A.M. 1759–1871.
[5] National Museum of Wales, Cardiff.

over Turner from about 1795 to 1798.[1] It has been difficult, at times, for students to decide whether certain drawings shadowed with the pale mixture of Indian ink and blue, which Dayes recommended, should be attributed to him or to Turner. Cold, bluish-grey, used for gradations of distance and sky, is a noticeable feature in the early work of both Turner and Girtin.

Dayes' established position is shown by the fact that he was called upon to draw the first plate, a view of Oxford, for *Walker's Copper Plate Magazine*, published in monthly parts, at 1s. or 1s. 6d., from 1792 to 1802. This publication is mentioned here not only on account of Dayes but because Girtin appears as the designer of a view of Windsor in 1792, and Turner with a view of Rochester in 1794. Girtin was only seventeen in 1792, and his first commission was probably secured for him by his master.

Dayes became a student in the Royal Academy Schools in 1780. He is said to have learned the art of mezzotint from William Pether, and practised this method, making some plates after Morland's subjects, besides producing some attractive miniatures. His work in miniature is rare, but two good examples are in the Victoria and Albert Museum.[2] As a painter of landscapes, architecture, and figure subjects in water-colour, he exhibited at the Royal Academy from 1786 to 1804, and at the Society of Artists in 1790 and 1791. He was employed by James Moore, F.S.A., 'to stiffen the weak drawing and possibly enliven the feeble colouring of twenty-eight of his sketches made on the Scottish tour of 1792, and he shared the work with Girtin'.[3] At one time he must have made a useful stay at Tintern. It is not known where his original drawings are, but the colour aquatints by F. Jukes suggest the fine draughtsmanship, the admirable balance and design, which the originals must have possessed.

His works as a writer included *An Excursion through Derbyshire and Yorkshire, Instructions for Drawing and Colouring Landscapes* and *Professional Sketches of Modern Artists*. They were collected for publication in one volume by E. W. Brayley, and issued in 1805, with the title *The Works of the late Edward Dayes*. The volume appeared a year after Dayes' death by suicide in May 1804, and the *Professional Sketches* bear evidence of his querulous, unbalanced, violent nature. They contain many venomous and malicious statements, among them his attack upon Girtin, which is as unfair as his description of Alexander Cozens as 'blot-master general to the town'. The technical notes in the first two portions of the book are of great value as a contemporary description of the tinted method which was in general use in the latter half of the eighteenth century.

The method described is fully exemplified in his own work; first, the completed outline; then, the dead colouring with a mixture of blue and Indian ink; then, the washes of warm colour over cold; with it all, the avoidance of 'introducing the colour of an object in its shade', a fallacy which Girtin was to expose. Dayes' preliminary work with the pen is

---

[1] *Life of J. M. W. Turner, R.A.*, 1939, p. 22.
[2] B. S. Long, *British Miniaturists*, 1929.
[3] C. F. Bell, *op. cit.* p. 79.

delicate and precise; he draws landscape and buildings pleasantly and with accuracy; his figures and animals, singly or in groups, are cleverly placed; but it must be admitted that, now and then, he can be slipshod and slovenly. The blue effect of his drawings is atmospheric, but it is an artificial atmosphere, and not so true in effect as the work of Rooker and Hearne. His tree drawing is characteristic, the foliage at the edges spreading out into shapes resembling bunches of bananas or fingers spread open; sometimes, as in a drawing of *Walsingham Abbey*, 1792,[1] it is in quick, often separated, curves, as of brittle, falling autumn leaves. One of his most important works is *Buckingham House, St. James's Park*, 1790[2] (Pl. 194). Here he seems to have set out to vie with Debucourt's *Promenade du Palais-Royal*, and with Rowlandson, whose *Vauxhall Gardens* had been painted some years before. The colour-print by F. D. Soiron of *Buckingham House* is prized by collectors. In the drawing it will be noted that the architecture is secondary and is very slightly rendered, while the artist's liveliness, dexterity, and restrained gaiety of colour are lavished on the fashionably-attired figures in the foreground. They are well studied and full of spirit, but they lack Rowlandson's vigour of touch and keen characterisation. The liveliness of rhythm in this drawing is secured by a false relationship in the placing of the heads, the background figures seeming to be standing on chairs. There is a similar falsity of scale and perspective in the figures of his *Greenwich Hospital*, 1788,[3] but the architecture is drawn with special care and refinement. In *Buckingham House* it will be noted that the pen-work changes from delicate drawing with a fine point in the figures, to a much bolder and stronger line in darker ink for the trees; and that the shadow washes are undisturbed by the overlaid tints. An example of Dayes at his best is a *View of St. Augustine's Gateway, Canterbury*, in the foreground a group of farm labourers with the Cathedral in the distance, dated 1787.

Apart from these more ambitious works, where groups of animated figures are a main interest, Dayes painted slight landscapes in simple blue and grey tones. A. J. Finberg describes them as 'brilliantly clever and wrought with astonishing ease and grace',[4] and adds that 'most of them have in recent times been attributed to Turner, and their merits render the attribution possible'. In his opinion *Corfe Castle*[5] and *Henley-on-Thames*[6] are wrongly ascribed to Turner and are both by Dayes. Finberg proves also that a whole group of sketches in the Turner Bequest, hitherto tentatively ascribed to Turner or Girtin, are actually by Edward Dayes.

There is still another side of Dayes' work which is little known and very confusing. Towards the close of the century he was painting large classical, historical and religious subjects very closely in the style of Blake. The figures have Blake's mannerisms in the

[1] Whereabouts unknown.
[2] V.A.M. 1756–1871.
[3] V.A.M. 1769–1900.
[4] *Life of J. M. W. Turner, R.A.*, 1939, pp. 112, 357, 358.
[5] V.A.M. 2961–1876.
[6] Whitworth Art Gallery, Manchester.

treatment of flowing robes, the patriarchal bearded heads, and the exaggeration of height and gesture; and they are painted with Blake's simplified scheme of colour. A *Fall of the Angels*[1] doubtless in this manner, was exhibited by him in 1798. I have seen two which would have been very puzzling if it had not been for the signature 'Edward Dayes, 1797'. *St. Gregory the Great and the British Captives*,[2] long attributed to Blake, was at one time re-christened as Dayes, and has again, rightly or wrongly, been given back to Blake.

A little bit of a hack, a little too versatile, of a rather spiteful and unpleasant character, Dayes was clearly a good teacher, and ranks high in accomplishment among the topographers.[3] His place is well suggested by an extract from a poem by Ange D. Macquin[4]:

> *. . . For henceforth, when thick cov'ring dust*
> *Shall bury to the smallest bust*
> *The Gothic pride of Castles Drear,*
> *Of Abbeys old with cloisters near,*
> *The magic spell of Indian ink,*
> *The simple cake of Brown or Pink,*
> *In* Dayes's *or in* Carter's[5] *pages,*
> *Shall still retain the dear images.*

As the poem, his work is of his period, sedate and well designed.

James Miller (Exhib. 1773–1791), a somewhat neglected artist, is worth noting as one of the most exact of the topographers, with considerable charm of drawing, colour and atmosphere. No biographical details about him are known, and there was more than one artist of this name exhibiting towards 1800. It may be assumed, however, that the painter of several topographical subjects in the Victoria and Albert Museum can be identified with the James Miller who exhibited views of London, Richmond, Chatham, etc., from 1773 to 1791 at the Incorporated Society of Artists, and from 1781 to 1788 at the Royal Academy. His *Cheyne Walk, Chelsea*[6] (Pl. 196), dated 1776, shows a meticulous attention to detail and is noteworthy for the beauty of the clear, firm transparent shadows which fall across the buildings. So few drawings by Miller are known that one is tempted to surmise that some of his work has been assigned to one or other of the outstanding topographers.

The discovery in 1921 of the diary of Joseph Farington,[7] together with a large number of sketch-books and drawings by him, provided a completely fresh source of knowledge.

---

[1] Whereabouts unknown.
[2] V.A.M. A.L.–6868.
[3] See Appendix to this chapter. Methods expounded by Dayes in his *Works*.
[4] Quoted by C. F. Bell, *op. cit.* p. 83.
[5] John Carter, 1748–1817, architectural draughtsman.
[6] V.A.M. 731–1893.
[7] The *Diary* and drawings, together with the silverplate presented to him by the Royal Academy came from the estate of Miss M. L. E. Tyrwhitt of Northwood Lodge, Wallington, Surrey, and was auctioned by Messrs. Puttick & Simpson, December 9, 1921. The *Diary* was bought by the *Morning Post* who published extracts serially from January 1922 to October 1923, edited by James Grieg. During 1922–1928, he produced an eight volume edition, which, although extensive, did not contain the whole of the important contents. Later, the proprietor of the *Morning Post* presented the complete manuscript to the Royal Library, Windsor, and a typescript from this can be seen in the British Museum.

The *Diary*, vast in length and covering the dates 1793 to 1821, presented an unrivalled account of the life of artistic London at the turn of the eighteenth century. It reveals, through the eyes of a shrewd observer, characters like Fox, Pitt, Burke, Napoleon and George III, and throws many sidelights on the manners of the nobility and their patronage of art. In the centre of the stage is Farington himself, within his own sphere one of the most powerful men in the London of his time.

The first entry in the *Diary* is dated July 13, 1793, and the last was written on the day of Farington's death in 1821. In an instruction to his Executors with regard to his *Diary*, Farington explains that he kept it chiefly for his own amusement—'much also I was induced to put down in writing as being curious Anecdote and useful to the Biographer'. He had intended, he says, to destroy the diaries before his death, but on second thoughts decided to leave them in the family: 'The Diary's I direct shall be given to my Brother, Richard Atherton Farington, who will find leisure to look into them if He be so disposed to do.' They were to be kept for 'inspection and perusal' by his three brothers. There is no hint of any possibility of publication.

The *Diary* amplifies and illuminates the previously known facts about Joseph Farington's life. He was born on November 21, 1747, at Leigh in Lancashire, and was the second son of the Rev. William Farington, B.D., Vicar of Leigh, and afterwards Rector of Warrington. His mother was Hester Gilbody, a miniature of whom, probably by John Plott, is in the Victoria and Albert Museum. According to his own statement, in a letter to Sir Thomas Lawrence dated 1820, Farington came to London in 1763,[1] and became a pupil of Richard Wilson. He was awarded several premiums by the Incorporated Society of Artists, where he exhibited from 1765, and was elected a member of the Society in 1768. The Society had for some time been rent by internal dissension, and matters came to a head in 1768 when several important members, among whom was Richard Wilson, seceded from the Society to found the Royal Academy of Arts. The Royal Academy schools were opened in 1769, and Farington was one of the first pupils. In 1773 he withdrew from the Incorporated Society, and in June of that year went to Houghton Hall, Norfolk, the seat of the Earl of Orford, to make drawings from the pictures there for the purpose of engraving. His younger brother George assisted him in the task, which was commissioned by Alderman Boydell and required no less than three years for its accomplishment. The Houghton Hall collection was sold in 1779 to the Empress Catherine of Russia for £40,555, the valuation put upon it by Benjamin West and Cipriani, to the astonishment of Horace Walpole.

In July 1776 Farington returned to the North, and spent some years in the Lake District, making many drawings and studies. From Keswick in 1778 he sent his first contribution to the Academy, *A Waterfall*. In 1780 he returned to London and settled down at 35 Upper Charlotte Street, Fitzroy Square. We may presume that he continued to be

[1] G. S. Layard, ed., *Sir Thomas Lawrence's Letter-Bag*, 1906, p. 161.

closely associated with Richard Wilson, and when Wilson died in 1782 Farington was already well established. He was elected an associate of the Royal Academy in 1783, defeating Opie by 15 votes to 2, and a full member in 1785 in the place of Joseph Wright of Derby, defeating among other candidates Ozias Humphry, John Russell and William Hamilton. He deposited *A Coast Scene* as his Diploma work.

The next few years of his life were apparently uneventful. He was exhibiting steadily at the Academy and laying the foundations of that far-reaching influence in its councils which brought him later more reputation than he ever earned by his pictures. He had made his first continental tour in 1767, when he travelled through Belgium. A sketch-book[1] which he used on this tour, contains a copy of a French permit of August 26, 1767, allowing Farington and 'Thomas d'Jour, Anglois'[2] to embark at Calais for England.

At the time when the *Diary* opens in 1793 Farington was a prominent figure in the social life of his day, and seems to have found time to combine the functions of the man-about-town, the artist, and the energetic man of business ruling the affairs of the Royal Academy. He was constantly in request for social functions, constantly appealed to for his support in favour of some candidate for artistic honours or a pension from the Academy funds. Every young artist coming up to London tried to obtain an introduction to the great man, as did young Constable in 1798, and those on whose behalf his activities were enlisted found him prepared to fulfil more than the letter of his promises. His immense influence in the Academy was probably due mainly to his flair for business.

In the *Life of Sir Martin Shee*,[3] President of the Royal Academy, we read:

> The principal spokesman was Mr. Farington, whose name was associated with every proceeding of the Royal Academy, in whose movement for good or evil he exercised so powerful a control as to procure for him the appellation of the dictator of the Academy. He possessed a degree of weight in the deliberations of the councils of the body far beyond what any other member could hope to attain or excel.

William Sandby aptly summed Farington up in a well-known passage[4]:

> He took an active part in the government and management of the Royal Academy: he first brought forward, as one of the auditors, the plan for increasing the income of the Academy which was adopted in 1809, and proposed some important resolutions in regard to the pension fund. In recognition of these services the Academy voted £50 to be employed in the purchase of a piece of plate to be presented to him. By his great personal influence over many of his brother Academicians, resulting from his unceasing attention to the interests of the institution combined with great diplomatic tact, and many other effective elements of social popularity, he possessed a degree of weight in the councils of the Academy, far beyond any other member—so much so that with some he bore the appellation of Dictator of the Royal Academy.

---

[1] V.A.M. P.76–1921.
[2] Probably the miniature painter Thomas Day (1732–1807).
[3] Martin Archer Shee, *Life of Sir Martin Shee*, 1860, I, p. 210.
[4] William Sandby, *The History of the Royal Academy of Arts*, 1862, I, p. 194.

184

But there were others who professed to find less worthy motives for his ambition. Northcote said[1]:

> How Farington used to rule the Academy! He was the great man to be looked up to on all occasions; all applicants must gain their point through him. But he was no painter; he cared nothing at all about pictures; his great passion was the love of power—he loved to rule. He did it, of course, with considerable dignity: but he had an untamable spirit, which, I suppose, was due to the fact that he had lost the game as a painter, and that it was too late to mend the matter.

It is not easy to mark the steps in Farington's rise to power in the Academy. From the very nature of his influence it follows that it was the result of work chiefly unspectacular and solitary among the Academy's books and business sheets. In actual policy his part was active but never very prominent. When Sir Joshua Reynolds, then President, offered his resignation on account of the Bonomi affair in 1790, Farington was one of the deputation requesting the withdrawal of the resignation, and when Benjamin West succeeded to the Presidency in 1792, Farington came more to the front. He was one of the witnesses against James Barry, the Professor of Painting, who was expelled in 1799, and in 1803 was mainly instrumental in securing the election of Dr. Burney, Lawrence's friend, to the post of Professor of Ancient History. In 1805 he himself came into conflict with the Academy authorities, and a general assembly of Academicians censured him severely. He was charged with admitting Northcote's *Young Roscius* after the time for receiving pictures had expired, of altering the position of Beechey's *Lord St. Vincent*, and of allowing Flaxman to arrange his own models. A paragraph in the *Morning Post* said that 'the meeting came to an unanimous resolution, that Mr. Farrington (*sic*) by his conduct as a member of the committee to whom the choice and placing of the pictures sent to Somerset House for exhibition was entrusted, had been guilty of a gross violation of the laws of the Academy'.

After the turn of the eighteenth century Farington's contributions to the Academy became more infrequent. He exhibited in 1801 and 1804, and not again until 1811. The date of his last exhibit is 1813. Perhaps his multifarious activities were becoming too great a strain, for there are no signs of diminution in his enthusiasm for his profession. His sketching expeditions were very frequent, and the jottings he kept of his travelling expenses show that his means must have been considerable. In September 1800 he toured in Wales, and in August 1801 he went to Scotland for several months, where he called on Alexander Nasmyth, 'who is in high reputation as a landscape painter'. He also saw Raeburn, whom he considered greatly superior to Nasmyth, despite the esteem in which the latter was held. In August 1802, after the horrors of the Revolution had ended and the Peace of Amiens had brought a period of uneasy quiet, he went to Paris with Fuseli, where he saw Greuze, 'a middle-sized, slender old man of a healthy appearance', taking his evening stroll; visited the Salon of Madame Récamier; and from a window in the Tuileries gazed upon Napoleon reviewing troops and, with strangely prophetic vision, thought that

---

[1] Ernest Fletcher, ed., *Conversations of James Northcote, R.A. with James Ward*, 1901, p. 165.

the First Consul 'would be a very passable figure on an English quarter-deck'. They returned in October 1802 and on landing in England Farington noted: 'What must be the nature of that mind that would not feel grateful that it was his lot to be an Englishman; a man entitled from his Birth to participate in such advantages as in no other country can be found.'

The latter part of his life was uneventful. His wife, Susan Hammond, a relation of the Earl of Orford, had died in 1800, and one of the few signs of emotional feeling in the *Diary* occurs when he speaks of her death. His own death in 1821 came when he was staying at Didsbury, near Manchester.

Strangely little is known about his work. His oil pictures are now rarely seen, and there is little evidence for estimating their quality. His contemporaries varied between the opinion expressed by Northcote—'he was no painter'—and the more favourable view which he noted in the *Diary* on July 17, 1804, on the occasion of a visit to Edridge. Edridge had been commissioned to find an artist to paint a companion picture to a Wilson owned by a certain Mr. Boldero Barnard, and 'Edridge said he applied to me from really thinking I was the person to be preferred—that there was a certain fashionable mode of painting which prevailed, but He most approved of that sober and natural manner which He observed in my pictures. . . . He declared that He thought I stood at the head of my profession and in applying to me He had acted conscientiously'. This confirms the opinion which one would deduce from such of his works as we know, that he remained within the following of Wilson. He was never a prolific exhibitor, for in the thirty-six years from 1778 to 1813 he sent only eighty-three pictures to the Academy, and these must include drawings as well as paintings. The influence of Wilson is naturally very strongly evident in his paintings, but he was also influenced by the Dutch. In one of his sketch-books[1] he notes that drawing after drawing is to be 'all Van Goyenish—silver warmth—simple colour', and another sketch-book[2] of 1808, contains copious notes about the work of Cuyp, Ruysdael and other Dutch artists, as well as of Gainsborough and Wilson. Claude seems to have impressed him less than might be expected, and he considered that all the grandeur in his pictures was derived entirely from their subjects.[3]

For most of us the chief interest of Farington lies in his *Diary*, but the main concern of this book is with his drawings. He was a topographical draughtsman, working chiefly in monochrome, with an eye on the engraver. Many of his drawings were engraved in the large topographical publications so popular in the late eighteenth and early nineteenth centuries. *Views of the Lakes, etc. in Cumberland and Westmoreland* appeared in 1789, and was sufficiently successful to warrant a new edition in 1816. *Views of Cities and Towns in England and Wales* was published in 1790, and the *Britannia Depicta* of Lysons, 1806, contains some of his drawings. His best work of this description was the *History of the River Thames*, which

[1] V.A.M. P.84–1921.
[2] V.A.M. P.92–1921.
[3] *Diary*, March 20, 1797.

186

appeared in two volumes in 1794, with seventy-six hand-coloured plates aquatinted by J. C. Stadler. The text was written by William Combe, the author of *The Three Tours of Dr. Syntax*. The plates vary a good deal in merit, but at their best, as in *Windsor Bridge*, show a fine sense of composition combined with very delicate draughtsmanship.

Until the sale of 1921 any estimate of Farington as a draughtsman had to be based upon these illustrations and upon the few drawings contained in public collections, for the Victoria and Albert Museum had only ten, and the British Museum two. The sale, however, brought to light hundreds of drawings and sketch-books, and for the first time there was ample material for a judgment of his work. The Victoria and Albert Museum acquired twenty-five sketch-books, ranging in date from 1763 to 1812. Many of them were filled on his various expeditions to Hertfordshire, Lincolnshire, Derbyshire, Hastings, Dover, Scotland and Paris. Of particular interest are the two earliest, dated 1763 and 1764 and inscribed 'at Mr. Wilson's, Great Piazza, Covent Garden'. In these we see the student's first tentative drawings, rather tight and worried; and frequently Wilson has with a few sure strokes pulled together a tottering composition, or demonstrated the fundamental structure of a tree. The later sketch-books show an increasing power, though the breadth and certainty of his master's handling was always beyond his reach. Edward Dayes' contemporary criticism[1] was too harsh, but there is in it a certain amount of truth:

> To remark that this artist is among the best of Wilson's pupils, is but a negative compliment; nor do I mean to include among the number, Sir George Beaumont, who is the only one that may be said to do great credit to his instructor. The artist who is the subject of the present sketch shows but a callow capacity, when he draws upon the stock of his own ideas . . . Farington made a long stay at the Lakes of Cumberland; but the grandeur of those scenes does not appear to have infused any of their dignity into his imagination; and the representations he has given of those spots are by no means great; nor has he caught any of their fine massy light and shade. Though his composition is poor, his colouring is often clear, brilliant and transparent, and sometimes accompanied with a breadth of *chiaro-oscuro*: his penciling is free and firm, but at times carried to excess; so much so, as to produce a hardness that effectually destroys repose. If these are the reflections of a nice critic, they are not those of an ill-natured one; and it is but justice to remark, that I have seen some firm, spirited, and well-colored pictures by this artist.

Though Farington, as Dayes implies, was not an artist of much imagination, his work in a narrow field was attractive and accomplished as may be seen in the best of the drawings in the Victoria and Albert Museum. *Near Hastings*,[2] dated 1785, which was probably one of the two pictures exhibited under this title at the Royal Academy in 1787; *Lancaster*,[3] *Landscape with Peasants*[4] and *Carnarvon*[5] reveal his characteristic method at its best. He seems to have worked with a reed pen and usually a diluted ink, sometimes black and sometimes brown. Over his drawings he puts washes of grey, of the type of 'Payne's Gray',

[1] *The Works of the late Edward Dayes*, 1805, pp. 325–326.
[2] V.A.M. P.37–1922.   [3] V.A.M. 152–1890.
[4] V.A.M. 42–1895.   [5] V.A.M. P.36–1922.

to indicate the masses and to convey effects of light and shade. His first washes of colour are thin and slight, and his underwork with the pen extraordinarily free and summary. Trees are often indicated with a mere shorthand of scribbled loops and segments of circles, but none the less have vitality and are well composed. One cannot help thinking that Constable, who was in touch with Farington even before he entered the Royal Academy Schools, was influenced not merely (as has been stated) by the Girtin drawings belonging to Sir George Beaumont, but also by Farington's sketches, which he no doubt saw when he visited his studio.[1] Farington himself was very clearly influenced by Gainsborough in his monochrome studies of rural scenery and particularly of trees. His line is accurate and expressive but never intricate. In his sketches Farington was indifferent, as was Gainsborough, to the ordinary niceties of style; he sees the shape of things but is careless of their structure; he is swift and impulsive. But when he sits down coolly to a study of some architectural subject, such as *Carnarvon*[2] or of trees, as *The Lady Oak, near Cressage, Shropshire*,[3] he can be both free and searching at once, with a line at the same time firm and picturesque. Several large drawings of Valenciennes in ruins after the siege of 1793, and dating from that year, show wide prospects in the Girtin manner such as the *Convent of Clarisses*[4] (Pl. 199), though done some years before Girtin had arrived at his full powers, and several of the aquatints, notably those in the Thames series, show the same grasp of the possibilities of panoramic width and recession.

Though Farington cannot be regarded as a great water-colour painter, he nevertheless holds a significant place among the early masters of the British school. The limitations of his drawings are those of the man himself; his work like his character is sincere, capable, and polished, but uninspired and a little shallow.

When the editor of the *Monthly Mirror* wanted to publish a portrait of Farington and some account of his life and work, Farington records that he refused his consent, but added 'that there was no doubt but at a future time I should be noticed in the proportion as I ought to be'. Little did he think, when he made that prophetic utterance, that full fame and grateful remembrance would come as a result of the *Diary*, and this would bring his drawings into new and favourable notice after more than a hundred years of oblivion.

In their use of monochrome underpainting Dayes, Miller and their fellows were following the practice of painters in oil. It remained for Turner and Girtin, Cox and Constable, to depart from the use of dead colouring.

Before the close of the eighteenth century the tinted method was being superseded. It was no longer the general custom to use a neutral tint to serve indiscriminately for the shadows on land, sea, sky, mountain, tree or building. Artists were grasping the principle that shadows vary in colour according to material and atmosphere, and were working in cold tones over warm, thus entirely reversing the earlier process. It is much easier to con-

---

[1] Certain drawings by Constable up to 1801 in the V.A.M. show a similarity to Farington. See illustrations in Graham Reynolds' *Catalogue of the Constable Collection in the V.A.M.*, 1960. [Eds.]
[2] V.A.M. P.36–1922.   [3] V.A.M. P.44–1895.
[4] Coll. Mr. & Mrs. Paul Mellon.

172 'St Botolph's Priory'

B.M. 1930.12.13.1 $13\frac{1}{4} \times 21\frac{3}{4}$: 337 × 552   *Water-colour, signed on the back*

Theodosius FORREST (1728–1784)

173 'View of London from the Terrace of York Buildings'

V.A.M. P.11–1931 $13\frac{7}{8} \times 21\frac{5}{8}$: 352 × 550   *Water-colour*

Theodosius FORREST (1728–1784)

174 'Italian Coast Scene'
Coll. Mrs Eleanor Williams $10\frac{5}{8} \times 16\frac{1}{4}$: 270 × 413   *Grey wash*
William MARLOW (1740–1813)

175 'The Amphitheatre at Nimes'
Coll. Mr John Mitchell   17 × 21: 432 × 534   *Water-colour, signed*
William MARLOW (1740–1813)

176 'A Game of Bowls'
Coll. Mr & Mrs Paul Mellon $8\frac{3}{8} \times 10\frac{3}{4}: 213 \times 273$ *Water-colour, signed*
Michael Angelo ROOKER, A.R.A. (1743–1801)

177 'Farmyard, Thetford'
B.M. 1857.2.28.210 $6\frac{1}{2} \times 8\frac{5}{8}: 165 \times 219$ *Water-colour, signed*
Michael Angelo ROOKER, A.R.A. (1743–1801)

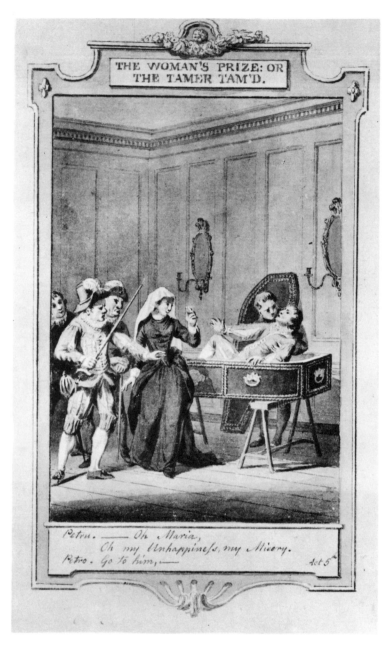

178 'The Woman's Prize', Act V. Sc. 4
B.M. 1859.7.9.87　　$6\frac{5}{8} \times 3\frac{7}{8}$: 168 × 98　　*Water-colour*
Michael Angelo ROOKER, A.R.A. (1743–1801)

179 'Bury St Edmunds'
V.A.M. 51–1881 $14\frac{1}{2} \times 18\frac{1}{4}$: 368 × 463   *Water-colour, signed*
Michael Angelo ROOKER, A.R.A. (1743–1801)

180 'Elvet Bridge, Durham'
B.M. 1859.5.28.207   8 × 10: 203 × 254   *Water-colour*
Thomas HEARNE (1744–1817)

181 'Sir George Beaumont and Joseph Farington Sketching a Waterfall'

Coll. Sir Francis Beaumont Bt. $17\frac{1}{2} \times 11\frac{1}{2}$: 445 × 292   *Pen and ink and wash*

Thomas HEARNE (1744–1817)

182 'Wooded Glen at Downton, Herefordshire'
V.A.M. 2933–1876 $12\frac{5}{8} \times 13\frac{3}{4}$: 321 × 349   *Indian ink and sepia, signed*
Thomas HEARNE (1744–1817)

183 'Scene in the West Indies'
B.M. 1872.5.11.531 $14\frac{3}{4} \times 21\frac{1}{4}$: 375 × 540
Indian ink and water-colour, signed and dated 1779
Thomas HEARNE (1744–1817)

184 'Stalls at St George's Chapel, Windsor'

Coll. Mr Roy Strong   14½ × 6 : 368 × 153   *Pen and brown wash*

John CARTER (1748–1817)

185 'Royal Crescent, Bath'
Victoria Art Gallery, Bath   14¼ × 21 : 362 × 533
Pen and water-colour, signed and dated 1777
Thomas MALTON II (1748–1804)

186 'The Strand, with Somerset House'
V.A.M. 1725–1871   13 × 19 : 330 × 483   *Water-colour*
Thomas MALTON II (1748–1804)

187 'Provost's House, Trinity College, Dublin'
B.M. 1878.7.13.1276 $10\frac{1}{8} \times 14\frac{5}{8}$: 258 × 372   *Pen and water-colour*
James MALTON (?1766–1803)

188 'Design for a Hunting Lodge'
Royal Institute of British Architects (G6/30) $8 \times 12\frac{1}{2}$: 203 × 317   *Water-colour*
James MALTON (?1766–1803)

189 'On the Coast at Broadstairs'
V.A.M. 108–1879   9½ × 13¼: 242 × 337   *Water-colour, signed*
Benjamin Thomas POUNCY (d. 1799)

190 'St George's or Newin Gate, Canterbury'
V.A.M. 75–1920   9 × 13⅛: 229 × 333   *Water-colour, signed and dated 1795*
Benjamin Thomas POUNCY (d. 1799)

191 'Lympne Castle'
Laing Art Gallery, Newcastle upon Tyne $17\frac{1}{4} \times 21\frac{1}{2}$: 438×546 *Water-colour*
Edward DAYES (1763–1804)

192 'Greenwich Hospital'
V.A.M. 1769–1900 $16\frac{1}{4} \times 22\frac{3}{8}$: 412×568 *Water-colour, signed and dated 1788*
Edward DAYES (1763–1804)

193 'Terrace at Windsor Castle'

Coll. Mrs Cecil Keith $12\frac{1}{2} \times 15\frac{1}{2}$: 318×394 *Water-colour, signed and dated 1783*

Edward DAYES (1763–1804)

194 'Buckingham House, St James's Park'

V.A.M. 1756–1871 $15\frac{1}{2} \times 25\frac{1}{2}$: 318×648 *Water-colour, signed and dated 1790*

Edward DAYES (1763–1804)

195 'Queen Eleanor's Cross, Waltham Cross, Herts.'
V.A.M. 407–1885   10 × 7¾: 254 × 196
Water-colour, signed and dated 1793 (at the back)
Thomas Richard UNDERWOOD (d. 1836)

196 'Cheyne Walk, Chelsea'

V.A.M. 731–1893 $16\frac{1}{8} \times 24\frac{7}{8}$: 409 × 623   *Water-colour, signed and dated 1776*

James MILLER (Exhibited 1773–1791)

197 'A Street in a Thames-side Locality'

Coll. Mr D. F. Snelgrove $7\frac{1}{2} \times 12\frac{1}{2}$: 190 × 317   *Water-colour*

James MILLER (Exhibited 1773–1791)

198 'Town Hall at King's Lynn'
B.M. 1881.10.8.91 $11\frac{3}{4} \times 12\frac{1}{8}$: 298 × 308
Pen and Indian ink and sepia, signed and dated 1787
Joseph FARINGTON, R.A. (1747–1821)

199 'Convent of Clarisses Valenciennes after the Siege of 1793'
Coll. Mr & Mrs Paul Mellon $13\frac{3}{8} \times 20\frac{1}{8}$: 340 × 510   *Pen and grey wash, signed*
Joseph FARINGTON, R.A. (1747–1821)

vert a warm rich colour into a cool state, than to give warmth to a neutral tint by any covering wash. With new methods came a new outlook and enlarged possibilities. The topographers gave the precise physical facts of landscape and architecture. A pale uniform sunshine pervades their drawings, and atmosphere was rarely taken into account. It was for Girtin and Turner, and more particularly Turner, to renew the outlook of Gainsborough and Cozens, and with a different emphasis to show that art could go beyond the plain record of facts. The business of the new generation of artists was not to convey topographic information, but to express emotion, the individual mood, the quality of awe or wonder with which their subject inspired them.

The exposition of contemporary methods given by Dayes has much interest for the student of eighteenth-century water-colour, as may be realised from the following extracts from his *Works*:

Pages 129/130 (note):

> Should the beauty of the scenery at Fountains Abbey prompt the student to sketch, the retirement of the place will afford him an opportunity of colouring from nature. The whole effect of the light and shade may be acquired by the aid of Indian ink, indigo, (Or Prussian blue), and Indian red: after which, the tints may be obtained from burnt Terra de Sienna, or Roman ochre, (according to their brilliancy), combined with more or less of the Indigo for the vegetation. The two latter colors will give the tones of the building, provided the parts which require to be kept down, are previously lowered with Indian ink, just warmed with a small quantity of Indian red. After the above process, all that will be requisite, is, to warm and retouch the strong parts of the shadows on the foreground, with some Cologne earth, or Van-Dyke brown; playing with it, for harmony's sake, a little among the light parts. These materials are enough in the hand of a master to do anything with, from the slightest sketch to the most finished drawing.

Page 281:

> It was premised, the use of water-colors only was meant to be treated of; for which purpose the following articles will be wanted: a drawing-board, with a pannel, to strain the paper when damped; a T square, compasses, black-lead and camel-hair pencils, Indian rubber, and the following colors: *yellows*, gamboge, raw terra de Sienna; *reds*, lake or carmine, vermillion, burnt terra de Sienna, Indian red; *blue*, dark Prussian; *brown*, Van Dyck. In addition to these, a decoction of bistre, or wood-soot, will be found of excellent use to tone with.

Page 283:

> When the outline is completed, by every part being marked as correctly as possible, the first part to begin to work on with color, must be the sky, then the distance, next the middle-ground, and, lastly, the fore-ground; laying each part in with care, but not attempting to finish either, only to do what the painter calls to dead color; taking care to keep the parts more cold and tender than in the original; and always to work from a cold state to a warm one, as a grey or soft purple may be easily over-come; but a yellow, brown, or red, never: then, when gone over a second or third time, give the true tone; and lastly, put in the spirited touches, or those touches of shadow in shade, that give animation to the picture.

Page 302:

> In washing up a drawing, the hair-pencils should be used as large as the parts worked on will admit. The shadows and middle tints being worked up to a sufficient degree of power, coloring will be the next operation. This must be done by beginning in the distant parts, coming on stronger and stronger, coloring light and middle-tint to the fore-ground; and, lastly, retouch the darker part of the fore-ground with Van-Dyck brown.

Page 303:

Whether the drawing is made by dead coloring, and worked up as in oil, or the light and shadow made first, with blue and Indian ink, the method of preceeding in both will be the same; that is, by beginning with the sky, then the distance, &c. Another care will be to color colder than the drawing is intended to be when finished: the necessity of this practice arises from the warm colors easily affecting the cold ones; but when once a part is made too yellow, or too red, it never can be overcome. From this it will be easily seen, that if a drawing is brought up in grey, (that is, in blue and Indian ink,) it will be susceptible of receiving the warm tones of an evening; the grey being by red convertible into a purple, and the warmer tints of the light operating in an equal proportion. To illustrate the matter further, grey by red (as lake or carmine) will become a purple; and that by a yellow (raw terra de Sienna, or gamboge) an orange; but an orange can never be made a red, or red a grey.

Page 306:

The vegetation should not be colored too green; that is, with a raw, hungry color of blue and yellow, but by uniting a red, as burnt terra de Sienna, or lake, with it, to give it a more solemn or autumnal hue; as nothing can have a more common or vulgar air, than too much green. The student must distinguish between a glaring and a glowing color, as we admire what is fine, before we can discern what is beautiful; for color is the attire of the art, and not the patches and paint of a courtezan.

CHAPTER XI

William Blake and Henry Fuseli

Blake, the greatest imaginative artist of the British school, remains isolated and remote, so remote that C. E. Hughes dismissed him in a single paragraph on the ground that 'his paintings cannot be regarded as essentially a part of the English school of water-colour.'[1] That statement embodies a false verdict upon Blake's own work and fails to recognise the importance of his influence upon contemporaries such as Flaxman and Fuseli (who used to declare that 'Blake is damned good to steal from'), Varley, Palmer and Calvert, and subsequently upon the Pre-Raphaelites and many later painters. I can well appreciate that Hughes was daunted by the impossibility of compressing into a few pages any adequate history and criticism of this great poet, mystic philosopher, painter, engraver and book-illustrator, the many aspects of whose genius has occasioned a whole library of volumes.

William Blake (1757–1827) was born at 28 Broad Street, Golden Square, where his father had a moderately prosperous hosiery business. As a boy he was quiet and dreamy, with a strong desire to use a pencil and a keen love of solitary rambles in the country. It was during one of these excursions that, as a child of about eight, he saw his first vision, 'a tree filled with angels, bright angelic wings bespangling every bough like stars'. When he related the incident at home on his return, it was only through his mother's intercession that he escaped a thrashing from his father for telling a lie. He did not expect others to share his visions, but for himself they remained natural and normal. His friends appear to have been impressed by the truth of his visionary communion with the spiritual world. It was a solid stockbroker, John Giles, who referred to Blake as 'the divine Blake, who has seen God, sir, and talked with angels'. The man who inspired that sort of belief in John Giles, Thomas Butts, John Linnell, George Richmond and Samuel Palmer, in hard-headed business men and artists alike, was no madman.

In 1767, at the age of ten, Blake was sent to Henry Pars' drawing-school in the Strand, which subsequently became Ackermann's showroom; and his father encouraged him by buying casts of the Gladiator, the Venus de Medici, the Hercules and other examples of ancient sculpture, that the boy might continue drawing at home. At an early age he was a constant frequenter of sale-rooms and, at a time when auctioneers took threepenny bids, became a collector of prints in a limited way. It is significant that Raphael and Michel-

[1] *Early English Water-colour*, 1913, p. 157.

192

angelo were his first choice; indeed, Michelangelo—never from first-hand knowledge—was the great inspirational influence throughout Blake's art.

At the age of fourteen Blake exchanged the drawing-school of Pars for the workshop of James Basire, the engraver, in Great Queen Street, Lincoln's Inn Fields. There had been some talk of apprenticing him to William Wynne Ryland, a much better engraver than Basire, but either the premium demanded was too onerous for the paternal pocket or the boy jibbed at the proposal. When they were leaving after a visit to consult Ryland in his studio, young Blake turned to his father and said: 'I don't like the man's face; it looks as if he would live to be hanged'. Ryland was then engraver to the King, a prosperous man of fine presence and prepossessing manner, honoured by the most distinguished leaders of art, letters and society. But the boy's prophetic vision was right, and twelve years later Ryland was hanged for forgery. Both Blake and Varley possessed some uncanny power of seeing a little beyond the veil.

Under Basire—the seven years' apprenticeship began in 1771—Blake's main work was the drawing of monuments in Westminster Abbey and other London churches, to be engraved for Richard Gough's *Sepulchral Monuments of Great Britain*. This task fed his romantic imagination and kindled a love of Gothic art. It was an influence curiously alternating with that of Michelangelo in Blake's mingling of massive and muscular human figures and the ornamental tracery of his designs. Apart from the mental results of this allotted task he had little else for which to thank Basire, except a careful grounding in the mechanical side of the engraver's art, leading to his own decision that firm, determinate outline was all in all. Hubert Gravelot, the French engraver, who was in London from 1732 to 1755, once said to Basire: 'De English may be very clever in deir own opinions, but dey do not draw de draw.' That saying may be further defined by Blake's own statements: 'Painting is drawing on Canvas, & Engraving is drawing on Copper, & Nothing Else; he who pretends to be either Painter or Engraver without being a Master of drawing is an Imposter,' and, 'In a work or Art it is not Fine Tints that are required, but Fine Forms; fine Tints without, are nothing. Fine Tints without Fine Forms are always the Subterfuge of the Blockhead.'

During the evenings Blake helped Basire to engrave selections of his Abbey studies, or made drawings from his imagination and from English history. It was during his apprenticeship to Basire that Blake wrote the poems, published in 1783 with the title *Poetical Sketches*. In 1779 he studied for a time in the school of the Royal Academy, exhibited there in 1780, and earned a humble livelihood by engraver's journey-work for the booksellers. These were days of courtship also, for in 1782 he married Catherine Boucher, who was to become so loving, patient and practical a helpmeet. She was uneducated, but soon learned to help him with his work; and, along with her practicality and common sense, had an entire belief in all his ideas and in the visionary beings who were as real to Blake as actual sitters. Without her unshakable faith and constant support, Blake might have stayed in the valleys and never have climbed exultantly to mountain tops.

Their married life began in lodgings at 23 Green Street, on the east side of Leicester Square. Hogarth had lived just round the corner, and on the west side of the Square Sir Joshua Reynolds had his handsome house and noble gallery. Blake detested Reynolds' opinions and his manner of painting. He wrote of him in a copy of Reynolds' *Discourses* as a 'man hired to depress Art', and continued: 'Having spent the vigour of my youth and genius under the oppression of Sir Joshua, and his gang of cunning, hired knaves—without employment, and, as much as could possibly be, without bread—the reader must expect in all my remarks on these books, nothing but indignation and resentment. . . . Reynolds and Gainsborough blotted and blurred one against the other, and divided all the English world between them. Fuseli, indignant, almost hid himself. I AM HID.' But they met on quite affable terms. 'Well, Mr. Blake,' Reynolds said, 'I hear you despise our art of oil-painting.' 'No, Sir Joshua,' Blake answered, 'I don't despise it, but I like fresco better.'

On the death of his father in 1784, Blake returned from Green Street to Broad Street, and at No. 27 started a business as printseller and engraver next door to his birthplace, where the family business was continued by his brother Robert. He entered into partnership with James Parker, who had been a fellow-apprentice, but the union proved unsatisfactory, and when his brother died in 1787 Blake dissolved the partnership and moved to 28 Poland Street, Mrs. Blake being now his sole pupil and assistant. From Broad Street in 1785 he sent four water-colours to the Royal Academy, a scene from Gray's *Bard*, and three subjects from the story of Joseph, executed with the soft tranquil beauty of his earlier style. By 1788 he had in readiness a new volume of poems with the proposed title, *Songs of Innocence*. He had even completed the illustrative designs in colour to accompany the poems, but lacked both ways and means of publishing them. For days and nights the question of how he could become author, printer and publisher, formed the subject of anxious thoughts and dreams, until in a vision during the night his brother Robert appeared before him and revealed a means of producing with his own hands a facsimile of song and design. On rising in the morning Mrs. Blake was sent out with half a crown—the only money they possessed—to spend one shilling and tenpence on the necessary material for the fulfilment of the dream. Thus began the series of poems and writings illustrated by coloured plates, which became the most efficient means of revealing Blake's genius to the world.

The method employed for producing the *Songs of Innocence* and later books was a system of etching which left both words and designs in relief. 'Instead of etching the blacks, etch the whites,' is Blake's memorandum. The artist wrote his verses and drew his illustrations and marginal ornaments, probably using as his medium the ordinary stopping-out varnish employed by etchers. He then applied acid, which bit away the surface on all the remainder of the plate. The text and designs now stood in relief like the lines of a woodcut, and could be printed in black or any colour, while the bitten parts would not touch the paper and would leave it white. Commentators on Blake's work have not realised, or have not emphasised, that he had no need of a cumbrous copper-plate printing press. His plates could be proved by hand, like a wood-block. As a rule the written part of the plate was printed in red, and the other portions inked with whatever colour was to be dominant. The print thus produced was finished with colour applied by hand in every variety of tint. Alexander Gilchrist tells us that Blake ground and mixed his water-colours himself on a piece of statuary marble, adding diluted carpenter's glue after the manner of the early Italians, a secret revealed to him in a vision of Joseph, the sacred carpenter. Mrs. Blake was his constant helper, soon learning to take off the impressions, to tint them with great artistic feeling, and finally to bind the little books.

The *Songs of Innocence*, to which the complementary *Songs of Experience* were added in 1793, are poems which, with their melody of rhythm and their tender simplicity, bring recollections of the heaven that lay about us in our infancy. They belong to a period before Blake, visionary though he already was, had adopted a mystical clothing for his thoughts. One of the poems describes their origin:

> *I pluck'd a hollow reed*
> *And I made a rural pen*
> *And I stained the water clear,*
> *And I wrote my happy songs*
> *Every child may joy to hear.*

The drawings are straightforward illustrations of the poems, decoratively expressed, but without any allegorical or cryptic symbolism. They show simple, domestic and rural scenes, but have a grandeur of style and conception, presaging the larger and fuller development of his decorative schemes. Text and designs, as in the later books, mingle and interweave, showing a grasp of ornamental treatment as strange to the times in which the artist lived as the poems themselves. Blake used his new discovery, with greater accomplishment and elaboration, in a whole series of further volumes, *The Book of Thel* (1789), *The Marriage of Heaven and Hell* (1790) and others, ending with *Jerusalem: the Emanation of the Giant Albion* and *Milton* in 1804. Thereafter, from the plates which he always retained, he printed separate sheets for sale, or whole volumes, finishing the printed pages in water-colour like miniatures. In a book such as this, one is absolved from any attempt to wrestle with the meaning of Blake's prophetic and symbolic books, or to discuss the influence of Swedenborg and other writers on his religious and ethical thought, or to refute the foolish notion of a minority of his contemporaries that Blake was mad.

In one or two of the symbolic books, notably the *Song of Los*, *Athania* and *Urizen*, and in his so-called 'colour-printed drawings', the method of colouring becomes more complicated. Examples of the finest of the colour-printed drawings were presented in 1940 to the Tate Gallery by W. Graham Robertson: *The Good and the Evil Angels*,[1] *Elohim Creating Adam*,[2] *Hecate*,[3] *Nebuchadnezzar*,[4] *Newton*,[5] *Lamech and his two Wives*,[6] *The Lazar House*,[7] *Pity*[8] and *Elijah in the Chariot of Fire*[9] (Pl. 200). All of them were executed in or about 1795, and the group contains masterpieces, of an inherent greatness and controlled accomplish-

[1] 5057   [2] 5055   [3] 5056   [4] 5059   [5] 5058   [6] 5061   [7] 5060   [8] 5062   [9] 5063

ment, which Blake rarely surpassed in his later days. It is strange that when this method produced such brilliant and astonishing results, Blake after 1795 ceased to make colour-printed drawings. As to the method which he employed, Graham Robertson has been able to supplement information given by Gilchrist and Frederick Tatham with results of his own knowledge and experience.[1] It seems that for the printed drawings Blake took a piece of thick and absorbent millboard and made his drawing upon it in strong and firm ink outlines which formed, as it were, his key design. He then worked over these outlines with brown or reddish paint, using a medium, probably yolk of egg, which, though practically an oleate, allowing of the extraction of an essential oil, would not leave heavy stains upon the paper. (Actually, it often leaves some stain, as in the case of Jacob Le Blon's experimental work with oil colour printed from a mezzotint plate.)[2] He painted quickly, without leaving time for the colour to dry, and an impression from the painted millboard was stamped upon paper while the colour was still wet. Then, with the same medium, shadows and dark masses were filled in on the millboard and transferred to the paper. When the colour on the paper was thoroughly dry, he proceeded to work over the whole subject in water-colour, making this possible by covering his picture with a thin transparent wash of glue, as in his 'frescoes'. *The Lazar-House of Milton*[3] is an example of this method. A picture thus made has in its earlier stages a curiously mottled appearance, obviously caused by the pressure of a flat surface covered with oily paint, which has adhered slightly and then been withdrawn. The granulation was intentionally used. Hazards and accidents, the foreseen and the unexpected, were skilfully adapted to his purpose, and in Tatham's words, 'the accidental look they had was very enticing'. When Blake had completed his printing, the pigment could be wiped from the millboard, leaving the inked outline for further reprinting and colouring. The inherent flaw in the method, since Blake was looking for means of multiplying his drawings, was that the first copy printed had a clarity and quality which could not be exactly repeated. In later versions the design would remain roughly the same, but the colouring would necessarily vary and would have to be more elaborated.

It is impossible to express adequately the imagination and the compass of Blake's actual colouring in his illustrations, his water-colours and his printed drawings. There can be no terms of comparison, for his work is unique. Here is Samuel Palmer's description of *The Marriage of Heaven and Hell*:

> Blake had worked so much & illuminated so richly that even the type seemed as if done by hand. The ever fluctuating colour, the spectral pigmies, rolling, flying, leaping among the letters; the ripe bloom of quiet corners—the living light & bursts of flame, the Spires & Tongues of fire vibrating with the full prism, made the pages seem to move and quiver within its boundaries; and you lay the book down tenderly, as if you had been handling something which was alive.

[1] Note by Ruthven Todd (Everyman Library), *Life of William Blake*, p. 395.
[2] Martin Hardie, *English Coloured Books*, 1906, pp. 44–53, 75, 76.
[3] B.M. 1885. 5.9.1616.

196

They are marvels of colouring; such tender harmonies of delicate greens, and blues, and rosy pinks; such brilliancy of strong golden and silver lights; such gorgeous depths of purples and reds; such pictures of the dark chasms of the nethermost pit, lit up and made lurid by unearthly glare of flame tongues—it has been in the power of no mortal brain to fancy, and no mortal hand to depict.

One other side of Blake's technique must be mentioned, and that is his 'fresco' painting, which was to all intents and purposes tempera or water-colour. According to Linnell's explanation, Blake founded his claim to the name 'fresco' on the material he used, which was water-colour on a plaster ground made of whiting and glue. He laid this ground in much the same way as the early painters laid it upon a wall. But when Blake's ground, with glue as a component, was laid on canvas or linen, it was apt to crack and, in some cases, went to ruin from want of care and protection from damp. Some of his 'fresco' pictures painted on panels, and even a few on canvas, have been preserved in good condition. Outstanding examples are the *Canterbury Pilgrims*,[1] *Adam naming the Beasts*,[1] and *Satan Smiting Job*.[2]

What Palmer said about Blake's book illustrations applies to his 'printed drawings' and 'frescoes', and to his work in direct water-colour as well. Fire seems to be the underlying motif in many of them. Drawing after drawing is a furnace glowing with bursts of flame that leap and quiver in prismatic iridescence. All through the long dark evenings of winter, when candles were scarce and dear, and a handful of coals all that he could afford, Blake must have sat and gazed into the glowing caverns among the embers on his hearth. 'All beautiful things,' he said 'have lain burningly on the Divine hand.' Flames, heating, cleansing, invigorating, leaping and dying, now molten red, now incandescent yellow, with their heat, their flickering tongues, their spiral curves, became part of his burning soul, part of heaven as well as hell, the essence and symbol which were to inform his work. With his richness of imagery, his intensity of mystic feeling, running at times near violence, he uses line and colour with an ecstasy which makes them like the flames, supple and quivering, creative and evocative. In no other water-colours of the British school is there the same spiritual uplift and imagination. But though he loved a riot of burning and flaming colour for giving form and substance to his vision of the intangible world, some of his finest drawings are radiant with quietened colours of the rainbow juxtaposed. Those rainbow tints are subtly used in *The River of Life*,[3] in *Beatrice in the Car*,[4] one of the Dante drawings, or in the colour print *Glad Day*.[5] Other drawings are light and silvery, such as *The Angel rolling away the Stone from the Sepulchre*,[6] and *The Infant Jesus Praying*.[7] We see here, as in J. R. Cozens, the value of subdued tones, where 'the impress of a single emotional mood is undistracted and undisturbed by colour'. And it should be noted that all through

[1] Coll. Sir John Stirling Maxwell.
[3] Tate Gallery (5887).
[5] B.M. 1856. 2.9.417.
[7] Coll. Mrs. Sydney Morse.

[2] Tate Gallery (3340).
[4] B.M. 1918. 4.13.5.
[6] Coll. Mrs. Sydney Morse.

his life, whatever experiments he made with powerful colour upon a printed basis, Blake clung to the traditional use of Indian ink and wash as a monochrome ground, with slight tints laid over the grey foundation. To take one of Blake's most superb drawings, *The Wise and Foolish Virgins*,[1] the method, so far as mere method goes, is that of Rowlandson or Dayes.

In 1793 Blake quitted Poland Street and moved across Westminster Bridge to Lambeth, where he occupied a humble but pleasant house at 13 Hercules Buildings. It was, says Tatham, 'a pretty, clean house of eight or ten rooms', and it gave Blake the space needful for the printing and drying-out of his colour prints. From his workroom he looked over gardens towards Lambeth Palace and the Thames. It was here that he produced most of his colour-printed work. Much later, in a letter to George Cumberland written four months before his death, he gave his reasons for having produced no more books or colour-printed drawings except in response to a definite commission. 'I cannot Print more except at a great loss,' he wrote, 'for at the time I printed these things I had a whole house to range in.'

At Lambeth, in 1796, he was detached from his colour-printing by an engagement to illustrate an expensive edition of Young's *Night Thoughts*, and for this he made 537 drawings[2] in transparent water-colours, forty-three of which were engraved by himself for the volume published in 1797. During his seven years at Lambeth, Blake worked incessantly on his frescoes and drawings, on his books, and on engravings commissioned by booksellers. Relief came to the appalling strain, mental and physical, under which he suffered, when Flaxman introduced him to William Hayley, poetaster, and biographer of Cowper: Byron describes him, 'For ever feeble and for ever tame'. Hayley invited Blake to come and live near him at Felpham in Sussex, offering employment in the making of engravings for his *Life of Cowper*. In September 1800, Blake with Mrs. Blake and his sister set out from Lambeth between six and seven a.m. The journey lasted till 11.30 p.m., involving six changes of chaise and driver for themselves and their sixteen heavy boxes and portfolios, yet 'All was Chearfulness & Good Humour on the Road'. In his cottage at Felpham Blake found a haven of peace and inspiration. 'Felpham,' he wrote, 'is a sweet place for Study, because it is more Spiritual than London. Heaven opens here on all sides her golden Gates; her windows are not obstructed by vapours; voices of Celestial inhabitants are more distinctly heard, & their forms more distinctly seen.' It was here that he wrote and illustrated his *Jerusalem: the Emanation of the Giant Albion*, a poem descriptive of the 'spiritual acts of his three years' slumber on the banks of Ocean'. It was here that for the first time he saw the open sea, and made his small but superb drawing, *The Spirit of God moves upon the Face of the Waters*.[3]

In the autumn of 1803 Blake returned from Felpham to London, taking lodgings at

[1] Tate Gallery 5196; five other versions are recorded.
[2] B.M. 1929. 7.13.1–270.
[3] Coll. Esmond Morse.

198

17 South Molton Street, where he remained for nearly seventeen years. A tablet on the house records his residence there. Much hard toil in the making of engravings for Hayley and for booksellers continued. 'I curse & bless Engraving alternately,' he wrote, 'because it takes so much time and is so untractable, tho' capable of such beauty and perfection.' He was fortunate, however, in having a consistent patron for his frescoes, water-colours and colour-printed drawings in the person of Thomas Butts, the only large buyer he ever knew until he met John Linnell. 'For years,' said Samuel Palmer, 'Butts stood between the greatest designer in England and the workhouse—that designer being, of all men whom I have ever known, the most practically sane, steady, frugal and industrious.' As early as 1797 Blake wrote: 'My Work pleases my employer, and I have an order for Fifty small pictures at one Guinea each, which is something better than mere copying after another artist.' Butts filled his house in Fitzroy Square with Blake's work, sometimes taking a drawing a week, and remained his firm friend and supporter until the end of his life.

In 1808 Blake, after a lapse of nine years, exhibited two works at the Royal Academy, *Christ in the Sepulchre guarded by Angels*[1] and a fresco, *Jacob's Dream*[2]. In 1809, in the hope of gaining public recognition, he determined to hold an exhibition of his own, on the first floor of James Blake's shop in Broad Street, Golden Square. It comprised sixteen 'Poetical and Historical Inventions', nine 'frescoes' and seven drawings; and the motto of the advertisement was 'Fit audience find tho' few'. The *Descriptive Catalogue*, now a very rare volume, was included in the half-crown charge for admission, and besides being a commentary on the exhibits is a manifesto eulogising Raphael and Michelangelo at the expense of Titian and Correggio, Rubens and Rembrandt. Charles Lamb was among the appreciative visitors, and long afterwards, recalled the exhibition, describing Blake as one of the most extraordinary persons of the age. Southey retained his catalogue, quoting from it in 1830, and saying: 'The colouring of all was as if it had consisted merely of black and red ink in all intermixture. Some of the designs were hideous, especially those which he considered as most supernatural in their conception and likenesses. In others you perceived that nothing but madness had prevented him from being the sublimest painter of this or of any other country.' The exhibition brought neither pecuniary profit nor access of fame, and again for long years Blake was dependent mainly upon his work as illustrator and engraver, was exploited by Cromek, and quarrelled with Thomas Stothard over their rival paintings and engravings of *The Canterbury Pilgrims*[3] and his pictures of the *Spiritual Forms of Pitt and Nelson*, guiding Behemoth and Leviathan respectively.[4] Here again his genius was overlooked, but in 1818 new light came into his life, for he won the friendship of John Linnell and, through him, gathered a group of young and devoted disciples who

[1] Coll. Sydney Morse.
[2] B.M. 1949. 11.12.2.
[3] Blake's Version, tempera on canvas, Coll. Sir John Stirling Maxwell.
[4] Tate Gallery 1110 and 3006.

cheered the last years of his life and encouraged him to fresh productiveness. More will be said in later chapters about Blake's relationship with John Varley, Samuel Palmer and Edward Calvert. Linnell, who was only twenty-six, and already on the way to becoming a prosperous painter, not only admired Blake's work but backed his admiration by commissions. Darrell Figgis[1] well stresses the fact that owing to Linnell's sympathy and support Blake entered upon a new space of creative power after his years of darkness and obscurity. He even turned to what was for him an entirely new technique, and produced the superb wood-cuts for Dr. Thornton's *Pastorals of Virgil*, which were to exercise a profound and stimulating influence upon Palmer and Calvert. The commission for the Virgil wood-cuts was probably due to Linnell, for Thornton was his family doctor.

In 1823 Linnell induced Blake to prepare a duplicate set of his drawings for the *Book of Job* at a price of £150, the largest sum which the artist ever received in any one payment. The original set had been bought some three years earlier by Blake's old patron, Thomas Butts. (They passed later into the possession of Lord Houghton.) Linnell was willing to finance the publication of an engraved *Book of Job*, which appeared, though with no resulting profits, in 1827. The illustrations to the *Book of Job* (four sets in all are known, three of them in colour, besides the engraved series) were edited in 1935 by Laurence Binyon and Sir Geoffrey Keynes for the Pierpont Morgan Library, New York. More than one hundred and thirty drawings are reproduced, seventy of them in colour.[2] From his earliest days Blake was haunted by the story of Job's prosperity and disaster, his humiliation by Satan, and his redemptive humiliation by God. Blake never made a nobler drawing than that which illustrates: 'Where wast thou when I laid the foundations of the earth . . . when the morning stars sang together, and all the Sons of God shouted for joy?' The glory and radiance of that drawing illustrate Blake's own saying, that 'painting, as well as poetry and music, exists and exults in immortal thoughts'. It helps, in the understanding of Blake's anthropomorphic conception of God and all his ecstatic visions in this and other drawings, to consider how much he shared the belief and religious attitude of his day. It was during Blake's life-time that Sir Robert Grant wrote:

> *The Ancient of Days*
> *Pavilioned in splendour,*
> *And Girded with praise.*

And Bishop Heber, his contemporary, pictured cherubim and seraphim, and all the saints:

> *Casting down their golden crowns*
> *Around the glassy sea.*

What to us is symbolic pageantry, was profound reality to Blake and to the writers of those hymns.

---

[1] *The Paintings of William Blake*, 1925.
[2] Since 1955 the William Blake Trust has been publishing Blake books in facsimile through the Trianon Press in Paris. These include *Songs of Innocence and Experience, Jerusalem, Milton, The Marriage of Heaven and Hell, Europe* and *America*.

200

In 1821 the Blakes removed to 3 Fountain Court, Strand, renting the first floor of a house occupied by Mrs. Blake's brother-in-law. Blake was worried by financial difficulties, sold his collection of prints, and received a grant of £25 from the Royal Academy. The entry in the minutes states: 'Read a letter from Mr. Collins, R.A., signed also by Mr. Abraham Cooper, R.A., recommending to the charitable consideration of the Council Mr. William Blake, an able designer and engraver, labouring under great distress.' But in spite of financial stress during these last years of his life, he was happy among the eager band of young disciples, Varley, Palmer, George Richmond, Calvert, Finch and others, to whom Linnell had introduced him. They called themselves 'The Ancients', and forestalled the Pre-Raphaelites in their approval of nothing but primitive art. They found their modern ideal in Blake, whom Palmer described as 'a fit companion for Dante . . . his ideal home was with Fra Angelico'. For the youthful enthusiasts Fountain Court was the 'House of the Interpreter'.

In 1825 Linnell again came forward with a commission, this time the mighty task of illustrating Dante's *Divine Comedy*, and Blake was still occupied with it when he died in 1827. In this series he made sixty-eight drawings for the *Hell*, twenty for the *Purgatory*, and ten for the *Paradise*. Only a few were fully coloured, but among them are two of striking beauty, the *Whirlwind of Lovers*[1] and the *Pageant of the Church*.[2] In the water-colours he is escaping from the repressive effect of rigid outline; his colour is free and fertile.

Blake's favourite tenet was that 'all things exist in the human imagination alone'. Again and again he insists upon this as the fundamental basis of his art:

> Shall painting be confined to the sordid drudgery of facsimile representation of merely mortal and perishing substances, and not be, as poetry and music are, elevated to its own proper sphere of invention and visionary conception?
> 'What' it will be questioned, 'When the Sun rises, do you not see a round disk of fire somewhat like a Guinea?' 'O no, no, I see an Innumerable company of the Heavenly host crying "Holy, Holy, Holy is the Lord God Almighty"' I question not my Corporeal or Vegetative Eye any more than I would Question a Window concerning a Sight. I look thro' it & not with it.'

More than any other British painter he had the power of interpreting inner vision and of communicating through line and colour and richness of imagery his intensity of subjective thought. Blake, with the prophets of old and Milton, was 'skilled to sing of time and eternity'. In the words of Hosea he might say, 'I have used similitudes'.[3] And in those similitudes nothing is more striking than his largeness of design. Expand in our minds such subjects as *The Ancient of Days* or *Elijah in the Chariot of Fire* (Pl. 200) to the scale of a big fresco, and they will fill the space with their inherent bigness and force. As Sir Herbert Read has said[4]: 'Nowhere else in the whole range of plastic art, unless in Giotto, is the

---

[1] Birmingham City Art Gallery.
[2] Whereabouts untraced.
[3] *Hosea*, XII, 10.
[4] 'English Art', *Burlington Magazine*, 1933, LXIII, pp. 243–269.

capacity of the line for rendering three-dimensional form so aptly demonstrated, and nowhere is solidity so compatible with movement and ethereal light.'

Samuel Palmer, chief among Blake's disciples, was impressed by a saying of Bacon, that 'In every great art is some element of strangeness'. 'Art,' said Thomas Hardy much later, 'is a disproportioning of realities.' Those elements of strangeness and disproportion were present in Palmer's best work of his Shoreham period, done under Blake's influence and sometimes under Blake's eye. In Blake's own case they took the form of distortion, false perspective, exaggeration, over-emphasis, elongated limbs, strained pose, stressed muscle. 'Natural objects always did and do weaken, deaden and obliterate imagination in me,' he wrote towards the end of his life. And on this account his drawings, like his poems, are marked at times by awkwardness of construction and by technical imperfection. In the poetry of Donne, another mystic, there is something tortured and difficult, as though mind and heart, reason and imagination, were at war. But in poems and pictures alike irregularities and licenses—used with a child's innocent blindness to the incongruous and absurd—overcome our more realistic outlook and inherited canons by their melody and sweetness of rhythm or the hammer-stroke of their crushing power. In Blake we always find, as Hazlitt found in some musty folio, 'cool springs, and green sunny spots, and the whirlwind and the lion's roar, and the shadow of angelic wings'. And as a fitting *finis* to anything written about Blake his own words may be quoted: 'I should be sorry if I had any earthly fame, for whatever natural glory a man has is so much detracted from his spiritual glory. I wish to do nothing for profit; I want nothing; I am quite happy.' He died singing hymns of joy.

To Samuel Palmer, at Shoreham, George Richmond wrote on August 15, 1827:

My Dr Friend
　　Lest you should not have heard of the Death of Mr. Blake I have written this to inform you. He died on Sunday Night at 6 Oclock in a most glorious manner. He said He was going to that Country he had all His life wished to see & expressed Himself Happy hoping for Salvation through Jesus Christ. Just before he died His Countenance became fair. His eyes Brighten'd and He burst out into singing of the things he saw in Heaven. In truth He died like a Saint as a person who was standing by Him observed. He is to be Buryed on Fridayay (*sic*) at 12 in Morng.

Fuseli may have found Blake 'damned good to steal from', but the older man was always a friend to Blake personally and championed his cause. Blake too had a firm belief in Fuseli and owed much to his influence and encouragement. He felt that Fuseli was a hundred years in advance of his own generation, as indeed he was himself; and modern appreciation of Blake has connoted a better understanding of Fuseli's imaginative power. Henry Fuseli (1741–1825), son of J. C. Füssli, a portrait and landscape painter, was born at Zurich. He came to England about 1763 and supported himself by literary work till in 1767 he met Reynolds, who gave him enthusiastic encouragement to devote himself to painting. For eight years he studied in Rome and became, like Blake, a worshipper of

Michelangelo. He exhibited at the Royal Academy from 1774, and after his return to England was elected A.R.A. in 1788, R.A. in 1790, and from 1799 held office as Professor of Painting and Keeper of the Academy Schools. His drawings, original, violent and fantastic at times, dealing with mythology, Gothic superstition and the invisible world, are theatrical, and lack Blake's feeling of profound experience. Peter Pindar said that he was the fittest artist on earth to be appointed hobgoblin painter to the devil. Like Blake, some of his delightful figure studies of ladies in flowing drapery (there is one at the V.A.M.) show him as belonging to the period of Flaxman, Barry, Mortimer and Romney, and made a more immediate appeal than his extravagant apparitions. Most of his work is in monochrome, but occasionally it is coloured, as in his powerful *Night Hag*,[1] a flying figure against a livid sky, his *Oedipus cursing his son Polynices*[2] and *Spirit in the form of a Beautiful Maiden rising before an Aged Pair*.[3] Walpole wrote of his picture *The Mandrake* that it was 'shockingly made, madder than ever, quite mad'; and a good idea of Fuseli and his work can be gathered from Haydon's description of a visit to his studio:

> I followed the maid into a gallery or showroom, enough to frighten anybody at twilight. Galvanized devils—malicious witches brewing their incantations—Satan bridging Chaos, and springing upwards like a pyramid of fire—Lady Macbeth—Paolo and Francesca—Falstaff and Mrs. Quickly—humour, pathos, terror, blood and murder, met me at every look! I expected the floor to give way—I fancied Fuseli himself to be a giant. I heard his footsteps and saw a little bony hand slide round the edge of the door, followed by a little white-headed, lion-faced man in an old flannel dressing-gown tied at the waist with a piece of rope and upon his head the bottom of Mrs. Fuseli's work-basket. . . . Weak minds he destroyed. They mistook his wit for reason, his indelicacy for breeding, his swearing for manliness, and his infidelity for strength of mind.

Dayes, as perverse about Fuseli as about Girtin, says that 'one of the most severe reflections on the understanding of would-be connoisseurs is the taking this man's *chimeras dire* for efforts of the sublime; they have always appeared to me more like the dreams of a lunatic than the productions of a sound mind'. He ends with an amusing tale about Fuseli: 'General Vernon said that when he was some years ago returning from Italy through Switzerland, he was struck with certain odd scramblings of figures on the walls of the inns, and traced them all the way to England; and that when he some time afterwards arrived in London, he knew the man by the same extravagancies in his pictures.' Fuseli, with his foreign manner and accent, was apt to be a butt for his English fellows. Genial and eccentric, he posed as being touchy and full of rages, of which he was the first to see the comic side. 'Sophia, my love,' he once said to his over-jealous wife, 'Why don't you swear? You don't know how much it would ease your mind.'[4]

Fuseli was buried in St. Paul's Cathedral, and the esteem in which he was held by his brother artists and the public at large was evidenced by the crowds at his imposing

[1] B.M. 1885. 3.14.200.
[2] V.A.M. 698.
[3] V.A.M. Dyce 782.
[4] For this, and much about Fuseli, see Alan Cunningham, *Lives of the Painters*, 1879/80.

funeral. Four days after his death Sir Thomas Lawrence, one of his most sincere admirers, wrote to Uwins in Rome, after some remarks on Michelangelo:

> We have just sustained the loss of kindred genius, if not of greater, in the original and lofty conceptions of Mr. Fuseli. In poetic invention it is not too much to say he has had no equal since the fifteenth and sixteenth centuries, and if his drawings and proportions were mannered and sometimes carried to excess, still it was exaggeration of the grandeur of antique form, and not—as in many, enlargement of the mean and ordinary in nature.

200 'Elijah in the Chariot of Fire'
Tate Gallery, London (5063)   17 × 21 : 431 × 532
Colour print and water-colour, signed with initials and dated 1795
William BLAKE (1757–1827)

201 'The Inscription over the Gate'
Tate Gallery, London (3352)   20⅝ × 14½: 525 × 370
Pen and water-colour, signed with initials
William BLAKE (1757–1827)

202 'Beatrice addressing Dante from the Car'

Tate Gallery, London (3369) $14\frac{5}{8} \times 20\frac{5}{8}$: 370 × 525   *Pen and water-colour*

William BLAKE (1757–1827)

203 'The Wise and Foolish Virgins'
Fitzwilliam Museum, Cambridge (P.D. 50–1950)   14¼ × 13¾: 363 × 337
Water-colour, signed
William BLAKE (1757–1827)

204 'Œdipus cursing his son Polynices'
V.A.M. 698   20¼ × 18¼: 514 × 464   *Water-colour*
Henry Fuseli, R.A. (1741–1825)

205 'Odin on Horseback'

The Art Institute of Chicago; The Leonora Hall, Gurley Coll. $22\frac{7}{8} \times 17\frac{1}{2}$: 581×445

Pen and wash

Henry Fuseli, R.A. (1741–1825)

206 'The Toilet'

Coll. Mr Brinsley Ford   17½ × 11½: 450 × 295   *Pencil and water-colour*

Henry FUSELI, R.A. (1741–1825)

207 'Ariadne Watching the Struggle of Theseus with the Minotaur'

Coll. Mr & Mrs Paul Mellon $23\frac{1}{4} \times 18\frac{1}{2}$: 591 × 470   *Oil and body-colour*

Henry FUSELI, R.A. (1741–1825)

CHAPTER XII

Thomas Rowlandson and other figure and animal painters

*Thomas Rowlandson   Henry W. Bunbury   James Gillray
Robert Dighton   George M. Woodward   John Nixon
Isaac, Robert and George Cruikshank   Henry Alken   Samuel Howitt*

In many books dealing with our water-colour school Thomas Rowlandson (1756–1827)
wins only scant and almost apologetic reference, or is passed over entirely as a mere caricaturist. C. E. Hughes[1] and Alfred Rich[2] omit him altogether; Cosmo Monkhouse[3] says
merely that he 'used the brush with much skill'. Joseph Grego gave rise to a widespread
misconception when in 1880 he entitled the two volumes, which were the first serious study
of the artist and his career, *Rowlandson the Caricaturist*. Rowlandson was more fairly, though
not quite satisfactorily, described in an obituary notice of 1827 as a 'graphic humourist'.
He deserves much more. One of the great masters of line, he made caricatures which were
boisterous, extravagant, sometimes vulgar, but always brilliant. He did not, however, deal
merely with 'pert low comedy'. In his portraits, such as his charming study of *George
Morland*[4] (Pl. 214), his more serious figure subjects where there are only hints of caricature in subsidiary groups, and in his rustic subjects of landscapes he revealed the hand
and mind of a superb draughtsman, an interpretative and creative artist, picturing the
whole life of his time. To think of Regency England is to think in terms of Rowlandson.

His style remained consistent, without any particular growth or development, throughout his life of seventy-one years, and except for clues given by costume it is often difficult
to assign a date to specific drawings. When dates exist upon the drawings they are un-
reliable, because in the carefree dishonesty of his later days he produced drawings and
countless repetitions of them, affixing dates quite casually, and often assigning them to an
earlier year for purposes of sale. A case in point is the *Portsmouth Harbour* showing French
prizes being brought in after Lord Howe's victory in 1794, of which there are two versions
in the Dyce Collection.[5] The earlier one is the better; the second, not improved by the

---

[1] C. E. Hughes, *Early English Water-colour*, 1913.
[2] A. W. Rich, *Watercolour Painting*, 1918.
[3] Cosmo Monkhouse, *The Earlier English Watercolour Painters*, 1890.
[4] B.M. 1868. 3.28.335.
[5] V.A.M. D. 790, 791.

introduction of more figures, bears after the signature the impossible date of 1780. In other drawings A. P. Oppé[1] has noted autographic dates which are obviously ten years earlier than the watermark on the paper. In his words, 'drawings are traced, copied, placed in new contexts, reduced, diversified, adapted'. At least this shows that Rowlandson's industry was enormous, and his serious belief in himself and his art can have been no less. All the same, he was not above copying and plagiarising. Randall Davies owned a drawing by him obviously copied in reverse from Dürer's *Venus and Cupid*; and Rowlandson was probably unaware that Dürer had derived his subject from an engraving by Marc Antonio, based on a design by Raphael.

He was not content with tracing and copying. Just as Francis Nicholson found a method of duplicating his drawings by rubbing black-lead into the lines of a soft-ground etching and taking repeated impressions which he could clothe with colour, so Rowlandson sought a labour-saving device.[2] He drew with printer's ink, which is made with any powdered colour and burnt oil (as an etcher, he was used to handling the muller and could mix his inks to a fluid state in varying shades of brown and red). Running his drawing through a printing-press with a piece of damp paper over it, he obtained an offset which he could colour up as an original, often retouching it and strengthening any weak portions with pencil or ink. *House and figures*, formerly called *The Richmond Green*,[3] is an example. The offsets often have loose pencil or chalk work added to suggest that they began as direct and spontaneous sketches with rough outlines. Three or four versions, getting lighter each time, could be produced from the same outline drawing without renewing the ink. The original drawing can frequently be recognised by a sort of double outline, the ink having been sucked from the centre of the drawn line in its passage through the press, leaving the edges dark. Often it is left weak and exhausted after the taking of several impressions. If the offsets were to be strictly topographical, the original drawing (as in Nicholson's case, the etching) must be made in reverse, an everyday task for Rowlandson the etcher. Originals and offsets of the same subjects are constantly to be found, and it may be difficult to decide what is their order and which the first version. A. P. Oppé considered that Rowlandson used the process 'for a variety of different purposes, but chiefly for the repetition of the topographical subjects with many figures dating from after 1800 which then, as now, were the most likely to attract more than one purchaser'. The Victoria and Albert Museum possesses two versions of *Scene on a Towing Path*,[4] the only actual *pair*, original and reverse, which Oppé had ever seen in conjunction. Besides the original penwork, they both show much working up, and in places almost a complete re-working of the detail.

To assign dates for reasons of style is accordingly hazardous, the more so because Row-

---

[1] *Thomas Rowlandson, his drawing and water-colours*, 1923.
[2] *Notes and Queries*, 1869, IV, p. 89; Grego, *op. cit* I, p. 30; and Oppé, *op. cit.*, p. 28.
[3] V.A.M. 1817–1900.
[4] V.A.M. E.4162, 3–1923.

landson was strangely uninfluenced by new movements in water-colour art. Twenty-five years after Girtin's death and Turner's election as a member of the Royal Academy, Rowlandson was still working in the manner which he had formed before either of them was born. Constantly meeting with his work of 1800 and later, we are apt to forget that he was born as far back as 1756, and in view of that fact it is difficult to understand why, like Blake, he should ever have been thought to stand apart from the true water-colour tradition. He was at the very centre of it; he helped to establish the method, inherited from Sandby, of using tint over a pen drawing and monochrome wash, which was the general practice among the topographers and others in the last quarter of the eighteenth century. It is significant that he was born seven years before Dayes, the teacher of Girtin.

In his own time he had immense popularity. The shops were full of the drawings and caricatures which he produced with unceasing vigour and prolific ease. Only a few wise collectors realised his greatness. Even for Grego he was mainly a producer of prints. But in later years came a better understanding of the finer aspects of his work, thanks to a number of discriminating collectors such as Captain Desmond Coke, Henry Harris, Dyson Perrins and Sidney L. Phipson. Rowlandson's place as an artist is established, his themes and his treatment are fully explained by A. P. Oppé's introduction. For an attempt to study his work one goes to Joseph Grego, and then to Oppé's comprehensive and more scholarly review, which is supported by a valuable series of reproductions.

Like Oppé, we are concerned here with Rowlandson as draughtsman and water-colour painter, not as the maker of hundreds of caricature sheets which for the most part were hasty cartoons dealing with the questions of the hour. The caricatures, issued by Tegg in Cheapside, and crudely coloured, are too often marred by an offensive taste going far beyond the broad humour which is acceptable and enjoyable in Smollett and Fielding and Sterne. In many of his drawings, which were never intended for use as prints, the same coarseness will be found, but it is not proper to confound art with morality. Rowlandson belonged to an age which was brutal and coarse beneath the veneer of Society, an age when miscreants were hanged as a public spectacle, when the press-gang used the methods of the *Gestapo* in kidnapping its victims, when cock-fights and the goring of dogs in the bull-ring and the battering of ungloved boxers were popular amusements. He did not live in the same circle as Reynolds and Farington, and did not frequent exalted company like his friend Henry Angelo; he was of the people and portrayed their faults and follies, rollicking humour and grossness. But in all the squalor he saw lightning-like flashes of beauty and could be intensely serious, more serious indeed than is often imagined. Many of his drawings may be compared with the grotesque gargoyles and miserere seats in Gothic churches. Hazlitt rightly notes that 'the Greatest grossness sometimes accompanies the greatest refinement, as a natural relief, one to the other'.

In Rowlandson's case, mingled with his love for the purity of nature, co-existing with the precision and clarity of his work, was the impulse described, not very accurately, as *la nostalgie de la boue*, which many artists of every type have possessed. It led Rowlandson into taverns and gaming-houses, among bawdy crowds and sordid surroundings, just as it led Lord Byron into the depths of debauchery at Venice. Rowlandson certainly, I think, could have maintained that his appetite for the gross pleasures of living was not self-indulgent but directed and controlled. He was an objective observer far more than a participant, just as was Aldous Huxley when he wrote about a place of cure in Italy: 'Huge jellied females overflowed the chairs on which they sat. Sagging and with the gait of gorged bears, old men went slowly shambling. Rich fat burgesses strutted with dignity behind their bellies. There was a hungry prowling of gaunt emaciated men and women, yellow-skinned and with tragical, bile-injected eyes.' That is a Rowlandson drawing perfectly translated.

Rowlandson was born in the Old Jewry the same year as Isaac Cruikshank, six years after Bunbury, and a year before Gillray. Attending 'a scholastic symposium of celebrity', presided over by Dr. Barrow in Soho Square, he had as his schoolfellows Jack Bannister,[1] the celebrated actor, and Henry Angelo, son of the Angelo, fencing master to the Royal Family. Even in his schooldays Rowlandson's genius for humorous drawing began to assert itself, and the margins of his books were filled with grotesque sketches of masters and schoolfellows. In 1771 he was invited to Paris by his widowed aunt, a French lady whose maiden name was Chatelier, and who had married a Thomas Rowlandson of a generation earlier. She paid the expenses of his education at a Parisian art school. His two years of study were spent to good advantage, and he learned there the dash and brilliance which characterised French art at a time when Fragonard was still alive and painting. Returning in 1772, he entered the Royal Academy schools, where his nude studies were thought to rival even those of J. H. Mortimer, regarded by a whole generation as their model of excellence. He gained the silver medal of the Academy in 1777. In 1775, the year when Turner and Girtin were born, he exhibited his first picture at the Academy, *Delilah paying Samson a visit while in prison at Gaza*.[2] From 1777 we find him settled in a studio at 133 Wardour Street, and devoting himself to making stained drawings and small water-colour portraits, several of which appeared on the Academy walls between 1780 and 1787. It is a mistake on the part of Grego and others to imply that he was an heroic painter *manqué*, or that he lapsed from serious portraiture into easy paths of caricature. In 1778 he was travelling on the continent, filling his sketch-books with notes of travellers and coaches, ordinaries and inn-yards, foreigners and their habits. By 1780 he had discovered his true vein.

About this time Rowlandson appears to have plunged into a career of dissipation, facilitated by the receipt of a legacy of seven thousand pounds, with plate and other

[1] Bannister in his youth was a student at the Royal Academy schools, and retained his interest in art. His collection, sold by Messrs. Foster in 1849, included Turner's oil-painting *Boats in a Gale*, now in the Fogg Museum at Harvard, five paintings by Wilson, one by Constable, with two water-colours by Girtin and two by Turner.
[2] Whereabouts unknown.

valuables, left to him on the decease of this aunt in Paris. He became a familiar figure in the gaming-houses of London. Henry Angelo, his friend of forty years' standing, who wrote the obituary notice in the *Gentleman's Magazine* of 1827, says that on Rowlandson's own word he had 'frequently played through a night and the next day; and that once, such was his infatuation for the dice, he continued at the gaming-table nearly thirty-six hours, with the intervention only of the time for refreshment'. That is related here partly to account for Rowlandson's obvious insight into the seamy side of London life and his clear knowledge of material which he turned to his own purpose, and partly because it perhaps contributed to his early abandonment of the legitimate in art. But he was no wastrel; when his means were exhausted he sat down to produce a series of new designs, saying 'I have played the fool, but'—holding up his reed pen—'here is my resource.' Success came with his drawing of *Vauxhall Gardens* (see p. 212), exhibited at the Academy in 1784, and his series of caricatures published during the excitement of the celebrated Westminster Election in the same year. From then onwards he produced a huge annual output of prints and drawings. His application and inventiveness never ceased, and he always had irons in the fire. From 1812 he was working year after year on his famous *Tours of Dr. Syntax.*

Rowlandson excelled in what Blake called 'the bounding line and its infinite inflections and movements'. For many of his brilliant sketches he used a pencil, but in everything developed from them the work was done with a reed pen charged with black ink, or more often with brown or bistre, sometimes with a mixture of vermilion. He frequently used inks of different strength and colour in the same drawing. His ink, as a rule, was so watered that it flowed from his pen with extreme fluency. A. P. Oppé thought that, particularly in his early work, he used a fine pen probably a quill, and contrasts it with the thick reed pen. But a reed can be cut and sharpened to a fine point like a quill; and Rowlandson's contemporaries always referred to his 'reed' pen. His *Almsgiving*,[1] cited by Oppé as being drawn with a fine pen, seems to me to show all the characteristics of work produced by the reed.

Partly as a result of his vast amount of rapid and constant etched work on copper for caricatures and book-illustrations he developed an extreme economy of line in his drawings and the quality of an etched line in his pen-work. In Rowlandson's case the immediate influence is French; and, as Mr. Osbert Sitwell notes, he had a 'Gallic liking for curly, rococo lines and a use of them that seems yet to be peculiarly apt as a medium for rendering our landscape, trees and people'.[2] No water-colour painter was ever so calligraphic as Rowlandson, so cursive and fluent in his rendering of life and form with swift curves and arabesques. Where others supplemented outline with tentative subsidiary lines and suggestions, with hatchings and discreet touches, he secured his sense of volume

[1] Coll. Dyson Perrins.
[2] *Sing High, Sing Low*, 1944, p. 124.

with single sweeping lines. He was influenced perhaps by Gainsborough, particularly in his landscape sketches, for he drew with an essentially free-flowing line of loops and curves, not of jerks and breaks and irregularities, as is the case with Samuel Prout, to take an extreme example of another manner. It is interesting to compare Rowlandson's *Waterfall*,[1] with a *Waterfall*[2] by Farington: Rowlandson's work, like that of Gainsborough and Farington, is free and creative, not depending upon any nervous, crumbling touches to give an air of artificial picturesqueness. But though he was of their school, he invented his own style for his own subjects.

His colour was limited to thin and simple tints laid with a full brush within the confines of his pencil or pen drawing. Form was given by underlying monochrome washes. It was the method of the topographers, and like them, Rowlandson's constant work for reproduction no doubt led him to use simple washes of primary colour as far as was possible. He must have visited the offices of Ackermann or Tegg almost daily, like the leader-writer of a newspaper, making a swift drawing or etching of some topical subject, then taking up a proof and adding washes of colour for the assistants in the atelier to follow throughout a whole edition. In his drawings which were not made for reproduction he used a similar method, but his colour—only now and then are his drawings heavily coloured—is delicate, transparent, opalescent, giving by its luminosity a calm suggestion of atmosphere and space. His colour harmonies are often quite subtle, and it was a very unobservant critic who said, in a broadcast criticism of the Rowlandson in the Leslie Wright collection at the Royal Academy, that they were outlines filled in with 'heraldic' tints. The vibration and movement which others gain chiefly by colour are given by his line. He wisely never attempted an 'effect', even in his independent water-colours. His drawing in itself was so vital and expressive that the merest hint of colour was sufficient.

In Rowlandson's interiors or street scenes we have to accept an occasional recklessness, or deliberate obtuseness, with regard to perspective. With his wish to suggest animated groups and violent contrasts of features or movements, he overcame the problem by seeing his rooms, in many instances, from somewhere near the ceiling, his streets partly as from the ground and partly as from a window, and by this means he obtained a recession, allowing head to rise above head, and group above group. Again and again, the perspective of figures, or of walls, windows, buildings, trees, is quite untrue and unrelated, showing two angles of vision. In the spirited and delightful *Assembly Room, Bath*,[3] the figures are drawn and placed with an absolute disregard of the laws of perspective and proportion. The bird's eye views of Cambridge colleges show the buildings on the summit of a hill. Similarly, in some of his seashore scenes, the boats are entirely out of scale with the figures.

No drawing is more typical of Rowlandson, his distortion of an interior to his own ends,

[1] A. P. Oppé, *op. cit.*, pl. 21.
[2] *Diary*, V, p. 97.
[3] Coll. S. L. Phipson.

his motives, and his masterly skill, than the *Exhibition Stare-Case*, which belonged to Henry Tonks. Here, as in so many other of his drawings, each figure is studied and has its own character, yet each is a unit in a crowd. The drawing was made about 1800, and the staircase is that of Somerset House, where the Royal Academy exhibitions were held from 1780 to 1837. In this superb drawing the whole idea of what Binyon calls 'the absurd cascade of figures' is wildly exaggerated, but the movement and exhilaration and the lovely arabesque of the design quite overwhelm the triviality or indelicacy of its elements. Oppé puts this well when he says: 'There is such life in the drawing that it even produces an illusion of elegance.'

He is at his best again in an early drawing, *The Reception of a New Member into the Society of Antiquaries in 1782.*[1] The new member, in blue and white, with his hat in his hand and a roll under his arm, is being welcomed by the President, Dr. Jeremiah Miller, Dean of Exeter, a stout clergyman in black, while other aged antiquaries look on with genial expressions. The scene is natural and the types are observed and recorded with humorous insight but with no particular stress upon caricature. Of the same nature is the purely imaginative scene of *Bookseller and Author*,[2] with its wonderful expressiveness of contrast in face and figure between the smug, stout, prosperous bookseller and the lean scarecrow writer who tries to win his interest for the publication of his manuscript, while a short-sighted scholar in the background peers into the pages of a book with complete absorption and detachment.

From 1780 to 1790 Rowlandson was at the very height of his power. Two drawings of this period which had lain in complete obscurity in the North of England, emerged at the beginning of the War.[3] In size, in variety of grouping, in brilliant execution, they rank among the finest examples of Rowlandson's art. They represent a royal visit, apparently an imaginary one, to the docks at Deptford. One of them in the Minto Wilson Collection, shows *King George III with Queen Charlotte driving in state through Deptford Broadway*. The state carriage and the preceding cavalry are relegated to the background. The picture is entirely one of the riotous crowds in the dusty highway, their jollities and junketings, portrayed with Rowlandson's eager perception of a humorous figure or a bustling group. In the companion *Deptford Docks*[4] we pass from noise and riot to a sunlit expanse of water, with frigates on the left. There are boatloads of rollicking figures in the foreground, but the eye is carried over these into the great luminous space of air and calm water. Surely, in this pair of drawings, Rowlandson was deliberately contrasting gabled houses with the wooden walls of ships, and the drab and dusty highway with the peaceful shimmering waterway. In 1784 Rowlandson had two notable exhibits at the Royal Academy. One was the *Vauxhall Gardens*, which was brilliantly reproduced in Juke's aquatint of 1785 and

[1] Society of Antiquaries.
[2] H.M. The Queen.
[3] A. P. Oppé, 'Rowlandson the Surprising', *Studio*, November 1942. These two drawings are there fully described and included in a series of interesting reproductions of Rowlandson's work.
[4] V.A.M. P.21–1948

clearly inspired Debucourt's well-known colour-print, *Promenade de la Galerie du Palais Royal*, issued in 1787. In 1945 a version of the original drawing of *Vauxhall Gardens* appeared at Christie's and created a saleroom sensation by fetching 2600 guineas. This now belongs to Mr. Alfred E. Pearson.[1] Angelo spoke of the drawing as the *chef d'oeuvre* of Rowlandson's caricatures, but to describe it as a caricature, in our modern acceptance of the term, is to do it an injustice. It is no more a caricature than Debucourt's *Promenade*. Each of them is an historic document, portraying with realistic skill an assemblage of 'the quality' and each combines superb grouping and dramatisation with faithful study of individual characters and costumes set in surroundings familiar at the time. Only in the subordinate parts of Rowlandson's drawing is there any touch of levity. The gay façade of the boxes, where the musicians perform, and the trees, lit at their edges by gleams of artificial light and drawn with fine brushwork over summary pencil touches, show Rowlandson's growing power in dealing with subjects other than figures.

The second drawing exhibited at the Academy in 1784 was *Skating on the Serpentine*, now belonging to Mr. Brian Clutton; a replica, made two years later and slightly inferior, is in the London Museum. Here there was opportunity for an animated crowd, for swift movement, for horseplay and tumblings. One is apt to become so intrigued by the gaiety, charm, movement and variety of the figures— variety helped by the attitudes and angles of the skaters—as to overlook that this is one of the most sympathetic of Rowlandson's landscape drawings, perfect in its suggestion of winter haze and feeling of frost, and in its delicate treatment of the bare trees, outlined with free touches of the pencil in contrast with the bold ink-work of the foreground. In the distance is the Ranger's cottage, which still remains, and on the right coaches are drawn up.

With this group of fairly early drawings may be included the *Entrance to the Mall, Spring Gardens*,[2] a brilliant study of landscape and costume, the figures not being specially ridiculed, with the exception of the obese burgher and his equally corpulent overdressed wife in the centre, and the macaroni on the left in his blue coat and cocked hat. A cleverly placed dog links the groups. The pen is hardly used in the landscape, and a black-and-white reproduction reveals that the brush-work of the foliage is somewhat reminiscent of that of Alexander Cozens. This drawing is one of an important group of twenty Rowlandson subjects bequeathed to the Victoria and Albert Museum by Captain Desmond Coke.[3] Of similar character to the *Entrance to the Mall*, with regard to landscape and well-placed figures, are *Sion House Gates* and *Boley Hill and Castle, Rochester*[4] (Pl. 215).

At the Royal Academy in 1786 his chief exhibits were *The French Review* and *The English*

---

[1] Lent to the exhibition 'The First Hundred Years of the Royal Academy', R.A. 1951–1952 (No. 473). Another version, in the Mr. & Mrs. Paul Mellon Collection (Pl. 213) shows notable differences such as the inclusion of a one-legged soldier in the front rank standing next to the only child in the picture, who has been changed from a boy to a girl.

[2] V.A.M. P.110–1931.

[3] Desmond Coke, when giving up his London residence, sold a third of his collection at Christie's in November 1929. See his letter in the *Daily Telegraph*, November 25, 1929.

[4] V.A.M. P.123–1931.

212

Review, bought at the time by the Prince of Wales and now in the Royal Library. Both the *Reviews* depend for their interest upon the assemblage of spectators, their mishaps and their merriment, rather than upon the movements of the troops, though the French troops are goose-stepping with precision. Royal patronage is shown again by *George III returning from Hunting*,[1] a cavalcade passing through Eton, with Windsor Castle in the background, and by a set of six fox-hunting scenes, executed about 1786–1788 for George IV when Prince of Wales. A series of these subjects, from which etchings were published, belonged to Lord Carnarvon and passed into the collection of Leslie Wright in 1934.

Rowlandson's reputation has rested, and may well rest, on drawings such as those mentioned; on scenes of the tavern and gaming-house, such as *Smoking a French Buck, The Hazard Room*,[2] *Boodle's Club Fête at Ranelagh*, and *The Hunt Supper*[3] (Pl. 209); on comedy and contrast between the sexes, *The Milksop*,[4] *Fille de Chambre*, so reminiscent of Sterne, or *Purchases at a Convent*; his studies of grotesques like *Death in the Bowl*,[5] or the interesting roundel of *Bull-Baiting*,[6] painted about 1810, one of a set of four illustrating the sports of England commissioned by Lord Byron for the decoration of a screen. But in comparison with drawings of that nature his high place as a landscape painter has been unduly ignored and neglected. He was sensitive to every kind of natural beauty. The man of the town, the student of the underworld and the demi-monde, the recorder of faces and bodies ravaged by greed and vice, was also a master of pastoral idylls. Very often, like Gainsborough, he drew rural scenery for its own sake. There is no deep emotion or seriousness in his landscapes, as there is in those of Cozens or Girtin or De Wint. He took landscape, as he took life, lightly, but though he regarded it with a certain gaiety and insouciance, he loved it for its freshness and variety and innocence. In the presence of rural nature he seemed to forget, perhaps with relief, the sordid and seamy side of human life which he recorded so wittily, so cruelly, so inimitably.

From the outset of his career Rowlandson was an indefatigable sketcher on all his excursions round London and further afield. In 1782, on hearing the news of the disastrous foundering of the Royal George at Spithead, he arranged a tour to visit the scene with his friend, Henry Wigstead. This excursion resulted in the production of some seventy water-colour drawings[7] portraying the incidents of the road, the places where they found a lodging for the night, episodes on land and water—material used again and again in his later life. Frequently he spent the summer months at Hengar House, Cornwall, the country seat of his friend and patron, Mitchell the banker. It was due to this association that he produced such numerous and delightful studies of Cornish towns, villages and coast scenery. His best landscape work was the outcome of annual tours, to Cornwall, Devon and Somerset (and notably Bath) with Mitchell; to Sussex, Hampshire, the Isle of Wight, North and South Wales, with Wigstead.

[1] H.M. The Queen. [2] V.A.M. P.116–1931. [3] V.A.M. P.119–1931.
[4] V.A.M. P.42–1917. [5] Ashmolean Museum, Oxford. [6] A. P. Oppé, *op. cit.*, pl. 81.
[7] Sixty-nine of these drawings are in the Huntington Library, San Marino, California. See *Rowlandson's drawings for a Tour in a Post Chaise*, with an Introduction and notes by Robert R. Wark, Huntington Library, 1963.

213

One of the most charming of his rural drawings, carried unusually far with regard to colour, is the *Landscape with Bridge, Horseman and Figures*.[1] This, like many other similar subjects, was probably worked up later, and improved in composition, from one of his original free pencil sketches, which were usually of small size. Sometimes he used one of these sketches for a set piece on a comparatively large scale, like the *Clovelly*[2] with its cottages nestling under wooded cliffs, and boats at anchor in the small harbour. His method here is the same as in the earlier sketches, but the loops of the pen-work are enlarged, and though possibly in consequence the design is a little empty, it shows his fertility, his swing and freedom as a landscape draughtsman. It seems clear, however, that the sky has been entirely repainted by a restorer, who was probably getting rid of some foxing marks: Rowlandson never modelled out the curves and folds of a cloud with minute stippling. In much of his work he shows the same panoramic sense as De Wint later, and many of his drawings were made, like De Wint's, across a double page of his sketch-book. This applies specially to the attractive subjects which he found in the Isle of Wight. Of the same type as these sketches is the slight but masterly *Fish-market at Brighthelmstone*[3] (Pl. 212), one of many lovely drawings of seaports with boats drawn up upon the beach or floating under a luminous sky upon a calm sea. In spirit and method the *Lymington*[4] is very close to Girtin, although actually this was drawn in 1782 when he was only seven years old. The unfinished *Netley Abbey*,[5] on Whatman paper, of 1794, is a good example of a drawing made across two pages. There is no pen-work in this, but slight traces of a pencil outline are apparent; and the forms and outlines are all experimentally touched in with the point of a brush. The colour is slight but very varied, and the grey-greens and hint of autumn russet are in subtle contrast with sunnier greens and yellows. Another unfinished drawing, of great interest and charm, apart from the fact that it shows the artist's technical approach to his subject, is *Cheyne Walk, Chelsea*.[6] His methods and experiments are also well illustrated by a set of three drawings of *The Mitre, Paddington Canal*,[7] wrongly described by Desmond Coke in his *Confessions of an Incurable Collector* as 'Eel Pie Island'. The Mitre was formerly a favourite resort of excursionists and was reached by boats plying on the Grand Junction Canal.[8] The drawings seem to show three stages of the same composition, with the addition or subtraction of a group of trees in the centre. Two drawings especially typical of English country life are *The Gardener's Offering*[9] and *The Country House*.[10] In the former the figures, varieties of foliage, and details of glasshouses and flower-beds, are drawn with unusual care and precision, obviously on the spot, perhaps at Mitchell's house. It is not often that Rowlandson allows himself such leisurely realism. *The Country*

[1] V.A.M. D.798. [2] Fine Art Society, 1943.
[3] H.M. The Queen (13689). [4] A. P. Oppé, *op. cit.*, pl. 3.
[5] V.A.M. P.198–1929. [6] London Museum. [7] V.A.M. P.128–1931.
[8] See J. T. Smith, *Nollekens and his Times*, and J. Hassell, *Picturesque Rides and Walks*, 1818, II, p. 247.
[9] A. P. Oppé, *op. cit.*, pl. 61.
[10] V.A.M. P.117–1931.

House, with its spacious landscape, its winding river, its house and the church nestling among trees, depicts all that was most gracious in English life and scenery.

In all of these landscapes the colour is just sufficient to suggest the warmth and glow of nature. What one values is their sensitivity and the astounding economy of the means by which the whole scene is realised. And in connection with Rowlandson's landscape work not enough attention has been paid to him as a draughtsman of animals, a much better draughtsman than Henry Alken, for all the latter's fame. Oppé rightly points out the 'vivid and almost monumental concentration of action and character' in the bulls and dogs of *Bull-baiting*. The monochrome study of *Two Greyhounds*[1] is masterly in its portrayal of animal traits. The drawing of horses in such subjects as *The Horse Fair at Southampton*[2] (Pl. 208) and *Horses*[3] is superb in its close study of form and movement. From his early days in London he was conversant with bull-baiting and had probably brought his keen observation to the study of every type of animal in the horse-drawn traffic as well as of pedestrians.

Rowlandson's continental drawings form a considerable part of his life-work. He toured the continent in company with Henry Angelo, J. R. Smith, Charles Westmacott and others, but his most frequent companion was Mathew Mitchell the banker. Henry Angelo's chatty *Memoirs* give several glimpses of Rowlandson on tours which, like Sterne's *Sentimental Journey* resulted in pictures of scenes and incidents, of habits and manners, of modes of travelling, observed with peculiar gusto and humour. In France, Flanders and Germany he made expressive notes, or complete pictures, of towns and villages, of travellers encountered on the way, of foreign aristocrats in gorgeous equipages, of waterside inn and canal boat, of country folk at their daily work. Records of these tramps abroad survive in hundreds of drawings, many of them elaborated on a large scale, such as *La Place de Meir, Antwerp*,[4] *Travelling in Holland*,[5] and *Hôtel de Flandre*.[6] The subjects are often drawn with casual haste and without any penetrating study of architectural form and detail, but in all of them he seizes the character and spirit of a place. With the same genius for summary impression he treated many English towns, such as the *Hertford Market Place*[7] or the *Cardiff*, of which there is a version in the National Museum of Wales, and a more finished one in the S. L. Phipson Collection.

No study, however brief, of Rowlandson and his work can be complete without reference to his book illustrations, particularly as many of the original water-colour drawings for them are in existence.[8] *The Loyal Volunteers of London*, 1799, the *Microcosm of London*,

[1] Coll. Mr. & Mrs. Paul Mellon.
[2] V.A.M. P.109–1931.
[3] Metropolitan Museum of Art, New York.
[4] V.A.M. D.389–1907.
[5] A. P. Oppé, *op. cit.*, pl. 34.
[6] A. P. Oppé, *op. cit.*, pl. 74.
[7] Hertford Museum.
[8] For Rowlandson as book-illustrator, see Martin Hardie, *English Coloured Books*, 1906.

1808,[1] and *The Miseries of Human Life*, 1808, all profusely illustrated with coloured plates, provided material after Rowlandson's own heart. But his great success came with the *Tours of Dr. Syntax*. The tale goes that the artist was seeking an idea for embodying his Cornwall and Devon sketches. 'I have it,' said Bannister, 'you must fancy a skin-and-bone hero, a pedantic old prig, in a shovel-hat, with a pony, sketching-stools and rattletraps, and place him in such scrapes as travellers frequently meet with—hedge alehouses, second and third-rate inns, thieves, gibbets, mad bulls, and the like.' Bannister almost certainly had in mind a caricature, *An Artist travelling Wales*, issued by Rowlandson in 1799 and depicting a spectacled artist on a sorry pony, carrying green umbrella, and laden with palette, easel, portfolio, and all the paraphernalia of his craft.[2] It is most likely that in 1799 Rowlandson was satirising the Rev. William Gilpin, who toured the countryside in this fashion for the preparation of his *Essays on Picturesque Beauty*. But Syntax and his horse have prototypes in Don Quixote and Rosinante, and in Yorick and his unnamed lean and lanky jade. Following up his early print and Bannister's suggestion, Rowlandson took some sketches to his patron, Rudolph Ackermann, the well-known publisher of coloured books, who saw that they might contribute to the success of his new *Poetical Magazine*, if a suitable narrative in verse could be supplied to accompany the drawings. It was arranged that the artist should forward an illustration each month to William Combe, for the latter to 'write up'.

The man who thus became librettist to Rowlandson's drawings, is a figure of no ordinary interest in the history of English literature. Born in 1741, and educated at Eton and Oxford, Combe spent his *Wanderjähre* in accompanying Sterne on part of the tour through Europe that resulted in the *Sentimental Journey*. Returning to London, he inherited a fortune, quickly scattered in gaming-houses and among the fashionable amusements of Cheltenham, Bath and Tunbridge Wells. Living in a princely style, he kept his carriages and a retinue of servants, and was notorious in town as 'Count Combe' or 'The Duke'. In 1768 his fortune was squandered; he became by turns a soldier, teacher of elocution, under-waiter in a Swansea tavern, soldier of France, and cook in the refectory of a French monastery. In 1772 he settled down in London, and devoted his really fine talents to literature. He was a most voluminous author. Satire, history, theology, politics, topography, humour, all poured from the point of his versatile pen. Between 1773 and his death in 1823, he wrote and edited over a hundred books, and contributed to a score of journals. For some time he was in receipt of £200 a year as a retainer for his literary support to the Pitt party, and for ten years or so, from about 1797 was acting editor of *The Times*.[3] Of Combe's scores of works, remarkably few bear his own name. The truth

---

[1] A very fine and unusual copy of the *Microcosm* was once in the possession of Desmond Coke, who wrote about it in his *Confessions of an Incurable Collector*. It belonged originally to Augustus Pugin, who collaborated with Rowlandson and supplied the architectural material for the illustrations.
[2] A coloured reproduction is given in *Hogarth and English Caricature*, edited by F. D. Klingender, 1944.
[3] *The Times*, July 19, 1941, leading article, in honour of the bicentenary of Combe's birth.

was that, like Captain Shandon in Thackeray's *Pendennis*, who was similarly gifted and similarly employed, he spent a great part of his life as a prisoner for debt 'within the rules' of King's Bench Prison. When Ackermann applied to him in 1809, he had reached the age of sixty-eight, his affairs were in a more depressed condition than usual, and he had just been writing seventy-three sermons as a clergyman's hack. *Dr. Syntax* turned the tide, and a writer in the *London Cyclopaedia* of 1829, who had formerly known Combe, draws a vivid picture of how he used 'regularly to pin up the sketch against a screen of his apartment in the King's Bench, and write off his verses as the painter wanted them'. Combe himself, in the preface to the second edition tells the exact story of how Rowlandson's sketches were used. 'The designs,' he wrote, 'to which this volume is so greatly indebted, I was informed would follow in a Series, and it was proposed to me to shape out a story from them. An etching or a drawing was accordingly sent to me every month, and I composed a certain proportion of pages in verse, in which of course the subject of the design was included: the rest depended upon what would be the nature of the second; and in this manner, in a great measure, the artist continued designing, and I continued writing every month for two years, till a work containing near ten thousand lines was produced: the artist and the writer having no personal communication with, or knowledge of each other. This vast collection of verses, however, appeared to advance the purposes of the Magazine, in which they grew into such an unexpected accumulation. Mr. Ackermann was satisfied with my services, and I was satisfied with the remuneration for it. I felt no parental fondness for the work, though it was written at that very advanced period of life, when we are apt to attach importance to any little unexpected exertion of decaying strength.' Six years after this, Combe was merrily writing an *English Dance of Death* to accompany the illustrations of Rowlandson!

The *Tour of Dr. Syntax in Search of the Picturesque*, which thus appeared in the *Poetical Magazine*, was so popular a success that in 1812 it was issued in book form at one guinea, with the text revised and augmented. A new set of plates, with very slight variations, was prepared, the old ones having been somewhat worn in printing. The illustrations in this first separate edition were thirty-one, three new subjects being added. Rowlandson's good-natured, quixotic, moralising school-master became a public character and a general favourite. Syntax was the popular title of the day, and shop windows were full of Syntax hats, Syntax wigs and Syntax coats. Figures of the famous Doctor, modelled by Edward Keys, were issued from the Derby China factory at prices from five shillings to twelve shillings and sixpence each. A racehorse, named after the popular favourite, had won by 1822 more cups, plates and money than any other racer known. The book met with such rapid and extensive demand that four editions appeared within twelve months, a fifth in 1813, a sixth in 1815, a seventh in 1817, and an eighth in 1819. It was followed by a host of imitations and parodies, and by a French and German edition in 1821 and 1822.

The success of the first tour led Ackermann to arrange with Rowlandson and Combe for a second series. Dr. Syntax's termagant spouse is decently buried early in the new volume, and an excuse thus found for further travels—*Dr. Syntax in Search of Consolation.* This was published in 1820, uniform with the first volume, and was speedily followed, in 1821, by a third and final tour—*Dr. Syntax in Search of a Wife.* For all three volumes the illustrations were etched by Rowlandson himself on the copper plates, and were then finished in aquatint, and coloured by hand in exact imitation of the artist's original water-colour sketches. Seventeen water-colour drawings by Rowlandson for the *Tours* are in the Victoria and Albert Museum, though only three of these actually appear in the published volumes.

Finally, here are two early pictures which help to an understanding of Rowlandson and his work as seen against a contemporary background:

> Well, Sirs, Master Caleb was on his way up the hill in the Adelphi to his post at the Society of Arts, and who should he stumble upon at the corner of James Street, just turning round from Rowlandson's, but Master Mitchell, the quondam banker, of old Hodsoll's house. Mitchell had, as usual, been foraging among the multitudinous sketches of that original artist, and held a portfolio under his arm; and as he was preparing to step into his chariot, Caleb accosted him— 'Well, worthy Sir, what more choice bits—more graphic whimsies, to add to the collection at Enfield, hey? Well, how fares it with our friend Rolly?' (a familiar term by which the artist is known to his ancient cronies.) 'Why, yes, Mister Caleb Whiteford, I go collecting on, though I begin to think I have enough already, for I have some hundreds of his spirited works; but somehow there is a sort of fascination in these matters, and—heigh-ha-ho-hoo,' (gaping) 'I never go up-up-up-Bless the man! why will he live so high?—it kills me to climb his stairs,' holding his ponderous sides. 'I never go up, Mister Caleb, but I find something new, and am tempted to pull my purse-strings. His invention, his humour, his—his oddity is exhaustless.' 'Yes,' said Whiteford. 'Master Rolly is never at a loss for a subject; and I should not be surprised if he is taking a bird's-eye view of you and I at this moment, and marking us down for game. But it is not his drawings alone; why he says he has etched as much copper as would sheathe a first-rate man-of-war; and I should think he is not far from the mark in his assertion.'
>
> 'Yes,' replied the banker, 'he ought to be rich, for his genius is certainly the most exhaustless, the most—the most—No, Mister Caleb, there is no end to him; he manufactures his humorous ware with such unceasing vigour, that I know not what to compare his prolific fancy to, unless—unless it be to this increasing population,' turning round, as he held the two sides of the door-way to his chariot, and looking with astonishment at the shoals of young folk who were pressing on for admittance to the Society's great rooms. It was on a day for the delivery of prize-medals.[1]

The second picture is by Henry Angelo, who records that Gillray sometimes met 'his ingenious compeer, Rowlandson' at one of the taverns which represented the social side of life to their generation:

> They would perhaps exchange half-a-dozen questions and answers upon the affairs of copper and aquafortis, swear all the world was one vast masquerade, and then enter into the common chat of the room, smoke their cigars, drink their punch, and sometimes early, sometimes late, shake hands at the door, look up at the stars, say 'It's a frosty night', and depart, one to the Adelphi, the other to St. James's Street, each to his bachelor's bed.

---

[1] E. Hardcastle (W. H. Pyne), *Wine and Walnuts*, 1824, Vol. II, pp. 323–325.

Those two quotations, one feels, convey a better impression of Rowlandson's associations and manner of life than exaggerated tales of his carelessness and debauchery. Add to this that if he had gambling debts they were always paid, and that his will, which Oppé was the first to rediscover, was witnessed by the highly respectable head of his bank, Mitchell's partner, Hodsoll, and was admitted for probate at about £3000, in those days a sum not likely to be left by any reckless rake and debaucher.

In this context should be mentioned some caricaturists who were Rowlandson's contemporaries: John Collet has been referred to in a previous chapter as a link between Hogarth and Rowlandson. With regard to Henry Wigstead (d. 1800), mentioned above as Rowlandson's friend and travelling companion, some association in their work has caused obscurity. Rowlandson appears to have worked up Wigstead's sketches, as many contemporary landscape painters did for their friends and patrons. Oppé points out the connection between Rowlandson's *Poet and Author*, a print of which was issued in 1784 bearing Wigstead's name, and a drawing by Wigstead of *Poet and Bookseller* exhibited that year in the Royal Academy. Many prints bearing Wigstead's full name or his initials are obviously based upon drawings by Rowlandson, whose anonymity was perhaps voluntary, and intended as a help to his friend. In 1785 Wigstead had three exhibits at the Academy, *Traffic Jews buying Old Clothes*, *The Back of the Boxes at the Theatre, Covent Garden* (obviously related to Rowlandson's *Box-Lobby Loungers*), and *The History of John Gilpin*.[1] The St. James's Chronicle remarked that: 'The humorous and excellent drawings we make no doubt to be the production of Mr. Rowlandson; and we wonder anyone should exhibit them as his own whose abilities are known to be unequal to the invention or execution of such drawings. And what shall we say of the penetration of the Rulers of the Academy who could not see in them the hand of Rowlandson?' Perhaps Rowlandson in the simpler and more Hogarthian vein of such drawings as *Poet and Author* owed something to the ideas and outlook of a man whose execution was much more feeble than his own. Wigstead remains a mystery, and his dates are not known. The contemporary critic obviously knew who he was—evidently an amateur—possibly (the name is uncommon) the Justice Wigstead, mentioned by Farington in 1801.

Henry William Bunbury (1750–1811) was born five years before Rowlandson. In the Victoria and Albert Museum are six monochrome drawings by him illustrating Boswell's *Journal of a Tour in the Hebrides*,[2] and these were etched by Rowlandson. Bunbury was the second son of the Rev. Sir William Bunbury, Bart., of Mildenhall, Suffolk. He was educated at Westminster School and St. Catharine's, Cambridge; became Colonel of the West Suffolk Militia, and in 1787 was appointed Equerry to the Duke of York. As an artist of caricatures and of humorous drawings, such as *Hints to Bad Horsemen*, he was compared by Walpole to Hogarth, but his work, however amusing, hardly deserves this

[1] V.A.M. P.22–1951. Lent to the exhibition. *The First Hundred Years of the Royal Academy*, R.A. 1951–1952 (No. 472): see the catalogue note.
[2] V.A.M. D.754–7.

commendation and indeed is much inferior to that of Rowlandson and Gillray. His water-colours are usually rather weak portraits or sentimental book-illustrations such as *Florizel and Autolycus*[1] and *The Water Sprite*.[2] His caricatures, without political aim and without personalities, were very popular in his time. They had none of the pungent satire, the *saeva indignatio*, with which James Gillray (1757–1815), Rowlandson's junior by one year, lashed the royal family and the leading politicians of his day. Gillray executed some fifteen hundred prints, mostly issued by Miss Humphrey at 29 St. James's Street, Piccadilly, where he lived; but his work was mainly done with pencil, pen and etching needle, and he hardly comes into our story except as Rowlandson's friend. His *Very Slippy Weather*[3] (1808) caricatures fill each square of the bow window. This was a time when rival print shops advertised permanent exhibitions of 'the largest collection of caricatures in the world, entrance 1s.' and when portfolios of political and personal satires, hot from the printing press, were hired out for the evening.

Robert Dighton[4] (1752–1814) was contemporary with Gillray and was one of his rivals as a caricaturist of men and manners. He possessed, however, a happy and charitable sense of humour, and was free from Gillray's liking for savage invective and ferocious attack. Dighton later showed versatile talent as painter, actor, dramatic writer, singer, caricaturist, collector and thief. He made his first appearance at the Royal Academy in 1775, when he exhibited 'a frame of stain'd drawings', and between that year and 1799 showed five monochrome portraits and *A View at Covent Garden during the Election, 1784, a teinted sketch*. This last drawing is now in the Royal Collection at Windsor Castle; Dighton also recorded the *Westminster Election of 1788* and *Westminster Election of 1796*, both of these drawings are in the London Museum. Dighton lived in the constituency, at Spring Gardens, during most of his active life, was clearly interested in its affairs, and found that the hurly-burly of an election crowd supplied him with subjects which provided not only animated movement but a contrast between aristocratic candidates with their supporters dressed in the height of fashion, and a tatterdemalion mob.

Dighton's finest ability as a water-colourist is shown by his *A Windy Day*[5] (Pl. 220). The scene is outside the shop of Bowles, the print-seller, in St. Paul's churchyard, and the window is lined with identifiable prints of the period. The artist has not concentrated, as Rowlandson would have done, on any revelation or exposure of the human form, but on the splendid rhythm of flying draperies, tossing like waves on a stormy sea. Another drawing, *Fortune Distributing her Gifts*,[6] fails in its conjunction of allegory and realism, and has not the same felicity of design. These two drawings and his *Men of War bound for Port of Pleasure*[7] are set down with vigorous and expressive pen line, reinforced by powerful light and shade in monochrome. The coloured washes that turn each into a 'teinted sketch' are clean and harmonious. After the period from about 1780 to 1790, to which these attractive

---

[1] V.A.M. 1702–1871.   [2] B.M.1890. 5.12.18.   [3] B.M. *Satires*, No. 11,100.
[4] Ralph Edwards, 'The Water-colour Drawings of R. Dighton', *Apollo*, XIV, 1931, pp. 98–102.
[5] V.A.M. D.843–1900.   [6] V.A.M. P.22–1931.   [7] B.M. 1875. 3.13.49.

drawings belong, Dighton seems to have settled down to producing a long series of portrait etchings which are without malice or excess of caricature. After Rowlandson he takes a very high place, and if his water-colours had been more numerous and had repeated the drama and design of *A Windy Day* his reputation would have been secure.

As dealer and collector Dighton went astray, and between about 1795 and 1806 made a practice of abstracting some of the most valuable prints from the portfolios in the British Museum. His practice was to bring his own portfolio of prints for comparison, and the Rev. William Beloe, who was the custodian, used to leave him alone in the Print Room. Thus it was that many of the Cracherode Rembrandt etchings disappeared but were fortunately recovered and may still be recognised by the letter *D* on the palette, the collector's stamp with which Dighton was brazen enough to decorate his acquisitions. Beloe, unfortunately for him, had accepted presents of 'geese, fowls, fish, peas at a guinea a quart, etc.' and was dismissed from his office, which brought a salary of '£200 a year with very good apartments & fire and Candle'. In spite of his offence, Dighton remained an active producer of caricatures for many years afterwards.[1]

George Moutard Woodward (1760–1809), born in Derbyshire, was a dilettante writer of light verse and a designer of social caricatures which were highly popular through etchings by Rowlandson and Isaac Cruikshank, both of them his seniors by a year or two. I have not seen it suggested, but suspect the 'Moutard' was a cognomen adopted to fit the nature of his work. Among four characteristic drawings by him in the British Museum is one of *Lunardi ascending in his Balloon*, 1784, the first aerial journey made in England. His drawings, in the manner of his time, depended upon firmly outlined pen-work, reinforced by shading with Indian ink, and finished with slight washes of colour. A large subject by him, *Ladies and Gentlemen at the Edge of a Wood*, 1792,[2] is less in the nature of a caricature than most of his work and shows that he was influenced by Wheatley.

John Nixon (*d.* 1818) was an amateur like Wigstead, and the date of his birth is unknown. A merchant in Basinghall Street, he was incidentally an artist, drawing landscapes, book-illustrations and caricatures. His drawings, such as his *Edmonton Statute Fair*[3] (Pl. 223) and his *Morning View of Sands at Worthing*[4] are of high quality and owe something perhaps to his contemporary, Rowlandson. *The Cove, Cork*[5] (Pl. 222), 1794, gives an amusing picture of a busy scene on the shore near Cork at a time when the port was full of naval activity owing to the French Wars. Nixon was for many years secretary to the Beefsteak Club. An early newspaper cutting (undated) in the Victoria and Albert Museum has this about him: 'Alas, my old friend John. Who among the wits and wags of the day has not to say, "I have taken my mutton with Jack Nixon in Basinghall-street?" John was a noted draughtsman of humorous subjects. He gave good dinners, the hospitable worthy: military time at five.'

[1] A. M. Hind, *Short History of Etching and Engraving,* and *Diary,* July 11, 1806.
[2] Fine Art Society, 1947. [3] V.A.M. P.46–1923.
[4] V.A.M. P.69–1920. [5] V.A.M. P.195–1929.

221

Isaac Cruikshank[1] (1756/7–*c.* 1811) was Rowlandson's exact contemporary and in some sort a rival, so far as political and social caricatures are concerned. Born in Edinburgh, he came to London about 1788 and earned a precarious living as book-illustrator, caricaturist, and water-colour painter.

Cruikshank made hundreds of humorous burlesques and political caricatures. His home became a sort of manufactory, with his wife colouring prints which he had etched on copper. Blanchard Jerrold describes him as a 'fair painter in water-colours' but his work of this nature is rare, and *The Dame School*[2] (Pl. 224) does not represent him at his best. He has the caricaturist's eye for pose, gesture, movement and a comic situation, as in Mr. Ralph Edwards' *Moses in the Bull-Rushes*. His work is good at times but lacks the brilliant sub-structure of pen-work which gives life to a Rowlandson drawing. His two sons Isaac Robert (generally known as Robert Cruikshank) and George, assisted their mother in colouring their father's prints and grew up to produce work of the same character as that of their father. The varying signatures—I.CK., I.R.CK., R.C.K., and G.CK.—have caused natural confusion among dealers, printsellers and collectors.

Robert (1789–1856) was the elder of the two sons. He was so inspired by the stories related by his mother's lodger, Mungo Park, that he went to sea as a midshipman in the East India Company's service. Abandoning this career, he settled in London and worked in partnership with his younger brother, George. For a time they vied directly with Rowlandson, assailing the same abuses and censuring the same crimes. The Regent, Napoleon, the 'delicate investigation', and Queen Caroline, attracted these three satirists together. Ackermann, Fores[3] and Fairburn came with plentiful commissions, and the leading prizefighters of the day were made equally at home in their studio, which enabled the two brothers to form an extensive acquaintance with the 'Tom and Jerry' life which they so admirably depicted. Their illustrations in 1821 to Pierce Egan's *Life in London* won a success comparable only with that of the *Tours of Dr. Syntax*. All London read it, and twenty years later Thackeray still remembered the leather gaiters of Jerry Hawthorn, the green spectacles of Bob Logic, the hooked nose of Corinthian Tom, and in a charming essay recalled his schoolboy's delight in these heroes.

George Cruikshank (1792–1878) was the most famous of the family. He illustrated numberless periodicals and humorous works, and his was once a household name for his illustrations to Dickens and his prints in support of the temperance cause. Publishers found that he could treat any subject with resource and sympathy, and his remarkable fecundity is shown by the five pages of cross-references under his name in the British Museum catalogue of books and by the 5,625 entries in Reid's catalogue of his work, of which 669 refer not to single prints but to whole sets of illustrations. Like all the cari-

[1] Ralph Edwards, 'Isaac Cruikshank', *Burlington Magazine.* LII, 1928, p. 184.
[2] V.A.M. 144–1890.
[3] In his essay on *Merry England,* Hazlitt writes: 'I should suppose there is more drollery and unction in the caricatures in Fores' shop-window than in all the masks in Italy, without exception.' ('Fores' wrongly printed as 'Fore's' in the *World Classics.*)

caturists of the period he used etching as a cheap and convenient method of reproducing his work. Ruskin, writing about Cruikshank's etchings, speaks of their 'pure unaffected rightness of method, utterly disdaining all accident, scrawl, or tricks of biting'. Cruikshank's published work conveys no idea of the painstaking study and endless elaboration by which it was produced. For every illustration he would make several studies in pencil or ink, adding in the margin numerous little sketches suggesting alterations in a figure or an expression. Whether his illustration was intended for publishing in colours or not, he often finished his pencil drawing in water-colour, perhaps because by this means he obtained a fuller idea of light, shade, atmosphere, and the whole spirit of the scene. His colouring was of the simplest, consisting of slight washes of yellow, green and blue, in pure tints, with here and there a suggestion of red.

His methods were amply illustrated in the *George Cruikshank Collection* of etchings and drawings, selected by the artist himself, and exhibited at Exeter Hall in 1863. This collection subsequently passed into the possession of the Westminster Aquarium, whose managers bought it from the artist in 1876 for £2500, with a life annuity for himself or his wife of £35. When the Aquarium premises (so well known to the Tom and Jerry of the naughty 'nineties) were disposed of in 1903, the Cruikshank collection was sold at Sotheby's. Among a large number of water-colour and pencil sketches for book-illustrations were the twenty water-colour drawings made for Harrison Ainsworth's *The Miser's Daughter*, and twenty for the *Irish Rebellion*. These two sets, together with some Oliver Twist drawings (a special commission from the artist by F. W. Cosens in 1866), were admirably reproduced in *Cruikshank's Water-Colours*, published in 1903 with an introduction by Joseph Grego. The British and Victoria and Albert Museums contain vast collections of his work, given by his widow or bequeathed by his executors; and many oddments from the 1903 sale and other sources appear at times in the market.

George Cruikshank was a mannered draughtsman, with little refinement in his handling of line and composition, and poor notions of how to draw a horse or a tree. Yet he was a keen observer of character, possessing high qualities of imagination, wit, fancy, and tragic power; and his work is always spirited, expressive and spontaneous. With these qualities was combined an exuberance of invention, which drove him to crowd humorous details into every corner of his picture and to concentrate upon episode and incident to the sacrifice of artistic unity. He was not an artist of the stature of Rowlandson or Charles Keene, but as Thackeray said, 'he has given a thousand new and pleasant thoughts to millions of people'; and Ruskin, while feeling that his services were recklessly lost in illustrating the Irish Rebellion and the career of Jack Sheppard, spoke of 'the great, grave (I use the word deliberately and with large meaning), and singular genius of George Cruikshank'.

Henry Alken[1] (1784, *d.* after 1849), maker of sporting prints and drawings, serious and

[1] W. Shaw Sparrow, *Henry Alken*, 1927; and catalogue of Exhibition of Original Drawings by Henry Alken, Ellis and Smith's Galleries, Grafton Street, with introduction by J. Gilbey Ellis, 1949.

humorous, of hunting and racing subjects, may be linked with the caricaturists. Henry Thomas Alken, to give him his full name, was born at 3, Dufours Place, Golden Square, the third son of Samuel Alken, architect and engraver. Henry received lessons from J. T. Barber,[1] the miniature painter, and as early as 1801 exhibited a miniature at the Royal Academy. In his *Art and Practice of Etching*, published in 1849, he speaks of 'forty years of practice in the various methods of engraving' and of his giving lessons during a great portion of that time 'in the library, parlour and drawing-room'. There seems to be no authority for the frequently printed statement that he was huntsman stud groom, or trainer to the Duke of Beaufort. There is certainly a gap in our information about his early years and no explanation as to how he came to be associated with well-to-do and aristocratic sportsmen in the Shires. He speaks of himself as owning horses and as 'having been much in the habit of riding young and violent horses with foxhounds' and 'having had four or five falls a day on a buck-leaping mare'. In the period 1810 to 1820 he was winning fame by hunting prints and drawings issued under the pseudonym of 'Ben Tally Ho', and the Meltonians, recognising their own countryside and characters, were puzzled about the unknown artist in their midst. They never suspected 'their own familiar friend, the man with whom they had for years taken sweet council', until he 'blabbed it out one night to Sir Francis Burdett'.[2] This implies that Alken was never seen with a sketch-book in hand and must have made his drawings in the studio from memory.

In his earlier days Alken used pure water-colour without appreciable pencil-work. In what Ellis describes as his second period, from 1820 to about 1831, he was using pencil or crayon, rather in the Morland manner, as the basis of his work; his tints, delicately laid, did not conceal the underlying structure. From 1830 onwards we find him forsaking his pencil-work and returning to broader and more direct handling of water-colour, with much stronger colour and more search for pictorial effects. His health began to fail, and with it his perception and skill.

Alken's sporting prints made from his drawings, and the best of them etched or engraved by himself, had and still have considerable vogue. Even in his more serious work in water-colour he ranks well below Rowlandson in design, character study, and movement. His appeal is to the sportsman who wishes every horse to be depicted a creature of breeding and spirit. He tends to exaggerate height and to make his horses' heads and necks and hoofs far too slender and small for even a thoroughbred. With first-hand knowledge he portrays horsemen who sit well and firmly on their saddles and move with the movements of their mount. He gives convincingly the metre and rhythm of a walk or a trot, but his galloping horses have the straddled gait always found in pictures before the invention of cinematography.

Ruskin complained that he could 'get at the price of lumber any quantity of British squires flourishing whips and falling over hurdles', and too much of Alken's work belongs

---

[1] In about 1830 became known as J. T. Barber Beaumont.
[2] Christopher North, *Blackwood's Magazine*, 1824.

208 'Horse Fair, Southampton'
V.A.M. P.109–1931   7¾ × 16: 197 × 407   *Water-colour*
Thomas ROWLANDSON (1756–1827)

209 'The Hunt Supper'
V.A.M. P.119–1931   8¾ × 12⅜: 222 × 314   *Water-colour*
Thomas ROWLANDSON (1756–1827)

210 'A French Postillion'
Coll. Mrs Dorian Williamson   8 × 11¼: 203 × 286   *Pen and water-colour*
Thomas ROWLANDSON (1756–1827)

211 'Castle on a Rocky Cliff'
Coll. Mr & Mrs Paul Mellon   9½ × 12: 243 × 306   *Water-colour*
Thomas ROWLANDSON (1756–1827)

212 'Fishmarket at Brighton'

H.M. The Queen (13689) $7\frac{5}{8} \times 11\frac{7}{8}$: 194 × 301   *Pen and water-colour*

Thomas ROWLANDSON (1756–1827)

213 'Old Vauxhall Gardens'

Coll. Mr & Mrs Paul Mellon $13\frac{1}{8} \times 18\frac{1}{8}$: 334 × 461   *Pen and water-colour*

Thomas ROWLANDSON (1756–1827)

214 'George Morland'

B.M. 1868.3.28.335   12½ × 8½: 318 × 216   *Pen, Indian ink and water-colour*

Thomas ROWLANDSON (1756–1827)

215 'Boley Hill and Castle, Rochester'

V.A.M. P.123.1931 $10\frac{1}{4} \times 14\frac{3}{4}$: 260 × 375   *Pen and water-colour*

Thomas ROWLANDSON (1756–1827)

216 'Patience in a Punt'

Coll. Mr & Mrs Paul Mellon   8 × 12⅜: 203 × 314   *Black chalk and water-colour*

Henry BUNBURY (1750–1811)

217 'The Water Sprite'

B.M. 1890.5.12.18   11 × 15½: 280 × 394   *Pen and water-colour, signed and dated 1796*

Henry BUNBURY (1750–1811)

218 'Cymon and Iphigenia'

Coll. Mr Pierre Jeannerat $9\frac{1}{2} \times 8\frac{3}{4}$: 241 × 213   *Pen and ink and water-colour*

James GILLRAY (1757–1815)

219 'A Brigade-Major at Weymouth'

Coll. Mr Osbert Lancaster   10 × 8 : 254 × 204   *Pen and ink and water-colour, signed*

James GILLRAY (1757–1815)

220 'A Windy Day'

V.A.M. D.843–1900   12⅝ × 9⅝ : 321 × 245   *Water-colour*

Robert DIGHTON (1752–1814)

221 'A Favourite Cat choaked with a Fish Bone'
Coll. Mrs Eleanor Williams   12 × 19: 305 × 483   *Water-colour, signed and dated 1790*
George Moutard WOODWARD (1760–1809)

222 'The Cove, Cork'
V.A.M. P.195–1929   19⅝ × 26¾: 505 × 680   *Water-colour, signed and dated 1794*
John NIXON (d. 1818)

223 'Edmonton Statute Fair'

V.A.M. P.46–1923 $25\frac{7}{8} \times 39\frac{3}{4}$: 657×1010 *Water-colour, signed and dated 1788*

John Nixon (d. 1818)

224 'The Dame School'

V.A.M. 144–1890 $7 \times 9\frac{1}{4}$: 178×235 *Water-colour*

Isaac Cruikshank (1756 or 1757–c. 1811)

225 'The Sailor's Sweetheart'

B.M. 1878.7.13.1256 $11\frac{1}{2} \times 8\frac{7}{8}$: 293 × 226   *Pen and water-colour*

Isaac CRUIKSHANK (1756 or 1757–c. 1811)

226 Illustration to 'Oliver Twist'

B.M. 1888.8.6.2   4 × 3¾: 102 × 95   *Pencil and water-colour, signed*

George CRUIKSHANK (1792–1878)

227 'Ring of Fairies Dancing beneath a Crescent Moon'
B.M. 'Cruikshank Coll.'   12¼ × 16: 312 × 407   *Water-colour, signed*
George CRUIKSHANK (1792–1878)

228 'Night Riders of Nacton: Preparing to Start'
Coll. Mr & Mrs Paul Mellon   10½ × 14½: 267 × 369
Water-colour and gouache on brown paper
Henry ALKEN (1784–after 1849)

229 'Charging a Flight of Rails'
B.M. 1939.7.14.130   9½ × 12: 242 × 305   *Pencil and water-colour*
Henry ALKEN (1784–after 1849)

230 'Fox Cubs'

Coll. Mr & Mrs Paul Mellon   5¼ × 7⅛: 133 × 181   *Water-colour, signed*

Samuel HOWITT (1756–1822)

231 'Exhibition Battle between a Tiger and a Buffalo'

B.M. Nn.7-39.279/1   11¼ × 16½: 286 × 420   *Pen and ink and water-colour*

Samuel HOWITT (1756–1822)

to this class. But the real Henry Alken, as opposed to the tired and over wrought Henry Alken, and as opposed to his many fraudulent imitators, has his moments of triumph. He was not a born designer, but now and then he dealt ably with a long frieze-like composition of horses and riders in the streaming skirmish of the hunt. It is of interest that in his series of the Quorn Hunt and elsewhere he puts in skies that are lightsome and breezy like those of Thomas Collier of later date. And in his drawing *Exercising Horses*,[1] on Newmarket Heath showing three thoroughbreds with stable lads up and the trainer on his hack in the background, he produced what seems to me his masterpiece, entirely happy in its composition and movement and in its characterisation of men, steeds and landscape.

A predecessor of Alken in the picturing of animals and sporting scenes was Samuel Howitt (1756–1822), who may well be included here because he was born the same year as Rowlandson,[2] and married Rowlandson's sister. Howitt, who was self-educated as an artist, became a drawing-master and for a time taught drawing at Dr. Goodenough's academy at Ealing. In 1783 he exhibited three 'stained drawings' of hunting subjects with the Incorporated Society of Artists, and was an exhibitor at the Royal Academy from 1784. He never visited Bengal, as has been stated by Redgrave and others, the probable reason for the error being that he worked up some drawings by Captain Williamson for the *Oriental Field Sports* which Williamson published in 1807. *The British Sportsman*, 1812, and other publications contain engravings from Howitt's drawings of animals and hunting scenes. His illustrations of such subjects are spirited and accurate. The Rowlandson influence is apparent sometimes in his style, particularly in some caricatures. *Foxes*[3] is a good example of his use of colour to enhance a lively draughtsmanship. It was probably drawn when Howitt was designing fifty-six plates for *The Fables of Aesop*, 1811.

[1] Coll. Mr. J. E. Ellis.
[2] Hitherto the date of Howitt's birth has been given as 1765 or 'about 1765'. The actual date, 1756, was recently discovered by Mr. G. E. Kendall in the Registers of St. James's Church, Piccadilly.
[3] Coll. Mr. & Mrs. Paul Mellon.

CHAPTER XIII

Marine painters

The Van de Veldes   Peter Monamy   Samuel Scott   Dominic Serres
Charles Brooking   John T. Serres   Charles Gore   Nicholas Pocock
John and Robert Cleveley   John Webber   William Anderson   Samuel Atkins

If marine painters are grouped in this and a later chapter, it is not because their work should be separated from the main stream of the history of art, but because several of our best water-colour painters have specialised in painting the sea and shipping and coastal scenery.

By the middle of the seventeenth century, the old conventions of European marine painting were being abandoned. The sea was no longer depicted in an endless repetition of jagged waves standing up with the dentated regularity of a curry-comb or a saw. Free movement and atmosphere, a new study of the form of waves and clouds, came into the picture. New conventions were tried out, for, in Ruskin's words: 'The sea never has been, and I fancy, never will be nor can be painted; it is only suggested by means of a more or less spiritual and intelligent conventionalism: and though Turner has done enough to suggest the sea mightily and gloriously, after all it is conventionalism still.'

The Dutch, in experiment and observation, led the van in the art, and for some time our painters sailed, as it were, in convoy under the Dutch flag. Bakhuyzen, in Holland, was one of the first artists who attempted to represent the actual movement of the sea, the tossing of ships, the unrest of the sky; and it is said that he used to employ mariners to take him afloat in order that he might study at first hand the configuration of storm-tossed water. His influence and that of the Van de Veldes, father and son, can be traced through the later Dutch painters to our own British school. From Willem Van de Velde the elder was inherited that passionate love of minute and meticulous detail which set a standard of technical accuracy, to be recognised and followed later in the work of such men as G. Chambers and E. W. Cooke. From Willem Van de Velde the younger came the realisation of the play of light over air and water, and the subtle placing of ships in a rhythmic design. 'It was the son,' says Callender,[1] 'who set down, with a few flecks of the brush, the movement of the sea and the wind in the sails, or with a clean flat wash recorded with facile truthfulness the appearance of a ship becalmed in a morning mist.'

[1] Exhibitions of drawings from the Ingram Coll. held at Messrs. Colnaghi, 1936 and 1937, introductions by Sir Geoffrey Callender. The Sir Bruce Ingram Collection was sold at Sotheby's during 1964 and 1965.

226

The Van de Veldes made their home in England in the early part of the year 1673. Among the papers of Mr. Secretary Pepys was a Warrant from King Charles II, February 20, 1674, which Vertue quotes[1]:

> Charles the Second by the Grace of God King of England Scotland France and Ireland defender of the faith. To Our Dear Cousin Prince Rupert and the rest of our Commissioners for Executing the places of Lord High Admiral of England. Greeting. Whereas wee have though fitt to allow the Salary of One hundred pounds p.Annm unto William Van de Veld the Elder for taking and making of Draughts of seafights, and the like Salary of One hundred pounds p. Annm unto William Van de Velde the Younger for putting the said Draughts into Colours for our particular use. Our Will and pleasure is and wee do hereby Authorize and require you to issue your Orders for the present and future Establishment of the said Salaries. . . . Given under Our privy seal at our pallace of Westminster. the 20 day of February. the 26 of our Reign.

Their official position alone, apart from the merit of their work, would account for their influence. Again to quote Callender: 'In the later phases of their genius they set a stamp on English marine art whose impress has never been quite obliterated, and whose pristine sharpness, indeed, for a century and a half, can hardly be said to have diminished.' Their influence counts as a vital and stimulating force in the work of our earlier painters such as Peter Monamy, Charles Brooking, John Cleveley, J. T. Serres, Dominic Serres, Nicholas Pocock and William Anderson.

Those who are depressed by the idea of 'marines' are probably thinking not of the lively work of Bakhuyzen and the younger Van de Velde, but of the more conventional output of eighteenth-century painters in oil. Every year on the walls of the Royal Academy were displayed records of historic sea-fights, or ship portraits, faithful in every detail of sails, masts and rigging, the ships static in a very dynamic world of the ocean.

About the end of the eighteenth century the attitude of painters and public underwent a revolutionary change. Up till then the value of the sea-coast as a health resort, the delights of bathing, salt water and sea breezes were still unknown or unrealised. Very few of those who dwelt inland had thought of visiting the seaside for health or pleasure until George III went to Weymouth by medical advice, and bathed to strains of *God save the King*, emitted by a hidden band. In 1750 Dr. Richard Russell published a dissertation recommending sea-water for certain glandular diseases, and it reached a sixth edition by 1769. The doctor built himself a house at Brighthelmstone, then a small seaside village, which later branched out into the Brighton which we know to-day. Dr. Johnson spent six weeks with the Thrales at Brighthelmstone in the autumn of 1776.

Brighton was already a gay bathing-place when *Pride and Prejudice* was published in 1813. By 1791 Bognor was well on its way to becoming a fashionable watering-place, thanks to Sir Richard Hotham, a retired hatter. Felpham, where Blake went to live in 1800, was only a few miles away, and from Bognor or near it Blake had his first glimpse of the sea. At a much earlier date bathing machines were introduced at Margate by one Beale, 'in

---

[1] Walpole Soc. XXVI, 1938. Vertue V, p. 75.

order that bathing should be conducted with safety and propriety'. Other fishing villages were transformed into seaside resorts.

Public and painters alike flocked to the coast for their holiday recreation and began to discover the charm of coastal landscape and the infinite variety of the sea. All round our coasts little villages followed the example of Brighthelmstone and Bognor, and blossomed out into towns with hotels, boarding establishments, concert-halls, reading-rooms and marine parades. Trim terraces and crescents were built, with fanlights above the doors, and balconies commanding a prospect of the sea, or bow windows that extended the view. Charles Lamb wrote of Hastings as 'a place of fugitive resort, an heterogeneous assemblage of sea-mews and stock-brokers, Amphitrites of the town, and misses that coquet with the Ocean. If it were what it was in its primitive shape, and what it ought to have remained, a fair honest fishing-town, it were something'.

The artist, for his part, began to realise that the vogue for the sea-coast was like the growing vogue for continental travel; that the sea, like the mountains, lakes and towns of the Continent, stood to the public for romance. Even Byron, of whom Lady Blessington observed that he 'had little taste for the fine arts', and who was, in Trelawney's words, 'indifferent to painting, sculpture and music', was induced to give thought to the work of sea-painters. He may have been blind to the appeal of the visual arts, but like Swinburne and Shelley he had a passion for the sea. In 1821, when 'sensibility reigned supreme, he wrote:

> Did Mr. Bowles ever gaze upon the sea? I presume that he has, at least upon a sea-piece. Did any painter ever paint the sea *only*, without the addition of a ship, boatwreck, or some such adjunct? Is the sea itself a more attractive, a more moral, a more poetical object, with or without a vessel breaking its vast but fatiguing monotony? . . .
>
> Even a ship laid up in dock is a grand and poetical sight. Even an old boat, keel upwards, wrecked upon the barren sand, is a 'poetical' object, whilst a long extent of sand and unbroken water, without the boat, would be as like dull prose as any pamphlet lately published. . . .
>
> Let us examine a little further this 'babble of green fields' and of bare nature in general as superior to artificial imagery for the poetical purposes of the fine arts. In landscape painting the great artist does not give you a literal copy of a country, but he invents and composes one. Nature in her natural aspect does not furnish him with such existing scenes as he requires. Even where he presents you with some famous city, or celebrated scene from mountain or other nature, it must be taken from some particular point of view, and with such light, and shade, and distance, etc., as serve not only to heighten its beauties, but to shadow its deformities. The very sky of his painting is not the *portrait* of the sky of nature; it is a composition of different *skies*, observed at different times and not copied from any *particular* day. And why? Because nature is not lavish of her beauties; they are widely scattered, and occasionally displayed, to be selected with care, and gathered with difficulty. Nature, exactly, simply, barely nature, will make no great artist of any kind.

The artist of 1821, in following the public taste, found for his part that ships tossed by the wind were a substitute for trees in his design, standing out light or dark against a fisherman's wooden shed, an old ketch or cobble lying over high and dry upon the beach, a windlass, coiled rope, a tangle of nets, brown sails spread out to dry, gave as much opportunity for picturesque drawing and colour as the thatched cottage and the farmyard with all their traps and trappings. Many landscape painters made excursions to the sea. Turner, Constable, Cotman, Cox, Prout, De Wint, Copley Fielding and others, painted seascapes which hold a definite place in their art, but remain a class or section of their work. Others, however, devoted themselves almost entirely to a specialised preference for coast views and the seascape. Most of them were born at the beginning of the nineteenth century and painted their coastal and sea subjects in response to the rising popular affection for the seaside, or indeed because they shared in it, just as Prout shared in the popular feeling of romance inspired by crumbling buildings in old towns of the Continent.

Among the early masters of the subject were Monamy and Samuel Scott. Peter Monamy (c. 1670–1749)[1] was born of poor parents in Jersey. He was sent to London as a boy and was apprenticed to a house-painter whose premises were on London Bridge. Born within sight and sound of the sea, the boy could still look from his master's windows upon a wide waterway. Within easy walking distance he could watch coaling ships and fishing craft discharging their cargoes, and larger vessels, 'that mysterious forest below London Bridge', lying at anchor in the Pool. Or he might wander down stream on a holiday and study men-of-war at Deptford and Woolwich. In house-painting and interior decoration he learned to handle brush and paint, like David Roberts in later days, and took the same professional road. Marine painting, naturally, was his subject. His inspiration came, directly or indirectly, from the Van de Veldes. The Dutch influence is very apparent in the slightly tinted *Old East India Wharf*,[2] a charming and careful study of an ancient timbered building, an uptilted cart and a sleeping dog. The tints are graded from a cold grey in the distance to a cool brown and a warmer brown in the foreground, with a hint of pale red on some tiles to the right. The drawing continues the Dutch tradition, but in its washes of transparent, almost monochromatic pigment, links with the early Thames-side drawings of Turner and Girtin about fifty years later. Though there are other existent drawings of this type by him, Monamy is best known as a painter of marine subjects in oil.

In the year of Monamy's death in 1749, Vertue made the following entry in one of his Note-books[3]:

Mr. Peter Monamy painter of ships & sea prospects born in Jersey—came to London when young & being put to ordinary painting, but haveing an Early affection to drawing of ships and vessels of all kinds and the Imitations of other famous masters of paintings in that manner. Van de Veldes &c by constant practice he distinguisht himself and came into reputation—besides his industry and understanding in the forms & buildings of shipping with all the tackles ropes & sails &c which he thoroughly understood made his paintings of greater value besides his neatness and clean pencilling of sky and water by many was much esteemed especially sea-faring people officers and others marchants &c

To remember his fame his picture was painted & done in messotint print under writt.

[1] M. W. Knott, 'Peter Monamy', *Walker's Monthly*, February 1936.
[2] V.A.M. 644.
[3] Walpole Soc. XXII, 1934, p. 145.

Petrus Monamy navium et prospectuum marionorum
Pictor Londini Vandeveldo soli secundus 1731.

He livd some years latter part of his life at Westminster near the River side. for the Con-
venency in some measure of viewing the Water & Sky. tho' he made many excursions to wards
the Coasts & sea ports of England to Improve himself from nature. Thus having run thro' his
Time about 60 years of age being decayd and Infirm some years before his death which
happend at his house in Westminster the beginning of Feb. 174$\frac{8}{9}$—leaving many paintings
begun and unfinished. his works being done for dealers at moderate prices kept him but in
indifferent circumstances. to his end.

Samuel Scott (*c.* 1702–1772), 'sea schap painter', as Vertue calls him, was born in
London in 1702 according to William Marlow. From Farington comes the entry:

Marlow said He went as a Pupil to Scott about the year 1756, and was with him 5 years.—
Scott resided in Covent Garden, on the South Side.—He had much business; and gained by his
profession about 7 or 800 pounds a year. He had for a picture of 6 feet, by 4 feet, 60 or 70
guineas.—For a half length 40 guineas, and for a kitcat 25 guineas, & so on in proportion.—He
was much afflicted with the gout, but applied to his profession. He died at the age of 70 at
Bath.[1]

Further additions are given to our scanty knowledge of Scott's life by another entry in
1797:

Scott, [Sawrey] Gilpin's Master, Had originally abt. £1000 with which he purchased the place
of Clerk or Deputy Clerk of Accounts to the Stamp Office which produced him £100 a yr.—
and obliged him to attend the office 2 Hours 3 times a week.
   In the latter part of his life He sold the place.—He was not intended for painting,—but
having spare time, took it up as an amusement. Zinck encouraged him to proceed. He copied
Vandevelde well. He never was at Sea, except once in a Yatch which was sent to Helvotsluys
to bring George 2d. from Hanover.—Scott was a warm tempered man, but good natured.—
In the latter part of his life He passed sometime at Ludlow with his only Child a daugr. married
there. She dying He went to Bath and continued there to his death . . . Taverner was
acquainted with Scott . . . Gilpin once saw Brooking. He was a man of sickly appearance.—
He had been much at Sea.—Scott greatly admired his works.—Gilpin went to Scott in the year
1749 and remained with him 9 years, being 2 years longer than his apprenticeship.[2]

Though, like Monamy, Scott made his reputation by his pictures in oil of marine or
Thames-side subjects, he may be described as one of the primitives of our water-colour
school; and Horace Walpole, who collected his work, claimed him as the father of that
medium in England. *A Shipbuilder's Yard*,[3] the only known drawing of detailed ship building
by Scott, is a good example of his somewhat timid handling. In the British Museum is
a delicate drawing by Scott of *St. Paul's and Blackfriars Bridge*,[4] sketched with ink and grey
wash over pencil, and finished with slight tints. The drawing is squared out; probably he
made, or intended to make, an oil-painting from it. In front of this and similar drawings it

[1] *Diary*, July 31, 1796.
[2] *Diary*, February 8, 1797.
[3] Huntington Art Gallery, California.
[4] B.M. 1868. 3.28.338.

230

is difficult to understand the statement made by Edward Dayes that Scott 'was the first to make his drawings approach the strength of oil pictures'—apparently a quite unjustifiable assertion. Scott became a friend of Hogarth, and accompanied Hogarth, Thornhill, Tothall, and Ebenezer Forrest on a May morning in 1732 on the famous Five Days' Peregrination in the Isle of Sheppey (see p. 66).

Close on the heels of Monamy and Scott followed Dominic Serres (1722–1793), born at Auch and said to have been a nephew of the Archbishop of Rheims. His parents destined him for the Church, but the boy envisaged for himself a more romantic career, ran away from home, was a vagabond in Spain, shipped as a common seaman, and rose finally to be master of a vessel trading to Havannah. About 1758, in conflict with a British frigate, during the Seven Years' War, he was taken prisoner and brought to England. Being released on parole he settled in Northamptonshire and set to work as an artist. On coming to London he received assistance and encouragment from Charles Brooking (1723–1759), a year his junior, who had been brought up in Deptford dockyard, became a ship painter, and learned his ships. Taking to art, Brooking had painted marine views and sea-fights, was fortunate in having Taylor White, Treasurer of the Foundling Hospital, as his discoverer and patron, and was beginning to gain deserved reputation, when he was attacked by consumption and died, apparently in great poverty, in Castle Street, Leicester Square. He was an adroit and accomplished painter, and much was lost by his premature death, but he left Dominic Serres as part of his legacy to art. By 1768 Serres had won such success that he became one of the foundation members of the Royal Academy. His seascapes in oil at Greenwich and at Hampton Court are somewhat dull and heavy; his drawings, influenced by the Van de Veldes, of whose work he was a collector, are much more lively. Writing about a study by Serres of the *Culloden* in the Ingram collection, Sir Geoffrey Callender says that 'his inferiority [to the great Dutch Masters] proclaims itself in the flatness of the wash and the defective draughtsmanship of the subtle curves of the ship's side'.[1] His drawings, vigorous and interesting for their period, are forerunners of more accomplished work by his successors.

His son, John Thomas Serres (1759–1825), was born in London, exhibited sea-pieces at the Royal Academy, the British Institution and Suffolk Street from 1780, and for a time was drawing-master at Chelsea Naval School. In 1793 he succeeded his father as marine painter to the King, and was appointed to the more lucrative post of draughtsman to the Admiralty. In 1791 he had made an unfortunate marriage, while she was still under age, with his pupil Olive Wilmot, daughter of Robert Wilmot, a Warwick house-painter. His wife was a born intriguer, brilliant and heartless, a parasite upon wealthy aristocrats, and caused scandal by her unfounded claims to be the legitimate daughter of the Duke of Cumberland. This lost Serres the Royal favour. A theatrical speculation made Serres insolvent; he left his wife, was arrested for debt and attempted to commit suicide. Broken

[1] See footnote (p. 1).

in health and spirit, he toiled on in prison, and died on being removed into the rules of the King's Bench.[1] When Serres called on Farington in 1813, the diarist notes that 'he now resides at Covent Garden Chambers, where He paints transperiences & executes such other commissions as come to Him. He spoke of His Brother, & sd. He was till lately very well circumstanced. He taught drawing & had several schools, & got from 12 to £1500 a year, but He lived expensively & saved nothing; and from some cause His head (understanding) has been affected; which has caused the loss of His schools & reduced Him to a state of necessity.' The brother, whom Farington mentions, was Dominic M. Serres (dates unknown), a younger son of Dominic Serres, R.A.; he exhibited landscapes at the Royal Academy at intervals from 1778 to 1804.

J. T. Serres was somewhat akin to Hearne and Rooker. He is not such a good draughtsman; his work is more open and his line, drawn with a dark brown or black ink, is more loosely handled, with an approach to the Rowlandson manner. Most of his subjects were nautical, but his typical treatment is well seen in his *Exchange at Waterford*,[2] which is dated 1787 and was exhibited at the Royal Academy in 1789. He is represented in the Herbert Powell Collection (N.A.C.F.) by a drawing of *Whitby*. A pleasant landscape, with the abbey, church and town on the left, is seen from the sea, where a cutter and barque lean over in a fresh breeze. It is a sparkling drawing, the clear blue, strong and well preserved; and the ships set well down into the water.

Dominic and John Serres published the *Liber Nauticus*, a manual of instruction for marine painters, with copious illustrations. In their introduction they gave some general advice which may appropriately be recorded here: 'Many are the obstacles to a proficiency in drawing marine subjects, particularly as it is not only requisite that a person desirous of excelling in this art should possess knowledge of the construction of ships, or of what is denominated "Naval Architecture", together with the proportion of the masts and yards, the width, depth and cut of sails, etc., but he should likewise be acquainted with seamanship.'

Information about Charles Gore (1729–1807) was scanty and diffused until it was collected and amplified in the account of his work given by C. F. Bell,[3] from whom much of what follows has been borrowed. Bell points out that Gore was the only Englishman honoured by long and close intimacy with Goethe, who in his *Philipp Hackert*, 1811, gave several pages to an account of Gore, dwelling particularly upon his artistic accomplishments. Gore was not, as has hitherto been stated, a shipwright in his youth, but was a Lincolnshire landowner. From Farington[4] we learn that he was the son of a City Merchant and was educated at Westminster School. 'He married the daughter of a Rope maker at Scarborough with a fortune of £40,000'; and this probably accounts for the

---

[1] *Diary*, vol. II, pp. 253, 254.
[2] V.A.M. 1758–1871.
[3] Walpole Soc. XXIII, 1934–1935, pp. 8, 9.
[4] *Diary*, March 31, 1810.

legend that he began life as a shipwright. The legend is more plausible from the fact that he had a lifelong passion for the sea and ships, and was a skilled amateur draughtsman, marine architect and yachtsman. In Farington's words: 'His great pleasure was in sailing, having a Yacht for that purpose, & in sketching vessels and Sea views in which He so much excelled as to be very generally spoken of for His superior taste in Art.' Apart from his own original sketches it was his practice to buy faded Van de Velde drawings and to work over them with a pen and slight colour washes. After 1773, for the sake of his wife's health, he wintered at Lisbon, and in 1774 a captain of a British thirty-two gun frigate offered to convey Gore and his family to Italy. They halted at Gibraltar and Port Mahon, in both of which places Gore made drawings. Drawings dated 1775 and 1776 were made in Sicily, Elba, Antibes, Nice and Leghorn. In 1777 he was one of Payne Knight's party who made the round of Sicily from Milazzo to Messina. A large proportion of his extant drawings consists of careful studies of shipping and craft, and about one thousand of them are in the Thüringische Landesbibliothek at Weimar in five large folios handed over, by Gore's desire, after his death in 1807, to the Duke Karl August of Saxe-Weimar. The late Thomas Girtin, who examined them at C. F. Bell's request, was particularly struck by his drawings of shipping. From 1777 onwards he turned more to water-colour than pen drawing, producing such admirable works as the *View near Elsinore*, 1792, and *Southampton Water* in the Ingram Collection. In the British Museum are twenty-seven drawings dating from 1775 to 1794, bequeathed by Payne Knight.

To the same generation also belongs Nicholas Pocock (1741–1821).[1] Son of a Bristol merchant, his knowledge of the sea, like that of Brooking and Dominic Serres, was derived from actual experience as a mariner. In this they differed from later marine painters, landsmen who merely saw the picturesque possibilities lying about the lanes of the sea. In his 'twenties he had the command of vessels (he was master of the Lloyd in 1767, and later of the Minerva) owned by Richard Champion, a merchant-venturer of Bristol, who later became owner of a china factory, producing the fine porcelain known as Bristol ware.[2] He must have had some taste for drawing, and probably some instruction as a boy, for when at sea his graphic talent was in constant exercise. Six volumes of his log, illustrated by drawings in Indian ink of the principal incidents of each day, were once in the possession of Champion's grandson. A similar log of a voyage to Jamaica in 1776, is now owned by Mr. Robert Walter, of Ware Priory.

At the age of about forty, Pocock left the sea, took to art as his profession, working in oil and water-colour, and won encouragement from Sir Joshua Reynolds. His first exhibited works were in 1782, when he sent four to Somerset House. In 1789 he left Bristol and settled in London, where he soon rose to distinction as a painter of naval engagements during the long struggle for mastery at sea which followed the declaration of war with

[1] For a full account of Pocock and a list of his works, see Randall Davies, *Old Water-Colour Soc.*, V, 1927–1928. From this and from Roget much of my information is borrowed.
[2] For Pocock in this connection, see H. Owen, *Two Centuries of Ceramic Art in Bristol*, 1873, p. 49.

France in 1793. In 1804, then aged sixty-three, he became one of the original members on the foundation of the Old Water-Colour Society, contributing sixteen subjects to the first exhibition at 20 Lower Brook Street, in 1805. Though he left the Society when it was reconstituted in 1812, he continued to exhibit there till 1817. He showed in the gallery 183 works in all; they were not all sea-paintings, for he enjoyed painting landscape as well. During his life he was in constant touch with many Admirals and leading naval officers, and much of his work is still in the possession of old naval families. The Earl of Dundonald has one of the best collections, and Lady Hood another, while other works by him remain in the possession of his own descendants. His son, Isaac, became a well-known painter of portraits and figure subjects besides being a dramatic author, from whose pen came the once popular melodrama, *The Miller and his Men*. G. A. Fripp and A. D. Fripp were his grandsons.

Pocock's colouring is restrained and has the great charm belonging to the early stained drawings, but many of his water-colours have suffered from constant exposure to strong light. His reputation was helped by the pains which he took in the careful delineation of individual vessels and in securing detailed and accurate information as to the progress of naval engagements. The true disposition of the ships was more important to him than their value as part of a design; but, like Van de Velde, he did manage to seize the aspect of an engagement which allowed for compositional effect. His notes on four sketches belonging to Lady Hood, with such remarks as 'Bellerophon, fore and main topmasts gone, much shattered. . . . R. Sovereign much shattered t.gallant masts gone. . . . Queen Charlotte, Flag Signals "to wear", topmasts gone, yards much wounded', show the infinite trouble which he took in ascertaining facts. His close study of actual happenings is shown in the descriptive titles of his exhibited drawings, e.g. in 1812: 'View of His Majesty's Brig of War, Philomel, Captain Guion, chased by a French Squadron of eight Ships of the Line and four Frigates, and protected from Capture by the Intrepidity of Captain Halliday, in the Repulse, of 74 guns, who shortened Sail and engaged the advanced Ships of the Enemy, when the whole discontinued the Chase, and returned into Toulon, 31st August, 1810.' Trustworthy material for naval history could be obtained from those descriptive titles alone. In his accuracy he is very different from De Loutherbourg and other producers of machine-made battlepieces. There is a picture by De Loutherbourg[1] showing the *Queen Charlotte*, Lord Howe's ship, on the *Montagne*'s lee bow in the action of 1794. Bowen, the ship's master, is reported to have said, on seeing the picture: 'If we could have got the old ship into that position we must have taken the French Admiral.' Pocock's excellent drawing not only of shipping but of landscape and figures is seen in his *View of Basseterre, St. Kitt's*.[2]

John Cleveley (1747–1786) was born at Deptford, where his father is said to have worked in the dockyard as a shipwright or draughtsman. The son spent his childhood amid naval

[1] National Maritime Museum.
[2] V.A.M. 1635–1888

234

surroundings, so that his choice of material was a natural one, and at an early age he acquired skill in drawing ships and a sound understanding of marine subjects. He was instructed in water-colour painting by Paul Sandby, then drawing-master at the Royal Military Academy, Woolwich. Later he painted, but with much less ease, in oil. He exhibited at the Free Society and from 1770 at the Royal Academy. Having made a name by his riverside scenes and drawings of shipping on the Thames he was selected as draughts-man to accompany Sir Joseph Banks on his voyage to the Orkneys and Iceland in 1772, and in 1774 was draughtsman to the North Sea expedition undertaken by Captain Phipps afterwards Lord Mulgrave. Three water-colours made on this voyage are in the Print Room at the British Museum,[1] and one at the Victoria and Albert Museum[2] shows Lord Mulgrave's ships embedded in the ice of the polar regions. The extent of his travels may be judged from exhibition catalogues which include, in addition to his many Thames subjects, views at Gibraltar and on the Tagus, *Greenland Fishery*, *The King reviewing the Fleet at Spithead*, *A Gale off Dover*,[3] subjects in the Friendly Isles, and similar themes which bear witness to his catholicity and energy. Like Pocock he showed vivacity in his handling, and helped on the development of water-colour by showing that it could be applied to a wide range of subjects. His usual signature, up to 1782, was 'John Cleveley, Junr.', which indicates that his father also was known as a painter. He must not be confounded with his twin brother, Robert: possibly the only case of twins both becoming artists. Robert painted in water-colours, but is better known by his oil pictures of naval actions and other marine subjects, which gained him the honour of being marine painter to the Prince of Wales, and marine draughtsman to the Duke of Clarence. *A View of Billingsgate at High Water*,[3] by Robert Cleveley (1747–1809), exhibited first at the Royal Academy in 1792, is on Whatman paper of antiquarian size (53 in. × 31 in.)—I think one of the largest water-colours on paper which I have ever seen. His *Rowing Match at Richmond*,[4] almost of the same size, was exhibited at the Royal Academy in 1793; and in the Laing Art Gallery, Newcastle, is a small sketch for it dated 1792. The large drawing depicts the rowing match held in celebration of the birthday of H.R.H. the Duke of Clarence in 1792. In its skilful introduction of a large crowd of fashionable spectators it recalls Dayes' drawing, 1790, of the promenade in front of Buckingham House. Farington relates that Robert began life as a caulker in the yards at Deptford, at a time when caulkers and shipwrights were earning a pound a day, high wages considering the value of money at that time; and adds that his comrades used to laugh at him for working in gloves.[5] Perhaps he never made much more income as a painter, even if he could wear gloves without mockery.

John Webber (c. 1750–1793), born in London, was the son of a Swiss sculptor named Weber. After studying at Berne and in Paris he returned to London in 1775 and entered

[1] B.M. 1888. 12.11.1–3.
[2] V.A.M. 316–1887.
[3] The whereabouts of these drawings is not known.
[4] V.A.M. P.1–1944.
[5] *Diary*, February 22, 1795.

the Royal Academy Schools. He accompanied Captain Cook in 1776 as draughtsman on his third voyage round the world in the *Resolution*. He was present at Captain Cook's death, and made a drawing of the event which was engraved by Byrne and Bartolozzi. On his return to England in 1780 he was employed by the Admiralty in making finished drawings of his sketches for the official account of the expedition which appeared in 1784. In 1808 Boydell published *Views in the South Seas*, engraved by Webber from his original drawings preserved at the Admiralty. Meanwhile, in 1785 he was elected an associate of the Royal Academy, and a member in 1791. A good draughtsman and a delicate colourist, he is not unlike J. R. Cozens in his quiet scheme of silvery blues. Like Cozens, he did not apply his colour on the spot. In his *Near Dolgelly, 1790*,[1] the colours are carefully noted in pencil—'greenish', 'purplish', 'reddish hue', 'purplish hue'; but in the drawing as finished the whole range of mountains on which these notes appear is a uniform grey-blue. His foliage is distinctive, in that he employs as a unit a sort of ostrich-feather shape. Webber takes a high place, higher than has yet been recognised, among the fore-runners of Girtin and Turner.

William Anderson (1757–1837), like the Cleveleys, was brought up among shipwrights. Born in Scotland, he came to London and exhibited river and sea views at the Royal Academy from 1787 to 1834, which showed his expert nautical knowledge. He exhibited also at the Incorporated Society of Artists, British Institution and Suffolk Street. A set of views of the Battle of the Nile was engraved after him by W. Ellis. Sir Geoffrey Callender sums him up: 'In his most characteristic work Anderson displays an airy quality and a soft sense of colour reminiscent of Van de Capelle. His work is unequal. He is at his best when portraying ships in light airs, but in some of his drawings he develops a hardness comparable with that found in the later work of Pocock.' Anderson made skilful use of the sharp point of a knife to indicate wave forms.

Next to him in order of time comes Samuel Atkins (*fl.* 1787–1808). He first exhibited at the Royal Academy in 1787. Later he went to the East Indies and remained there from about 1796 to 1804. His work is rare, but its extremely high quality is shown by his *View of the Pool, below London Bridge*,[2] which may be dated about 1790. In 1788, following on his first appearance at the Royal Academy, he used the following advertisement:

MARINE DRAWING taught in an easy, pleasing and expeditious manner by S. Atkins No. 78, Corner of Salisbury-street, Strand, where specimens may be seen every day (Sundays excepted) from ten till four during the exhibition at the Royal Academy. N.B. Schools attended.

[1] V.A.M. 1732–1871.
[2] V.A.M. E.188–1911.

232 'Two Boats coming alongside a First Rater'
Coll. Mr & Mrs Paul Mellon   5¾ × 10½: 147 × 267   *Grey wash over blue chalk*
Samuel Scott (c. 1702–1772)

233 'Dutch Shipping'
Coll. Mr & Mrs Paul Mellon   6¾ × 9¼: 172 × 235   *Water-colour*
Dominic Serres (1772–1793)

234 'Shipping off the Coast'

Coll. Mr Basil Taylor $7\frac{5}{8} \times 10\frac{1}{8}$: 174×260 *Grey monochrome*

Charles BROOKING (1723–1759)

235 'An Armed Cutter in a Storm'

B.M. Oo–5–64 $7\frac{3}{8} \times 10\frac{3}{8} : 187 \times 264$ *Water-colour and some body-colour*

Charles GORE (1729–1807)

236 'Shipping off the Coast'
B.M. 1885.5.9.1647   9⅜ × 14:240 × 355   *Water-colour, signed and dated 1789*
John Thomas SERRES (1759–1825)

237 'Eastbourne, Sussex'
B.M. 1870.12.10.235   12⅞ × 17¾: 327 × 456   *Water-colour*
Nicholas POCOCK (1741–1821)

238 'The Ships of Lord Mulgrave's Expedition Embedded in Ice in the
Polar Regions'

V.A.M. 316–1887   14 × 18: 351 × 457   *Water-colour, signed and dated 1774*

John CLEVELEY (1747–1786)

239 'Pont y Pair on the River Oawen near Llanrwst'
Coll. Mr & Mrs Paul Mellon   13⅜ × 18¾: 340 × 476   *Water-colour*
John WEBBER, R.A. (1750–1793)

240 'English Ships of War'
V.A.M. 343–1872 $9\frac{1}{2} \times 15\frac{1}{4}:241 \times 387$ *Water-colour*
Robert CLEVELEY (1747–1809)

241 'Man O'War at Anchor, being Rigged'
Coll. Mr & Mrs Paul Mellon $8 \times 11\frac{1}{2}: 203 \times 292$ *Water-colour, signed*
Samuel ATKINS (working 1787–1808)

242 'Coast Scene'

V.A.M. 17–1878   8½ × 11¾: 216 × 298   *Water-colour, signed and dated 1795*

William ANDERSON (1757–1837)

INDEX

of Artists Mentioned in the Text

The numerals in *Italics* refer to the principal entries relating to each artist and those in **Bold** type refer to the *Figure Numbers* of the illustrations.

237